Power Graphics Using Turbo Pascal® 6

Wiley's Power Graphics books are designed as practical, hands-on guides that show programmers how to get the most out of graphics programing. They feature a step-by-step approach that will be welcomed by programmers whether they are new to graphics programming or experienced in the fundamentals of graphics.

Other Wiley Power Graphics books:

Power Graphics Using Turbo C++, Keith Weiskamp, Loren Heiny

Power Graphics Using Turbo C, Namir Shammas, Keith Weiskamp, Loren Heiny

Power Graphics Using Turbo Pascal, Keith Weiskamp, Namir Shammas, Loren Heiny

To order our Power Graphics books, call Wiley directly at (201) 469-4400 or check your local bookstore.

Power Graphics Using Turbo Pascal® 6

Coriolis Group Book

Keith Weiskamp
Loren Heiny

John Wiley & Sons, Inc.

New York • Chichester • Brisbane • Toronto • Singapore

Publisher: Therese A. Zak
Editor: Katherine Schowalter
Managing Editor: Nana D. Prior
Copy Editor: Shelley Flannery
Design and Production: Rob Mauhar and Lenity Himburg, The Coriolis Group

Turbo Pascal is a registered trademark of Borland International, Inc.

Library of Congress Cataloging-in-Publication Data

Weiskamp, Keith.
    Power graphics using Turbo Pascal 6: Coriolis group book /Keith Weiskamp, Loren
Heiny.
      p.   cm.
    Includes bibliographical references.
    ISBN 0-471-54736-0 (paper)
    1. Computer graphics. 2. Turbo Pascal (Computer program)
I. Heiny, Loren. II. Title.
T385.W463   1991
006.6'869--dc20   91-14337

Printed in the United States of America

10 9 8 7 6 5 4 3 2 1

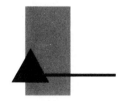

Contents

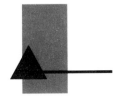

Preface

If you've picked up this book because you're interested in learning how to master graphics programming using Turbo Pascal 6.0, then you've come to the right place. In the past, programming graphics has been a difficult, time-consuming task. However, with Turbo Pascal 6.0 in hand, it's never been easier. To begin with, Turbo Pascal includes its own easy-to-use graphics tools, the Borland Graphics Interface (BGI). And now, Turbo Pascal 6.0 makes it possible for you to take full advantage of object-oriented programming (OOP) techniques. Combined, these language tools greatly simplify the work of creating two- and three-dimensional graphics programs.

A number of books have been written about graphics programming over the years; however, most of these books emphasize the "low road" approach to writing graphics. That is, they present techniques for developing low-level graphics tools such as simple line and arc drawing routines, clipping and filling algorithms, and graphics hardware drivers. This book, on the other hand, takes the "high road" approach by showing you how to use the graphics routines provided with the new Turbo Pascal to create real-world graphics applications.

If you have had some experience with Turbo Pascal programming and you're ready to take the next step and learn how to develop graphics programming techniques, you'll want a book that provides a hands-on approach to the art of developing graphics tools and applications. To fill this need, *Power Graphics Using Turbo Pascal 6* takes you inside Turbo Pascal and the powerful Borland Graphics Interface.

But this book does more than just show you how to program with the BGI. Along the way you'll learn how to apply the latest object-oriented programming techniques to create flexible and highly useful graphics tools and programs.

Here are some of the major highlights of this book:

- In-depth discussions of the major BGI functions
- Sidebars that present special graphics-related topics including BGI programming tips
- A hands-on approach to building object-oriented graphics tools
- Techniques for designing graphics-based user interfaces (GUIs)
- The fundamentals of two- and three-dimensional graphics programming
- Real-time animation
- Presentation graphics
- Interactive applications including a drawing and painting program

Who Should Read This Book

If you have always wanted to know how to master the BGI, develop your own practical set of object-oriented graphics tools, or write a major graphics application such as a CAD program, you'll enjoy this book. Whether you're new to graphics programming or experienced with the fundamentals of graphics, this book shows you, step-by-step, how to design tools and applications including presentation graphics, icon editors, graphics-based user interfaces, painting and CAD programs, and three-dimensional graphics viewing programs.

What You'll Need

To use this book you'll need Turbo Pascal 6.0 (or Turbo Pascal 5.5) as well as an IBM PC XT, AT, PS/2, or a compatible computer system capable of displaying graphics. Most of the programs are designed to work with the Virtual Graphics Array (VGA), Enhanced Graphics Adapter (EGA), Color Graphics Adapter (CGA), or Hercules graphics adapters. Because of the flexibility of the BGI and the programs presented, you can easily customize them to run on your own system.

The interactive graphics tools that we present, such as the icon editor, pop-up windows, and drawing routines, are designed to work with a Microsoft-compatible mouse. The mouse is an important component to interactive graphics systems; in fact, we've devoted a complete chapter to showing you how to support the mouse. In order to run the interactive graphics programs (Chapters 7 through 13), you'll want to make sure that your computer has a mouse installed.

A Look Inside

This book has evolved from the first edition, *Power Graphics Using Turbo Pascal*, which was originally written for Turbo Pascal version 5.0. Since the first edition, many people have called and written us with comments and suggestions which we've taken to heart and incorporated into this new book. We've also redesigned many of the tools and applications so that they take advantage of the power and flexibility of OOP. We've spent a number of years working with Turbo Pascal and graphics and this book contains the topics that we've found to be of the most interest to PC programmers.

Our new book, *Power Graphics Using Turbo Pascal 6.0*, progresses from fundamental graphics programming techniques to more advanced topics such as building interactive drawing tools and three-dimensional graphics programming. Whenever feasible, we've written the programs using the object-oriented features of Turbo Pascal 6.0 so that they can easily be modified and expanded. Although we had to limit the features of some of the programs because of space, you'll find that they are complete, well explained, and highly useful—unlike the typical "toy" programs found in most graphics programming books.

Chapter 1: *Introducing the BGI*. This chapter will show you how to use the BGI tools and Turbo Pascal to access your graphics hardware and write complete standalone graphics programs. Along the way, we'll also cover some of the OOP features of Turbo Pascal 6.0. After we cover the essentials, we'll show you how to develop a program to create fractal images.

Chapter 2: *The BGI Drawing Commands* explains how all of the major BGI drawing commands are used. You'll also learn how to work with colors and color palettes and fill regions with predefined and user-defined fill patterns.

Chapter 3: *BGI Fonts and Text* presents the tools for displaying text in graphics mode. You'll learn how to work with the bit-mapped and stroke fonts and how to magnify and clip characters. We'll also create some custom functions for supporting text input in graphics mode.

Chapter 4: *Presentation Graphics* shows you how to develop programs for generating high-quality presentation graphics. In this chapter, you'll learn how to combine the BGI fonts and drawing routines to display pie, bar, and coin charts.

Chapter 5: *Graphics Techniques in Two Dimensions* covers a variety of techniques for working with two-dimensional graphics. Some of the topics presented include transformations and rotating graphic objects.

Chapter 6: *Animation* shows you how to add animation effects to your two-dimensional graphics. You'll learn how to use the **GetImage** and **PutImage** procedures to move graphics images and how to use color palettes to simulate animation.

Chapter 7: *Creating Mouse Tools* presents a hands-on discussion of how to build a set of tools to control a Microsoft compatible mouse. In later chapters, we'll use the mouse tools to support graphics drawing programs.

Chapter 8: *Working with Icons* shows you how to build a useful icon editor. We'll use this icon editor to create the icons that we'll need to support our interactive drawing programs in Chapters 11 and 12.

Chapter 9: *Pop-Up Windows in Graphics* presents a set of tools for supporting pop-up windows in graphics mode.

Chapter 10: *Interactive Drawing Tools* shows you how to build a useful toolset of interactive drawing routines.

Chapter 11: *A Paint Program* presents a powerful painting program that includes a mouse-based user interface.

Chapter 12: *A CAD Program* presents a two-dimensional CAD program.

Chapter 13: *Three-Dimensional Graphics* explains the fundamentals of three-dimensional graphics programming. In this chapter you'll learn about clipping, projection, three-dimensional representation, and much more.

Where's the Code?

If you've read earlier versions of this book or if you've taken a few minutes to thumb through this one, you've probably noticed that we've included a number of tools and applications. To save you from having to type in all of this code, we're making the software available in electronic form. A disk order form is placed in the back of the book for your convenience. If you're in a hurry, you can call in an order with your credit card and we'll rush a code disk out to you.

Contacting the Authors

Whether you program graphics for sport or for pleasure, we'd love to hear from you. One of the reasons this book keeps growing is because of the valuable comments we get. If you have a suggestion or a problem with Turbo Pascal and graphics programming, send us postal or electronic mail and we'll try to help you out. You can reach us by post at *PC TECHNIQUES* Magazine, 7721 East Gray Rd, Suite #204, Scottsdale, AZ, 85260. If you have access to CompuServe, you can reach Keith Weiskamp at 72561,1536 and Loren Heiny at 73527,2365.

Introducing the BGI

These days, graphics play a more important role than ever before in the world of personal computers (PCs). The days of text-based programs are numbered, because PC users simply are demanding that programs be more visual and easy to use. Fortunately, the tools for creating these programs, such as Turbo Pascal 6.0 and the Borland Graphics Interface (BGI), are now readily available.

To help you get started writing graphics-based programs, in this chapter we'll take a brief look at the major features of the BGI. We'll also introduce a few of the powerful features of Turbo Pascal 6.0 such as *objects*. In later chapters, we'll cover the BGI in much greater detail and we'll show you how they can be used to develop applications such as icon editors, pop-up windows, and CAD and painting programs. Along the way, we'll also be presenting the major concepts of two- and three-dimensional graphics programming.

We'll begin our tour by discussing the basic structure of a Turbo Pascal graphics program. Then we'll show you how to use several of the BGI graphics routines, such as pixel plotting procedures, line drawing commands, polygon plotting routines, and text manipulation routines that work in graphics mode.

At the end of the chapter we'll develop an interesting program that creates fractals. This will give us as an opportunity to combine what we've learned so far into a very simple fractal program that displays computer-generated landscapes.

Getting Started

For each graphics program that you write, there are certain steps that must always be followed. For example, at the start of every graphics program you'll need to set your video display hardware to a graphics mode. In addition, you should restore the computer's screen to its normal display mode at the end of each program. In the following section, we'll show you what basic components are required in a typical Turbo Pascal graphics program.

Initializing the BGI

The first step every graphics program must take is to initialize the graphics hardware. By *hardware* we mean the video display adapter card that must be in your PC in order to display graphics. To complicate the issue, there are several different graphics cards available for the PC, each with numerous graphics modes. Fortunately, the BGI supports many of these graphics "standards." To start out, we won't cover all of the graphics cards and modes. Rather, we'll use the default mode of the BGI initialization routine, which allows us to set the currently installed graphics adapter to its highest-resolution mode.

The BGI procedure used to configure your computer to graphics mode is called **InitGraph** and has the following declaration:

```
procedure InitGraph(var GraphDriver, GraphMode: integer;
                    DriverPath: string);
```

The procedure **InitGraph** is defined in the Pascal unit **Graph** which must be included in the **uses** section of all of your graphics programs. This file contains the data structures, constants, procedures, and functions for the BGI.

The first two parameters of **InitGraph** specify which video adapter and mode to use and are set to one of the logical values defined in the **Graph** unit that your PC supports. After **InitGraph** is called, these parameters will contain the actual adapter and mode specifications that the BGI used to set the graphics system. The third parameter specifies the pathname where the Turbo Pascal graphics driver files are stored. (There is at least one graphics driver for each graphics adapter.) The driver files are the files that come with your Turbo Pascal distribution disk and end with the **.BGI** extension. The pathname can be represented as a full pathname, such as:

```
InitGraph(GDriver,GMode,'\compilers\turbo\graphics');
```

or it can be a partial pathname:

```
InitGraph(GDriver,GMode,'graphics\drivers');
```

In the second example, **InitGraph** searches the directory **drivers**, which is a subdirectory of the directory **graphics**. **Graphics** is, in turn, a subdirectory of the current directory. If the BGI graphics driver files are stored in the same directory that you are using to execute your program, you can call **InitGraph** with:

```
InitGraph(GDriver,GMode,'');
```

Here, the pathname is specified as the empty string.

Now let's see how we can use **InitGraph** to select the graphics mode. You can instruct **InitGraph** to use a particular graphics driver and mode by setting its first two parameters to particular values. Alternatively, you can let **InitGraph** automatically configure your PC's video adapter. We'll use this option.

If the first parameter is set to the constant **Detect**, a constant declared in the unit **Graph**, **InitGraph** will configure your graphics system to its highest-resolution mode. In this case, the second parameter in **InitGraph** does not need to be initialized to any value. After **InitGraph** is called, you can examine the value of these parameters to determine which graphics adapter and mode the BGI initialized. As a last requirement for setting your PC's video adapter, you'll need to specify the path to the BGI driver files.

When writing a graphics program, **InitGraph** is not complete without its companion routine **CloseGraph**. The procedure **CloseGraph**, which does not take any parameters, should be used at the end of all of your programs to shut down the BGI system and restore the monitor to the video mode it was in before the call to **InitGraph**.

Writing the Basic BGI Program

To summarize the initialization steps that we have been discussing, let's write a simple graphics program that uses **InitGraph** and **CloseGraph**. The following program is probably the shortest graphics program we can write in Turbo Pascal. It's shown here to emphasize the basic structure of the typical Turbo Pascal graphics program; you can also use it as a skeleton for your own programs.

```
program SmallestGraphicsProgram;
uses
  Graph;                                { Turbo Pascal graphics unit }
const
  GDriver: integer = Detect;           { Select the autodetect feature }
var
  GMode: integer;                      { For autodetection use a }
                                       { variable placeholder }
begin                                  { for the mode }
  InitGraph(GDriver,GMode,'\tp\bgi'); { Set the driver and mode }
  { ... put drawing commands here ... }
```

```
    CloseGraph;                        { Exit the graphics mode }
    end.
```

If you run this program without adding any graphics drawing routines, you'll see a couple of flashes on the screen and that's about it. The screen flicker is caused by your PC switching from its normal text mode to graphics mode and then back again to text mode (assuming the screen was in text mode before the call to **InitGraph**).

Let's take a closer look at the program. The code begins with the **uses** section which includes the Turbo Pascal unit **Graph**. Every graphics program must contain this statement. Remember that the unit **Graph** contains various predefined constants, type definitions, and all of the BGI routines.

The call to **InitGraph** automatically sets your video adapter because **Detect** is passed as the value for the first parameter. The second parameter, **GMode**, references the video mode and is not given a value; it simply acts as a placeholder in this example. After **InitGraph** is called, you can examine **GDriver** and **GMode** to see which video adapter has been loaded and which mode was initialized. The third parameter specifies the directory where the BGI driver files are kept, in this case the **\tp\bgi** directory. Throughout this book, we'll assume that this is the directory in which your BGI files are located. If you don't specify the correct directory, your program will fail to be initialized to graphics mode and won't display any graphics.

Fortunately, the BGI provides several error handling routines to handle this situation. One such function, **GraphResult**, obtains the error condition of the last graphics routine called. Another BGI function, called **GraphErrorMsg**, takes the value returned by **GraphResult** and displays an appropriate error message for you. We'll use these error detection functions in the next program we write to show you how to construct a much more robust version of our first program.

Error Checking

The most common error that can occur in a graphics program is caused when a Turbo graphics driver cannot be found. Remember, the third parameter of the function **InitGraph** specifies the path to the Turbo Pascal graphics driver files. If the path is incorrect and the graphics drivers can't be located, the graphics initialization will fail. In our first sample program, the path to the graphics drivers is set to the path **\tp\bgi**. If your BGI files are not in this directory, you'll need to set this path to the directory where they are stored.

Now let's modify our original example so that we can check for potential errors. Here is the program that you should type in, compile, and execute.

```
program GraphTest;
{ GRAFTEST.PAS: A simple graphics program to test whether the BGI
  is set up properly. }
uses
  Graph, Crt;
const
  GDriver: integer = Detect;              { Autodetect graphics mode }
var
  GMode, GError: integer;
begin
  InitGraph(GDriver,GMode,'\tp\bgi');  { Initialize the BGI }
  GError := GraphResult;                  { Get error flag value }
  if GError < 0 then begin                { If negative then error }
    Write('Graphics initialization error: ');
    WriteLn(GraphErrorMsg(GError));       { Print error message }
    Halt(1);
  end;
  { If a graphics error hasn't occurred, then print a greeting }
  OutText('Hello graphics world!    Press any key to exit ...');
  { Wait for the user to strike a key. If this weren't done, the
    program would immediately execute CloseGraph and the screen
    would be cleared and switched to text mode. }
  repeat until KeyPressed;
  CloseGraph;                             { Exit graphics mode }
end.
```

This program does a comprehensive job of error checking. If everything is okay, the message

```
Hello graphics world!    Press any key to exit ...
```

is displayed. If a problem occurs, however, an appropriate error message is displayed and the program is terminated. To ensure that your graphics environment is set up correctly, you should try running this program before going on to the next section.

One new routine in the program that we haven't seen yet is **OutText**, which is used to write a text string to the graphics screen. This is one of two specialized graphics text output routines provided with the BGI. There is also a BGI procedure called **OutTextXY**, which allows you to display a text string at a specified screen location. We'll look at both of these routines in much greater detail in Chapter 3 when we present the techniques for working with BGI fonts and text.

Working with Coordinates

As with most goals you wish to accomplish, it helps to know where you have been and where you are going. In graphics, we keep track of our positions by using *pixel coordinates.* Pixels are the very small dots you see on the screen, and they can be *addressed* by using a coordinate system that is similar to the way we access the rows and columns of a two-dimensional array data structure. This coordinate system is called the *Cartesian coordinate system.* Figure 1.1 illustrates how pixels are referenced with row and column coordinates.

The dimensions of your screen's coordinate system depends on the video adapter that you use. Fortunately, there are some standard techniques for handling pixel coordinates that you can use for any of the BGI supported video adapters. First, all graphics modes on the PC start their coordinates at the top left of the screen with the coordinate (0,0). The highest pixel coordinate is at the bottom right of the screen. Its value is dependent on your graphics mode; however, Turbo Pascal includes two functions, **GetMaxX** and **GetMaxY**, that you can call to get these values. They are typically used in statements such as:

```
MaxXCoordinate := GetMaxX;
MaxYCoordinate := GetMaxY;
```

It's good programming practice to exploit these function calls and create programs that can work equally well on several different graphics adapters and modes. Neither function requires that a parameter be passed to it, and both return the number of pixels in the x direction (the number of columns on the screen) and the number

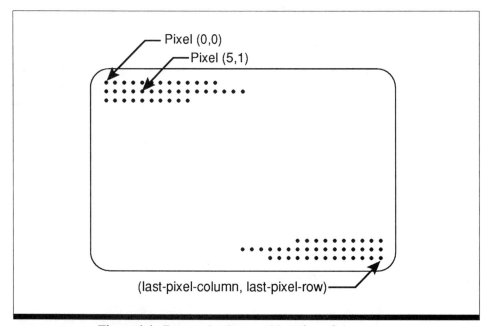

Figure 1.1. Row and column addressing of the screen

of pixels in the y direction (the number of rows), respectively. Therefore, the bottom-right coordinate is given by (**GetMaxX, GetMaxY**). With this information, we are now able to instruct the BGI where objects should be drawn on the screen. Next, let's investigate some of the drawing routines.

Drawing Commands

Turbo Pascal supports a wide variety of drawing routines that are amazingly simple to use. These extend from pixel-level screen commands to high-level routines that draw three-dimensional bar graphs.

For this part of our tour, we'll explore several of the BGI's drawing routines. We'll start with the lowest-level drawing routines in the BGI, the **PutPixel/GetPixel** routines, and then we'll work our way up to the higher-level ones.

Getting Down to Pixels

Both **PutPixel** and **GetPixel** can access only one pixel on the screen at a time. The **PutPixel** procedure sets a pixel at a specified location (coordinate) to a particular color. The **GetPixel** function, on the other hand, is used to determine the current pixel color of any location on the screen. These routines are defined as:

```
function GetPixel(X, Y: integer): word;
procedure PutPixel(X, Y: integer; Color: word);
```

Notice that **GetPixel** returns a word value that corresponds to the pixel's color at (x, y). A few sample calls for these routines are:

```
PutPixel(100,200,Red);
Color := GetPixel(20,50);
```

To see how both of these routines are used in a graphics program, let's write a program that randomly plots 1000 pixels on the screen using **PutPixel** and then relies on **GetPixel** to locate each pixel in order to thin them out. Here is the complete program:

```
program RandPixl;
{ RANDPIXL.PAS: This program randomly plots 1000 pixels on the
  screen and then erases every other one. }
uses
  Graph;
```

```
var
  GDriver, GMode: integer;
  MaxX, MaxY: integer;        { Maximum coordinates of screen }
  MaxColor: word;             { This mode's maximum color value }
  I, X, Y: integer;
  Color: word;
begin
  GDriver := Detect;
  InitGraph(GDriver,GMode,'\tp\bgi');
  Randomize;        { Initialize the random number generator }
  { Get the maximum x and y screen coordinates and the largest
    valid color for this mode }
  MaxX := GetMaxX;    MaxY := GetMaxY;
  MaxColor := GetMaxColor;
  { Now randomly plot the pixels }
  for I := 1 to 1000 do begin
    X := Random(MaxX+1);          { Add one to these since the }
    Y := Random(Maxy+1);          { Random function returns a }
    Color := Random(MaxColor+1);  { value between 0 and num - 1 }
    PutPixel(X,Y,Color);          { Color the pixel }
  end;
  { Now scan through the screen and thin out the nonblack pixels.
    Use the GetPixel command to locate the nonblack pixels. Every
    other pixel that is found is reset to black. }
  I := 0;
  for Y := 0 to Maxy do
    for X := 0 to MaxX do
      if GetPixel(X,Y) <> Black then begin
        if (I mod 2) = 0                { Only reset every }
          then PutPixel(X,Y,Black);     { other pixel }
        Inc(I);
      end;
  CloseGraph;
end.
```

The program starts by initializing the graphics mode using the BGI's autoconfiguration feature. After the graphics mode is set, the maximum x and y screen coordinates are determined by calls to the functions **GetMaxX** and **GetMaxY**. In addition, a similar call is made to **GetMaxColor**, which retrieves the highest color value that the currently installed video adapter can produce. This function gives us the full range of valid color values for the active video mode, since all colors lie between 0 and this number. The **GetMaxColor** function works much like **GetMaxX** and **GetMaxY** and is invaluable for writing device-independent programs. One final part of the initialization process involves a call to **Randomize** that seeds the random number generator we'll be using later.

Notice that no error checking has been performed in this program. Although it is good practice to check and ensure that the graphics system has successfully initialized itself, for the sake of brevity we'll ignore this possibility for now.

The first **for** loop generates the randomly drawn pixels. They are plotted throughout the screen in random locations and colors. The color values used range from zero (black) to the value returned in **GetMaxColor** (normally white). After this loop, your screen will portray an impressive looking night sky filled with stars.

The next **for** loop travels through these stars and erases every other non black one by resetting them to black. To locate the randomly drawn stars, a search is made of the screen pixels. This is accomplished by calls to the **GetPixel** function. Every other time **GetPixel** encounters a pixel other than black, **PutPixel** is called to reset it to black. The thinning process is assured by the variable **I**, which allows **PutPixel** to plot its black pixels on every even occurrence of **I**. The indexing of the screen is limited by the variables **MaxX** and **MaxY** that hold the maximum screen coordinates. These variables are set at the beginning of the program with calls to **GetMaxX** and **GetMaxY**.

Drawing Figures

Now that we've seen how to plot and read pixels, let's move on and take a look at how some of the Turbo Pascal BGI routines are used to draw figures. We'll start with the drawing routines that create outlines of figures and shapes. These are the **Arc**, **Circle**, **DrawPoly**, **Ellipse**, **Line**, and **Rectangle** routines. Each one of these six procedures has its own unique features and peculiarities and rather than go into them now, we'll simply develop a program that will serve to introduce you to them.

Each of these procedures have rather intuitive names and operate much as you might expect. For example, **Arc** draws an arc and **Circle** draws a circle. The **Circle** procedure requires three parameters: the x and y coordinates of its center and the radius of the circle. The other procedures are similar. The only odd one is **DrawPoly**. This routine takes an array of x and y points and the number of points in the array and plots line segments connecting the points. If the first coordinate in the list of points matches with the last, then a closed polygon is drawn.

The basic BGI drawing routines are powerful for drawing figures. You can control the color that figures are drawn in, the type of line style used to make their perimeter, and the aspect ratio used (in the case of the **Arc** and **Circle** procedures). In Chapter 2, we'll explore each of the drawing routines in much greater detail.

For now, let's write a program that illustrates how these six drawing procedures are used. The program is somewhat encumbered by the need to keep all of the indexes to the drawing routines device independent, but this is often the cost of generality.

The screen is divided into six sections in which figures are drawn for each of the drawing commands. In addition, it uses the **OutTextXY** text display function to write labels for each of the figures. Here is the program:

```
program ShowDraw;
{ SHOWDRAW.PAS: Displays most of the simple drawing routines in
  the BGI. These do not include the fill routines or the various
  line styles that are available. }
uses
  Graph, Crt;
var
  GDriver, GMode, MaxX, MaxY: integer;
  Color: word;
  Points: array[1..5] of PointType;
begin
  GDriver := Detect;                          { Autodetect the graphics mode }
  InitGraph(GDriver,GMode,'\tp\bgi');
  MaxX := GetMaxX;  MaxY := GetMaxY;     { Get screen resolution }
  { Draw an arc, circle, and polygon at top of the screen
    and an ellipse, line, and rectangle at the bottom }
  Arc(MaxX div 6,MaxY div 4,0,135,50);
  OutTextXY(MaxX div 6-TextWidth('Arc') div 2,0,'Arc');
  Circle(MaxX div 2,MaxY div 4,60);
  OutTextXY(MaxX div 2-TextWidth('Circle') div 2,0,'Circle');
  Points[1].X := MaxX * 5 div 6 - 20;
  Points[1].Y := MaxY div 4 - 20;
  Points[2].X := MaxX * 5 div 6 - 30;
  Points[2].Y := MaxY div 4 + 25;
  Points[3].X := MaxX * 5 div 6 + 40;
  Points[3].Y := MaxY div 4 + 15;
  Points[4].X := MaxX * 5 div 6 + 20;
  Points[4].Y := MaxY div 4 - 30;
  Points[5].X := Points[1].X;
  Points[5].Y := Points[1].Y;
  DrawPoly(5,Points);
  OutTextXY(MaxX*5 div 6-TextWidth('DrawPoly') div 2, 0,'DrawPoly');
  Ellipse(MaxX div 6,MaxY*3 div 4,0,360,75,20);
  OutTextXY(MaxX div 6-TextWidth('Ellipse') div 2,
            MaxY-TextHeight('l'),'Ellipse');
  Line(MaxX div 2-25,MaxY*3 div 4-25,MaxX div 2+25, MaxY*3 div 4+25);
  OutTextXY(MaxX div 2-TextWidth('Line') div 2,
            MaxY-TextHeight('L'),'Line');
  Rectangle(MaxX*5 div 6-30,MaxY*3 div 4-20,
            MaxX*5 div 6+30,MaxY*3 div 4+20);
  OutTextXY(MaxX*5 div 6-TextWidth('Rectangle') div 2,
            MaxY-TextHeight('R'),'Rectangle');
  repeat until KeyPressed;   { Show screen until key is pressed }
  CloseGraph;
end.
```

The display produced by this program is shown in Figure 1.2. The main drawing routines spotlighted are the calls to the drawing routines of the form:

```
Arc(X,Y,StAngle,EndAngle,Radius);
Circle(X,Y,Radius);
DrawPoly(NumberOfPoints,ArrayOfXYPoints);
```

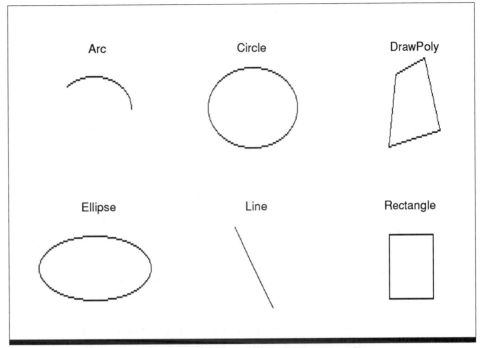

Figure 1.2. Output of SHOWDRAW.PAS

```
Ellipse(X,Y,StAngle,EndAngle,XRadius,YRadius);
Line(X1,Y1,X2,Y2);
Rectangle(Left,Top,Right,Bottom);
```

The different calculations and offsets are included in the program so that you can see what type of code is typically needed to generate device-independent scenes in Turbo Pascal. In particular, note that we are using the **TextHeight** and **TextWidth** procedures to determine the size of the text strings that are displayed. Both of these routines will be covered in more detail in Chapter 3.

Keep in mind that we are only showing some of the powerful features of these drawing routines in our sample program. For example, several of the routines shown earlier let you set their line styles and they all let you control the color used to draw them. However, we've avoided these for now so that we can show you their basic features in our quick tour.

Filling Figures

In the previous section we experimented with routines to draw outlines of objects. Turbo Pascal also has a set of graphics routines that can draw and paint solid objects or objects filled with patterns. These routines are **Bar, Bar3D, FillPoly, FillEllipse, PieSlice,** and **Sector**. As in the figure drawing routines, these procedures are very flexible. Most support different fill patterns, colors, and even different line styles. The procedural declarations for each of these routines are:

```
procedure Bar(Left, Top, Right, Bottom: integer);
procedure Bar3D(Left, Top, Right, Bottom: integer;
                Depth: word; TopFlag: boolean);
procedure FillEllipse(X, Y: integer; XRadius, YRadius: word);
procedure FillPoly(NumberOfPoints: integer; var ArrayOfXYPoints);
procedure PieSlice(X, Y: integer; StartAngle, EndAngle, Radius: word);
procedure Sector(X, Y: integer; StartAngle, EndAngle,
                 XRadius, YRadius: word);
```

The procedures **Bar, Bar3D, PieSlice, FillEllipse,** and **Sector** are useful routines for creating impressive looking graphs and charts. In Chapter 4 we'll explore these and other routines in much greater detail when we develop several presentation graphics applications. The remaining routine, **FillPoly**, works much like its companion routine **DrawPoly**, except that it both draws and fills a polygon using the current drawing color and fill pattern.

Now let's write a program that uses each of these routines to draw some basic graphic objects. The program divides the screen into six regions and draws a different figure in each region. The display produced by the program is shown in Figure 1.3. The offset calculations make the code a bit cumbersome, but once again this is the cost of the generality. Here is the complete program:

```
program ShowFill;
{ SHOWFILL.PAS: Displays various filled figures. }
uses
  Graph, Crt;
var
  GDriver, GMode, MaxX, MaxY: integer;
  Color: word;
  Points: array[1..5] of PointType;
begin
  GDriver := Detect;
  InitGraph(GDriver,GMode,'\tp\bgi');
  MaxX := GetMaxX;  MaxY := GetMaxY;
  { Draw a bar, a 3d bar, and a filled polygon on the top portion
    of the screen and a pieslice, a filled circle, and a filled
    elliptical region on the bottom portion }
  Bar(MaxX div 6-20,MaxY div 4-30,MaxX div 6+20,MaxY div 4+20);
  OutTextXY(MaxX div 6-TextWidth('Bar') div 2,0,'Bar');
  Bar3d(MaxX div 2-20,MaxY div 4-30,MaxX div 2+20,
        MaxY div 4+20,10,True);
  OutTextXY(MaxX div 2-TextWidth('Bar3d') div 2,0,'Bar3d');
  Points[1].X := MaxX*5 div 6-20;
```

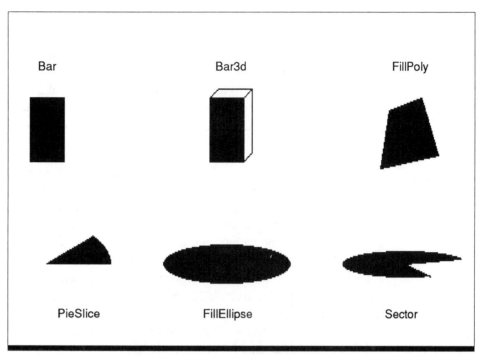

Figure 1.3. Output of SHOWFILL.PAS

```
Points[1].Y := MaxY div 4-20;
Points[2].X := MaxX*5 div 6-30;
Points[2].Y := MaxY div 4+25;
Points[3].X := MaxX*5 div 6+40;
Points[3].Y := MaxY div 4+15;
Points[4].X := MaxX*5 div 6+20;
Points[4].Y := MaxY div 4-30;
Points[5].X := Points[1].X;
Points[5].Y := Points[1].Y;
FillPoly(5,Points);
OutTextXY(MaxX*5 div 6-TextWidth('FillPoly') div 2,
          0,'FillPoly');
PieSlice(MaxX div 6,MaxY*3 div 4,0,45,75);
OutTextXY(MaxX div 6-TextWidth('PieSlice') div 2,
          MaxY-TextHeight('l'),'PieSlice');
FillEllipse(MaxX div 2,MaxY * 3 div 4,75,15);
OutTextXY(MaxX div 2-TextWidth('FillEllipse') div 2,
          MaxY-TextHeight('F'),'FillElipse');
Sector(MaxX*5 div 6,MaxY*3 div 4,25,295,75,10);
OutTextXY(MaxX*5 div 6-TextWidth('Sector') div 2,
          MaxY-TextHeight('l'),'Sector');
repeat until KeyPressed;
CloseGraph;
end.
```

You may now be wondering, how do the fill commands know what type of fill pattern to use? Basically, each time you call one of the fill commands it uses the current fill style and color. In our program, we did not explicitly set the fill style, so the program defaults to a solid fill painted in the maximum color available on the video adapter. Turbo Pascal provides a procedure called **SetFillStyle** that is used to change the fill style. As an example, if we added the statement:

```
SetFillStyle(HatchFill,Blue);
```

immediately after the call to **InitGraph,** our program would have drawn all of the objects with a blue (on an EGA or VGA system) hatch pattern. The values for **HatchFill** and **Blue,** along with other colors and fill styles, are defined in the **Graph** unit. In Chapter 2 we'll show you how you can create your own fill patterns.

You may also be wondering whether Borland has provided enough fill commands in their BGI toolset. For example, there isn't a circle fill command; or is there? Actually, several of the Turbo Pascal graphics commands serve dual roles. In the case of a circle, the **FillEllipse** procedure can be used to paint a filled circle. The trick is to call **FillEllipse** with x and y coordinates that are adjusted so that they draw a circular figure. The **FillPoly** procedure is the real powerhouse, however. It has a tremendous amount of flexibility because you can use it to fill objects of any shape.

Text and Fonts

When it comes to text output and fonts, the BGI is quite impressive. In the past, text output in graphics mode on an IBM PC has been a bit of a disappointment. For example, in graphics mode the IBM PC provides only characters of a fixed size that are in some cases of poor quality. However, with the BGI tools you can easily add high-quality text to your graphics displays. The BGI includes a stroke font package that is well suited for drawing characters of various heights and widths. In addition, it is also capable of drawing vertical text.

Our next task is to write a program that displays a single line of text at varying scales and in both horizontal and vertical orientations. The program uses the sans serif stroke font to display the message "Turbo Pascal" centered on your screen. The program will allow you to interactively rescale the size of the text. The s key is used to shrink the text, and the g key to make the text grow in size. The space bar will switch the text between a horizontal and a vertical format. Finally, pressing the q key will quit the program.

The following program takes a slight departure from the other programs we've presented because it uses Turbo Pascal's new object-oriented features. In fact, the majority of the program is designed around a new language construct called an *object*. In simple terms, an object is much like a record, but it can also contain procedures and functions. If you are new to objects, you should read the sidebar called "Creating Objects with Turbo Pascal" on page 19 to help you get up to speed with this powerful new language feature.

This program is built around one primary object, which we've labeled to be of a type called **TextObj**. The **TextObj** object type houses a number of elements such as the variables **MultX**, **DivX**, and **MultY** used to control the size of the text to display, and the routines **Erase**, **Display**, and **UpdateSize**, which are used to display the text. By using an object we're able to combine all the data and functions required to display and process a text string under one roof, in this case the object type **TextObj**.

Here's the complete program:

```
program ShowText;
{ SHOWTEXT.PAS: This program displays a line of text that you can scale as
  you please. The program allows the following user interaction:
       s        shrink the text
       g        grow or enlarge the text
       space    switch between horizontal and vertical text format
       q        quit the program
  Unlike the other programs in this chapter, ShowText uses an
  object-oriented style. Take a good look at it because later in
  the book we'll be using OOP techniques extensively. }
uses
  Graph, Crt;
const
  Incr: integer = 10;        { Change text this much when resized }
type
{ Define an object that specifies what text to display and how
  to display it }
TextObj = object
  { The data components of the object type are: }
  MultX, DivX, MultY, DivY,  { Text scaling factors }
  NewDir, CurrentDir,        { Orientation flags of text }
  CX, CY,                    { Text is centered to this point }
  SW, SH: integer;           { String pixel width and height }
  TextString: string;        { The string to display }
  { The methods of the object type are: }
  constructor Init;          { Initializes the object }
  procedure Erase;           { Erases the text }
  function UpdateSize: char; { Changes the size of the text }
  procedure Display;         { Displays the text }
end;

var
  GDriver, GMode: integer;
  Text: TextObj;             { Declare a TextObj object }
  Ch: char;
```

```
constructor TextObj.Init;
{ Constructor procedure for TextObj. It initializes the object. }
begin
  MultX := 100;          DivX := 100;           { Start with this size }
  MultY := 100;          DivY := 100;
  { Display text horizontally }
  CurrentDir := HorizDir;  NewDir := HorizDir;
  TextString := 'Turbo Pascal';                  { String to display }
  SetFillStyle(SolidFill,GetBkColor);            { Set fill color }
  CX := GetMaxX div 2;   CY := GetMaxY div 2;    { Center text }
  SetTextJustify(CenterText,CenterText);
end;

procedure TextObj.Erase;
{ Erase the existing string by painting over it with a solid bar
  that is set to the color of the background }
begin
  SW := TextWidth(TextString) div 2;
  SH := TextHeight(TextString) * 3 div 2;
  if CurrentDir = HorizDir then begin { Where to erase text }
    if SW > CX then SW := CX + 1;     { depends on whether text }
    if SH > CY then SH := CY + 1;     { is written horizontally }
    Bar(CX-SW,CY-SH,CX+SW,CY+SH);
  end
  else begin                          { The text is vertical }
    if SH > CX then SH := CX + 1;
    if SW > CY then SW := CY + 1;
    Bar(CX-SH,CY-SW,CX+SH,CY+SW);
  end;
  CurrentDir := NewDir;               { Update direction flag }
end;

function TextObj.UpdateSize: char;
{ Resize the text based on the character the user has pressed }
var
  Ch: char;
begin
  Ch := ReadKey;                      { Get user input }
  { Resize the text as long as the scale won't go to zero }
  if Ch = 'g' then begin              { Grow the text }
    if DivX > Incr then begin
      Dec(DivX,Incr);  Inc(MultX,Incr);
    end;
    if DivY > Incr then begin
      Dec(DivY,Incr);  Inc(MultY,Incr);
    end;
  end
  else if Ch = 's' then begin         { Shrink the text }
    if MultX > Incr then begin
      Dec(MultX,Incr); Inc(DivX,Incr);
    end;
    if MultY > Incr then begin
      Dec(MultY,Incr); Inc(DivY,Incr);
```

```
      end
    end
  else if Ch = ' ' then              { Change orientation of text }
    if NewDir = HorizDir then NewDir := VertDir
      else NewDir := HorizDir;
  UpdateSize := Ch;
end;

procedure TextObj.Display;
{ Display the text with the new text specifications }
begin
  SetUserCharSize(MultX,DivX,MultY,DivY);
  SetTextStyle(SansSerifFont,CurrentDir,UserCharSize);
  OutTextXY(CX,CY,TextString);
end;

begin
  GDriver := Detect;
  InitGraph(GDriver,GMode,'\tp\bgi');
  Text.Init;                   { Initialize the text object }
  repeat
    Text.Display;              { Display the text with its current settings }
    Ch := Text.UpdateSize;     { Update text settings }
    Text.Erase;                { Erase the existing text }
  until Ch = 'q';
  CloseGraph;
end.
```

The **ShowText** program might at first appear a little odd to you because of its object-oriented style. Let's take a closer look. Note that at the beginning of the program we have defined the object type **TextObj**. It specifies which variables and routines are available to a **TextObj**. The routines themselves are only listed using procedure and function headings in the definition of **TextObj** and are actually defined later in the program.

Note that the first routine we've defined, **Init**, has a rather unusual procedural heading:

```
constructor Init;
```

In fact, it is a special procedure, called a constructor, that is used to initialize an object of type **TextObj**. Although not all object types must have constructors, we've included one here so you can see how it can be used. In Turbo Pascal, a constructor must be called once after an object is declared, but before any of its routines are used. For example, if we declared an object variable called **Text** to be of type **TextObj**:

```
var Text: TextObj;
```

we could later initialize it by calling its constructor using the statement:

```
Text.Init;
```

Note that the name of the object precedes the name of the routine in the object that is to be executed, in this case the constructor **Init**.

Later in the program you'll find the actual definition of the **Init** routine. You'll see that it initializes each of the variables of the **TextObj** object to a known state. In this case, we've set the initial scale of the text, the direction to draw the text, and finally which text string to display.

The other routines in our sample program, **Erase**, **UpdateSize**, and **Display**, are defined more like traditional Turbo Pascal routines. One of the obvious differences is in how these procedures are defined. As you can see in the code, the name of the object type with a period precedes the name of the routine. For instance, the **Erase** routine has the header:

```
procedure TextObj.Erase;
```

This information tells the compiler which object type the routine belongs to, in this case the **TextObj** type. To emphasize that routines such as this are tightly coupled with an object type, procedures and functions in an object are usually referred to as methods. This hints at the different role that routines play in an object-oriented program as opposed to a more traditional program.

That is, instead of writing programs that consist of procedure and function calls made by a main program or other routines, you can use objects to control the show. When an object calls a method, the object's data can be used by the routine to perform computations on itself. In one sense, you can think of an object as a miniature self-contained program, where an object's behavior depends on which methods are available to it.

Fractal Landscapes

Our tour of the BGI is almost over, but before we finish let's put together a program that uses many of the BGI features that we have been discussing. Of course, this program won't demonstrate everything that we have learned in this chapter, but it will show you the simplicity and the power of graphics programming with the BGI.

The program uses BGI tools to draw landscape scenes that are generated using fractal geometry. Each scene is designed with a mountain skyline and an ocean shoreline topped off with a glowing red sun. A sample scene created by the pro-

Creating Objects with Turbo Pascal

In many respects objects are merely an extension of Turbo Pascal's records. This change gives Turbo Pascal its object-oriented personality. Like records, objects begin as templates defined in the **type** section of a program by defining an *object type*. The primary difference, however, is that an object type is defined using the **object** keyword rather than **record**. In addition, an object can contain both data and procedures and functions, whereas ordinary records can contain only data. Once defined, an object type can be used to declare object variables in the **var** section of a program.

The two most important features that objects provide are *encapsulation* and *inheritance*. Encapsulation is the ability to package data and routines in an object so that they can be hidden from the rest of an application or at least kept together. Inheritance is the technique of building object types from other object types. This is one of the most important components of OOP because it allows us to easily reuse and share code.

The basic syntax used for declaring an object type is:

```
<object type name> = object
  private:
  { Private data and methods go here }
  public:
  { Public data and methods go here }
end;
```

There are two basic components of an object type: its data (called *instance variables*) and its procedures and functions (called *methods*). As the general syntax shows, these components can be declared to be either *public* or *private*. If an object component follows the **private** keyword, then that member can be accessed only by that object, much like a local variable can be accessed only inside the function that defines it. Unless otherwise noted, all members of an object type are public and can be accessed anywhere it is legal to access the object that contains them. However, outside of the object, you must use the name of the object to reference any of the object's instance variables or methods. For example, Figure 1.4 shows an object type called **Str** and illustrates how to declare an object of type **Str** and access its instance variables and call some its methods.

```
type
  Str = object
        S : String;            } Instance variables
        Len : integer;
        procedure Init;
        procedure AppendChar(Ch : char);  } Methods
        procedure DisplayString;
  end;
var  StringObj : Str;
begin
  StringObj.Init;
  StringObj.AppendChar('S');
  StringObj.DisplayString;
end.
```

Figure 1.4. Using an object in Turbo Pascal

gram is shown in Figure 1.5. The contours of the mountains and the shoreline are both created with fractals. We'll discuss fractals shortly, but first let's look at an important BGI routine used in the program that we have not yet discussed.

The sky, the water, and the sun are all painted using a procedure called **FloodFill**. This routine simply fills a bounded region of any size or shape with the current fill settings and drawing color. The procedure declaration for **FloodFill** is:

```
procedure FloodFill(X, Y: integer; BorderColor: word);
```

Here the parameters **X** and **Y** specify what is called a *seed point* and the parameter **BorderColor** indicates the color of the border of the bounded region. The seed point should be a coordinate point that is somewhere inside the bounded region.

Now let's take a quick look at fractal geometry. Fractal technology was created by mathematical researchers who were attempting to efficiently model the complexity of nature. By using mathematical formulas, these researchers found it possible to create realistic three-dimensional scenes of mountains complete with trees, lakes, bolts of lightning, and many other natural objects.

Our example program uses a fractal routine to generate a view of a coastal range against a shoreline. The contour lines of the mountains and the ocean actu-

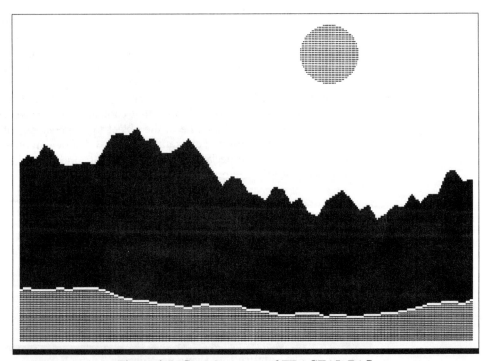

Figure 1.5. Sample output of FRACTAL.PAS

ally begin as straight horizontal lines that extend across the screen. A procedure called **Fractal** is invoked to contort these lines so that they take on the jaggedness of a mountain skyline or the meanderings of a shoreline.

The **Fractal** procedure calls the routine **Subdivide**, which actually performs the *fractalization*. This routine takes a line segment, which is passed to it as two endpoints, calculates the midpoint for the line segment, and then uses the midpoint to *bend* the line up or down. The line is bent by a random amount. This adjusted midpoint, which will later correspond to the y value to be used when drawing the line at that point, is saved in a global array called **Frctl**. The fractalization continues by taking the line segments to the left and right of the midpoint and bending them at their midpoints, too. Their segments are subdivided and bent in a similar fashion and the process is repeated until the segments become too small to subdivide. The resulting line is a connected series of small segments that vary in the y direction. Figure 1.6 shows the stages of the fractalization of a sample line segment. Note that the amount the line segment is bent decreases as the line segment is subdivided into smaller pieces.

The amount that the midpoint is bent, or perturbed, is randomly calculated. This gives the line a reasonably natural look. However, there are several variables that we'll be using to help control the way that the lines are generated. Let's start by examining the parameters used with the **Fractal** procedure. Here is its declaration:

```
procedure Fractal(Y1, Y2, MaxLevel: integer; H, Scale: real);
```

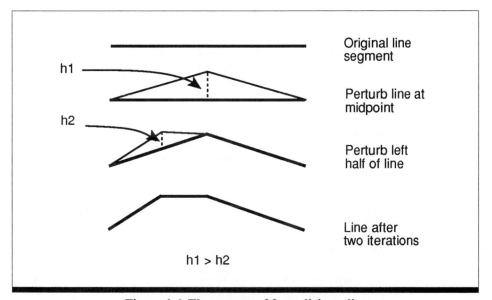

Figure 1.6. The process of fractalizing a line

The last parameter in **Fractal**, called **Scale**, partially defines the amount of the perturbation at each step in the fractalization. In addition, the preceding parameter called **H** specifies a decay factor that is multiplied against the current perturbation value in **Scale** at each subdivision of the line to reduce the size of **Scale** with each smaller and smaller line segment. In other words, initially, line segments vary greatly, but as they get smaller they are perturbed less and less. This creates a realistic roughness in many scenes. In fact, it is the combination of these two values, **Scale** and **H**, that we'll use to control the outcome of the fractal line. For example, the mountain skyline is much rougher than the shoreline so its H decay factor is set to only 0.5 (1 is the smoothest and close to 0 is the roughest). In addition, the mountains should be large, so **Scale** is initially set to a rather large value of 50. The shoreline, however, is supposed to be much smoother, so its **H** factor is 0.9, and **Scale** is assigned a value of 30.0.

The key to fractal geometry is the randomness that is applied to the line, surface, or shape that is being fractalized. Here, the Turbo Pascal routines **Random** and **Randomize** are combined to return a random value based on the clock in the PC. These random values are used to determine how much to perturb each line segment. Since the clock is used in the random number process, the program generates a different landscape scene each time it is run.

Finally, you may also want to try experimenting with the **H** and **Scale** values passed to the fractal routine for the mountains and shoreline in order to see what effect these parameters have on the fractalized surface.

```
program FractalProgram;
{ FRACTAL.PAS: This program combines several of the features of
   the BGI with a fractal routine to create a fractalized
   landscape scene. The scene will be slightly different each time
   you run it. Press any key to quit the program after the scene
   is displayed. This program requires a graphics adapter that can
   display CGA. }
uses
   Graph, Crt;
const
   MaxSize  = 1000;   { The fractalized array has this much room }
   MaxLevel = 6;      { Number of times line is cut in half }
   Water    = 1;      { Color of the water  on CGAC3 = blue }
   Sun      = 2;      { Color of the sun — on CGAC3 = red }
   Sky      = 3;      { Color of the sky — on CGAC3 = white }
var                   { Array used to hold fractalized lines }
   Frctl: array[1..MaxSize] of real;
   GDriver, GMode: integer;

function Power(Num, Pow: real): real;
{ Returns Num to the Pow }
begin
   if Num = 0 then Power := 0
```

```
        else Power := Exp(Pow * Ln(Num));
end;

procedure Subdivide(P1, P2: integer; Std, Ratio: real);
{ This is the workhorse routine for the fractalization process.
  It computes the midpoint between the two points: P1 and P2,
  and then perturbs it by a random factor that is scaled by Std.
  Next Subdivide calls itself to fractalize the line segments to
  the left and right of the midpoint. This process continues
  until no more divisions can be made. }
var
  MidPnt: integer;
  StdMid: real;
begin                              { Break the line at the midpoint }
  MidPnt := (P1 + P2) div 2;   { of point 1 and point 2 }
  { If midpoint is unique from point 1 and point 2, then perturb
    it randomly according to the equation shown }
  if (MidPnt <> P1) and (MidPnt <> P2) then begin
    Frctl[MidPnt] := (Frctl[P1] + Frctl[P2]) / 2 +
                     (Random(16) - 8.0) / 8.0 * Std;
    { Then fractalize the line segments to the left and right
      of the midpoint by calling Subdivide again. Note that the
      scale factor used to perturb each fractalized point is
      decreased each call by the amount in Ratio. }
    StdMid := Std * Ratio;
    Subdivide(P1,MidPnt,StdMid,Ratio);   { Fractalize left side }
    Subdivide(MidPnt,P2,Stdmid,Ratio);   { Fractalize right side }
  end
end;

procedure Fractal(Y1, Y2, MaxLevel: integer; H, Scale: real);
{ This is the main fractal routine. It fractalizes a line in one
  dimension only. In this case, the y dimension. The fractalized
  line is put into the global array: Frctl. The parameter
  MaxLevel specifies how much to break up the line, and H is a
  number between 0 and 1 that specifies the roughness of the
  line (1 is smoothest), and Scale is a scale factor that says
  how much to perturb each line segment. }
var
  First, Last: integer;
  Ratio, Std: real;
begin
  First := 1;                          { Determine the bounds of }
  Last := Round(Power(2.0,MaxLevel));{ array that will be used }
  Frctl[First] := Y1;                  { Use Y1 and Y2 as start }
  Frctl[Last] := Y2;                   { and endpoints of line }
  Ratio := 1.0 / Power(2.0,H);         { Set smoothness }
  Std := Scale * Ratio;                { and decay amount }
  Subdivide(First,Last,Std,Ratio);   { Begin the fractalization }
end;

procedure DrawFractal;
{ This routine displays a fractalized line. The Frctl array
```

```
    holds y values. The x values are equally spaced across the
    screen depending on the number of levels calculated. }
var
  I, X, XInc, L: integer;
begin
  { Number of points in Frctl used }
  L := Round(Power(2.0,MaxLevel));
  XInc := GetMaxX div L * 3 div 2;   { Calculate the x increment }
  MoveTo(0,100);                      { used to draw each line }
  X := 0;
  for I := 1 to L do begin           { Draw the lines using }
    LineTo(X,Round(Frctl[I]));        { the y values in Frctl }
    Inc(X,XInc);
  end
end;


begin
  GDriver := CGA;          { Sets the screen to CGAC3, which has }
  GMode := CGAC3;          { black=0, cyan=1, magenta=2, white=3 }
  InitGraph(GDriver,GMode,'\tp\bgi');
  Randomize;                               { Initialize Random function }
  Rectangle(0,0,GetMaxX,GetMaxY);          { Draw a frame for picture }
  SetColor(Sky);                           { Prepare to draw the sky }
  Fractal(100,100,MaxLevel,0.5,50.0);      { Fractalize the skyline }
  DrawFractal;                             { and then display it }
  SetFillStyle(SolidFill,Sky);             { Use FloodFill to draw }
  FloodFill(1,1,Sky);                      { color in the sky }

  SetColor(White);                         { Draw white shoreline }
  Fractal(170,170,MaxLevel,0.9,30.0);      { Use smoother settings }
  DrawFractal;                             { Color the screen below }
  SetFillStyle(SolidFill,Water);           { the shoreline with the }
  FloodFill(1,GetMaxY-1,White);            { color set by Water }

  SetFillStyle(SolidFill,Sun);             { Draw a sun using a }
  SetColor(Sun);                           { circle floodfilled with }
  Circle(GetMaxX-100,40,20);               { the color set by Sun }
  FloodFill(GetMaxX-100,50,Sun);
  repeat until KeyPressed;                  { Hold screen until key hit }
  CloseGraph;                              { Exit graphics mode }
end.
```

The BGI Drawing Commands

The heart of any graphics system consists of its drawing routines. As we saw in Chapter 1, the BGI provides a rich set of drawing procedures and functions that support several graphics hardware and video modes. In this chapter we're going to show you how you can use the basic drawing functions in your Turbo Pascal programs.

We'll begin with the fundamental BGI drawing routines—the pixel-oriented routines. We'll then work with the more general drawing procedures that include routines to draw rectangles, circles, ellipses, polygons, and other shapes. In addition, we'll explore region filling techniques and develop a program to help us experiment with our own fill patterns and designs. Along the way, we'll take a close look at the **PutImage** and **GetImage** procedures that we'll use to introduce programming techniques for creating animation.

Working with Pixels

As we've seen in Chapter 1, the pixel is the basic building block for PC graphics. By grouping pixels, we can draw lines, figures, textures, and other graphics objects. Of course, if we were to construct all our graphics scenes at the pixel level, we'd have a tremendous programming task before us. Nevertheless, pixels and the routines that can manipulate them are an essential element of a graphics toolkit.

The BGI includes two pixel routines, **PutPixel** and **GetPixel**, which we briefly introduced in our quick tour in Chapter 1. To refresh your memory, **PutPixel** displays one pixel at a specified screen location and **GetPixel** returns the current color of any pixel on the screen. In the following section we'll use both of these to illustrate how pixels are accessed and displayed.

Plotting a Single Pixel

The **PutPixel** procedure plots a pixel at an x and y coordinate using a specified color. It is declared as:

```
procedure PutPixel(X, Y: integer; PixelColor: word);
```

The location where the pixel is displayed is relative to the origin of the current viewport. Although the valid range of x and y depends on the size of the viewport, initially the full screen is used. Therefore, the functions **GetMaxX** and **GetMaxY** can be used to determine the maximum extents of x and y, respectively.

The **PixelColor** parameter specifies the pixel's color. Actually, the **PixelColor** parameter specifies the index location of the palette from which the color is chosen. This parameter, like the x and y coordinates, has a restricted range of values for each video mode. This range extends from zero to the maximum color value returned by the **GetMaxColor** function. In actuality, **GetMaxColor** returns the valid range of indexes into the palette table.

Working with Colors

We've shown how the color of individual pixels can be set using the **PutPixel** procedure. However, there is much more flexibility in controlling color than this. In particular, the routines that can manage the background and foreground drawing colors are listed in Table 2.1. Using the BGI's color system, however, is a little more complicated than you might think. The routines listed in Table 2.1 represent only half the story.

To use the BGI's color drawing and filling capabilities, you'll need to know how colors are displayed on your PC's screen. The available colors are stored in a color palette. Essentially, the *color palette* is a table that lists all of the colors that can be displayed at one time. Let's take a closer look.

When you specify that a particular color is to be displayed, you are really specifying an index into the color palette. It is the color stored in the palette that

Table 2.1. The main color routines

Routine	Description
SetBkColor	Sets the active background color
SetColor	Sets the active foreground color
GetBkColor	Returns the active background color
GetColor	Returns the active drawing color
GetMaxColor	Returns the highest index in the color palette

you actually see on the screen. For example, if you set the current drawing color to 0, then the color located in the 0th position of the color palette is used. The color indexing system is illustrated in Figure 2.1. Note that only the active colors in the palette can be displayed. The first entry in the palette table, (0), has a special meaning. It stores the color to be used for the screen's background. To allow you to access the color palette, the BGI provides seven special routines, which are listed in Table 2.2. The number of colors that can be displayed at the same time is determined by the size of the current color palette and depends on the graphics

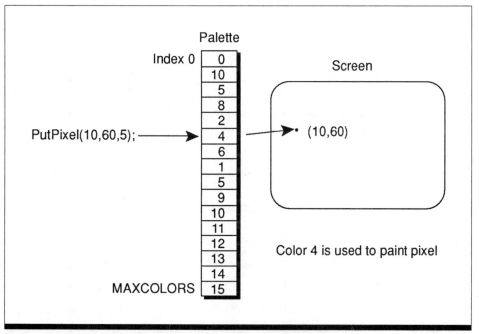

Figure 2.1. The color indexing system

Table 2.2. Routines for accessing the color palette

Routine	Description
SetPalette	Changes a palette color
SetAllPalette	Changes all palette colors
GetPalette	Returns information about the color palette
GetDefaultPalette	Returns the default palette for the current driver
GetPaletteSize	Returns the size of the color palette
SetRGBColor	Changes a color in the palette for 256-color displays
SetRGBPalette	Changes the palette for 256-color displays

mode being used. As an example, the color palette for the CGA adapter in one of its modes contains four colors, and the palette for EGA's supported modes contains 16 colors. Because each adapter works a little differently, we'll consider each one separately. For a list of the adapters and modes that the BGI supports, refer to the sidebar on page 29, "Working with the Graphics Hardware."

CGA Colors

A low-resolution and high-resolution mode are supported on the CGA. In the low-resolution mode, four different colors can be displayed at the same time. The colors that are available are listed in Table 2.3 (modes 0 to 3). In the high-resolution mode (mode 4), only two colors can be displayed, and the background color must always be black. The foreground color can be set to any of the colors in Table 2.4.

Table 2.3. CGA colors (low-resolution mode)

Mode	Background Color (0)	Foreground Colors (1,2,3)
0	User selectable	Light green, light red, yellow
1	User selectable	Light cyan, light magenta, white
2	User selectable	Green, red, brown
3	User selectable	Cyan, magenta, light gray

Working with the Graphics Hardware

Although the BGI supports a variety of graphics adapters and modes, the basic concepts for working with each of these adapters and modes is the same. In each mode, the screen is divided into rows of pixels and each pixel is represented as an addressable memory location. The number of pixel rows and columns available is called the *resolution* of the screen. The upper-left corner of the screen is referenced as (0,0) and the lower-right corner as (last-pixel-column,last-pixel-row).

Each graphics adapter supported by the BGI provides a set of selectable modes. The mode determines the resolution of the screen and the number of colors available. In addition, some of the modes provide multiple pages of memory so that you can switch between different screens. The table below lists the adapters and modes supported by the BGI. The more popular adapters such as the CGA, EGA, and VGA are listed first. Note that multiple drivers are provided for the EGA. The label component is the symbolic name of the mode that the BGI supports. These names can be used with routines such as **InitGraph**, **DetectGraph**, **GetModeName**, **GetModeRange**, and so on to initialize the graphics system. They are defined in the unit **Graph**.

Adapter	Mode	Resolution	Colors	Pages	Mode Label
CGA	0-3	320x200	4	1	CGAC0,CGAC1, CGAC2,CGAC3
	4	640x200	2	1	CGAHi
EGA	0	640x200	16	4	EGALo
	1	640x350	16	2	EGAHi
EGA64	0	640x200	16	1	EGA64Lo
	1	640x350	4	1	EGA64Hi
EGAMono	0	640x350	2	1	EGAMonoHi
VGA	0	640x200	16	2	VGALo
	1	640x350	16	2	VGAMed
	2	640x480	16	2	VGAHi
MCGA	0-3	320x200	4	1	MCGAC0, MCGAC1, MCGAC2, MCGAC3
	4	640x200	2	1	MCGAMed
	5	640x480	2	1	MCGAHi
Herc	0	720x348	2	2	HercMonoHi
ATT400	0-3	320x200	4	1	ATT400C0, ATT400C1, ATT400C2, ATT400C3
	4	640x200	2	1	ATT400Med
	5	640x400	2	1	ATT400Hi
PC3270	0	720x350	2	1	PC3270Hi
IBM8514	0	640x480	256	—	IBM8514Lo
	1	1024x780	256	—	IBM8514Hi

Table 2.4. Selectable palette colors

Value	Symbolic Name
0	Black
1	Blue
2	Green
3	Cyan
4	Red
5	Magenta
6	Brown
7	LightGray
8	DarkGray
9	LightBlue
10	LightGreen
11	LightCyan
12	LightRed
13	LightMagenta
14	Yellow
15	White

In the low-resolution mode, the foreground colors are predefined. For example, if you choose mode 2 as shown in Table 2.3, the foreground colors are green, red, and brown. You can, however, choose your own background colors by using any of the colors listed in Table 2.4.

Before we leave CGA colors, there are a few key issues we must discuss. If you are working with the low-resolution modes, you can select one of the four color sets (modes 0 to 3) by using the **SetGraphMode** procedure. For example, the call

```
SetGraphMode(2);
```

would select mode 2 and the three foreground colors would be green, red, and brown.

If you are using the high-resolution mode, you can set the foreground color using the **SetBkColor** procedure. This might not seem correct; however, in the high-resolution mode, the foreground color is treated as the background by this routine.

EGA and VGA Colors

The supported modes on the EGA and VGA are much more powerful than the CGA when it comes to colors. Both adapters provide a color palette that can be changed at any time. The color palette contains 16 entries that are by default set to the colors listed in Table 2.4. There are, however, a total of 64 colors from which you can choose. The routines listed in Table 2.2 are used with the EGA and VGA either to change one or more of the colors in the active palette or determine which colors are currently available.

The functions **SetAllPalette**, **GetPalette**, and **GetDefaultPalette** use the **PaletteType** record type to represent the palette of the installed graphics adapter:

```
PaletteType = record
  Size: byte;
  Colors: array[0..MaxColors] of ShortInt;
end;
```

The **Size** field gives the number of colors in the palette and the **Colors** field contains the actual color value for each entry in the palette.

Overview of Drawing Commands

Although you can draw almost anything using pixels, Turbo Pascal furnishes numerous drawing procedures and functions that simplify the task. These drawing routines can be divided into the following categories:

- Lines
- Rectangles
- Polygons
- Arcs, circles, and ellipses

Let's now take a closer look at each of these categories.

Drawing Lines

Although a line is always the shortest distance between two points, Turbo Pascal provides three different ways of drawing one. Table 2.5 presents a list of the line drawing and related positioning routines. As shown in the table, there are essentially two types of line drawing procedures: absolute and relative. Both, however, always use the current drawing color and line style when drawing a line.

Table 2.5. Line drawing and positioning routines

Routine	Description
Line	Draws a line from (x1,y1) to (x2,y2)
LineTo	Draws a line from the current position to the point (x,y)
LineRel	Draws a line from the current position in the relative direction (dx,dy)
MoveRel	Moves the current position a relative amount
MoveTo	Moves the current position to the point (x,y)

Drawing Lines with Absolute Coordinates

Our discussion of the line drawing routines starts by looking at the two procedures, **Line** and **LineTo**, which use absolute coordinates. Let's begin by looking at the procedure **Line**. It takes two x and y coordinate pairs that specify the endpoints of the line that it is to draw. A typical call to **Line** is:

```
Line(5,30,200,180);
```

This statement, if executed, will draw a line from the point (5,30) to the point (200,180). Similarly, a triangle with the vertices (X1,Y1), (X2,Y2), and (X3,Y3) can be drawn using the following code sequence:

```
Line(X1,Y1,X2,Y2);
Line(X2,Y2,X3,Y3);
Line(X3,Y3,X1,Y1);
```

An alternative technique for drawing lines consists of using the **LineTo** and **MoveTo** procedures that allow you to draw lines by moving in discrete steps. Both of these routines take one coordinate pair as a parameter. The **LineTo** procedure is used to draw a line from the current position to a coordinate specified by **LineTo**. After a call to **LineTo**, the current position is updated to the coordinate pair specified with **LineTo**.

The **MoveTo** procedure is used to move the current position as needed. Normally, it is needed only when setting the beginning of a line segment. The current position may be affected by other graphics functions, too. For example, when you open a viewport the current position is always set to (0,0).

To draw the same triangle that was presented in our previous example using **MoveTo** and **LineTo**, you would use:

```
MoveTo(X1,Y1);
LineTo(X2,Y2);
LineTo(X3,Y3);
LineTo(X1,Y1);
```

In some cases, **LineTo** provides a more convenient way of drawing line figures. For instance, if you are calculating points for a figure while you are drawing it but are not saving them as you go, the **MoveTo** and **LineTo** pair may be an ideal way of drawing the lines.

Drawing Lines with Relative Coordinates

In some of your applications, you may need to draw lines using relative coordinates. For instance, you may want to draw lines relative to other points or lines. The **LineRel** and **MoveRel** procedures are provided for this reason.

For example, our triangle can be drawn using:

```
MoveTo(X1,Y1);
LineRel(X2-X1,Y2-Y1);
LineRel(X3-X2,Y3-Y2);
LineRel(X1-X3,Y1-Y3);
```

Of course, this example is rather poor, since it leads to a lot of extra operations, so clearly it's not the best solution for this case. However, if we were calculating our way along a curved surface, the **LineRel** and **MoveRel** routines might be the best choice.

Setting a Line Style

In the previous section we explored several ways to draw lines using the BGI. The BGI also allows us to specify the color of a line, its thickness, and its style. By default, all lines are drawn as solid lines, one pixel wide using the current drawing color. However, we can change each of these drawing parameters.

For instance, in Chapter 1 we learned how to change the current drawing color with the **SetColor** procedure. In addition, the BGI supports four predefined line patterns as well as user-defined line styles. In the next section, we'll look at how we can change the line style and its thickness.

Predefined Line Patterns

The BGI provides the **SetLineStyle** procedure to alter the line type and width of all lines drawn. Its declaration is:

```
procedure SetLineStyle(LineStyle, Pattern, Thickness: word);
```

The **LineStyle** parameter, which can be set to one of five values as defined in the unit **Graph**, specifies the line type that is used when a line is drawn. Its possible values are:

Constant	Value
SolidLn	0
DottedLn	1
CenterLn	2
DashedLn	3
UserBitLn	4

The first four constants specify predefined line patterns and are shown in Figure 2.2. These enable you to draw solid lines, dotted lines, and dashed lines. You can also create your own line style by using the **UserBitLn** constant.

The second parameter in **SetLineStyle** is used when a user-defined line pattern is desired. If, however, you're using one of the four predefined patterns, you should use a value of 0 for this parameter. The last parameter, **Thickness**, specifies the thickness that all lines are to be drawn. There are two possibilities here:

Constant	Value	Line Thickness
NormWidth	1	1 pixel thick
ThickWidth	3	3 pixels thick

Combining this information, suppose we want to draw a series of dashed, thick lines using the current drawing color. In order to do this, we must first make a call to **SetLineStyle**:

```
SetLineStyle(DashedLn,0,ThickWidth);
```

Once this is done, all lines that are drawn will use these line settings.

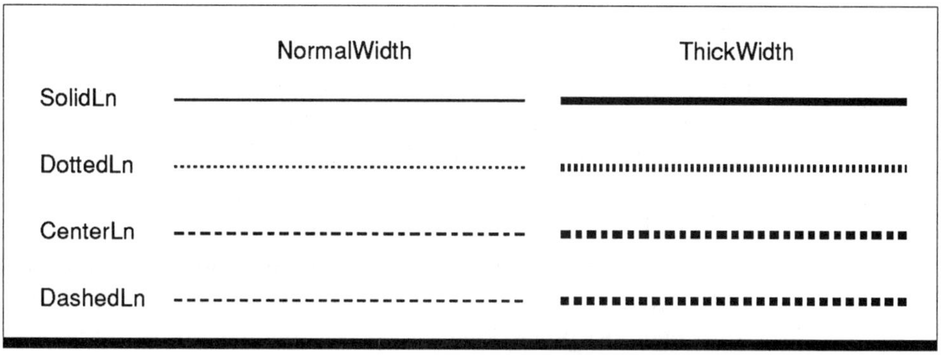

Figure 2.2. The four predefined line styles

Determining the Current Line Style

Now let's look at how the BGI enables us to determine the current line settings. This feature is particularly useful when we need to save the current line settings so that they can be changed and later restored. Fortunately, the BGI provides the procedure **GetLineSettings**, which is specifically designed for this task. To understand how it works, we must introduce the record type **LineSettingsType** that is used for storing the current line settings. It is defined in **Graph** as:

```
LineSettingsType = record
  LineStyle: word;
  Pattern: word;
  Thickness: word;
end;
```

This record type is important because **GetLineSettings** expects a record of this type to be passed to it and will return the various line parameters within its fields. The procedural declaration for **GetLineSettings** is:

```
procedure GetLineSettings(var LineInfo: LineSettingsType);
```

Therefore, to retrieve the current line settings, you can use the statements:

```
SavedLineInfo: LineSettingsType; { Declare line record }
GetLineSettings(SavedLineInfo); { Save line settings }
```

Later, to restore the line settings, you can use the **SetLineStyle** procedure:

```
SetLineStyle(SavedLineInfo.LineStyle,SavedLineInfo.Pattern,
         SavedLineInfo.Thickness);
```

User-Defined Line Styles

Besides the four predefined line styles shown in Figure 2.2, the BGI also provides us with a way of defining our own line styles. This is accomplished with the **SetLineStyle** procedure and involves setting the first two of its three parameters.

As mentioned before, the leftmost parameter of **SetLineStyle** declares the type of line that is used and must in this case be set to **UserBitLn** or a value of 4. The second parameter, however, actually defines the line pattern. It is a 16-bit binary pattern that encodes the way that lines are to be drawn. Each bit in the pattern is equivalent to 1 pixel along a 16-pixel stretch of a line. If the bit is on, all pixels in its corresponding position on the line are displayed with the current drawing color. If the bit is a 0, its corresponding pixels are not painted or changed. Therefore, a user-defined line pattern that defines a solid line can be created by the procedure call:

```
SetLineStyle(UserBitLn,$FFFF,NormWidth);
```

The hex value $FFFF will turn all pixels on and will effectively create solid lines. Similarly, to draw a dashed line where every other pixel is on, you merely need to use a bit pattern with every other bit set to a 1. This can be accomplished with the line:

```
SetLineStyle(UserBitLn,$AAAA,NormWidth);
```

Figure 2.3 shows numerous line patterns that can be generated by varying the user-defined line pattern.

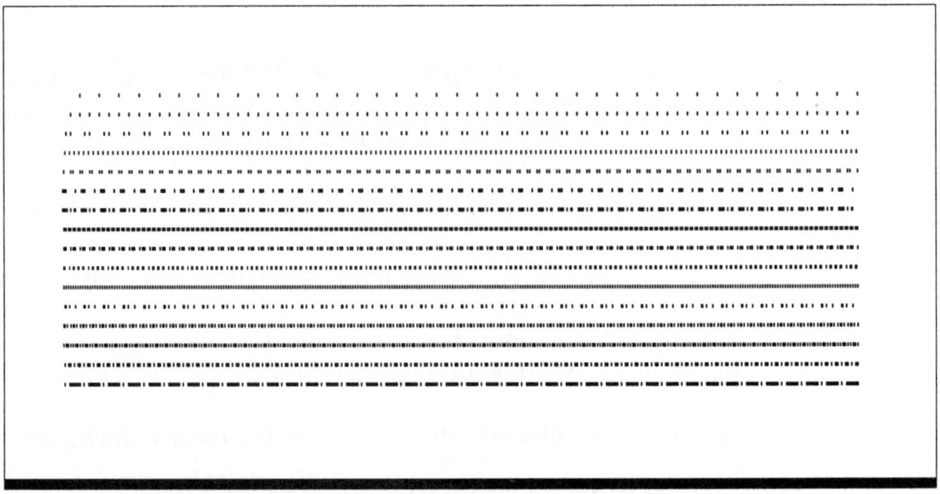

Figure 2.3. Several user-defined line patterns

Drawing Rectangles

All the PC graphics that we'll create throughout this book could be produced with the pixel and line drawing procedures that have been presented. The BGI, however, also provides several higher-level drawing routines that can help us generate graphics. The first of these procedures we'll present is **Rectangle**. It is used for drawing rectangles. Its declaration as given in **Graph** is:

```
procedure Rectangle(Left, Top, Right, Bottom: integer);
```

The four parameters specify the pixel coordinates of the top-left and bottom-right corners of the rectangle. When using **Rectangle**, keep in mind that it draws only the perimeter of a rectangle. In later sections of this chapter, we'll see how the **Bar** and **Bar3D** procedures can be used to draw filled rectangles. Like most of the procedures we'll cover from here on, **Rectangle** uses the current drawing color and line style settings and is drawn relative to the current viewport.

Working with Polygons

The BGI also includes a generic routine to draw polygons, appropriately called **DrawPoly**. It takes an array of points and draws line segments between the points using the current line style and drawing color. In effect, **DrawPoly** is comparable to making a series of calls to a line routine. Here is how it is declared in **Graph**:

```
procedure DrawPoly(NumPoints: word, var PolyPoints);
```

The first parameter specifies the number of *coordinates* that are sent to **DrawPoly**. The second parameter, **PolyPoints**, is an untyped parameter pointing to an array of records of type **PointType** that specify x and y coordinates that are to be joined by line segments. The record **PointType** is defined in the unit **Graph** as:

```
PointType = record
  X, Y: integer;
end;
```

Therefore, if we want to draw an open three-sided figure, **NumPoints** should be set to a value of 3 and the array of coordinate points should contain three **PointType** structures that specify the three line endpoints. For example, let's say that the three points are (10,30), (300,30), and (100,90). The following lines of code would draw this figure for us.

```
Points: array[1..3] of PointType = ((X:10,  Y:30), (X:300, Y:30),
                                     (X:100, Y:90));
DrawPoly(3,Points);
```

The **DrawPoly** procedure does not automatically close off the polygon. If you want a closed polygon, the last point must be the same as the first. Therefore, to close the polygon presented in this example, we can use:

```
Points: array[1..4] of PointType = ((X:10,  Y:30), (X:300, Y:30),
                                     (X:100, Y:90), (X:10,  Y:30));
DrawPoly(4,Points);
```

Note that the first and last coordinate pairs in the **Points** array are the same and that the **NumPoints** parameter has been increased by one to accommodate this.

Arcs, Circles, and Ellipses

By now you're probably wondering if the BGI can do more than draw lines. Fortunately, it can. The BGI provides the procedures **Arc, Circle, Ellipse, PieSlice, FillEllipse,** and **Sector** that can each draw curved figures. We'll begin by looking at the first three of these. The **PieSlice, FillEllipse,** and **Sector** procedures will be presented when we discuss filled regions later in this chapter.

Each of the curve drawing routines uses the current drawing color. They are, however, not completely affected by the line styles. In particular, the perimeters of the objects are always drawn solid, yet they are affected by the current setting of the line thickness. In addition, like all the procedures thus far, the coordinates of these routines are taken relative to the current viewport. Let's look at the **Arc** procedure.

Drawing Arcs

The **Arc** procedure draws a portion of a circle or a complete circle. It is defined as:

```
procedure Arc(X, Y: integer; StAngle, EndAngle, Radius: word);
```

The first two parameters specify a screen coordinate for the center point of the arc. The **StAngle** and **EndAngle** parameters are angles that specify the sweep of the arc. These values are in degrees and are measured counterclockwise starting from the 3 o'clock position. The last parameter dictates the radius of the circle. This value is measured in pixels from the center of the arc along the current row until it intersects the arc or the location on the screen where it would intersect the arc if it were swept to its 0 angle. This description is important when you consider that the aspect ratio of a given screen mode may cause the radius to actually be a different number of pixels in size at different angles along the circle.

For example, suppose we want to draw an arc that extends 15 degrees from the horizon. For the sake of this example, let's center the arc at (200,100) and give it a radius of 100. The line of code that will produce this arc is:

```
Arc(200,100,0,15,100);
```

If you count the pixels along the radius of this arc, you'll be able to verify that the radius is 100 pixels along its horizon.

Arc Endpoints

Sometimes it is useful to tell where the endpoints of an arc are located. For example, there are times when you may want to connect a line with the endpoints of an arc or link a series of arcs together. To accomplish this, the BGI provides the procedure **GetArcCoords**. Its procedural declaration is:

```
procedure GetArcCoords(var ArcCoords: ArcCoordsType);
```

The only parameter of **GetArcCoords** is a record of type **ArcCoordsType**. This record stores the endpoints of the last arc drawn and its center location. It is defined in **Graph** as:

```
ArcCoordsType = record
  X, Y: integer;
  XStart, YStart: integer;
  XEnd, YEnd: integer;
end;
```

By way of example, suppose we want to draw the perimeter of a hemisphere. To do this we can use a combination of the **Arc** and **Line** procedures. To properly connect the arc with a line segment, we'll use **GetArcCoords** to determine exactly where the endpoints of the arc are and consequently where the line should be drawn. The following program demonstrates this process by drawing a hemisphere at the center of the screen with a radius one-fourth its width.

```
program HemiSphere;
{ HEMI.PAS: Draws a hemisphere at the center of the screen }
uses
  Graph;
```

```
const
  GDriver: integer = Detect;
var
  GMode: integer;
  ArcCoords: ArcCoordsType;
begin
  InitGraph(GDriver,GMode,'\tp\bgi');
  Arc(GetMaxX div 2,GetMaxY div 2,0,180,GetMaxX div 4);
  GetArcCoords(ArcCoords);
  Line(ArcCoords.XStart,ArcCoords.YStart,
       ArcCoords.Xend,ArcCoords.YEnd);
  ReadLn;
  CloseGraph;
end.
```

Circles and Ellipses

Although **Arc** can be used to draw a complete circle (by specifying a start angle of 0 degrees and an ending angle of 360 degrees), a better method of accomplishing the same task is to use the BGI's **Circle** procedure. It is declared as:

```
procedure Circle(X, Y: integer; Radius: word);
```

The **X** and **Y** parameters specify the center of the circle and the last parameter—its radius. As is the case with **Arc**, the radius of the circle refers to the number of pixels from the center of the circle along its horizontal axis to its perimeter.

Note that **Circle** draws only the perimeter of a circle. In order to draw a filled circle, you must use **FillEllipse**, **PieSlice**, or alternatively flood fill the region as we will see later.

Another curved shape supported by the BGI is an ellipse. This shape is drawn with the procedure **Ellipse**, which operates much like **Arc**, since it can be used to draw all or part of an ellipse. The procedural declaration for **Ellipse** is:

```
procedure Ellipse(X, Y: integer; StAngle, EndAngle: word;
                  XRadius, YRadius: word);
```

Most of these parameters function the same as they have with the two previous routines. However, in order to achieve a wide variety of elliptic shapes this function allows you to specify the radius in the y direction as well as the x direction. The **Ellipse** procedure does not affect the interior of each ellipse that it draws. As we'll see, the **Sector** and **FillEllipse** procedures are used to draw filled elliptic regions.

Fundamentals of Animation

Let's take a break from the drawing commands so that we can focus on the **GetImage** and **PutImage** procedures. These procedures will be needed in the next section when we develop an interactive program to create our own fill patterns.

Basically, **GetImage** and **PutImage** are used to manipulate rectangular regions of the graphics screen. Using these procedures, we can easily cut, paste, move, or change regions of the screen without having to worry about screen memory addresses. We can, therefore, concentrate on using **GetImage** and **PutImage** for tasks such as animation effects, supporting pop-up windows, or allowing graphics objects to be easily edited and moved.

The declaration for **GetImage** is:

```
procedure GetImage(Left, Top, Right, Bottom : integer; var BitMap);
```

The first four parameters specify the top-left and bottom-right pixel boundaries of a rectangular region on the screen that is to be copied. This copied image is saved into memory pointed to by its last parameter, **BitMap**. The size of the memory **BitMap** points to is dependent on the size of the screen image being saved and the current graphics mode. Remember that each mode supports a different screen resolution that requires different amounts of memory. To determine the size of a screen image, the BGI provides the **ImageSize** function. This function takes the same pixel boundaries as **GetImage** to calculate the size of the screen that is to be saved. Based on these boundaries, the function returns the number of bytes that should be allocated for the **BitMap** array. For example, suppose we want to copy the region of the screen bounded by (10,10) and (100,100). First, we need to declare and allocate space for the **BitMap** as shown:

```
ScreenImage: pointer;
GetMem(ScreenImage,ImageSize(10,10,100,100));
```

Next, the image can be copied into the **ScreenImage** block of memory by a call to **GetImage**:

```
GetImage(10,10,100,100,ScreenImage^);
```

Note that the ^ symbol must be used to properly reference the **ScreenImage** memory when calling **GetImage**. Now that we have a copy of the screen image in **BitMap**, we can copy it to a different screen location with **PutImage**. The declaration for **PutImage** is:

```
procedure PutImage(Left, Top: integer; var BitMap; Op: word);
```

The first two parameters specify the top-left location where the image passed to the procedure is to be placed. Note that **PutImage** does not require the bottom-right boundaries, since this information is encoded within the **BitMap** memory. The last parameter of **PutImage**, called **Op**, specifies how **BitMap** is supposed to be copied to the screen. It can take on the following values:

Constant	Value	Description
CopyPut	0	Copy bit image to screen as is
XorPut	1	Exclusive-or bit image and screen
OrPut	2	Inclusive-or bit image and screen
AndPut	3	And bit image and screen
NotPut	4	Copy inverse of bitmap to screen

Therefore in our example, if we want to copy the bitmap image to the location (110,10) on the screen, we could use the statement:

```
PutImage(110,10,ScreenImage^,CopyPut);
```

Once again note that the ^ symbol must be used to properly access the **ScreenImage** memory. Similarly, if we want to invert the portion of the image that we saved earlier we could use the statement:

```
PutImage(10,10,ScreenImage^,NotPut);
```

This can be useful in highlighting portions of a screen. Figure 2.4 shows the effects produced by each of the image copying options listed previously.

Another extremely useful possibility with **PutImage** is to use the **XorPut** operation. It exclusive-ORs the bitmap image with the screen image. At a binary level the exclusive-OR operation sets all bits in the screen memory to a 1 if either but not both corresponding bits in the bit image and screen image are a 1. If both bits are 0 or 1, then the corresponding bit in the screen image is set to a 0. What makes this particular feature so useful is that once an image has been exclusive-ORed it can be removed by repeating the process. This can be valuable for some types of animation. In a program later in this chapter we'll use the **XorPut** option to help move a cursor across the screen without having to worry about modifying the screen as it is moved. Note that the results of a **PutImage** operation using the exclusive-OR function will depend on the current colors on the screen and the colors in **BitMap**.

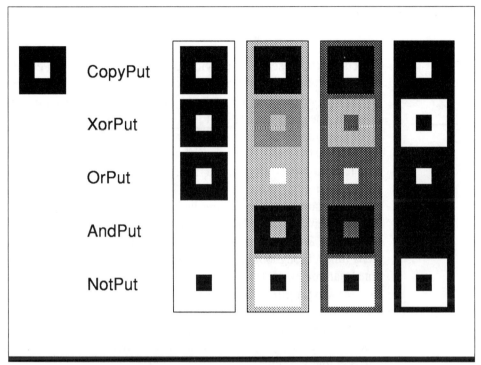

Figure 2.4. Effects created using PutImage

The other two operations supported by **PutImage** are the **AndPut** and **OrPut** selections. The **AndPut** option performs a bitwise and of the bitmap image and the screen where it is placed. Similarly, the **OrPut** option performs a bitwise or operation.

Finally, there are a few considerations that you should keep in mind while using **GetImage** and **PutImage**. First, although these procedures are positioned relative to the current viewport coordinates, they are not affected by viewport clipping. However, if any portion of the **BitMap** image extends beyond the screen boundaries, the whole image operation may be clipped. This may cause problems when moving objects about a region; however, most of the time this is what you want.

Another area that may lead to a restriction when using **GetImage** and **PutImage** is related to the maximum size allowed for any bitmap. These procedures are designed to accept images that are 64k in size or smaller. This may seem like more than enough memory for any situation; however, when dealing with graphics screens this memory restriction can quickly become a problem. For example, in many of the 640 by 200 modes we would be unable to save the entire screen at once, since it would require more than 64k for the bitmap memory. The best we can do is divide the screen into sections and use multiple calls to **GetImage** to capture the whole screen.

Filling Regions

Thus far we have looked only at the graphics routines that draw the outlines of objects. Turbo Pascal also provides several procedures that can draw figures filled with either one of several predefined patterns or a user-defined pattern.

Before we proceed, let's take a quick look at the procedures listed in Table 2.6. (Refer to the program SHOWFILL.PAS in the section "Filling Figures," Chapter 1, for a demonstration of how these routines work.) The **Bar** and **Bar3D** procedures are similar, but have two key differences. The **Bar3D** procedure draws a three-dimensional bar while the **Bar** routine simply draws a filled rectangular region. We'll explore this more in Chapter 4. Actually, **Bar3D** can also be used to draw a two-dimensional bar, by setting its depth to zero. However—and here is the other major difference—**Bar3D** draws an outline to its region in the current drawing color while **Bar** does not have any outline. This distinction will become important many times throughout this book. You should also be aware that **Bar3D** has an additional parameter. If **True**, the procedure shades the top of the three-dimensional bar. Drawing a three-dimensional bar without a top can be useful if you want to stack several bars on top of one another.

The procedure **FillPoly** is also much like its counterpart **DrawPoly**. Both are used the same way. The only difference is that **FillPoly** paints the interior of the polygon that it draws.

Finally, **PieSlice** and **Sector** can draw filled pie slices and filled elliptical shapes, respectively. Each has parameters to specify where the pie slice or sector is supposed to start and end. Both angles begin at the 3 o'clock position relative to the center point (x,y) of the figures.

Table 2.6. The BGI draw and fill routines

Routine	Description
Bar	Draws a filled bar without an outline
Bar3D	Draws a three-dimensional filled bar with an outline
FillPoly	Draws a filled polygon
FillEllipse	Draws a filled elliptic region
PieSlice	Draws a pie slice and can be used to draw a filled circle
Sector	Draws a filled elliptic region with an outline

A final note on **PieSlice, FillEllipse**, and **Sector** is in order. Recall that the BGI does not directly include a procedure that can draw a filled circle. We've suggested that the **PieSlice** and **Sector** procedures can be used. The idea is to use a start angle of 0 degrees and an end angle of 360 degrees to draw a completely filled circle. However, note that both of these routines draw a perimeter in the current drawing color that will surround the shape as well as extend into its center. If the interior and border are different colors you will see a line extending from the center of the circle to the 3 o'clock position on the border of the circle. The only way to avoid this is to make the border and the fill pattern the same color. Another possibility is to use **FillEllipse** with balanced x and y dimensions that are adjusted for the screen's aspect ratio.

Now let's get back to the fill patterns. The BGI supplies 12 predefined fill patterns that the procedures listed in Table 2.6 can use. They are enumerated in **Graph** and are listed in Table 2.7. Figure 2.5 displays each of these fill patterns as they appear in a filled rectangle. Besides the predefined fill patterns, you can use **UserFill** to add your own fill pattern. We'll soon look at this. By default all fill operations use **SolidFill** and paint the interior regions with the color returned by **GetMaxColor**—most often this will be white.

Table 2.7. Predefined fill patterns

Constant	Value	Description
EmptyFill	0	Fill with background color
SolidFill	1	Fill completely with fill color
LineFill	2	Fill with horizontal lines
LtSlashFill	3	Fill with thin left to right slashes
SlashFill	4	Fill with thick left to right slashes
BkSlashFill	5	Fill with thick right to left slashes
LtBkSlashFill	6	Fill with thin right to left slashes
HatchFill	7	Fill with a light hatch pattern
XHatchFill	8	Fill with a heavy crosshatch
InterleaveFill	9	Fill with interleaving lines
WideDotFill	10	Fill with widely spaced dots
CloseDotFill	11	Fill with closely spaced dots

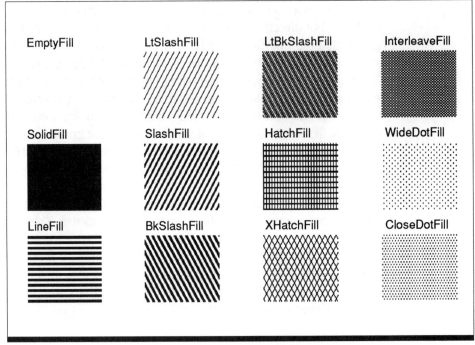

Figure 2.5. Predefined fill patterns

Setting the Fill Pattern

The fill pattern is selected by the **SetFillStyle** procedure. The declaration for this routine is:

```
procedure SetFillStyle(Pattern, Color: word);
```

The **Pattern** parameter is one of the fill styles listed in Table 2.7. The **Color** parameter is the color to be used for drawing the interior. All parts of the interior that are not part of the pattern are painted with the background color. One quirk that you may run across here is that in CGA high-resolution mode, all black patterns are drawn the same as white patterns.

User-Defined Fill Patterns

Defining a user-defined fill pattern is not done through **SetFillStyle**. Instead, the procedure **SetFillPattern** is used. As shown below, **SetFillPattern** is passed an 8 by 8 binary pattern representing the fill pattern to use and the color in which it is to be drawn. Its declaration is:

```
procedure SetFillPattern(Pattern: FillPatternType; Color: word);
```

The first parameter, called **Pattern**, is a byte array that specifies the pattern to use in the fill operation. Its type, **FillPatternType**, is predefined in the unit **Graph** as:

```
FillPatternType: array[1..8] of byte;
```

It is an array 8 bytes long where each byte represents one row of 8 pixels in the pattern. For example, a solid fill pattern can be defined as:

```
FillPattern: FillPatternType = ($FF, $FF, $FF, $FF, $FF, $FF, $FF, $FF);
```

Similarly, a checker pattern of alternating on and off pixels can be declared as:

```
FillPattern: FillPatternType = ($AA, $55, $AA, $55, $AA, $55, $AA, $55);
```

To set the current fill pattern to one of these user-defined patterns you can use a statement such as:

```
SetFillPattern(FillPattern,GetMaxColor);
```

Getting the Fill Pattern

As is the case with line styles, it is sometimes useful to be able to retrieve and save the current fill settings. This is often invaluable when you want to temporarily alter the fill settings. The procedure to access the current fill settings is:

```
procedure GetFillSettings(var FillInfo: FillSettingsType);
```

As you can see, it uses a record of type **FillSettingsType** to return the fill settings. This record is defined in the unit **Graph** as:

```
FillSettingsType = record
  Pattern: word;
  Color: word;
end;
```

Retrieving the fill settings is somewhat complicated by the user-defined fill patterns. If you are not using user-defined fill patterns all you need to do is call

GetFillSettings and it will return the pattern style and the fill color. However, if the current fill style is a user-defined fill pattern, the **Pattern** field in the record will be set to **UserFill**. Clearly, this can be used to tell that a user-defined pattern is being used, however, it doesn't tell what the pattern is. Thus whenever you want to save a user-defined pattern you must make an additional call to a procedure called **GetFillPattern** to retrieve the user-defined fill pattern.

The procedure **GetFillPattern** is defined as:

```
procedure GetFillPattern(var FillPattern: FillPatternType);
```

It copies the user-defined fill pattern that is currently being used into the array **FillPattern** (of type **FillPatternType** defined earlier), which is passed to it.

Putting all this together, let's say that we want to save the current fill settings, no matter what they are, perform some operations, and then restore the settings. To accomplish this, the following excerpted lines of code can be used:

```
SaveUserPtrn: FillPatternType;    { Declare space for the }
SaveFill: FillSettingsType;       { user-defined pattern }
                                  { and the fill settings }
GetFillSettings(SaveFill);        { Retrieve fill settings }

if SaveFill.Pattern = UserFill then      { If user-defined fill }
  GetFillPattern(SaveUserPtrn);          { pattern, save it }

{ ... code that can change fill settings ... }
if SaveFill.Pattern = UserFill then { Restore fill settings }
  SetFillPattern(SaveUserPtrn,SaveFill.Color)
else
  SetFillStyle(SaveFill.Pattern,SaveFill.Color);
```

Experimenting with User-Defined Fill Patterns

There are many possible user-defined fill patterns. Visualizing these patterns is a rather complicated thing to do; so instead, we'll develop a standalone program that will enable us to interactively explore different fill patterns.

The USERFILL.PAS program (see Listing 2.1) has three main components. First, there is a rectangular polygon drawn on the upper-right portion of the screen that shows a user-defined fill pattern. Adjacent to it is an exploded view of the pattern that you can edit. Using the arrow keys on the PC's keypad you can move a cursor through this pattern and toggle portions of the pattern on and off by pressing the space bar. This will automatically update the current fill pattern displayed in the rectangle on the right side of the screen. In addition, along the lower portion of the screen you will see a valid Pascal declaration that you can use in a program to declare the pattern you see on the screen. You won't have to figure out the bit patterns by hand.

Using the Arrow Keys

The USERFILL.PAS program relies on the keyboard for user input. More specifically, the arrow keys on the keypad are used to move the cursor around the enlarged fill pattern. These keys require special handling because each of the arrow keys generates a 2-byte sequence rather than the normal single character that most of the keyboard keys produce. Consequently, it takes two calls to **ReadKey** to acquire the full key code for the arrow keys. The question then becomes, how can we tell if we have an extended key code where we must make two calls to **ReadKey** or a normal character in the keyboard buffer? Luckily, for the keys that we are interested in, this is not much of a problem. It turns out that the first byte of each of the arrow keys is always a zero and that none of the other regular keys on the keyboard generates a single character equal to zero. Consequently, when our program reads a zero character, it knows that an extended key code is in the buffer and that it must read another byte from the keyboard buffer. This second byte can be used to decipher which arrow key was pressed. A list of these values is shown in Table 2.8.

In the mainline of USERFILL.PAS the **case** statement tests for the extended key codes by checking for a zero value in the character that is read by **ReadKey** at the beginning of the **while** loop. If this value is zero, it assumes that an arrow key was pressed, and reads another character from the keyboard buffer. This is the

Table 2.8. Extended key codes for arrow keys

Arrow Key	First Byte	Second Byte
Home	$00	$47
Up	$00	$48
PgUp	$00	$49
Left	$00	$4b
Right	$00	$4d
End	$00	$4f
Down	$00	$50
PgDn	$00	$51

value that is actually used in the **case** statement to decide which arrow key was pressed and which action to take. These are the values listed in the third column of Table 2.8.

• Listing 2.1. USERFILL.PAS

```
program UserFill;
{ USERFILL.PAS: This program enables the user to interactively experiment
   with various user-defined fill patterns. The user actually manipulates
   an 8 by 8 enlarged version of the pattern that is drawn on the left
   side of the screen. On the right side of the screen is a rectangle
   filled with the current fill pattern. At the bottom of the screen is
   the Pascal code for an array declaration that could be used to generate
   the current fill pattern. The user interaction allowed is:
      Arrow keys on keypad — moves cursor in the enlarged fill pattern
      Space bar           — toggles the current pixel under the cursor
      Esc                 — terminates the program }
uses
   Graph, Crt;
const
   GDriver: integer = Detect;
   PLeft        = 20;     { Left column of the big pattern }
   PTop         = 50;     { Top row of the big pattern }
   BigPixelSize = 8;      { The big pixels are 8 by 8 in size }
   { A few titles: }
   BigPatternTitle: string[17] = 'User Fill Pattern';
   PolyTitle: string[12] = 'Test Polygon';
   { Contains the fill pattern. Initially, it is all set off. }
   Fill: FillPatternType = (0, 0, 0, 0, 0, 0, 0, 0);
var
   BigPixel: pointer;     { Image used to hold a big pixel }
   Cursor: pointer;       { Cursor image }
   Ch: char;
   X, Y, GMode: integer;

procedure InitImages;
{ This initialization routine is called once to create the images that
   are used for the big pixel and the cursor }
var
   PX, PY, I, J: integer;
   Size: word;
begin
   { Create the image of a big pixel. Do this at the top-left
     corner of the big pattern. Once it is created, erase it by
     exclusive-ORing its own image with itself. }
   PX := PLeft;  PY := PTop;
   for J := PY+1 to PY+BigPixelSize do
      for I := PX+1 to PX+2*BigPixelSize do
         PutPixel(I,J,GetMaxColor);
   Size := ImageSize(PX+1,PY+1,PX+2*BigPixelSize,PY+BigPixelSize);
```

```
    GetMem(BigPixel,Size);
    GetImage(PX+1,PY+1,PX+2*BigPixelSize,PY+BigPixelSize,BigPixel^);
    PutImage(PX+1,PY+1,BigPixel^,XorPut);      { Erase the big pixel }
    { Next, create a small cursor image where the big pixel just was }
    PX := PX + 3;    PY := PY + 3;
    for J := PY to PY+BigPixelSize-5 do
      for I := PX to PX+2*BigPixelSize-5 do
        PutPixel(I,J,GetMaxColor);
    Size := ImageSize(PX,PY,PX+BigPixelSize*2-5,PY+BigPixelSize-5);
    GetMem(Cursor,Size);
    GetImage(PX,PY,PX+2*BigPixelSize-5,PY+BigPixelSize-5,Cursor^);
  end;

procedure DrawEnlargedPattern;
{ Using a series of horizontal and vertical lines, draw an outline
  for the 8 by 8 large pattern on the left side of the screen. Use
  dotted lines for these and when done, call InitImages to create
  the big pixel and cursor images. }
var
  I, Right, Bottom: integer;
begin
  SetLineStyle(DottedLn, 0, NormWidth);
  Right := 2 * (PLeft + (BigPixelSize-1) * (BigPixelSize + NormWidth));
  Bottom := PTop + 8 * (BigPixelSize + NormWidth);
  for I := 0 to 8 do begin               { Draw outline of big pixels }
    Line(PLeft,PTop+I*(BigPixelSize+NormWidth),Right-1,
    PTop+I*(BigPixelSize+NormWidth));
    Line(PLeft+2*(I*(BigPixelSize+NormWidth)),PTop,
    PLeft+2*(I*(BigPixelSize+NormWidth)),Bottom);
  end;
  InitImages;               { Initialize the big pixel and cursor }
end;

procedure DrawTestPolygon;
{ This routine draws a rectangular region on the right-hand side of the
  screen using the current user-defined fill pattern. Before it displays
  the pattern it erases the existing rectangle on the screen by drawing a
  black rectangle. }
begin
  SetLineStyle(SolidLn,0,NormWidth);     { Erase the old filled }
  SetFillStyle(SolidFill,Black);         { rectangle }
  Bar3D(400,PTop,500,PTop+50,0,False);
  SetFillPattern(Fill,GetMaxColor);      { Set to the new fill }
  Bar3D(400,PTop,500,PTop+50,0,False); { pattern and show it }
end;

function InttoStr(L: longint): string;
{ Convert an integer into a string }
var
  S : string;
begin
  Str(L,S);
  InttoStr := S;
end;
```

```pascal
procedure ShowPatternCode;
{ Show Pascal code that can be used to declare the fill pattern
  currently shown }
const
  X: integer = 20;
  Y: integer = 150;
var
  Buffer: string[80];
begin
{ Erase the old text on the screen by drawing a filled rectangle.
  The rectangle extends across the screen and is 8 pixels high since the
  default font is used. }
  SetColor(Black);
  SetLineStyle(SolidLn,0,NormWidth);
  SetFillStyle(SolidFill,GetBkColor);
  Bar3D(X,Y,GetMaxX,Y+8,0,False);
  { Convert the values to a string that can be printed out by OutTextXY }
  Buffer := 'Fill: FillPatternType = (' + InttoStr(Fill[1]) +
            ', ' + InttoStr(Fill[2]) + ', ' + InttoStr(Fill[3]) +
            ', ' + InttoStr(Fill[4]) + ', ' + InttoStr(Fill[5]) +
            ', ' + InttoStr(Fill[6]) + ', ' + InttoStr(Fill[7]) +
            ', ' + InttoStr(Fill[8]) + ');';
  SetColor(White);             { Restore the drawing color to white }
  OutTextXY(X,Y,Buffer);       { Display the Pascal code for the pattern }
end;

procedure TogglePixel(X, Y: integer);
{ Toggle the value for the indicated pixel stored in the user-defined
  pattern }
var
  Mask : byte;
begin
  Mask := $01;
  Mask := Mask shl (8-X);
  Fill[y] := Fill[Y] xor Mask;
end;

procedure ToggleBigPixel(X, Y: integer);
{ This routine should be called each time a pixel in the user-defined
  pattern is toggled. It will toggle the current big pixel by
  exclusive-ORing the current cell with the bigpixel image. It then
  calls TogglePixel to toggle the pixel in the pattern array. }
var
  PX, PY: integer;
begin
  PX := PLeft + (X-1) * 2 * (BigPixelSize + NormWidth) + 1;
  PY := PTop + (Y-1) * (BigPixelSize + NormWidth) + 1;
  PutImage(PX,PY,BigPixel^,XorPut);
  TogglePixel(X,Y);
end;

procedure ToggleCursor(X, Y: integer);
{ Toggle the cursor image on the screen by using the exclusive-OR
```

```
        feature of the PutImage procedure }
var
  PX, PY : integer;
begin
  { Calculate screen location of cursor }
  PX := PLeft + (X-1) * 2 * (BigPixelSize + NormWidth) + 3;
  PY := PTop + (Y-1) * (BigPixelSize + NormWidth) + 3;
  PutImage(PX,PY,Cursor^,XorPut);          { Toggle cursor }
end;

begin
  X := 1;  Y := 1;
  InitGraph(GDriver,GMode,'\tp\bgi');
  OutTextXY(PLeft,PTop-20,BigPatternTitle);  { Write the titles }
  OutTextXY(400,PTop-20,PolyTitle);
  DrawEnlargedPattern;                    { Create the enlarged pattern }
  DrawTestPolygon;                        { Draw the test filled polygon }
  ShowPatternCode;                        { Show the code for the pattern }
  Ch := ReadKey;
  while Ch <> #27 do begin               { While the user doesn't type ESC }
    if Ch = ' ' then begin               { If it is a space, then toggle }
      ToggleBigPixel(X,Y);               { the big pixel and update the }
      DrawTestPolygon;                   { polygon and code that shows }
      ShowPatternCode;                   { the pattern }
    end
    else if Ch = #0 then begin           { If character was a 0, then it }
      Ch := ReadKey;                     { may be an extended code for }
      ToggleCursor(X,Y);                 { an arrow key, get next ch }
      { Move the cursor through the big pixel pattern according to the
        arrow key that is pressed }
      case Ch of
        #75 : if X > 1 then Dec(X);      { Left arrow }
        #77 : if X < 8 then Inc(X);      { Right arrow }
        #72 : if Y > 1 then Dec(Y);      { Up arrow }
        #80 : if Y < 8 then Inc(Y);      { Down arrow }
        #71 : begin
                if X > 1 then Dec(X);    { Home key }
                if Y > 1 then Dec(Y);
              end;
        #73 : begin
                if X < 8 then Inc(X);    { PgUp key }
                if Y > 1 then Dec(Y);
              end;
        #81 : begin
                if X < 8 then Inc(X);    { PgDn key }
                if Y < 8 then Inc(Y);
              end;
        #79 : begin
                if X > 1 then Dec(X);    { End key }
                if Y < 8 then Inc(Y);
              end;
      end;
      ToggleCursor(X,Y);                 { Restore cursor to screen }
```

```
      end;
      Ch := ReadKey;
    end;
    CloseGraph;                              { Exit graphics mode }
  end.
```

Working with Flood Fills

So far all the fill operations that we have discussed have been oriented around various shapes. Sometimes, you may want to fill a region with a particular fill pattern that is bounded by a set of lines or objects. To accomplish this, you can use an operation called a flood fill where you specify a location to begin filling and then the filling process floods an area, making sure it doesn't cross over any pixels that match the border color specified.

The declaration for the BGI flood fill operation is:

```
procedure FloodFill(X, Y: integer; Border: word);
```

Here, the values of **X** and **Y** specify the starting location of the fill operation, commonly called the *seed point*. The **Border** parameter indicates the color that the **FloodFill** uses to determine when it has reached the border of the region it is filling. The procedure uses the current fill settings when filling the region.

One place where the flood fill operation may come in handy is when you want to draw a filled circle. This can be done with **PieSlice**, **FillEllipse**, or **Sector**; however, we can also draw a filled circle by first drawing a circle and then filling it with a call to **FloodFill**. The following code performs this sequence of operations.

```
SetColor(White);              { Use White for the circle }
Circle(100,100,50);           { Draw a circle }
FloodFill(100,100,White);     { Fill the circle starting }
                              { from its center }
```

Note that the color of the circle must be the same as the border color specified in the **FloodFill** procedure in order for this technique to work correctly.

3

The BGI Fonts and Text

This chapter continues our in-depth examination of the BGI with a closer inspection of its text manipulation routines. Although the BGI has several unique and powerful drawing and filling features, its character generation capabilities are some of its most distinguished.

We'll begin by outlining the two forms of character generation supported by the BGI: bit-mapped characters and stroke fonts. We'll then demonstrate how you can exploit these two techniques in a typical graphics program. We'll continue by discussing the complete set of routines that are used to specify the font style, set the character magnification, determine the text dimensions, define the text justification, and more.

In this chapter we'll also develop a useful unit containing enhanced text manipulation tools. These new routines will perform such tasks as automatically enclosing text within a border, sizing text to fit in an existing window, and supporting text input with screen echo.

Text in Graphics Mode

The BGI provides two methods for writing characters to the screen in graphics mode. The default text scheme uses bit-mapped characters. An optional, more powerful, approach uses *stroke* fonts. The method that you select for an application will depend on the size of the text you want to write, the degree of quality of text you need, and the font style you desire. In the following sections, we'll look at both methods for displaying text.

The Bit-Mapped Font

A bit-mapped font is automatically built into every program that you write under the BGI. By default, bit-mapped characters are displayed whenever you perform text output operations to the screen with one of the BGI text functions.

Each character in the default bit-mapped font is represented by an 8 by 8 pixel pattern where each bit in the pattern corresponds to a screen pixel. If the bit in the pattern is a 1, a corresponding pixel is displayed on the screen in the current drawing color. If the bit is a 0, the pixel is set to the background color. Since all characters are stored and displayed in the same manner, the bit-mapped characters are easy to work with and can be displayed quickly. Figure 3.1 presents an exploded view of a bit-mapped character.

By default, these bit-mapped patterns produce characters that are 8 pixels wide and 8 pixels high. Later, we'll see how we can change the size of bit-mapped characters and even write them vertically.

The Four Stroke Fonts

Although bit-mapped characters are adequate for most applications, the BGI also provides stroke fonts that are invaluable for displaying high-quality text output in graphics mode. Stroke fonts are not stored as bit patterns; instead, each character is defined as a series of line segments called strokes. The size of a character's description depends on its complexity. For example, the character "M" requires more strokes than the character "T." Therefore, characters with curves or numerous segments may take dozens of strokes to be properly defined. Figure 3.2 displays a sample stroke character. You should compare this character with the bit-mapped character in Figure 3.1.

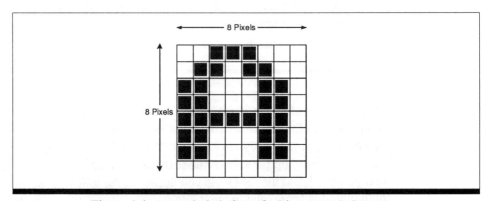

Figure 3.1. An exploded view of a bit-mapped character

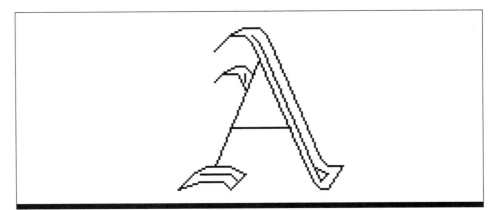

Figure 3.2. A stroke font character is made up of line segments

The BGI includes four different stroke font styles: Small Font, Sans Serif, Triplex, and Gothic (see Figure 3.3). You'll find that these font styles will supply you with enough flexibility for most applications.

The BGI Text Functions

In addition to the fonts, the BGI provides nine text-related routines, listed in Table 3.1. Throughout this chapter we'll be discussing most of these routines in detail and we'll present different techniques for using them. As you can see by studying the table, the text-processing routines furnish a great deal of flexibility for working with both bit-mapped and stroke font styles. Keep in mind that two of the routines, **SetUserCharSize** and **RegisterBGIFont**, work only with stroke fonts.

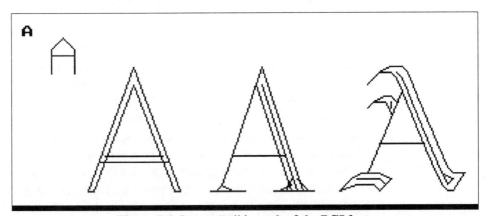

Figure 3.3. Letter "A" in each of the BGI fonts

Table 3.1. The BGI text-related routines

Routine	Description
GetTextSettings	Retrieves the current font, direction, size, and justification of the text
OutText	Displays a string of text at the current position
OutTextXY	Displays a string of text at the location (x,y)
RegisterBGIFont	Used to link a font file into the program's executable file
SetTextJustify	Defines the justification style used by OutText and OutTextXY
SetTextStyle	Sets the font style, direction, and character magnification
SetUserCharSize	Sets the magnification factor used by stroke fonts
TextHeight	Returns the height of a string in pixels
TextWidth	Returns the width of a string in pixels

Writing Text to the Screen

Since the BGI supports several different video modes, multiple font styles, and variable sized text, it provides its own text routines that should be used to display all screen output. The two routines for displaying text are **OutText** and **OutTextXY**.

The routine **OutText** displays an ASCII string at the current screen position in the current viewport. It is declared in the unit **Graph** as:

```
procedure OutText(TextString: string);
```

The parameter **TextString** is the character string that is displayed. By default, all text is written horizontally and is left justified with respect to the current position. When the default settings are used, a call to **OutText** updates the current position to the rightmost side of the text. Therefore, the next call to **OutText** places its string immediately to the right of the previously displayed string.

You'll see later that if you switch between fonts or use a text arrangement other than the one specified earlier, then **OutText** will not automatically update the current position after each call and you must keep track of its position yourself. We'll describe this process in the section "Determining Character Dimensions."

Writing Text to a Pixel Location

A companion text output routine of **OutText** is **OutTextXY**. It displays a string of text to the screen, just as **OutText** does; however, with **OutTextXY**, the text is displayed with respect to a pixel coordinate that you specify. Here is the declaration for **OutTextXY**:

```
procedure OutTextXY(X, Y: integer; TextString: string);
```

The first two parameters specify the pixel coordinate about which the string is justified. As before, **TextString** is the string displayed. When using **OutTextXY**, keep in mind that this routine does not change the current drawing position after a text string has been displayed.

An Example of Text Display

The program shown in this section, called TEXTTEST.PAS, demonstrates how text is displayed with the **OutText** and **OutTextXY** routines. It begins by initializing the graphics mode using Turbo Pascal's autodetect feature. As long as the initialization succeeds, several strings are displayed on the screen. The program uses the default settings for all the displayed text. Consequently, bit-mapped characters are used and the text is left justified and written horizontally. Here is the complete program:

```
program TextTest;
{ TEXTTEST.PAS: This program demonstrates the BGI OutText and
  OutTextXY functions. }
uses
  Graph;
const
  GDriver: integer = Detect;
var
  GMode: integer;
begin
  InitGraph(GDriver,GMode,'\tp\bgi');
  if (GDriver < 0) then begin
    WriteLn('Graphics initialization failure.');
    Halt(1);
  end;
  OutText('This sentence is printed using OutText ');
  OutText('in the default font. ');
  OutTextXY(GetMaxX div 2,GetMaxY div 2, 'OutTextXY printed this.');
  OutText('This sentence is also printed using OutText.');
```

```
        OutTextXY(0,GetMaxY-20,'Press Return ...');
        ReadLn;
        CloseGraph;
end.
```

The first two text strings are displayed with **OutText**. Since this program uses the default justification, **OutText** updates the current position after each call. As a result, the two strings are displayed next to each other. The next statement is **OutTextXY**, which is used to display a string originating at the middle of the screen. The functions **GetMaxX** and **GetMaxY** retrieve the width of the screen and are used to calculate the screen midpoint. This is accomplished by the line:

```
OutTextXY(GetMaxX div 2,GetMaxY div 2, 'OutTextXY printed this.');
```

The next call is to **OutText**. Note that since **OutTextXY** does not update the current drawing position, **OutText** displays its text after the string printed by the last call to **OutText** and not the string printed by **OutTextXY**. Finally, the program calls **OutTextXY** to display a status line at the bottom-left corner of the screen, informing you to press any key to continue.

How Turbo Pascal Accesses Fonts

Unlike the default bit-mapped characters, the stroke fonts are not automatically built into every graphics program. In addition, only one stroke font at a time is normally available in memory while your program is running. Turbo Pascal does this to avoid excessive use of memory, but it has several implications.

First, each stroke font is stored in a separate font file. These files are included with your Turbo Pascal disks and end with a .CHR extension (see Table 3.2).

If you plan to use the stroke fonts, the stroke font files must be accessible to your program at runtime. If they are not accessible, an error will occur. In addition, if you use more than one stroke font, the program must have access to the stroke files each time a different font style is selected.

Selecting and Loading a Font

To use one of the stroke fonts you must explicitly load a font file. This is done with the **SetTextStyle** procedure. It's declared as:

```
procedure SetTextStyle(Font, Direction, CharSize: word);
```

Table 3.2. The BGI stroke font files

Filename	Description
GOTH.CHR	Stroked gothic font
LITT.CHR	Stroked font of small characters
SANS.CHR	Stroked sans serif font
TRIP.CHR	Stroked triplex font

The **Font** parameter is a numeric value specifying the font file to be loaded. To represent the codes for font files, the BGI provides the following set of constants that are defined in the unit **Graph**:

Constant	Value
DefaultFont	0
TriplexFont	1
SmallFont	2
SansSerifFont	3
GothicFont	4

The second parameter, **Direction**, specifies whether the text should be written horizontally or vertically. It can be set to one of two valid values that are also represented by constants defined in **Graph** as:

Constant	Value
HorizDir	0
VertDir	1

The last parameter, **CharSize**, specifies the character magnification factor that is used when text is displayed with **OutText** or **OutTextXY**. This parameter can be set to any integer value from 0 to 10. The effects of these various values in **CharSize** will be discussed shortly.

Before we leave this topic, let's look at a few examples of how **SetTextStyle** is called. The following sample statement loads the gothic stroke font file, defines the direction flag so that all text is written horizontally, and sets the character magnification to a factor of 4:

```
SetTextStyle(GothicFont,HorizDir,4);
```

The next statement selects the triplex font, forces all text to be displayed vertically, and sets the character size to the largest possible size, 10:

```
SetTextStyle(TriplexFont,VertDir,10);
```

Loading Fonts and Drivers Using the Linking Method

In this chapter we mentioned that calls to **SetTextStyle** cause a font driver to be loaded that corresponds to the font selected. Similarly, in Chapter 1 we explained that a graphics hardware driver is loaded in response to **InitGraph**. In both cases, when the appropriate driver is loaded, memory is allocated for the driver, and the appropriate .BGI or .CHR file is loaded from disk. Unfortunately, this process has two disadvantages; it slows down the execution of a graphics program and if the program is designed to run on other systems you must ensure that the appropriate driver files are available on the new system. Fortunately, there's a trick you can use to get around this problem: build the graphics device drivers and font drivers into your executable program. Let's look at how this is done.

Turbo Pascal provides the BINOBJ.EXE utility for converting driver and font files into .OBJ files so that they can be linked into a program. As a result, a driver or font file will be treated as an external procedure. To convert a file, you call BINOBJ using the following syntax:

```
binobj <driver or font filename> <object filename> <symbolic name>
```

The symbolic name can be any identifier you want to use to refer to the procedures in the object version of the appropriate BGI file. Once the object files are created, you can refer to them in your program file. For example, to add the EGAVGA.BGI driver to a program you would first create an object version of the driver

```
binobj egavga.bgi egavga.obj EgaVgaDriverProc
```

and then refer to the file it creates, EGAVGA.OBJ, in your program using the syntax:

```
procedure EgaVgaDriverProc; external;   { Declare as external }
{$L EGAVGA.OBJ }                        { Link with object file }
```

Errors in Loading a Font

If the appropriate font file cannot be found or loaded, an error state is initiated. After the call to **SetTextStyle**, you can make a call to **GraphResult** to check for an error. The possible error conditions are listed in Table 3.3.

The following excerpt of code could be used to change the currently used font, but will catch any errors if they occur. If there is a problem, the routine calls **GraphErrorMsg** to print out the reason for the error and the program terminates. Note, **grOk** is a constant defined in **Graph** for the value 0. It will be the value returned in **GraphResult** if no error occurs in **SetTextStyle**.

The final step that must be taken involves registering the drivers in your graphics program using the **RegisterBGIDriver** and **RegisterBGIFont** routines. Note that these routines require that you pass them the symbolic name that you specified with BINOBJ (**EgaVgaDriverProc** for EGAVGA.BGI, **SmallFontProc** for LITT.CHR, for instance.). A sample program that illustrates how a graphics and font driver are registered is:

```
program LinkBGI;
{ LINKBGI.PAS: Links the EGAVGA.BGI driver and LITT.CHR font
  file into this program. }
uses
  Graph;
var
  GMode, GDriver: integer;

procedure EgaVgaDriverProc; external;
{$L EGAVGA.OBJ}

procedure SmallFontProc; external;
{$L LITT.OBJ}

begin
  GDriver := Detect;
  { Drivers must be registered first }
  if RegisterBGIDriver(@EgaVgaDriverProc) < 0 then Halt(1);
  if RegisterBGIFont(@SmallFontProc) < 0 then Halt(1);
  InitGraph(GDriver,GMode,'\tp\bgi');
  Rectangle(0,0,GetMaxX,GetMaxY);
  OuttextXY(100,100,'Text displayed in small font');
  ReadLn;
  CloseGraph;
end.
```

Table 3.3. Possible errors from loading a font

Return Value	Description
-8	Font file not found
-9	Not enough memory to load font
-11	General error condition
-12	Graphics input/output error
-13	Invalid font file
-14	Invalid font number

```
procedure ChangeTextStyle(Font, Direction, CharSize: word);
var
  ErrorNum: integer;
begin
  GraphResult;
  SetTextStyle(Font,Direction,CharSize);
  ErrorNum := GraphResult;
  if ErrorNum <> grOk then begin
    CloseGraph;
    WriteLn('Graphics Error: ',GraphErrorMsg(ErrorNum));
    Halt(1);
  end
end;
```

Creating Custom Fonts

Now that we've covered the basics of how the built-in stroke fonts are used, let's take a slight detour and examine how we can create our own custom stroke fonts. Creating a new font is a lot easier than you might first think, especially because Borland has developed a special stroke font editor called FE.EXE. Although this utility does not come with Turbo Pascal 6.0, you can obtain it by downloading it from a network such as CompuServe. (The font editor is stored in the file BGI.ARC in the Lib0 section of the Borland forum BPROGB. To get to this forum, type GO BPROGB.) We are also including this utility with our code disks, which you can obtain by using the order form in the back of this book.

The font editor allows you to interactively edit and create .CHR font files by using the mouse. You can also preview characters on the screen and send your output to a plotter such as an HP 7470. To run this utility, you'll need to make sure you have a Microsoft-compatible mouse installed and that your system is

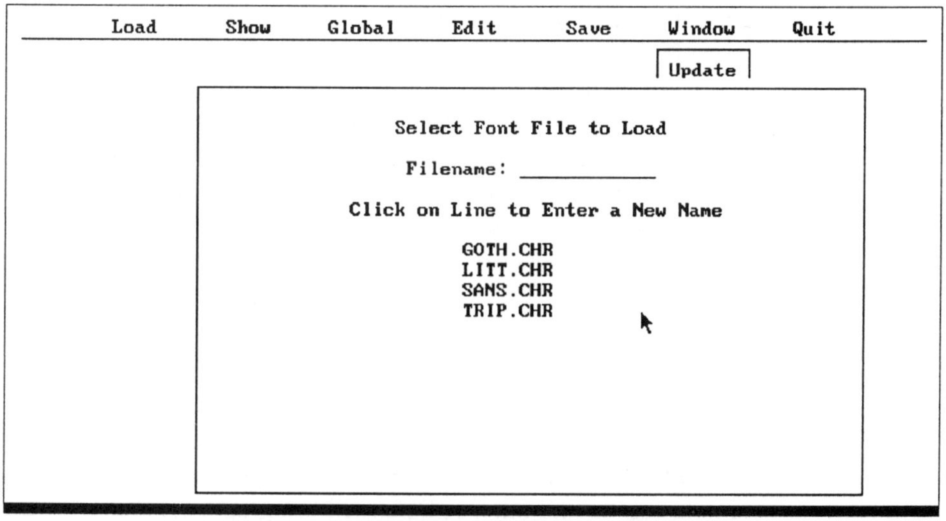

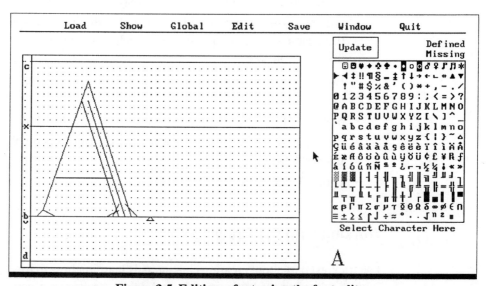

Figure 3.4. The font editor's opening screen

equipped with EGA or VGA display hardware. After you call up the font editor by typing in the filename FE, the screen shown in Figure 3.4 is displayed. Here, you must type in the name of an existing stroke font file, such as SANS.CHR, or the name of a new file. After the filename is entered, the screen will change to the one shown in Figure 3.5. Note that the editor is divided into three main sections: a main menu bar that provides the basic editing and file management commands, a font-drawing grid, and a font table, which is used to select the active character for

Figure 3.5. Editing a font using the font editor

editing. To edit or create a character, you simply select the desired character from the table, and then use the mouse with the drawing grid to edit or create the character. To draw a character, you must use straight-line segments, which the editor calls strokes. The editor does not support arcs or circles. When drawing strokes in the grid, remember that your strokes are shown in a magnified format. The character that you are drawing is shown at its actual size directly below the character selection table.

Working with the Menu Options

Each of the main menu options, Load, Show, Global, Edit, Save, Window, and Quit, can be selected by positioning the mouse cursor on the option name and clicking the right mouse button. Some of the options, such as Load, perform a simple action, and other options will bring up a submenu containing a new set of menu options. For example, when you select the Edit option, the menu bar changes and the options: CopyChar, Flip, Shift, ShowAlso, ClipBoard, and Exit, are displayed. (Note that whenever you are working with a submenu, you can select the Exit option to take you back to the main menu.) The following is a summary of the basic commands performed by the main menu options:

- Load—Loads in a new or existing stroke font file
- Show—Displays all of the characters that have been created with the font editor; you can also use this option to plot your characters
- Global—Allows you to set the left, right, and baseline spacings for the entire character set; an option is also included for copying characters from a different font file
- Edit—Provides a number of editing options including copying, flipping, and shifting
- Save—Saves the work created in the editor to a .CHR stroke font file
- Window—Provides a set of options for controlling how the character editing window is displayed
- Quit—Terminates the editor

Working with the Drawing Grid

The trickiest part about creating characters is learning how to use the drawing grid. With the drawing grid you can add and delete strokes, and copy, flip, and move characters. Before we get into the techniques of drawing characters, we'll explore the components of the drawing grid.

Figure 3.6 shows the grid with its key components labeled. Note that the grid contains four horizontal lines that represent the different heights of a character. The line used as the origin is called the *base height*. This height defaults to a setting of 0 and represents the base of a character.

Some characters, such as the lowercase letter p, contain a *descender*. In this case, the descender consists of the stem that extends below the circle that makes up the letter. On the drawing grid, the horizontal line labeled with the letter d represents the *descender height*. The line that is directly above the *base height* is the *lowercase height*. This line, which is labeled with an x, represents the height of each lowercase letter in a character set. The last line, labeled with a c, is the *capital height* because it represents the height of a capital letter.

When you draw characters, you should use the horizontal height markers as your guidelines. For example, if you want all the capital letters in a set to look uniform, make sure you start them at the *base height* and use the *capital height* as the top point of each character. The small triangle that intersects the *base height* serves as a marker to indicate where the next character will start. After you draw a character, you should move the triangle by clicking it and dragging it to the right so that a space will be placed after the character you are drawing and the next character in the alphabet.

The four horizontal dimensions we've just discussed are assigned a default setting when you start the font editor (*base height* = 0, *descender height* = -7, *lowercase height* = 20, *capital height* = 40). Because these dimensions are determined using the base dimensions of the characters 'M,' 'q,' and 'x,' you can change their

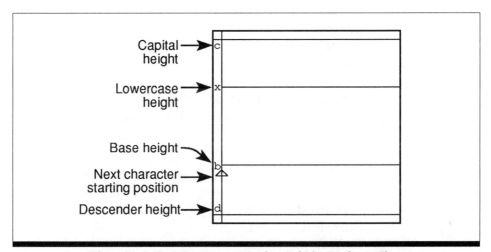

Figure 3.6. The character-drawing grid in the font editor

settings by calling up the font editor, drawing these characters, and saving them. The next time the font is loaded, the character dimensions will be used instead of the defaults.

Once your dimensions are set, you can draw the strokes for each character by clicking and dragging the mouse. The editor uses a "rubber banding" technique for drawing lines. To erase a line, you simply draw over a line. If you start to draw a line and then you don't like how it looks, move the mouse cursor outside the drawing grid and the line will go away.

Working with Text Justification

The BGI provides a handful of text justification settings that can be used to customize your graphics displays. These settings are used by the **OutText** and **OutTextXY** routines to determine how the text should be displayed relative to the current drawing position. By default, all text is left justified and displayed above the current position. These default settings can easily be changed by calling the **SetTextJustify** routine. Here is its declaration:

```
procedure SetTextJustify(Horiz, Vert: word);
```

The first parameter, **Horiz**, sets the horizontal justification style. It can be set to one of the following values:

Constant	Value
LeftText	0
CenterText	1
RightText	2

Similarly, the **Vert** parameter defines the vertical justification that is used in all calls to **OutText** and **OutTextXY**. Its range of values is:

Constant	Value
BottomText	0
CenterText	1
TopText	2

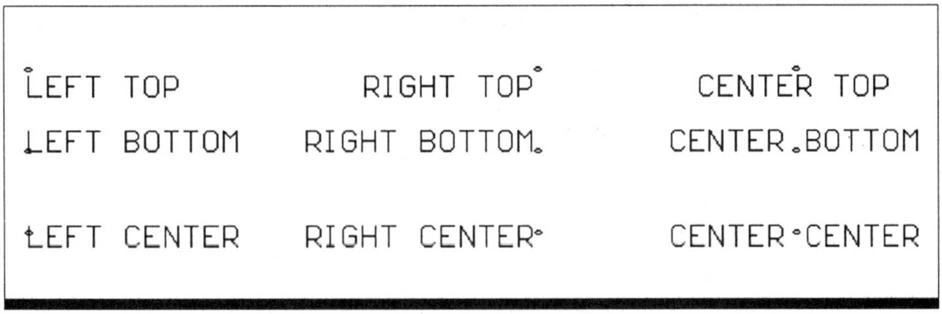

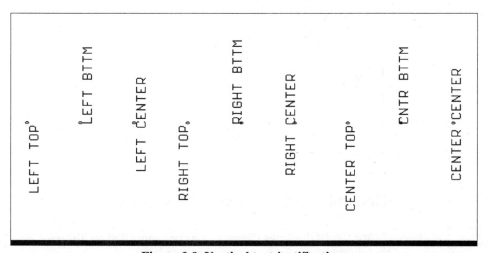

Figure 3.7. Horizontal text justifications

Figures 3.7 and 3.8 display a set of strings in both horizontal and vertical formats by using various combinations of the justification settings.

Determining the Current Text Settings

Turbo Pascal provides the procedure **GetTextSettings,** which can retrieve the current text settings. This routine is convenient to use when you want to temporarily change the text style and then restore it to its previous settings. The procedure is defined as:

```
procedure GetTextSettings(var TextInfo: TextSettingsInfo);
```

Figure 3.8. Vertical text justifications

To store information about a text font, a special data record named **TextSettingsType** is used. You'll find this record defined in the unit **Graph** as:

```
TextSettingsType = record
  Font: word;
  Direction: word;
  CharSize: word;
  Horiz: word;
  Vert: word;
end;
```

The record field **Font** contains the numeric code for the active font style. Remember that Turbo Pascal provides one default style and four stroke fonts; thus the range of values that are stored in this component span from 0 to 4. The second field, **Direction**, indicates whether the current text is to be displayed in a horizontal or vertical direction. Moving down the list, the component **CharSize** stores the magnification factor used to scale any text that is displayed.

The scale factor will be covered in greater detail later; but briefly, it can range from 0 to 10 where a value of 1 selects the standard size for bit-mapped characters (8 by 8), 2 dictates bit-mapped characters twice the size (16 by 16), and so on. Similarly, larger values of **CharSize** create larger stroke font characters. A **CharSize** of 0 is reserved for stroke fonts only and is used to select a secondary form of character magnification that we'll also see later. Finally, the last two fields, **Horiz** and **Vert**, define the justification attributes used for displaying text in the horizontal and vertical directions.

As you can see, a call to **GetTextSettings** will retrieve the font style, the direction flag, the character magnification, and the text justification settings and store this information in the **TextSettingsType** record. As an example, the following lines of code save the text settings, change them, and then restore the text specifications.

```
{ Declare a structure to save the settings in }
OldText: TextSettingsType;
{ Previous code ... }
GetTextSettings(OldText);
{ Change the text settings here ... }
{ Restore the text settings }
SetTextStyle(OldText.Font,OldText.Direction,OldText.CharSize);
SetTextJustify(OldText.Horiz,OldText.Vert);
{ Rest of the code ... }
```

Determining the Character Dimensions

Since the BGI allows characters to be magnified to different sizes, it is necessary to be able to determine the actual pixel sizes of any text written to the screen. This is particularly important when you are trying to align text or enclose a text string within a window. The BGI provides two functions to determine the text dimensions of a string. These routines are:

```
function TextHeight(TextString: string): word;
function TextWidth(TextString: string): word;
```

Individually, they return the height and width in pixels of the character string when it is displayed on the screen. The values returned by these functions are always determined with respect to the orientation of the characters and not the screen axes. In other words, **TextHeight** and **TextWidth** return the same values whether the text is displayed horizontally or vertically.

A bit-mapped character (remember that they are derived from an 8 by 8 bit pattern) with the default character magnification of 1, has a text width of 8 pixels. Similarly, its height is also 8 pixels. To better understand the effects that magnification has on the dimensions of a bit-mapped character see Figure 3.9. Here we are showing the dimensions of the letter A with magnifications of 1 through 10 times the default size.

A Note about Vertical Character Dimensions

Although **TextHeight** and **TextWidth** operate similarly whether text is written horizontally or vertically, they may confuse you when you are writing code. Re-

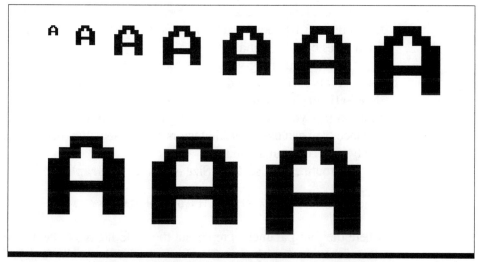

Figure 3.9. Magnification of a bit-mapped character

member that these functions return pixel dimensions that are oriented with respect to the character strings. For example, when a string is displayed horizontally, **TextWidth** returns the number of pixel columns that the text spans. However, when the text is displayed vertically, **TextWidth** returns the number of pixel rows that the text stretches across. You will need to be careful with **TextWidth** and **TextHeight** when writing routines that are designed to handle horizontal and vertical text in the same way.

Magnifying Characters

The BGI provides two methods for altering the size of text displayed by **OutText** and **OutTextXY**. The approach to use depends on whether bit-mapped or stroke fonts are being displayed.

The simplest way to change the size of text that is displayed is by altering the **CharSize** field in the **TextSettingsType** record introduced earlier. The **CharSize** component can be set by a call to the procedure **SetTextStyle**. Remember, it defines the scale factor that is applied to all text that is displayed by **OutText** and **OutTextXY** and can range from 0 to 10. If the **CharSize** value is between 1 and 10, it will affect both the default bit-mapped characters and the stroke fonts. In the case of bit-mapped characters, a **CharSize** of 1 will produce characters the default size of 8 by 8. Bit-mapped text written with a **CharSize** of 2 are twice as big as the default size (16 by 16) and so on up to a **CharSize** of 10, which produces characters 80 by 80 pixels in size.

The larger values of **CharSize** also serve to magnify the stroke fonts although they do not always generate characters of the same size as the bit-mapped characters. Figure 3.10 shows each of the stroke fonts and the default font using the **CharSize**s of 1, 2, 3, and 4.

The one remaining value of **CharSize**, 0, is reserved exclusively for stroke fonts. If it is used, a second group of scale factors, specified by calls to the procedure **SetUserCharSize**, are employed. These allow finer control over the stroke fonts so that you can adjust the height and width of the text independently. For instance, you can use the scale factors in **SetUserCharSize** to fit a text string precisely to a rectangular window.

The routine **SetUserCharSize** is defined in **Graph** as:

```
procedure SetUserCharSize(MultX,DivX,MultY,DivY: word);
```

where the four parameters represent the scale factors to be applied to the default size of the text displayed (a **CharSize** of 4 for the stroke fonts). The first two pa-

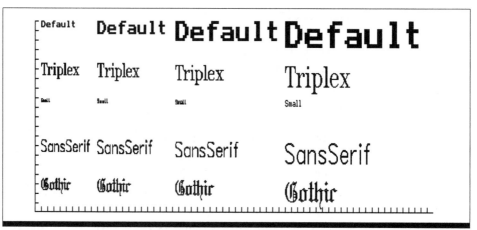

Figure 3.10. The BGI fonts using a CharSize of 1, 2, 3, and 4

rameters indicate the amount that the text is to be stretched or compressed in the horizontal direction. These parameters work as a pair and it is the ratio of these values that defines the scale factor that is applied. For example, to double the width of all text **MultX** can be set to 2 and **DivX** to 1. Similarly, to reduce the height of all text to one-third its default height, we can set **MultY** to 1 and **DivY** to 3. These numbers can take on any ratio of integers up to the screen width of the graphics mode being used. Therefore, in the CGA high-resolution mode (640 by 200), the ratio **MultX/DivX** cannot exceed 639 and similarly the ratio **MultY/DivY** cannot be larger than 199. Figure 3.11 shows how the scale factor ratios influence a stroke font character.

You should be aware that when using vertical text, the four parameters of **SetUserCharSize** are relative to the text itself and not the screen. Therefore, changing **MultX** and **DivX** when the text is vertical will change the number of rows that the text stretches across.

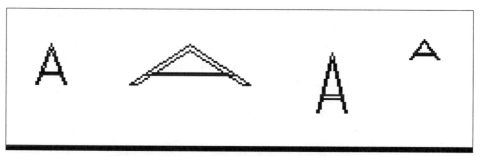

Figure 3.11. Scale factors influence stroke fonts

Fitting Text Inside a Box

By way of example, let's see how we can scale a stroke font text string so that it fits into a rectangular region. The program AUTOSCAL.PAS, shown in Listing 3.1, allows us to specify the dimensions of a rectangular region and the string to be centered inside it. The program automatically scales the text string so that it completely fills the inside of this region as shown in Figure 3.12. This program is worth looking over because of its use of the **SetUserCharSize** procedure.

The program includes two routines, **ScaleText** and **ScaleVertText**. The first routine scales the text so that it fits horizontally into the window specified in its parameters. The latter routine operates in the same way except that it places the text vertically in the window.

In each procedure, the parameters **Left**, **Top**, **Right**, and **Bottom** specify the bounds of the region in which the text is to be displayed. The text to display is contained in the array called **String**. The two routines center the text in both the horizontal and vertical directions so each contains the statement:

```
SetTextJustify(CenterText,CenterText);
```

Now let's take a closer look at how **SetUserCharSize** is used to scale the text string to fit inside the window specified. This is performed in the following statements included in each of the routines:

```
SetUserCharSize(1,1,1,1);
SetTextStyle(Font,HorizDir,UserCharSize);
{ Note the order of the box coordinates. Compare them with
  the ordering for vertical text. }
SetUserCharSize(Right-Left,TextWidth(Str),Bottom-Top,
                TextHeight(Str) * 3 div 2);
```

You'll probably first notice that there are two calls to **SetUserCharSize**. Let's start with the second one. As mentioned earlier, the *ratios* of the parameters in **SetUserCharSize** define the scale factors applied to the text string. Since we want the text to stretch across the window, we can set **MultX** to **Right-Left** and **DivX** to the length of the string. Actually, we need to ensure that the length of the string is calculated using the default text magnification, not the current settings, so this explains the earlier use of:

```
SetUserCharSize(1,1,1,1);
```

The height is similarly scaled to fit into the window. However, you'll note that the height returned from **TextHeight** is scaled by 1 1/2. This factor must be used in

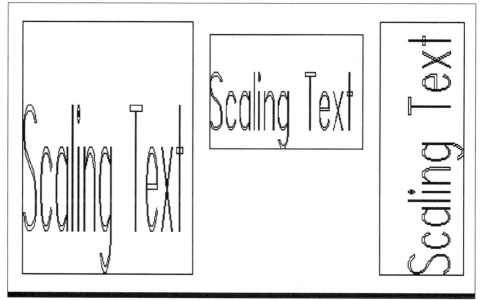

Figure 3.12. Output of AUTOSCAL.PAS

order to squeeze the characters into the box so that letters like p, g, and y, which extend below the text line, do not protrude from the bottom of the box.

• Listing 3.1. AUTOSCAL.PAS

```
program AutoScal;
{ AUTOSCAL.PAS: Given a box of a particular size, scale the text so
  that it fits inside it. Note that this program does not guarantee
  that the text will look good or that it will be readable. This
  can happen if the box is too small for the text. }
uses
  Graph, Crt;
const
  Str: string[12] = 'Scaling Text';
var
  GDriver: integer;
  GMode: integer;

procedure ScaleText(Left, Top, Right, Bottom: integer;
                    Font: integer; Str: string);
{ Scale Horizontal text to fit in a rectangle }
begin
  { Reset UserCharSize to all ones, so that the TextWidth, TextHeight
    functions will return the number of pixels on the screen that the
    default font size uses, not the current size, whatever it may be }
```

```
    SetUserCharSize(1,1,1,1);
    SetTextStyle(Font,HorizDir,UserCharSize);
    { Note the order of the box coordinates. Compare with the ordering
      for vertical text. }
    SetUserCharSize(Right-Left,TextWidth(Str),
                    Bottom-Top,TextHeight(Str) * 3 div 2);
    SetTextJustify(CenterText,CenterText);
    { Clear screen and draw a box where text is to be displayed }
    SetFillStyle(SolidFill,GetBkColor);
    Bar3D(Left,Top,Right,Bottom,0,False);
    { Write text string centered in the box }
    OutTextXY((Right+Left) div 2,(Bottom+Top) div 2,Str);
end;

procedure ScaleVertText(Left, Top, Right, Bottom: integer;
                        Font: integer; Str: string);
{ Scale vertical text to fit in a box }
begin
  { Reset UserCharSize to all ones, so that the TextWidth, TextHeight
    functions will return the number of pixels on the screen that the
    default font size uses, not the current size, whatever it may be. }
  SetUserCharSize(1,1,1,1);
  SetTextStyle(Font,VertDir,UserCharSize);
  SetUserCharSize(Bottom-Top,TextWidth(Str),
      Right-Left,TextHeight(Str) * 3 div 2);
  SetTextJustify(CenterText,CenterText);
  { Clear screen and draw a box where text is to be displayed }
  SetFillStyle(SolidFill,GetBkColor);
  Bar3D(Left,Top,Right,Bottom,0,False);
  { Write string centered in the box }
  OutTextXY((Right+Left) div 2,(Bottom+Top) div 2,Str);
end;

begin
  GDriver := Detect;
  InitGraph(GDriver,GMode,'\tp\bgi');
  ScaleText(0,0,200,GetMaxY,SansSerifFont,Str);
  ScaleText(220,10,400,100,SansSerifFont,Str);
  ScaleVertText(420,0,520,GetMaxY,SansSerifFont,Str);
  repeat until KeyPressed;
  CloseGraph;
end.
```

A Note on Clipping Text

Although the BGI supports clipping for both bit-mapped and stroke fonts, it handles the two slightly differently. If clipping is set for the current viewport, a bit-mapped character will be completely clipped if any portion of it extends beyond the borders of the viewport. A stroke font character, however, will have only that portion of the character that extends beyond the viewport clipped.

Displaying Characters and Numbers

Thus far we have only talked about writing text strings to the screen in graphics mode. You may be wondering how numeric values and the like can be displayed in graphics mode. After all, **OutText** and **OutTextXY** can only display text strings. The trick is to convert all values you want to display into ASCII strings and then display these strings through calls to **OutText** and **OutTextXY**. This can be accomplished for integers or real values using Turbo Pascal's **Str** function and its other string manipulation features. In the next section we'll look at this and other routines in detail.

Extended Text Manipulation Routines

Although the BGI text manipulation routines have great power, they do lack sufficient capabilities to perform interactive text input and output. For example, we need text output routines in graphics mode that have the versatility of the **Write** procedure and input routines that operate like their counterparts in text mode.

In the forthcoming sections, we'll be developing a set of enhanced text routines that we'll be using throughout the rest of this book when displaying text to the screen. These routines are all combined into a Turbo Pascal unit called GTEXT.PAS (see Listing 3.2). A list of the routines in GTEXT.PAS is shown in Table 3.4.

Table 3.4. Routines in GTEXT.PAS

Routine	Description
GWrite	Graphics print utility that mimics Write
GWriteXY	Graphics Write routine that displays text at the location (x, y)
GWriteCh	Puts a single character on the graphics screen
IntToStr	Converts an integer to a string
RealToStr	Converts a real value to a string
GReadStr	Allows user to enter a text in graphics mode
GReadReal	Allows user to enter real numbers in graphics mode

Graphics Version of Write

At first glance, both **OutText** and **OutTextXY** seem adequate for applications that manipulate text in graphics mode, but their limitations become apparent when we compare them with the Pascal routine **Write**. In particular, they only accept string arguments and they do not clear the screen where they write to the screen. In this section we'll develop a graphics version of the **Write** routine that will support the text features of the BGI. This routine will be called **GWrite** and is included in GTEXT.PAS.

The greatest difficulty in creating a routine that mimics **Write** comes from the fact that the routine will have to be able to process a variable number of parameters. Since Turbo Pascal doesn't provide an easy way for us to do this, we will limit our **GWrite** routine so that it only takes a single string parameter. Instead, we'll use support routines that assist us in converting any integer or real values that we wish to display into string values.

The unit **GText** includes two such support routines. They are called **IntToStr** and **RealToStr**. The first one converts an integer value into a string and the second similarly converts a real value into an equivalent string representation. The strings that these functions generate can then be concatenated to other strings or simply passed along to **OutText** or **OutTextXY** to be displayed.

As an example, let's look at the function **RealToStr**. It requires three parameters corresponding to the real value to be converted, the total character width that the conversion should have, and the number of decimal positions that should appear in the string. The string is returned in the function name. Here is the complete listing of the **RealToStr** function:

```
function RealToStr(N: real; Width, Decimals: integer): string;
{ Converts a real number to a string }
var
  S: string;
begin
  Str(N:Width:Decimals,S);
  RealToStr := S;
end;
```

Now let's see how we can use this routine to display the value 3.1, which is stored in the variable **X**. To accomplish this we can use the following statement:

```
OutText('The value of x = '+RealToStr(X,3,1));
```

It will display the line

```
The value of x = 3.1
```

on the graphics screen. The **IntToStr** function works in a similar fashion.

Now that we've seen how to write numeric values to a graphics screen, let's continue to see how we can improve on **OutText** and **OutTextXY**. One thing that is annoying about the BGI stroke fonts is that they make a mess when they over-write graphics already displayed on the screen. The reason for this is that stroke fonts only draw a series of line segments, they do not clear the space below the character as it is displayed. A way around this problem is to erase the screen where each character is to appear before it is displayed. This can be done by drawing a filled rectangular region the size of each character with the background color prior to writing the character. If you examine the **GWrite** routine in GTEXT.PAS, you'll see that **Bar** is used in conjunction with a **SolidFill** set to the background color to clear the screen underneath the string that is displayed.

Finally, in our **GWrite** routine, **OutText** is used to display the formatted ASCII string. Note that the text will be displayed and justified relative to the current position. If left justification and horizontal text styles are in force, then the current position will automatically be updated after a call to **GWrite**.

In addition to **GWrite**, GTEXT.PAS includes **GWriteXY**, which is a routine similar to **GWrite**. The main difference is that **GWriteXY** writes a character string at an (x,y) coordinate position. Like the BGI **OutTextXY**, **GWriteXY** does not update the current position.

One other text output routine in **GText** that you'll often find useful is the routine **GWriteCh**. It simply displays a single character to the graphics screen. It is often convenient when echoing user input while using a function such as **ReadKey**. Actually, all it does is load a string with the single character and pass it along to **GWrite**.

Working with Text Input

Another area that the BGI does not directly support is text input. Fortunately, we can easily build tools to provide text input features. One important input routine to have is a character input function that echoes the input to the graphics screen. As mentioned in the last section we could retrieve user input using the Turbo Pascal routine **ReadKey**, however, it does not support the backspace character or a cursor. We must handle these ourselves. This is the purpose of our next routine, **GReadStr**.

The routine **GReadStr** requires a string to be passed to it in which it will place all text typed until a carriage return is entered. While the text is typed, it will provide an underbar as a cursor and will support the backspace character. When using this **GReadStr**, you must make sure there is enough room in the character buffer passed to **GReadStr** to accept the whole string typed in.

The routine is rather lengthy but it has only two main elements. The first is a **while** loop that continually accepts any text typed by the user until a carriage return is pressed. Every character that is typed is entered into the string, **S**, passed to it by the statements:

```
Inc(CurrLoc);
S[0] := Chr(CurrLoc);
S[CurrLoc] := Ch;
```

where **CurrLoc** is the next location in the string. Remember that the 0 location in a string holds its length. This explains the purpose of the second statement in the code above.

The backspace character, which has a value of $08, is handled as a special case. It causes the last character to be rewritten in the background color, which effectively erases it, the current position to be moved left to where the character used to reside, and the **CurrLoc** index to be decremented.

When you enter a carriage return the **while** terminates and **GReadStr** erases the cursor and exits with a value of True. If the string entered is empty, then the function will return False.

Entering Numeric Values

Just as displaying numeric values in graphics mode is a problem, so is entering numeric values. The GTEXT.PAS source file also includes the routine **GReadReal** that can read real values typed while in graphics mode. It is much like an inverse of the **GWriteReal** function that we saw earlier. In particular, it uses the **GReadStr** function to retrieve an input text string and then calls the Turbo Pascal function **Val** to have it converted into a real value. Like **GReadStr**, it too is a Boolean function that only returns True if the user has entered an appropriate real value.

• Listing 3.2. GTEXT.PAS

```
unit GText;
{ GTEXT.PAS: An extended set of text routines for graphics mode. }
interface
const
  CR  = #13;
  ESC = #27;
  BS  = #08;
```

```
{ These routines are available to any programs that "use" this unit }
function IntToStr(Num: longint): string;
function RealToStr(N: real; Width, Decimals: integer): string;
procedure GWrite(S: string);
procedure GWriteXY(X, Y: integer; S: string);
procedure GWriteCh(Ch: char);
function GReadReal(var Num: real): boolean;
function GReadStr(var S: string): boolean;

implementation
uses
  Graph, Crt;

function IntToStr(Num: longint): string;
{ Converts an integer to a string }
var
  S: string;
begin
  Str(Num,S);
  IntToStr := S;
end;

function RealToStr(N: real; Width, Decimals: integer): string;
{ Converts a real number to a string }
var
  S: string;
begin
  Str(N:Width:Decimals,S);
  RealToStr := S;
end;

procedure GWrite(S: string);
{ Writes a string to the screen. Clears the screen below the text
  before writing the string. It will update the current position.
  It assumes that you are using the HorizDir and LeftText settings. }
var
  X, Y: integer;
  SaveFill: FillSettingsType;
begin
  GetFillSettings(SaveFill);
  X := GetX;   Y := GetY;
  SetFillStyle(SolidFill,GetBkColor);
  Bar(X,Y,X+TextWidth(S),Y+TextHeight(S));
  SetFillStyle(SaveFill.Pattern,SaveFill.Color);
  OutText(S);
end;

procedure GWriteXY(X, Y: integer; S: string);
{ Writes a string to the location (x,y). It does not update the current
  position, but it does clear the screen where it will write the text.
  It assumes that you are using the HorizDir and LeftText settings. }
var
  SaveFill: FillSettingsType;
```

```pascal
begin
  GetFillSettings(SaveFill);
  SetFillStyle(SolidFill,GetBkColor);
  Bar(X,Y,X+TextWidth(S),Y+TextHeight(S));
  OutTextXY(X,Y,S);
  SetFillStyle(SaveFill.Pattern,SaveFill.Color);
end;

procedure GWriteCh(Ch: char);
{ Writes a single character to the screen }
var
  S: string;
begin
  S[0] := #1; S[1] := Ch;
  GWrite(S);
end;

function GReadReal(var Num: real): boolean;
{ Reads a single real number followed by a carriage return from the
  graphics screen }
var
  S: string;
  Code: integer;
  T: boolean;
begin
  if GReadStr(S) then begin
    Val(S,Num,Code);
    if Code <> 0 then GReadReal := False
      else GReadReal := True;
  end
  else
    GReadReal := False;
end;

function GReadStr(var S: string): boolean;
{ A graphics-based text input routine. It returns the string entered.
  Echoes text as it is entered. It supports the backspace character and
  provides a cursor for easy typing. }
const
  Buff2: string[2] = 'c_';
var
  I, CurrLoc, MaxChars, OldColor: integer;
  View: ViewPortType;
  CharBuff: string[2];
  Ch: char;
begin
  S[0] := #0;
  CurrLoc := 0;
  CharBuff[0] := #1;
  GetViewSettings(View);
  MaxChars := (View.x2 - GetX) div TextWidth('M') - 1;
  if MaxChars <= 0 then Exit;
  GWriteXY(GetX,GetY,'_');
```

```
        Ch := ReadKey;
        while Ch <> CR do begin
          if Ch = BS then begin
            if CurrLoc > 0 then begin
              if CurrLoc <= MaxChars then begin
                OldColor := GetColor;
                SetColor(GetBkColor);
                CharBuff[1] := S[CurrLoc];
                Buff2[1] := S[CurrLoc];        { Erase last character in string }
                GWriteXY(GetX-TextWidth(CharBuff),GetY,Buff2);
                SetColor(OldColor);
                MoveTo(GetX-TextWidth(CharBuff),GetY);
                Dec(CurrLoc);
              end;
            end;
          end
          else begin                          { Show this character if room permits }
            if CurrLoc < MaxChars then begin
              OldColor := GetColor;
              SetColor(GetBkColor);
              GWriteXY(GetX,GetY,'_');              { Erase cursor }
              SetColor(OldColor);
              Inc(CurrLoc);
              S[0] := Chr(CurrLoc);
              S[CurrLoc] := Ch;
              GWriteCh(Ch);
            end
            else begin
              Sound(220); Delay(200); NoSound;  { Beep! No room }
            end
          end;
          if CurrLoc < MaxChars then
            GWriteXY(GetX,GetY,'_');
          Ch := ReadKey;
        end;
        if Currloc <= MaxChars then begin
          OldColor := GetColor;
          SetColor(GetBkColor);
          GWriteXY(GetX,GetY,'_');                  { Erase cursor upon exit }
          SetColor(OldColor);
        end;
        if Length(S) = 0 then GReadStr := False
          else GReadStr := True;
      end;

    end.
```

4

Presentation Graphics

It has been said that a picture is worth a thousand words, and if you have ever experienced a good art gallery, you'll probably agree. Of course, when it comes to communication, pictures not only have a place in the art world but in the fast-moving business world as well. And that's where microcomputers come in.

In the early days, most microcomputer users found it downright cumbersome to create useful and attractive presentations. Fortunately, the situation has changed. Now with the latest generation of fast PCs equipped with high-resolution video cards and displays, the field of presentation graphics has emerged. By presentation graphics we mean the technology of using the computer to represent complex information in the form of charts, graphs, and pictures.

In this chapter we'll show you how to use Turbo Pascal's graphics capabilities to produce high-quality business and scientific charts and graphs. In particular, we'll explore techniques for drawing pie charts, bar graphs, coin graphs, and animated charts. We will not be able to cover all of the types of graphs and charts that can be generated with the BGI tools, but by the end of the chapter, you'll know enough to be able to customize your own Pascal applications with presentation graphics.

The Basic Graph Types

The BGI provides three specialized routines for generating graphs and charts. These include a pie chart routine, a bar graph routine, and a three-dimensional bar graph procedure. With these high-level routines we can create professional looking charts and graphs with a minimum of effort. We'll explore each one of these in detail and, in addition, we'll use several of the other tools in the BGI to generate other types of charts and graphs including coin graphs and animated charts.

Getting Started

If you're looking for hard and fast rules for developing charts and graphs, you won't find any here. After all, a picture doesn't always tell the same story to everyone. Our major goal is to display information in a consistent and meaningful manner. However, meaningful does not mean boring. In fact, a good graph or chart is one that is visually pleasing. Therefore, along the way, you may want to experiment with various colors, backdrops, and the layout of the graphs. This chapter will give you a few sample programs that will help you get started; however, feel free to experiment with your own ideas.

Pie Charts

If you pick up almost any magazine or newspaper, you're bound to see pie charts. In fact you'll also find them in popular software applications such as Borland's Quattro. In this section we'll develop a utility called PIE.PAS that can automatically create a complete pie chart like that shown in Figure 4.1. All we'll need to do is provide PIE.PAS with the data and titles for the pie slices. It automatically sizes the pie chart to fit on the screen, creates a legend, and writes a title. The program, shown in Listing 4.1, is designed around Turbo Pascal's **PieSlice** procedure and a set of our own custom routines. Let's take a close look at PIE.PAS.

Drawing a Slice

In Chapter 2, we introduced the **PieSlice** procedure. We'll use it to draw the pie slices in our pie charts. Our task then is to determine how to relate a set of data to the various slices in the pie chart. Typically, each slice represents the proportion of a particular group of data in relation to the whole chart. In other words, each slice represents a percentage of the whole pie.

For our program, we'll assume that a series of percentage values are available for us to use. Each percentage value corresponds to one pie slice and all the slices total to 100 percent. In some applications, a set of raw data is used from which the program must calculate appropriate percentage values. To keep our program simple, we'll assume that these percentages are already available.

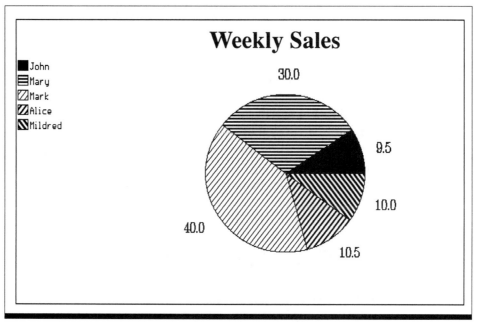

Figure 4.1. Output of PIE.PAS

Our enhanced version of the **PieSlice** procedure is called **PieceOfPie**. We'll invoke this custom routine for each pie slice of the chart that we need to draw. Here is the code for a simplified version of this procedure:

```
const
  StartPercentage: real = 0.0;
procedure PieceOfPie(X, Y, Radius: integer; SlicePercentage: real;
                     Color, Fill: integer);
var
  StartAngle, EndAngle: integer;
begin
  SetFillStyle(Fill,Color);
  StartAngle := Round(StartPercentage / 100.0 * 360.0);
  EndAngle := Round((StartPercentage+SlicePercentage) / 100.0 * 360.0);
  PieSlice(X,Y,StartAngle,EndAngle,Radius);
  StartPercentage := StartPercentage + SlicePercentage;
end;
```

The first three parameters to **PieceOfPie** define the center point and radius of the pie slice to be drawn. From the code, you can see that these values are simply passed along to the Turbo Pascal **PieSlice** procedure. However, we still need to determine the overall size of the pie slice, which is dependent on the value in **SlicePercentage**. But first, let's see how we determine the starting angle to begin drawing the current pie slice. This is the purpose of the real constant **StartPercentage**. It keeps a running total of the percentage of the circle that has already been displayed. The declaration initializes it to zero as shown:

```
StartPercentage: real = 0.0;
```

Each time **PieceOfPie** is called, **SlicePercentage** is added to the running total. The next pie slice is then drawn starting at this location. Therefore, **StartPercentage** specifies the starting angle for drawing the pie slice and **SlicePercentage** instructs the routine on how big to make the slice. Actually, these percentage values must be converted to angles before they can be used. The Turbo Pascal **PieSlice** procedure is expecting angles to be passed to it, not percentages. Therefore, we must convert these values to angles. This is accomplished by the two statements:

```
StartAngle := Round(StartPercentage / 100.0 * 360.0);
EndAngle := Round((StartPercentage+SlicePercentage) / 100.0 * 360.0);
```

The statements are similar. Each is based on the following ratio:

$$\frac{\text{Angle desired}}{360 \text{ degrees}} = \frac{\text{Percentage}}{100 \text{ percent}}$$

Note that this procedure sets the current fill style and color to the values specified with the last two parameters that are passed to it. These drawing parameters are set so that each pie slice can be drawn differently.

As it stands, our procedure, **PieceOfPie**, is ready to be called to create a pie chart. However, let's modify it slightly so that it will add labels for the percentage values alongside each pie slice.

Labeling Pie Slices

There are many different ways to add labels to a pie chart. We'll write the percentage value of each pie slice off to the side of the slice. This technique makes it easy for the viewer to determine the sizes of the pie slices. Some other possibilities are to write titles next to the pie slices or even write the titles or percentage values over the pie slices themselves. Listing 4.1 includes the updated listing of this procedure as well as the rest of the source code for our pie chart program.

When looking at the **PieceOfPie** procedure the first thing to note is that it contains a new variable called **LRadius**. This variable is used to determine the distance from the center of the pie chart to where the labels are written. For our application, the **LRadius** is set to be 1.2 times the radius of the pie chart by the statement:

```
LRadius := Radius * 1.2;     { Dependent on size of chars }
```

This calculation depends on how much room you have on the screen for the labels and the size of the text that you are using. You can derive a general equation for this, but to keep things simple we'll just use the multiplication constant 1.2.

By convention, each of the labels is placed at the middle of the pie slice. This angle is stored in **LabelAngle** and is half way between the start angle of the pie slice and its ending angle. In order to be used by the Turbo Pascal trigonometric functions, this value is converted into radians by the function **ToRadians**.

```
LabelAngle := (StartAngle + EndAngle) div 2;
LabelLoc := ToRadians(LabelAngle);
```

Next, the x and y coordinates of where the label is to be written are calculated by the following lines of code. Note that the y value must be adjusted for the aspect ratio of the screen.

```
X := X + Round(Cos(LabelLoc) * LRadius);
Y := Y - Round(Sin(LabelLoc) * LRadius * AspectRatio);
```

The following statements set the text parameters. First, the font style is set to the triplex stroke font. Next you'll find a series of nested if-then-else statements that determine which type of text justification to use. For instance, if the label is to be printed to the right of the pie slice, then its justification is set to **LeftText** and **CenterText**. However, if the text is to be written on the left side of the pie chart, its justification is set to **RightText** and **CenterText**. Finally, the text is written to the screen by **OutTextXY**.

```
SetTextStyle(TriplexFont,HorizDir,1);
{ Set text justification depending on location of pieslice }
if (LabelAngle >= 300) or (LabelAngle < 60) then
  SetTextJustify(LeftText,CenterText)
else if (LabelAngle >= 60) and (LabelAngle < 120) then
  SetTextJustify(CenterText,BottomText)
else if (LabelAngle >= 120) and (LabelAngle < 240) then
  SetTextJustify(RightText,CenterText)
else
  SetTextJustify(CenterText,TopText);
OutTextXY(X,Y,RealToStr(ShowPercentage,3,1));
```

Up to this point, we've seen how to draw each slice in a pie chart. To draw a complete pie chart we merely need to call **PieceOfPie** repetitively with the appropriate values.

Making Each Slice Different

One thing that you will probably want to do is draw each pie slice a different color or at least fill it with a different fill pattern. To accomplish this we'll sequence through the colors supported by the current graphics mode and 11 of the fill patterns. (We won't use the empty fill pattern since it doesn't generate a unique fill pattern in CGA high-resolution mode.)

The program in Listing 4.1 uses the procedure **NextColorAndFill** to sequence through each of the fill patterns and color combinations. It uses global variables to begin the fill patterns at 1 and the fill color at 0. When all of the combinations are used up, the procedure is written so that the program will exit. You may want to change this so that it cycles through the values again.

Creating a Legend

At the end of **PieceOfPie**, the **ShowKey** procedure is called to write out an entry in a color key on the left side of the screen. This legend shows each color and fill pattern used in the pie chart along with its corresponding label. The procedure **ShowKey** draws one rectangle for each pie slice starting from the top-left of the screen and working down. The **Bar3D** procedure is used with a depth of 0 in order to draw the filled region. The boxes are 16 pixels in width by 16 pixels in height times the aspect ratio. This correction is made in order to make the region square. The location of the square is maintained by the global integer constants **KeyX** and **KeyY**. The **KeyX** value is always equal to 3. However, the **KeyY** position is incremented by 18 pixels each time **ShowKey** is called.

• Listing 4.1. PIE.PAS

```
program Pie;
{ PIE.PAS: This is a demo of the pie chart capabilities of the BGI.
  Note this program uses the GText unit created in Chapter 3. You
  will need to have the GTEXT.PAS file in the same directory as this
  program to compile PIE.PAS. }
uses
  Graph, Crt, GText;
```

```pascal
const
  PercentValues: array[1..5] of real = (9.5, 30, 40, 10.5, 10);
  Labels: array[1..5] of string =
                  ('John', 'Mary', 'Mark', 'Alice', 'Mildred');
  NumValues: integer = 5;
  Title: string[12] = 'Weekly Sales';
  GDriver: integer = Detect;
  StartPercentage: real = 0.0;
  KeyX: integer = 3;
  KeyY: integer = 50;
  FFill: integer = 1;
  FColor: integer = 0;
var
  AspectRatio: real;
  I, X, Y, Radius, Color, Fill, GMode: integer;
  XAsp, YAsp: word;

function ToRadians(Degrees: integer): real;
{ Convert degrees to radians }
begin
  ToRadians := Degrees * Pi / 180.0;
end;

procedure ShowKey(Color, Fill: integer; TheLabel: string);
{ Each pie slice has an entry in a key on the left side
  of the screen showing the fill pattern used for the
  pie slice and a corresponding label for it. }
begin
  SetFillStyle(Fill,Color);
  Bar3D(KeyX,KeyY,KeyX+16,Round(KeyY+16.0*AspectRatio),0,False);
  SetTextJustify(LeftText,CenterText);
  SetTextStyle(SmallFont,HorizDir,5);
  OutTextXY(KeyX+20,Round(KeyY+8*AspectRatio),TheLabel);
  KeyY := KeyY + 18;
end;

procedure PieceOfPie(X, Y, radius: integer; ShowPercentage: real;
                     Color, Fill: integer; TheLabel: string);
{ Draw a single pie slice in the pie chart }
var
  StartAngle, EndAngle, LabelAngle: integer;
  LabelLoc, LRadius: real;
begin
  LRadius := Radius * 1.2;      { Dependent on size of chars }
  SetFillStyle(Fill,Color);
  StartAngle := Round(StartPercentage / 100.0 * 360.0);
  EndAngle := Round((StartPercentage + ShowPercentage) / 100.0 * 360.0);
  LabelAngle := (StartAngle + EndAngle) div 2;
  LabelLoc := ToRadians(LabelAngle);
  PieSlice(X,Y,StartAngle,EndAngle,Radius);
  X := X + Round(Cos(LabelLoc) * LRadius);
  Y := Y - Round(Sin(LabelLoc) * LRadius * AspectRatio);
  SetTextStyle(TriplexFont,HorizDir,1);
```

```
        { Set text justification depending on location of pieslice }
        if (LabelAngle >= 300) or (LabelAngle < 60) then
          SetTextJustify(LeftText,CenterText)
        else if (LabelAngle >= 60) and (LabelAngle < 120) then
          SetTextJustify(CenterText,BottomText)
        else if (LabelAngle >= 120) and (LabelAngle < 240) then
          SetTextJustify(RightText,CenterText)
        else
          SetTextJustify(CenterText,TopText);
        OutTextXY(X,Y,RealToStr(ShowPercentage,3,1));
        StartPercentage := StartPercentage + ShowPercentage;
        ShowKey(Color,Fill,TheLabel);
      end;

      procedure NextColorAndFill(var Color: integer; var Fill: integer);
      { Sequence through each of the possible fill patterns and colors }
      begin
        Inc(FColor);
        if FColor > GetMaxColor then begin
          FColor := 1;
          Inc(FFill);
          if FFill > 11 then begin
            CloseGraph;
            WriteLn('Too many calls to NextColor ...');
            Halt(1);
          end
        end;
        Fill := FFill;
        Color := FColor;
      end;

      begin
        InitGraph(GDriver,GMode,'\tp\bgi');
        Rectangle(0,0,GetMaxX,GetMaxY);
        { Write a header to the graph }
        SetTextJustify(LeftText,TopText);
        SetTextStyle(GothicFont,HorizDir,4);
        OutTextXY((GetMaxX - TextWidth(Title)) div 2,0,Title);
        X := GetMaxX div 2;  Y := GetMaxY div 2;
        GetAspectRatio(XAsp,YAsp);
        AspectRatio := XAsp / YAsp;
        Radius := Round(y * 5.0 / 9.0 / AspectRatio);
        Y := Y + TextHeight(Title) div 2;
        X :=  Round(x * 6.0 / 5.0);
        NextColorAndFill(Color,Fill);
        for I := 1 to NumValues do begin
          PieceOfPie(X,Y,Radius,PercentValues[I],Color,Fill,Labels[I]);
          NextColorAndFill(Color,Fill);
        end;
        repeat until KeyPressed;
        CloseGraph;
      end.
```

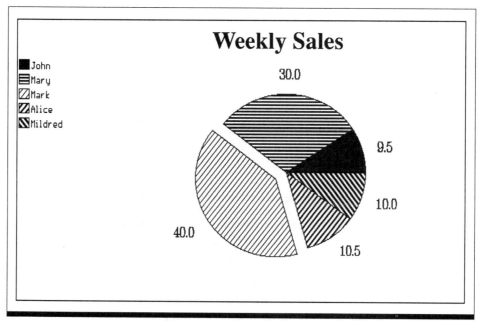

Figure 4.2. A pie slice can be offset for emphasis

Emphasizing a Slice

In some of your pie chart presentations you might need to emphasize one or more pie slices. There are several ways to accomplish this. One approach is to offset the pie slice from the rest of the pie chart by a small amount as shown in Figure 4.2. Although we won't add this feature to our previous example, we'll develop a procedure to implement it.

To offset the pie slice, we'll remove it from the rest of the pie chart by extending it out along the radius of the circle. For instance, let's offset the pie slice by a multiple of its radius. This offset must be added to the x and y coordinates that mark the "center" of the pie slice and its label. The amount that must be added to the x versus the y location depends on where the pie slice is to be drawn. We also need to take into account the aspect ratio of the screen. Figure 4.3 shows the scaling and offset calculations for a moved pie slice.

A procedure that generates an offset pie slice is presented next; it is called **PieceOfPie2** and is similar to our previous routine, **PieceOfPie**. The key difference is that **PieceOfPie2** contains an additional parameter—**OffsetFlag**. When this Boolean parameter is true, the procedure draws a pie slice offset from the rest of the pie chart as shown by the following statements. First, the amount of the offset is calculated by:

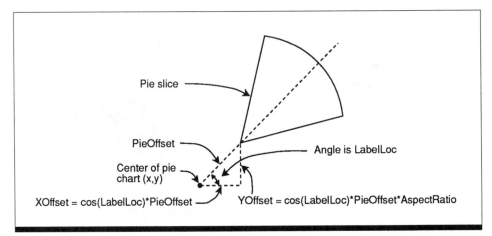

Figure 4.3. Calculations for offsetting a pie slice

```
XOffset := Round(Cos(LabelLoc) * PieOffset);
YOffset := Round(Sin(LabelLoc) * PieOffset * AspectRatio);
```

where **PieSlice** is an integer constant set to a value of 10. It defines how much offset will be used. Note that these statements are similar to the ones used to calculate the location of the label.

The call to **PieSlice** must be changed to reflect this offset:

```
PieSlice(X+XOffset,Y-YOffset,StartAngle,EndAngle,Radius);
```

In addition, the call to **OutTextXY** to write the text label must be changed to use the offset values as well:

```
OutTextXY(X+XOffset,Y-YOffset,Buffer)
```

The complete procedure is listed next. You can use the procedure like the last routine except that when you want to offset a particular pie slice all you need do is set the offset flag to true. Otherwise, if **OffsetFlag** is set false, the pie slice is drawn as before.

```
procedure PieceOfPie2(X, Y, Radius: integer; ShowPercentage: real;
              Color, Fill: integer; TheLabel: string; Offset: Boolean);
const
  PieOffset = 20;     { Amount a pie slice may be offset }
var
  StartAngle, EndAngle, LabelAngle, XOffset, YOffset: integer;
  LabelLoc, LRadius: real;
  Buffer: string[20];
```

```
begin
  LRadius := Radius * 1.2;    { Dependent on size of characters }
  SetFillStyle(Fill,Color);
  StartAngle := Round(StartPercentage / 100.0 * 360.0);
  EndAngle := Round((StartPercentage + ShowPercentage) / 100.0 * 360.0);
  LabelAngle := (StartAngle + EndAngle) div 2;
  LabelLoc := ToRadians(LabelAngle);
  if Offset then begin
    XOffset := Round(Cos(LabelLoc) * PieOffset);
    YOffset := Round(Sin(LabelLoc) * PieOffset * AspectRatio);
    PieSlice(X+XOffset,Y-YOffset,StartAngle,EndAngle,Radius);
    end
  else
    PieSlice(X,Y,StartAngle,EndAngle,Radius);
  X := X + Round(Cos(LabelLoc) * LRadius);
  Y := Y - Round(Sin(LabelLoc) * LRadius * AspectRatio);
  SetTextStyle(TriplexFont,HorizDir,1);

  { Set text justification depending on location of pieslice }
  if (LabelAngle >= 300) or (LabelAngle < 60) then
    SetTextJustify(LeftText,CenterText)
  else if (LabelAngle >= 60) and (LabelAngle < 120) then
    SetTextJustify(CenterText,BottomText)
  else if (LabelAngle >= 120) and (LabelAngle < 240) then
    SetTextJustify(RightText,CenterText)
  else
    SetTextJustify(CenterText,TopText);
  Buffer := RealToStr(ShowPercentage,3,1);
  if (Offset) then
    OutTextXY(X+XOffset,Y-YOffset,Buffer)
  else
    OutTextXY(X,Y,Buffer);
  StartPercentage := StartPercentage + ShowPercentage;
  ShowKey(Color,Fill,TheLabel);
end;
```

Creating Bar Graphs

The BGI provides two specialized procedures for drawing bar charts: **Bar** and
Bar3D. We briefly visited these two procedures in Chapter 2 and now we'll take a
closer look at how we can actually use them to create presentation bar charts.

Creating a bar chart is in itself simple. The complexity arises, however, when
we try to add various embellishments to make a professional looking bar chart or
to automate the chart generation process. This section presents a bar chart program
that automatically generates a bar chart from a set of data; however, it sacrifices
some generality for the sake of brevity. More specifically, the program uses the
BGI **Bar** procedure to create bar charts like the one pictured in Figure 4.4. A

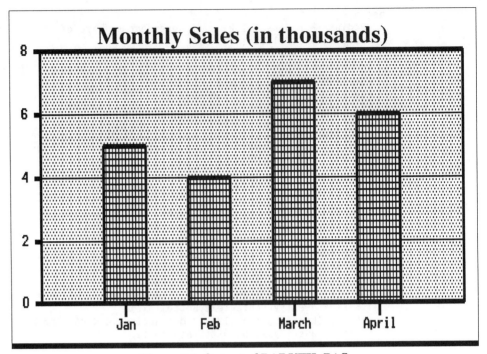

Figure 4.4. Output of BARUTIL.PAS

complete listing of the program is shown in Listing 4.2. The data that is displayed is contained in the variables shown here:

```
type
  ListOfStrings = array [1..4] of string;
  ListOfNums = array [1..4] of integer;
const
  YValues: ListOfNums = (5,4,7,6);
  XStrings: ListOfStrings = ('Jan', 'Feb', 'March', 'April');
  Title: string[36] = ' Monthly Sales (in thousands) ';
```

In this example, the bar chart depicts the sales figures for a business. The title of the chart is stored in the string **Title**. The data for the chart corresponds to the first four months of the year. The labels for these are listed in the array of characters stored in the **XStrings** array. These labels will appear below each bar on the horizontal axis. The data for the bars is placed in the **YValues** array. For simplicity, these values are restricted to integers. Finally, since there are four bars to be drawn, the global **NumBars** constant is set to four.

The first step in drawing the chart consists of calling the **DisplayChart** procedure, provided in Listing 4.2. As you can see, this procedure is passed the various values and titles that are to be displayed as well as a value called **NumRules**. This integer value specifies the number of horizontal divisions that are to be used in the chart. In our example, we'll use four horizontal rules. You may want to experiment with this value to produce different charts.

Essentially, **DisplayChart** is responsible for performing four important tasks. First, it calculates the bounds of the chart, which are based on the size of the screen and the pixel boundaries defined by **ScreenBorderX** and **ScreenBorderY**. Second, the title is written across the screen. To accommodate titles of varying lengths, a modified version of the **ScaleText** procedure that we developed in Chapter 3 is used to automatically adjust the text to fit across the top of the chart. This version of **ScaleText** is designed so that it favors stretching the text the same amount in both the x and y directions. This is done to try to avoid having the text stretch too much in one direction and become unreadable.

The third part of **DisplayChart** consists of a call to the **GetMax** function and a **while** loop that determines the maximum value for the y (vertical) axis. The **GetMax** function returns the maximum value in the array of values contained in **YValues**. This value is saved in **MaxYValue**. The **while** loop increments **MaxYValue** until it reaches a number that is a multiple of the number of horizontal rules that is defined in the call to **DisplayChart**. The **while** loop ensures that the program selects a maximum value for the chart that will produce whole numbers that can be labeled on the y axis at each horizontal rule on the chart.

Finally, **DrawChart** is called. This routine is also provided in Listing 4.2 (BARUTIL.PAS). It actually draws out a backdrop for the bar graph as well as the labels for the horizontal and vertical axes and the bars themselves. The backdrop is created by a call to **Bar3D**. Note that we are using this procedure instead of **FillPoly** because its parameters are easier to specify. The procedure **Bar** could easily be used in place of **Bar3D**; however, it would not draw a border to the backdrop.

Within **DrawChart**, the four lines following the call to **Bar3D** and the **for** loop are used to draw the horizontal rules across the backdrop and create thick hash marks and labels on the y axis. The distance between the hash marks is calculated and stored in the variable **Offset**, which is used within the **for** loop to place the rules across the chart. The two statements immediately following this **for** loop are used to write the label for the 0 value that corresponds to the horizontal axis.

Next, a scale factor is calculated that is later used to determine exactly how high each bar should be drawn. The statement that performs this calculation is:

```
Scale := (Bottom - Top) / MaxYValue;
```

As shown, the scale factor is dependent on the overall height of the chart and the maximum value determined in **DisplayChart**. Figure 4.5 shows the scale factor calculation for a bar.

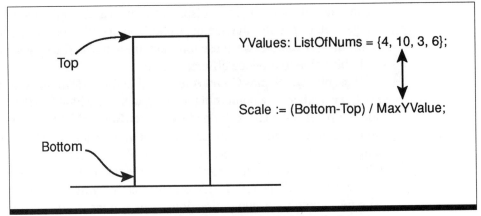

Figure 4.5. Calculating the height of a bar

The lines of code following this statement are similar to those discussed previously that create the vertical labels. However, this code now marks out the divisions and labels on the horizontal axis. The **for** loop uses the strings in the **XStrings** array as the labels. Also within the **for** loop is a call to **Bar3D**. This statement actually creates each of the bars. Once again note that these calls to **Bar3D** use a depth of 0 so that the bars are drawn without a depth. As with the backdrop, **Bar3D** is used instead of the simpler **Bar** procedure because it provides borders around each of the bars.

To adapt this chart program to your own data you will need to provide your own values in **XValues, YValues,** and **Title** as well as change the number represented by **NumBars** to correspond to the number of unique data points you have. Finally, you can choose a value for **NumRules** that will affect the number of horizontal rules drawn by the program and consequently the number of labels on the vertical axis.

Some additional things you might try adding are titles for the vertical and horizontal axes. Also you might want to change the program so that it accepts float values along the vertical axes rather than just integers. Of course, there are a great many other alterations you could try.

• Listing 4.2. BARUTIL.PAS

```
program BarUtil;
{ BARUTIL.PAS: Displays a professional looking bar graph. }
uses
   Graph, GText;
Const NumBars = 4;
type
   ListOfStrings = array [1..NumBars] of string;
   ListOfNums = array [1..NumBars] of integer;
```

```
const
  ScreenBorderY: integer = 20;        { 10-pixel border at top and bottom }
  ScreenBorderX: integer = 20;        { 10-pixel border on each side }
  UseRules: integer = 4;              { Use four rules on the backdrop }
  HashWidth: integer = 8;             { Make hash marks on rules this long }
  NumStrings: integer = 4;            { Four strings on x axis }
  GDriver: integer = Detect;
  YValues: ListOfNums = (5,4,7,6);
  XStrings: ListOfStrings = ('Jan', 'Feb', 'March', 'April');
  Title: string[36] = ' Monthly Sales (in thousands) ';
var
  MaxX, MaxY: integer;                { Dimensions of graphics screen }
  GMode: integer;
  Ch: char;

procedure ScaleText(Left, Top, Right, Bottom: integer; TheString: string);
{ Scale the text so it fits into the specified rectangle. This
  routine is a modification of the ScaleText routine in Chapter 3.
  It uses SetUserCharSize to try to scale the text so that it
  looks good. Uses Triplex font. }
var
  Height: integer;
begin
  SetTextJustify(CenterText,TopText);
  SetUserCharSize(1,1,1,1);
  SetTextStyle(TriplexFont,HorizDir,UserCharSize);
  { In height calculation make room for letters extending below line
    by multiplying TextHeight by 5/4 }
  Height := TextHeight(TheString) * 5 div 4;
  if Height > Bottom-Top then begin
    { Text is too tall so find how. Try scaling down x and y by
      same amount in order to keep text well proportioned. }
    SetUserCharSize(Bottom-Top,Height,Bottom-Top,Height);
    SetTextStyle(TriplexFont,HorizDir,UserCharSize);
    { Enough room — so write it }
    if TextWidth(TheString) <= Right - Left then
      OutTextXY((Right+Left) div 2,Top,TheString)
    else begin
      { Doesn't fit with equal scaling - so squash it in! }
      SetUserCharSize(1,1,1,1);
      SetTextStyle(TriplexFont,HorizDir,UserCharSize);
      SetUserCharSize(Right-Left,TextWidth(TheString),Bottom-Top,Height);
      SetTextStyle(TriplexFont,HorizDir,UserCharSize);
      OutTextXY((Right+Left) div 2,Top,TheString);
    end
  end
  { String is too long - try scaling equally }
  else if TextWidth(TheString) > Right-Left then begin
    SetUserCharSize(Right-Left,TextWidth(TheString),
        Right-Left,TextWidth(TheString));
    SetTextStyle(TriplexFont,HorizDir,UserCharSize);
    { Enough room — so write it }
    if TextHeight(TheString)* 5 div 4 <= Bottom-Top then
```

```pascal
        OutTextXY((Right+Left) div 2,Top,TheString)
      else begin
        { Doesn't fit with equal scaling - so squash it! }
        SetUserCharSize(1,1,1,1);
        SetTextStyle(TriplexFont,HorizDir,UserCharSize);
        SetUserCharSize(Right-Left,TextWidth(TheString),Bottom-Top,Height);
        SetTextStyle(TriplexFont,HorizDir,UserCharSize);
        OutTextXY((Right+Left) div 2,Top,TheString);
      end
    end
  else                  { Write out text — enough room }
    OutTextXY((Right+Left) div 2,Top,TheString);
end;

function GetMax(Values: ListOfNums): integer;
{ Finds and returns the largest value in the array of values }
var
  I, Largest: integer;
begin
  I := 0;  Largest := 1;
  for I := 1 to NumBars do
    if Values[I] > Largest then
      Largest := Values[I];
  GetMax := Largest;
end;

procedure DrawChart(Left, Top, Right, Bottom, NumRules: integer;
   MaxYValue: integer; XStrings: ListOfStrings; YValues: ListOfNums);
{ Draws the chart's backdrop }
var
  Scale: real;
  I, Height, Incr: integer;
  Buffer: string[10];
  Offset: integer;       { Draw horizontal rules this many pixels apart }
begin
  { Make a thick border around the backdrop }
  SetLineStyle(SolidLn,0,ThickWidth);
  SetFillStyle(CloseDotFill,Blue);
  { Use Bar3D with a depth of zero to draw a bar with a border }
  Bar3D(Left,Top,Right,Bottom,0,False);
  Offset := (Bottom - Top) div NumRules;
  Incr := MaxYValue div NumRules;
  SetTextJustify(RightText,CenterText);
  SetTextStyle(DefaultFont,HorizDir,1);
  for I := 1 to NumRules do begin
    { Draw rule as thin line }
    SetLineStyle(SolidLn,0,NormWidth);
    Line(Left,Top+(I-1)*Offset,Right,Top+(I-1)*Offset);
    { Show thick hash mark }
    SetLineStyle(SolidLn,0,ThickWidth);
    Line(Left-HashWidth,Top+(I-1)*Offset,Left,Top+(I-1)*Offset);
    Buffer := IntToStr(Incr * (NumRules - I + 1));
    OutTextXY(Left-HashWidth-TextWidth(Buffer),Top+(I-1)*Offset,Buffer);
```

```
    end;
    { Draw bottom hash mark }
    Line(Left-HashWidth,Bottom,Left,Bottom);
    OutTextXY(Left-HashWidth-TextWidth(Buffer),Bottom,'0');

    { Write out the values for the horizontal axis }
    { Figure the amount to scale all bars }
    Scale := (Bottom - Top) / MaxYvalue;
    SetFillStyle(HatchFill,Blue);        { Make all bars Hatch Fill }
    Offset := (Right - Left) div (NumStrings + 1);
    SetTextJustify(CenterText,TopText);
    SetTextStyle(DefaultFont,HorizDir,1);
    for I := 1 to NumStrings do begin
      { Show thick hash mark }
      SetLineStyle(SolidLn,0,ThickWidth);
      Line(Left+I*Offset,Bottom,Left+I*Offset,Bottom+HashWidth);
      OutTextXY(Left+I*Offset,Bottom+HashWidth+2,XStrings[I]);
      { Draw the bars for the values. Make the total width of one of the
        bars equal to half the distance between two of the hash marks on
        the horizontal bar. }
      Height := Round(YValues[I] * Scale);
      Bar3D(Left+I*Offset-Offset div NumBars,Bottom - Height,
      Left+I*Offset+Offset div NumBars,Bottom,0,False);
    end;
end;

procedure DisplayChart(Title: string; XStrings: ListOfStrings;
                       YValues: ListOfNums; NumRules: integer);
var
  MaxYValue, Left, Top, Right, Bottom: integer;
begin
  if NumRules < 0 then
    NumRules := 1;                     { Ensure NumRules is greater than zero }
  { Determine border points of backdrop }
  Left := ScreenBorderX + MaxX div 8;
  Top := ScreenBorderY;
  Right := MaxX - ScreenBorderX;
  Bottom := MaxY - ScreenBorderY;
  { Display the title at the top. Scale it to fit. }
  ScaleText(Left,0,Right,Top,Title);
  { Determine a maximum value for the chart scale. It should be at least
    as large as the largest list of values and a multiple of the number
    of rules that the user desires. NumRules should not be greater than
    MaxYValue. }
  MaxYValue := GetMax(YValues); { Get the largest y value }
  while (MaxYValue mod NumRules) <> 0 do
    Inc(MaxYValue);
  { Draw the backdrop }
  DrawChart(Left,Top,Right,Bottom,NumRules,MaxYValue,XStrings,YValues);
end;

begin
  InitGraph(GDriver,GMode,'\tp\bgi');
```

```
        MaxX := GetMaxX;  MaxY := GetMaxY;
        DisplayChart(Title,XStrings,YValues,UseRules);
        ReadLn;                              { Press Enter to quit program }
        CloseGraph;
      end.
```

Three-Dimensional Bar Graphs

In the last section we learned how to develop a bar graph utility that can create two-dimensional bar graphs. Next, we'll show you how to modify the program so that it can draw three-dimensional bar graphs. In fact, since **Bar3D** is already used to draw the bars, all we really have to do is change the depth parameter passed to **Bar3D** in the procedure **DrawChart** to get a three-dimensional bar chart.

Generally, if you set the depth of the bar chart to one-fourth the height of the highest bar you will get very pleasing results. Therefore an updated statement for **Bar3D** is:

```
Bar3D(Left+I*Offset-Offset div 4,Bottom-Height,
      Left+I*Offset+Offset div 4,Bottom,HeightOfHighestBar div 4,0);
```

You can easily change the depth of the bars by altering the next-to-the-last parameter in **Bar3D**. If the depth is too large, the bars may begin to merge. If this happens, you will have to place more spacing between the bars or use a smaller value for the depth.

Coin Graphs

Another modification you might try making to the BARUTIL.PAS program (Listing 4.2) is to alter it so that it can create coin graphs like the one shown in Figure 4.6. This coin graph represents the sales of computer monitors for four computer salespeople. In order to make the chart interesting, small pictures of the monitors are stacked on top of each other like coins in order to represent the sales totals.

Probably the most challenging task of making a good coin graph is coming up with the right picture to use. You may need to experiment with various sequences of BGI functions before you come up with a design that satisfies you.

In order to create a coin chart, the basic idea is to draw a small picture, capture its image with **GetImage**, and then redraw it as necessary using **PutImage**. The coin chart in Figure 4.6 was created from the BARUTIL.PAS program with only a few minor modifications. Rather than show the entire code over again and risk the possibility of obscuring these changes, let's simply outline them one at a time.

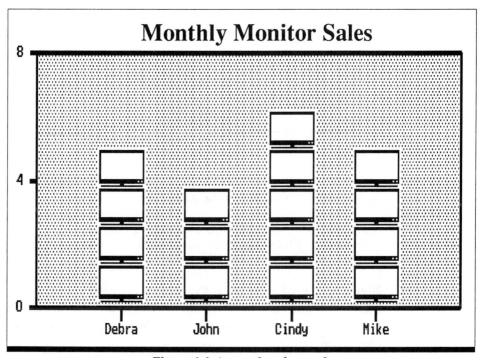

Figure 4.6. A sample coin graph

First, we'll need to declare a few new variables. We'll use two constants to define the pixel dimensions of one of the monitors—the image for the coin chart. In addition, we'll need an array to hold the image of the monitor. Therefore, the following lines must be added to the top of BARUTIL.PAS:

```
const
  PictHeight = 24;
  PictWidth = 32;
var
  Picture: pointer;
```

In addition, the program was modified to use the following values and titles in generating the chart:

```
YValues: array [1..4] of integer = (5,4,7,6);
XStrings: array [1..4] of string = ('Debra', 'John', 'Cindy', 'Mike');
Title: string[23] = ' Monthly Monitor Sales ';
```

The next change to make involves creating an image of the monitor. The monitor image used in Figure 4.6 was created from the following statements that were added to the mainline immediately after the graphics initialization.

```
{ The following lines create the picture of the monitor }
Bar(2,2,PictWidth-2,PictHeight-2);
SetFillStyle(SolidFill,0);
Bar(4,4,PictWidth-4,PictHeight-5);
SetColor(0);
Line(PictWidth-4,PictHeight-3,PictWidth-5,PictHeight-3);
Line(PictWidth-8,PictHeight-3,PictWidth-9,PictHeight-3);
SetColor(GetMaxColor);
SetFillStyle(SolidFill,GetMaxColor);
Bar(PictWidth div 2-2,PictHeight,PictWidth div 2+2,PictHeight);
Line(4,PictHeight,PictWidth-4,PictHeight);
```

Once the picture of the object is drawn, its image is copied into memory pointed to by **Picture** using the following statements:

```
GetMem(Picture,ImageSize(0,0,PictWidth,PictHeight));
GetImage(0,0,PictWidth,PictHeight,Picture^);
PutImage(0,0,Picture^,XorPut);
```

Note also that we must erase the original picture on the screen before we go on. This is accomplished by using the **XorPut** option as shown earlier. Now that we have an image to work with we are ready to call our chart program to create our coin graph.

This leads us to our next change. Within the **DrawChart** procedure, we need to replace the call to **Bar3D** that draws the bars with the code to draw a stack of the coin images. This can be done by replacing the call to **Bar3D** with a **for** loop that stacks images of **Picture** according to the height that represents the chart value. Here is the new **for** loop:

```
{ Stack images of the "coin" to represent the height of the bar }
NumImages := (Height - PictHeight) div PictHeight;
for J := 1 to NumImages+1 do
  PutImage(Left + I * Offset - PictWidth div 2,
           Bottom - (J * PictHeight) - 4,Picture^,CopyPut);
```

Note that this statement draws only whole copies of the coin image. It does not draw fractional images. If you need this additional capability you might try overwriting the percentage of the image you don't need by the background or backdrop color.

Animated Graphs

Graphs and charts do not have to be static and lifeless. One way to make a graph more interesting is by adding animation. This section discusses a way of animating bar graphs by using a technique called *inbetweening*.

Briefly, inbetweening is a process where an object's initial and final shapes are predefined and the program automatically calculates intermediate states between them. By sequencing through these intermediate states, the object is effectively animated. We'll look at inbetweening and other animation techniques in greater detail in Chapter 6.

For a bar in a bar graph, the initial state is simply a bar of zero height and the final image is the bar displayed at its full height. The intermediate images of the bar simply depict the bar at ever increasing heights. Figure 4.7 presents the final output of the animated bar chart program. The smoothness of the animation usually depends on the amount of change between the intermediate states of the object, that is, on the number of intermediate states that are used in the animation.

Shown in Listing 4.3 is a program that demonstrates the concept of inbetweening as it can be applied to bar charts. The code merely demonstrates the concept. If you want to experiment with it further you might try integrating it with the BARUTIL.PAS program created earlier.

• Listing 4.3. ANIMATE.PAS

```pascal
program Animate;
{ ANIMATE.PAS: Demonstrates how an animated bar graph can be created. }
uses
  Graph;
const
  NumSteps: integer = 10;      { Controls the "growth" rate of the }
                               { bars as they are animated }
  Title: string[23] = 'Animated Bar Graph Demo';
  GDriver: integer = Detect;
var
  GMode, Col: integer;

procedure AnimatedBar(Left, Top, Right, Bottom: integer);
var
  I, Inc: integer;
begin
  Inc := (Bottom - Top) div NumSteps;
  for I := 0 to NumSteps - 1 do
    Bar(Left,Bottom-Inc*I,Right,Bottom);
end;

begin
  InitGraph(GDriver,GMode,'\tp\bgi');
  { Write a header to the graph }
  SetTextJustify(LeftText,TopText);
  SetTextStyle(GothicFont,HorizDir,5);
  { Center the title on the first row of the screen }
  OutTextXY((GetMaxX - TextWidth(Title)) div 2,0,Title);
```

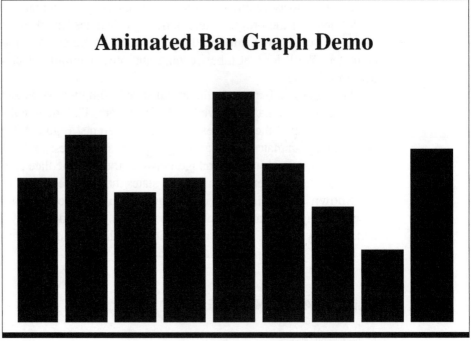

Figure 4.7. Final output of ANIMATE.PAS

```
        SetFillStyle(SolidFill,Magenta);
        { Draw and animate the bars one at a time }
        AnimatedBar(50,100,100,200);
        AnimatedBar(110,70,160,200);
        AnimatedBar(170,110,220,200);
        AnimatedBar(230,100,280,200);
        AnimatedBar(290,40,340,200);
        AnimatedBar(350,90,400,200);
        AnimatedBar(410,120,460,200);
        AnimatedBar(470,150,520,200);
        AnimatedBar(530,80,580,200);
        ReadLn;                         { Press the Enter key to quit }
        CloseGraph;
     end.
```

5

Graphics Techniques in Two Dimensions

In this chapter we'll lay the foundation for developing two-dimensional graphics programs. We'll begin by exploring the relationship between screen coordinates and world coordinates and we'll present techniques for mapping between these coordinates. In addition, we'll introduce the concept of transformations, which we'll use to describe how objects can be manipulated in two dimensions. As part of our exploration, we'll develop a package called MATRIX.PAS that applies many of the concepts presented.

Screen Coordinates

As we've seen earlier, the BGI supports various graphics adapters and modes, each with its own range of colors, resolution, and number of memory pages. Unfortunately, this flexibility introduces compatibility problems for the graphics programs that we develop. After all, how can we write a program so that it works equally well under the various graphics modes? One problem that we have already encountered is the issue of screen resolution. Not only must we consider the resolutions of the various modes, but we must also adjust for the aspect ratio of a screen in the various modes. Let's examine how this is done.

Working with Aspect Ratios

Each graphics mode has an aspect ratio associated with it. The aspect ratio is based on the ratio between the width and height of each pixel. This ratio is critical when we try to draw a figure of a particular size and shape on the screen. For instance, if we use the CGA 320 by 200 mode, each pixel is approximately twice as high as it is wide. Therefore, if we draw a 4 by 4 block of pixels we won't get a square on the screen. To actually draw a square we must adjust for the aspect ratio of the mode as shown in Figure 5.1.

Fortunately, the BGI provides the **GetAspectRatio** routine, which we can use to determine the aspect ratio of the current mode. It is defined in the unit **Graph** as:

```
procedure GetAspectRatio(var Xasp, Yasp: word);
```

The parameters **Xasp** and **Yasp** can be divided together to calculate the aspect ratio of the screen. In most modes, the pixels are taller than they are wide, therefore the BGI normalizes the **Yasp** value to 10,000 and returns some value less than 10,000 in **Xasp**. The aspect ratio of the screen, therefore, can be calculated as:

```
AspectRatio := Xasp/Yasp;
```

This value can then be multiplied against each y dimension in order to draw an object correctly proportioned and positioned. For instance, in Figure 5.1, the height of the 4 by 4 square shown becomes:

```
ScreenHeight := 4 * AspectRatio;
```

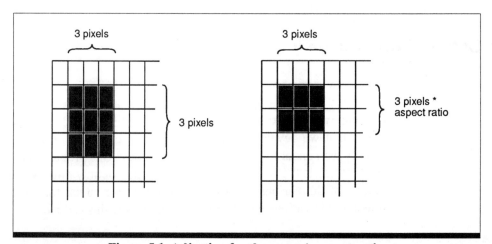

Figure 5.1. Adjusting for the screen's aspect ratio

Since **Xasp** is generally smaller than **Yasp, AspectRatio** is set to some fractional value and **ScreenHeight** is calculated as a value less than 4. This produces a correctly proportioned square as shown in Figure 5.1.

Screen and World Coordinates

In the last section we learned how to adjust for the difference between the x and y dimensions that exists in most of the graphics modes. Similarly, we must make adjustments to graphics objects so they retain their size when displayed in graphics modes with different screen resolutions. To achieve this, we'll use a standard coordinate system called world coordinates.

Up until now, we have been working only with screen coordinates. This approach can lead to problems when we work with graphics modes with different resolutions. For instance, a 10 by 10 square in a 320 by 200 mode appears quite different in a 640 by 200 mode. In addition, if we define an object to be located at (500,150) it would not even appear in the 320 by 200 mode. What we need is the ability to map objects so that they are displayed proportionally and correctly positioned. We'll do this by expressing objects in world coordinates (such as in inches, feet, meters, etc.), and then map them to screen coordinates so that they fit properly on the screen before they are drawn.

Mapping between Coordinate Systems

In general, we want to be able to map between world coordinates and screen coordinates as shown in Figure 5.2. To do this we can use the relations shown in Figure 5.3. The equations:

```
x' = a * x + b
y' = c * y + d
```

define how a point (x,y) in world coordinates can be mapped to a screen coordinate (x',y'). The values **L1, T1, R1,** and **B1** represent the range of values that we are considering in the world coordinates and similarly **L2, T2, R2,** and **B2** define the size of the screen area that the object is to be mapped into. Now let's put these equations into our unit MATRIX.PAS. The code for this file is shown later in this chapter.

First, we need two routines that can set the ranges of the world and screen coordinates. These procedures are called **Set_Window** and **Set_ViewPort**. Each

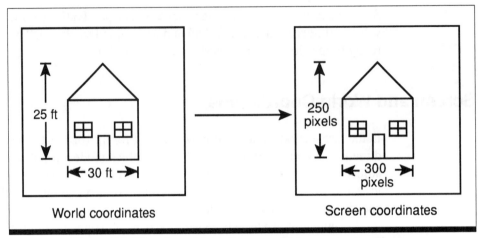

Figure 5.2. Mapping objects from world to screen coordinates

is called with the left, top, right, and bottom bounds of its region, and internally sets an appropriate group of global variables within MATRIX.PAS to these ranges. In addition, **Set_ViewPort** calculates the ratios shown in Figure 5.3. For example, the two statements:

```
Set_Window(0.0,0.0,3.0,3.0);
Set_ViewPort(0,0,GetMaxX,GetMaxY);
```

set the range of values in the world and screen coordinates so that all objects between (0.0,0.0) and (3.0,3.0) in world coordinates are mapped to the full screen. Objects outside this range are clipped and not displayed.

As another example, you could use the same world coordinate settings but define the viewport on the screen to be:

```
Set_ViewPort(0,0,GetMaxX div 2,GetMaxY div 2);
```

In this case, the same objects that would appear above would now appear in only the top-left half of the screen. Similarly, you can effectively zoom in on the objects displayed by decreasing the size of the region passed to **Set_Window**. Note that, as written, you must match each call to **Set_Window** with a succeeding call to **Set_ViewPort** in order to make changes take effect.

The routines in MATRIX.PAS that actually map between the coordinate systems are called **WorldToPC** and **PCtoWorld**. Each routine maps one point from one of the coordinate systems to the other. For example, **WorldToPC** maps a world coordinate to a screen coordinate by using the code:

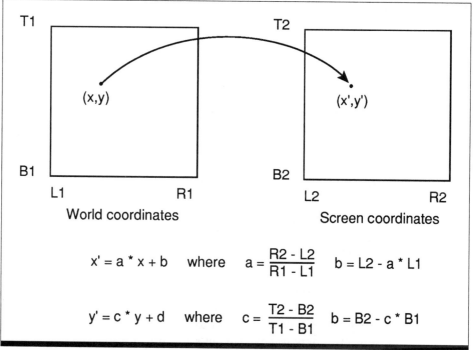

Figure 5.3. Equations for mapping from world to screen coordinates

```
procedure WorldToPC(Xw, Yw: real; var XPC, YPC: integer);
{ Converts a world coordinate to a screen coordinate }
begin
  XPC := Round(A * Xw + B);
  YPC := Round(C * Yw + D);
end;
```

The parameters **Xw** and **Yw** are the world coordinates to be mapped to the screen coordinates **XPC** and **YPC**. You should compare these statements with the equations shown in Figure 5.3. Similarly, **PCToWorld** maps a screen coordinate to world coordinates by the statements:

```
procedure PCToWorld(XPC, YPC: integer; var Xw, Yw: real);
{ Converts a screen coordinate to a world coordinate }
begin
  Xw := (XPC - B) / A;
  Yw := (YPC - D) / C;
end;
```

We'll be using these routines in the CAD program that we will develop in Chapter 12 to define how and where objects are displayed.

Transformations

In the last section, we learned how to map objects represented in world coordinates to the screen. Now let's explore ways to manipulate these objects so that they can be drawn at different locations, orientations, and scales. We'll use transformations to produce these effects.

Transformations are a basic mathematical operation in graphics programming. Quite literally, a transform is a function (or equation) that defines how one set of data is to be changed or transformed into another. For example, let's say that we have a picture of a wheel on the screen that we want to rotate. We can use a rotation transformation to determine how the wheel is supposed to be affected as it is moved.

The most common transformations are translation, rotation, and scaling. In this section we'll explore each of these transformations in detail and add routines to MATRIX.PAS to perform these operations. A list of the transformation routines that will be added to MATRIX.PAS is shown in Table 5.1.

The CAD program we'll develop in Chapter 12 uses the MATRIX.PAS unit to translate and rotate objects. When we explore three-dimensional graphics in Chapter 13 we'll rely on transforms to generate perspective views of three-dimensional objects. For now, however, let's concern ourselves with objects in two dimensions.

Translation

One of the simplest transforms produces a translation. Essentially, a translation defines how a point is supposed to be moved from one location in space to another.

Table 5.1. Two-dimensional transformations supported in MATRIX.PAS

Routine	Description
PCTranslatePoly	Translates a polygon in screen coordinates
PCScalePoly	Scales a polygon in screen coordinates
PCRotatePoly	Rotates a polygon in screen coordinates
PCShearPoly	Shears a polygon in screen coordinates
WorldTranslatePoly	Translates a polygon in world coordinates
WorldScalePoly	Scales a polygon in world coordinates
WorldRotatePoly	Rotates a polygon in world coordinates

For example, if we have a box drawn on the left-hand side of the screen and we want to move it to the right, we can use a translation transformation to specify how each point must be moved.

For instance, translating a pixel on the screen can be done by adding an appropriate value to each of the x and y coordinates to which the point is to be moved. This can be written in Pascal as:

```
NewX := X + TranslateX;
NewY := Y + TranslateY;
```

The values **TranslateX** and **TranslateY** can be either positive or negative and define how much the point (x, y) should be translated in the x and y directions, respectively.

Translating an object, like a polygon, is only a matter of translating each of the points that make up the polygon as illustrated in Figure 5.4. A routine in MATRIX.PAS that does this is called **PCTranslatePoly**.

```
procedure PCTranslatePoly(NumPoints: integer; var Poly: PCArray;
                          Tx, Ty: integer);
{ Translates a two-dimensional polygon by Tx and Ty. The polygon should be
  in screen coordinates. }
var
  I: integer;
begin
  for I := 0 to NumPoints-1 do begin
    Poly[I].X := Poly[I].X + Tx;
    Poly[I].Y := Poly[I].Y + Ty;
  end
end;
```

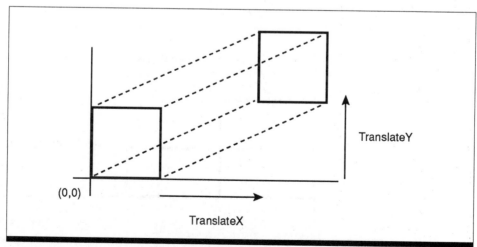

Figure 5.4. Translating an object

It is designed to work in screen coordinates since the translation amounts are specified as integers. A similar routine, **WorldTranslatePoly**, is included in MATRIX.PAS that is designed to translate a polygon specified in world coordinates. Because of this, **Tx**, **Ty**, and the array **Poly** are defined as using real values.

Scaling a Two-Dimensional Polygon

Scaling a two-dimensional polygon can be accomplished by multiplying each of the coordinates of the original polygon by a scale factor. For example, assume we want to scale the box shown in Figure 5.5 by 2 in the x direction and by one half in the y direction. This can be done by applying the following equations to each of the coordinates of the box:

```
ScaleDx := x * ScaleX;
ScaleDy := y * ScaleY;
```

A routine in MATRIX.PAS that performs this operation for a polygon in screen coordinates is called **PCScalePoly.**

```
procedure PCScalePoly(NumPoints: integer; var Poly: PCArray; Sx, Sy: real);
{ Scales a polygon by Sx in the x dimension and Sy in the y dimension.
  The polygon should be in screen coordinates. }
var
  I: integer;
begin
  for I := 0 to NumPoints-1 do begin
    Poly[I].X := Round(Poly[I].X * Sx);
```

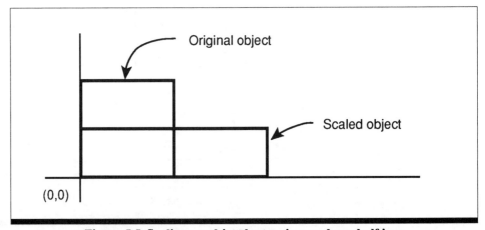

Figure 5.5. Scaling an object by two in x and one half in y

```
   Poly[I].Y := Round(Poly[I].Y * Sy);
  end
end;
```

A similar routine exists for polygons specified in world coordinates. It is called **WorldScalePoly**.

Merely calling **PCScalePoly** to scale an object does not always produce the results expected, however. Since each coordinate in the object is multiplied by a scale factor, the object may be moved as well as scaled as shown in Figure 5.6. That is, unless one of the coordinates is (0,0). This coordinate would stay the same. Therefore, if you want to scale an object, yet keep one of its points stationary so that the object doesn't move, two additional steps must be taken. First, the object must be translated so that the point you want to scale about (keep fixed) moves to the origin. Second, after applying the scaling transformation, the object must be translated back by the amount that it was translated earlier. The net effect is that the object is scaled, but the point that is translated to the origin and back remains stationary. This scaling sequence, as illustrated in Figure 5.7, is actually more useful than the first.

For example, the following code doubles the size of the polygon in the array **Poly** by translating it so that its first point is at the origin, scaling it, and then translating the polygon back.

```
Px := Poly[1].X;
Py := Poly[1].Y;
PCTranslatePoly(NumPoints,Poly,-Px,-Py);
PCScalePoly(NumPoints,Poly,2.0,2.0);
PCTranslatePoly(NumPoints,Poly,Px,Py);
```

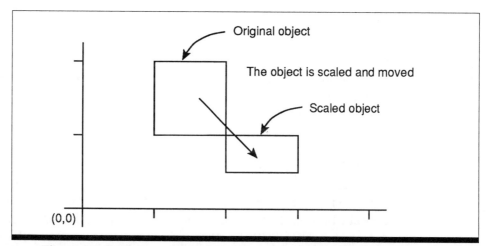

Figure 5.6. Scaling an object not at the origin changes its size and location

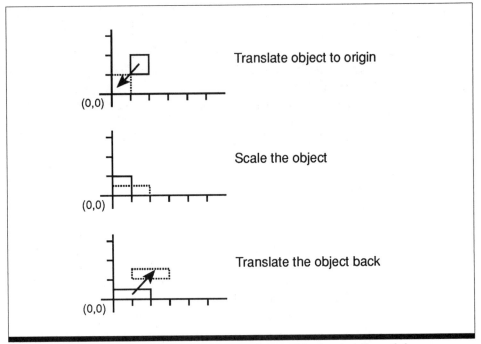

Figure 5.7. Process to properly scale an object not at the origin

Rotating a Two-Dimensional Polygon

Another useful transformation rotates an object around a point. The equations to perform the rotation are:

```
RotatedX := X * Cos(Angle) - Y * Sin(Angle);
RotatedY := X * Sin(Angle) + Y * Cos(Angle);
```

Rather than go into the geometry that derives these equations, let's look at them from a user's standpoint. The **X** and **Y** variables on the right side of the equation represent the point being rotated and the **Angle** variable specifies the angle on which the point is to be rotated. In Turbo Pascal this value needs to be expressed in radians. Since degrees are more natural for us to specify angles, we'll use the function **ToRadians** to convert angles in degrees to radians.

Actually, to rotate an object successfully we need to pick a point around which the object is to be rotated, translate it to the origin, rotate the polygon, and then translate the object back. The routine in MATRIX.PAS that performs the rotation operation is called **PCRotatePoly** and can be used to rotate a polygon as shown in Figure 5.8.

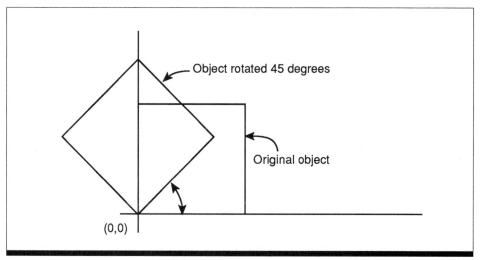

Figure 5.8. Rotating an object

```
procedure PCRotatePoly(NumPoints: integer; var Poly: PCArray; Angle: real);
{ Rotates a polygon by the number of degrees specified in Angle.
  The polygon should be in screen coordinates. }
var
  I: integer;
  X, Y, Radians, CosTheta, SinTheta: real;
begin
  Radians := ToRadians(Angle);
  CosTheta := Cos(Radians);    SinTheta := Sin(Radians);
  for I := 0 to NumPoints-1 do begin
    X := Poly[I].X;     Y := Poly[I].Y;
    Poly[I].X := Round(X * CosTheta - Y * SinTheta / AspectRatio);
    Poly[I].Y := Round(X * SinTheta * Aspectratio + Y * CosTheta);
  end
end;
```

Note that the **Y** values in the equations are adjusted by **AspectRatio**. This is required because this routine is operating with screen coordinates. The procedure **WorldRotatePoly** has similar code, except that since it is designed to work with world coordinates, it does not need these adjustments.

The Shear Transform

Some transformations produce some rather interesting effects. One of the more common transformations that falls into this category shears objects to which it is applied as shown in Figure 5.9. It involves multiplying each of the coordinates of

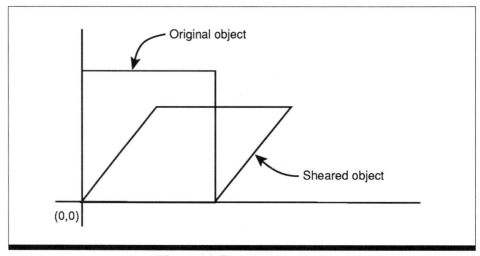

Figure 5.9. Shearing an object

the object by a scale factor and adding an offset. A pair of equations that produces the shear effect are:

```
ShearedX := X + C * Y;
ShearedY := D * X + Y;
```

As with rotations, we want to shear the polygon about a point, so we must translate the polygon to the origin, apply the shear transform, and then translate the object back. In addition, if we transform pixels on the screen we will need to compensate for the monitor's aspect ratio. The routine that can be used to shear a polygon situated at the origin is **PCShearPoly**. You should refer to MATRIX.PAS (Listing 5.1) for the complete routine.

• Listing 5.1. MATRIX.PAS

```
unit Matrix;
{ MATRIX.PAS: The following set of matrix operations are used in the
  two-dimensional graphics programs later in this book. }
interface
uses
  Graph;
const
  MaxPoint = 30;
type
  PCArray = array[0..MaxPoint-1] of PointType;
  WorldType = record
```

```
      X, Y: real;
    end;
    WorldArray = array[0..MaxPoint-1] of WorldType;
  var
    AspectRatio: real;          { Define the aspect ratio }
    XAsp, YAsp: word;


  { These are the procedures that MATRIX.PAS provides }
  function ToRadians(Degrees: real): real;
  procedure PCTranslatePoly(NumPoints: integer; var Poly: PCArray;
                            Tx, Ty: integer);
  procedure PCScalePoly(NumPoints: integer; var Poly: PCArray; Sx, Sy: real);
  procedure PCRotatePoly(NumPoints: integer; var Poly: PCArray; Angle: real);
  procedure PCShearPoly(NumPoints: integer; var Poly: PCArray; C, D: real);
  procedure CopyPoly(NumPoints: integer; var PolyFrom, PolyTo: PCArray);
  procedure WorldTranslatePoly(NumPoints: integer; var Poly: WorldArray;
                               Tx, Ty: real);
  procedure WorldScalePoly(NumPoints: integer; var Poly: WorldArray;
                           Sx, Sy: real);
  procedure WorldRotatePoly(NumPoints: integer;
                            var Poly: WorldArray; Angle: real);
  procedure CopyWorldPoly(NumPoints: integer; var PolyFrom,
                          PolyTo: WorldArray);
  procedure WorldToPC(Xw, Yw: real; var XPC, YPC: integer);
  procedure PCToWorld(XPC, YPC: integer; var Xw, Yw: real);
  procedure Set_Window(XMin, XMax, YMin, YMax: real);
  procedure Set_ViewPort(XMin, XMax, YMin, YMax: integer);
  procedure PCPolyToWorldPoly(NumPoints: integer; var PCPoly: PCArray;
                              var WorldPoly: WorldArray);
  procedure WorldPolyToPCPoly(NumPoints: integer; var WorldPoly: WorldArray;
                              var PCPoly: PCArray);

  implementation
  var
    A, B, C, D: real;              { Internal values set by }
    Xvl, Xvr, Yvt, Yvb: integer;  { Set_Window and Set_ViewPort }
    Xwl, Xwr, Ywt, Ywb: real;     { to map to screen coordinates }

  function ToRadians(Degrees: real): real;
  { Convert degrees to radians }
  begin
    ToRadians :=  Pi * Degrees / 180.0;
  end;


  procedure PCTranslatePoly(NumPoints: integer; var Poly: PCArray;
                            Tx, Ty: integer);
  { Translates a two-dimensional polygon by Tx and Ty. The polygon should
    be in screen coordinates. }
  var
    I: integer;
  begin
    for I := 0 to NumPoints-1 do begin
      Poly[I].X := Poly[I].X + Tx;
```

```
      Poly[I].Y := Poly[I].Y + Ty;
    end
end;

procedure PCScalePoly(NumPoints: integer; var Poly: PCArray; Sx, Sy: real);
{ Scales a polygon by Sx in the x dimension and Sy in the y dimension.
  The polygon should be in screen coordinates. }
var
  I: integer;
begin
  for I := 0 to NumPoints-1 do begin
    Poly[I].X := Round(Poly[I].X * Sx);
    Poly[I].Y := Round(Poly[I].Y * Sy);
  end
end;

procedure PCRotatePoly(NumPoints: integer; var Poly: PCArray; Angle: real);
{ Rotates a polygon by the number of degrees specified in Angle.
  The polygon should be in screen coordinates. }
var
  I: integer;
  X, Y, Radians, CosTheta, SinTheta: real;
begin
  Radians := ToRadians(Angle);
  CosTheta := Cos(Radians);   SinTheta := Sin(Radians);
  for I := 0 to NumPoints-1 do begin
    X := Poly[I].X;    Y := Poly[I].Y;
    Poly[I].X := Round(X * CosTheta - Y * SinTheta / AspectRatio);
    Poly[I].Y := Round(X * SinTheta * Aspectratio + Y * CosTheta);
  end
end;

procedure PCShearPoly(NumPoints: integer; var Poly: PCArray; C, D: real);
{ Shears a polygon by applying C to the x dimension and D to
  the y dimension. The polygon should be in screen coordinates. }
var
  I: integer;
  X, Y: real;
begin
  for I := 0 to NumPoints-1 do begin
    X := Poly[I].X;    Y := Poly[I].Y;
    Poly[I].X := Round(X + C * Y / AspectRatio);
    Poly[I].Y := Round(D * X * AspectRatio + Y);
  end
end;

procedure CopyPoly(NumPoints: integer; var PolyFrom, PolyTo: PCArray);
{ Copies from one integer polygon to another }
var
  I: integer;
begin
  for I := 0 to NumPoints-1 do begin
    PolyTo[I].X := PolyFrom[I].X;
```

```
      PolyTo[I].Y := PolyFrom[I].Y;
    end
  end;

procedure WorldTranslatePoly(NumPoints: integer; var Poly: WorldArray;
                             Tx, Ty: real);
{ Translates a polygon in world coordinates }
var
  I: integer;
begin
  for I := 0 to NumPoints-1 do begin
    Poly[I].X := Poly[I].X + Tx;
    Poly[I].Y := Poly[I].Y + Ty;
  end
end;

procedure WorldScalePoly(NumPoints: integer; var Poly: WorldArray;
                         Sx, Sy: real);
{ Scales a polygon in world coordinates by Sx and Sy }
var
  I: integer;
begin
  for I := 0 to NumPoints-1 do begin
    Poly[I].X := Poly[I].X * Sx;
    Poly[I].Y := Poly[I].Y * Sy;
  end
end;

procedure WorldRotatePoly(NumPoints: integer;
                          var Poly: WorldArray; Angle: real);
{ Rotates a polygon in world coordinates by the number of degrees
  in Angle }
var
  I: integer;
  Rad: real;
  CosTheta, SinTheta: real;
  X, Y: real;
begin
  Rad := ToRadians(Angle);
  CosTheta := Cos(Rad);
  SinTheta := Sin(Rad);
  for I := 0 to NumPoints-1 do begin
    X := Poly[I].X;    Y := Poly[I].Y;
    Poly[I].X := X * CosTheta - Y * SinTheta;
    Poly[I].Y := X * SinTheta + Y * CosTheta;
  end
end;

procedure CopyWorldPoly(NumPoints: integer;
                        var PolyFrom, PolyTo: WorldArray);
{ Copies one polygon in world coordinates to another }
var
  I: integer;
```

```
begin
  for I := 0 to NumPoints-1 do begin
    PolyTo[I].X := PolyFrom[I].X;
    PolyTo[I].Y := PolyFrom[I].Y;
  end
end;

procedure WorldToPC(Xw, Yw: real; var XPC, YPC: integer);
{ Converts a world coordinate to a screen coordinate }
begin
  XPC := Round(A * Xw + B);
  YPC := Round(C * Yw + D);
end;

procedure PCToWorld(XPC, YPC: integer; var Xw, Yw: real);
{ Converts a screen coordinate to a world coordinate }
begin
  Xw := (XPC - B) / A;
  Yw := (YPC - D) / C;
end;

procedure Set_Window(XMin, XMax, YMin, YMax: real);
{ Defines the window used in real world coordinates }
begin
  Xwl := XMin;    Xwr := XMax;
  Ywb := Ymin;    Ywt := YMax;
end;

procedure Set_ViewPort(XMin, XMax, YMin, YMax: integer);
{ Defines the region on the screen to which world objects are mapped }
begin
  Xvl := XMin;    Xvr := XMax;
  Yvb := YMin;    Yvt := YMax;
  A := (Xvr - Xvl) / (Xwr - Xwl);    B := Xvl - A * Xwl;
  C := (Yvt - Yvb) / (Ywt - Ywb);    D := Yvb - C * Ywb;
end;

procedure PCPolyToWorldPoly(NumPoints: integer; var PCPoly: PCArray;
                            var WorldPoly: WorldArray);
{ Converts a list of polygon points from screen coordinates
  to world coordinates }
var
  I: integer;
begin
  for I := 0 to NumPoints-1 do
    PCToWorld(PCPoly[I].X,PCPoly[I].Y,WorldPoly[I].X,WorldPoly[I].Y);
end;

procedure WorldPolyToPCPoly(NumPoints: integer; var WorldPoly: WorldArray;
                            var PCPoly: PCArray);
{ Converts a list of polygon points from world coordinates to
  screen coordinates }
var
```

```
    I: integer;
begin
  for I := 0 to NumPoints-1 do
    WorldToPC(WorldPoly[I].X,WorldPoly[I].Y,PCPoly[I].X,PCPoly[I].Y);
end;

end.
```

A Matrix Demo

Listing 5.2 presents a short program that you can use to test the matrix operations included in MATRIX.PAS. It applies several of the transformations developed in MATRIX.PAS to the polygon in the array **Points**. After displaying the result of each of the transforms, you must press a key to proceed to the next one.

• Listing 5.2. MTXTTEST.PAS

```
program MtxtTest;
{ MTXTTEST.PAS: Tests the transforms defined in the MATRIX.PAS unit. }
uses
  Graph, Matrix, Crt;
const
  GDriver: integer = Detect;
  NumPoints = 5;
var
  PolyCopy: PCArray;
  GMode, Px, Py, I: integer;
  Ch: char;
  Points: PCArray;
begin
  InitGraph(GDriver,GMode,'\tp\bgi');
  GetAspectRatio(XAsp,YAsp);
  AspectRatio := XAsp / YAsp;
  Rectangle(0,0,GetMaxX,GetMaxY);
  Points[0].X := 150;  Points[0].Y := 80;
  Points[1].X := 400;  Points[1].Y := 80;
  Points[2].X := 400;  Points[2].Y := 150;
  Points[3].X := 150;  Points[3].Y := 150;
  Points[4].X := 150;  Points[4].Y := 80;
{ Test translate polygon }
  DrawPoly(NumPoints,Points);
  CopyPoly(NumPoints,Points,PolyCopy);
  Px := PolyCopy[0].X;    Py := PolyCopy[0].Y;
  PCTranslatePoly(NumPoints,PolyCopy,-Px,-Py);
  DrawPoly(NumPoints,PolyCopy);
  Ch := ReadKey;
```

```
{ Scale the polygon about the point (Px,Py) }
CopyPoly(NumPoints,Points,PolyCopy);
PCTranslatePoly(NumPoints,PolyCopy,-Px,-Py);
PCScalePoly(NumPoints,PolyCopy,1.5,1.5);
PCTranslatePoly(NumPoints,PolyCopy,Px,Py);
DrawPoly(NumPoints,PolyCopy);
Ch := ReadKey;

{ Rotate the figure around the point (Px,Py) by 45 degrees }
CopyPoly(NumPoints,Points,PolyCopy);
PCTranslatePoly(NumPoints,PolyCopy,-Px,-Py);
PCRotatePoly(NumPoints,PolyCopy,45.0);
PCTranslatePoly(NumPoints,PolyCopy,Px,Py);
DrawPoly(NumPoints,PolyCopy);
Ch := ReadKey;

{ Shear the object about the point (Px,Py) }
ClearViewPort;
DrawPoly(NumPoints,Points);
CopyPoly(NumPoints,Points,PolyCopy);
PCTranslatePoly(NumPoints,PolyCopy,-Px,-Py);
PCShearPoly(NumPoints,PolyCopy,0,1);
PCTranslatePoly(NumPoints,PolyCopy,Px,Py);
DrawPoly(NumPoints,PolyCopy);
Ch := ReadKey;
CloseGraph;     { Exit graphics mode }
end.
```

Animation

Animation is an attractive graphics feature for several reasons. It can help draw attention to a portion of a display, demonstrate how something works, lay the foundation for interactive programs, or simply make a program visually more interesting. In this chapter we'll explore some of the various animation techniques that you can experiment with in your own graphics programs. Some of the techniques we'll present include inbetweening, moving objects by using **GetImage** and **PutImage**, animating objects by changing palette colors, and using multiple screen pages to create motion.

A Closer Look at Inbetweening

In Chapter 4 we briefly explored inbetweening by using it to animate a bar graph. Now we'll take a closer look at it to see how it can be used to produce more general animation effects.

The inbetweening technique is a simple one. The basic idea is to define the start and stop coordinates of an object and then calculate and display the object as it progresses from its initial state to its final one. Let's take a simple case. Suppose we want to animate a single point by moving it from one location to another. All we need to know is where the point starts, stops, and the number of intermediate steps it should take. For example, if our point starts at (0,0) and we want it to move to (150,150) in 15 steps, we must move the point in 10-pixel increments.

The next step is to write a program that can calculate and plot the intermediate steps of our animated point. The calculation is merely a linear interpolation between the start and stop positions of the point. In our case, we want to plot the point 15 times, by moving it 10 pixels each time in the x and y directions. Therefore, the code that can perform this is:

```
NumberOfSteps := 15;
StepSize := (StopX - StartX) / NumberOfSteps;
for J := 0 to NumberOfSteps-1 do begin
  IncAmount := Round(StepSize * J);
  PutPixel(StartX+IncAmount,StartY+IncAmount,White);
  PutPixel(StartX+IncAmount,StartY+IncAmount,Black);
end;
PutPixel(X+IncAmount,Y+IncAmount,White);
```

The variable **StepSize** determines the distance the point should be moved between each state. It is dependent on the number of intermediate states that are desired (in this case 15), and the total distance to travel. The **for** loop steps through each of the intermediate steps of the animation, plots the pixel by a call to **PutPixel** and then erases it by another call to **PutPixel**. The location of the pixel is determined by **IncAmount**, which continually moves the point closer to the final state as **J** increases toward 15. In this example, the x and y directions are incremented equally, but we can easily modify the code so that the x and y directions change by different amounts.

This example shows us how to move a point across the screen, but what about animating an object? The transition is simple. If we have an object that is drawn as a series of line segments, for instance, all we need to do is run our inbetweening algorithm on each of the endpoints of the line segments and draw the lines between the points at each step in the process. The following section looks at animating objects using this technique.

Animating a Line

Before we proceed with animating an object drawn from line segments, we need to reexamine the way we draw lines. In order to animate an object we must draw the object, remove it from the screen, draw it in its new position, erase it, draw it at the next location, and so on. However, if we remove the line segments from the screen by overwriting them with the background color, the screen may quickly become a mess if there are other objects on the screen that the animated object crosses over. Clearly, this is not what we want.

In Chapter 2, we learned that an object could be moved *cleanly* by using the **XorPut** option of the **PutImage** procedure. Although we won't use **PutImage** to animate a line segment, we can still use the same **XorPut** option to cleanly move a line across the screen.

The BGI allows us to set the line drawing routines so that they draw exclusive-OR lines. Because of the exclusive-ORing, we'll be able to remove any line from the screen by simply drawing it again. In order to turn the exclusive-OR capability of the line drawer on, we must use the **SetWriteMode** routine. It is defined in **Graph** as:

```
procedure SetWriteMode(Mode: integer);
```

The **Mode** parameter can be set to **CopyPut** or **XorPut**. By default the BGI uses **CopyPut**. This means that lines are drawn by setting each pixel along the line segment to the current drawing color. If the **XorPut** option is used, each pixel in the line segment is exclusive-ORed with the screen image. Therefore, if a line routine is called twice with the same coordinates when the **XorPut** option is used, the line will be drawn and then erased without the original screen being affected. Note that the **SetWriteMode** procedure works only with **Line**, **LineRel**, **LineTo**, **Rectangle**, and **DrawPoly**.

Working with Inbetweening

Now let's apply **SetWriteMode** to inbetweening so that we can animate a set of line segments. The code shown next, for instance, will move a rectangle across the screen (Figure 6.1).

The starting coordinates of the rectangle are defined in the array **StartPoints**, where the array contains a series of x and y coordinates. The final location of the

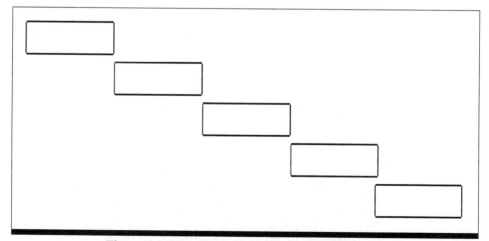

Figure 6.1. Time-lapsed output of INBETWN.PAS

rectangle is stored in the array **StopPoints**. Since **DrawPoly** is used to draw the lines, the arrays are declared so that their first and last coordinates are the same. An additional array, **Inbetween**, is also declared to be the same size as **StartPoints** and **StopPoints** so that it can hold and display each intermediate state of the animated rectangle. The constant **NumSteps** defines the number of intermediate steps used in the animation. In this example, **NumSteps** is set to a value of 100. Other than in the use of these variables, the inbetweening procedure, **InbetweenPoints**, is similar to the one presented earlier. Here is the complete program:

```pascal
program InBetwn;
{ INBETWN.PAS: Demonstrates an animation technique called inbetweening
  by moving a rectangle across the screen. }
uses
  Graph, Crt;
const
  Length = 5;                        { Number of coordinate pairs in arrays }
  NumSteps: integer = 100;           { Number of steps from start to end }
                                     { Also controls speed of movement }
  { Leave these statements in to move a rectangle across the screen }

  StartPoints: array[1..Length] of PointType = ((x:0;    y:0),
                                    (x:100; y:0), (x:100; y:20),
                                    (x:0;   y:20), (x:0;   y:0));
  StopPoints: array[1..Length] of PointType =  ((x:400; y:100),
                                    (x:500; y:100), (x:500; y:120),
                                    (x:400; y:120), (x:400; y:100));

{ Swap these two statements with those above to animate the process
  of a rectangle turning into a triangle }
{
  StartPoints: array[1..Length] of PointType = ((x:0;    y:0),
    (x:639; y:0), (x:639; y:199), (x:0;   y:199), (x:0;    y:0));
  StopPoints: array[1..Length] of PointType =  ((x:210; y:120),
    (x:315; y:60), (x:420; y:120), (x:210; y:120), (x:210; y:120));
}

  GDriver: integer = Detect;
var
  Inbetween: array[1..Length] of PointType;
  GMode, I: integer;

procedure InbetweenPoints;
var
  StepSize, IncAmount: real;
  I, J: integer;
begin
  StepSize := 1.0 / (NumSteps - 1.0);
  for I := 1 to NumSteps do begin
    IncAmount := (i-1) * StepSize;
    for J := 1 to Length do begin
```

```
      Inbetween[J].X := StartPoints[J].X + Round(IncAmount *
                      (StopPoints[J].X - StartPoints[J].X));
      Inbetween[J].Y := StartPoints[J].Y + Round(IncAmount *
                      (StopPoints[J].Y - StartPoints[J].Y));
    end;
    DrawPoly(Length,Inbetween);        { Draw lines }
    Delay(100);                        { Wait a while so line doesn't flicker }
    DrawPoly(Length,Inbetween);        { Erase line }
  end;
  DrawPoly(Length,Inbetween);          { Redraw the final lines }
end;

begin
  InitGraph(GDriver,GMode,'\tp\bgi');
  SetWriteMode(XorPut);
  InbetweenPoints;
  ReadLn;
  CloseGraph;
end.
```

One intriguing thing about inbetweening is that the first and last images of the object being animated do not have to be the same. Figure 6.2 shows the previous code modified so that the rectangle is turned into a triangle. The only restriction

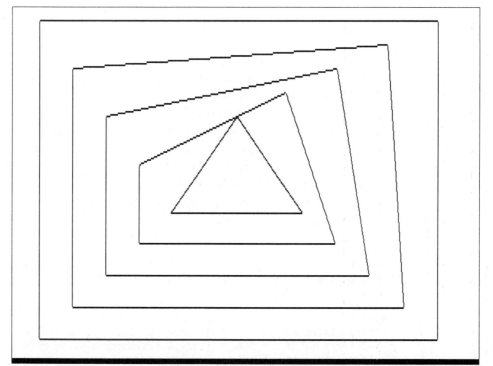

Figure 6.2. Using inbetweening to convert a rectangle into a triangle

here is that the number of line segments in the start and final states must be the same. Actually, we can break this rule by adding various figures to the final version of the animated object to produce interesting results. As an exercise you might try turning a square into a face, for instance. Of course, the difficulty here is coming up with the proper coordinates that can draw the shapes.

The following are two array declarations for **StartPoints** and **StopPoints** that you can use to replace the ones shown in the previous example. The coordinates in these two arrays will produce a picture of a rectangle turning into a triangle as described earlier. Since the number of line segments must be the same in the start and stop states, but clearly the rectangle and triangle have a different number of vertices, we have declared **StopPoints** so that the first and last coordinate is specified three times. In other words, one of the line segments in the rectangle shrinks to a line of zero length. Therefore, although there will be the same number of line segments declared in the arrays, it appears that the triangle has one less line.

```
StartPoints: array[1..Length] of PointType = ((x:0;  y:0),
   (x:639; y:0), (x:639; y:199), (x:0; y:199), (x:0; y:0));
StopPoints: array[1..Length] of PointType = ((x:210; y:120),
   (x:315; y:60), (x:420; y:120), (x:210; y:120), (x:210; y:120));
```

Working with GetImage and PutImage

One of the drawbacks to using inbetweening is that the animated object must be redrawn at each step along the way. For complex objects this process can be slow. An alternative method is to draw the image once and then move it across the screen using the **GetImage** and **PutImage** routines.

Chapter 2 introduced the **GetImage** and **PutImage** procedures and described the various placement options that are available with **PutImage**. In this section we'll focus on using them, rather than understanding how they operate. (See Chapter 2 for more specific details on these routines and how they function.)

Our first animation example using **GetImage** and **PutImage** shows a bicycle moving across the screen (see Figure 6.3). The code for this example is listed here.

```
program Bike;
{ BIKE.PAS: This program uses the BGI's GetImage and PutImage procedures
  to move a bike across the screen. }
uses
  Graph;
const
  Step: integer = 5;          { Number of pixels to move bike each time }
  GDriver: integer = CGA;     { Use CGA high-resolution mode }
  GMode: integer = CGAHI;
```

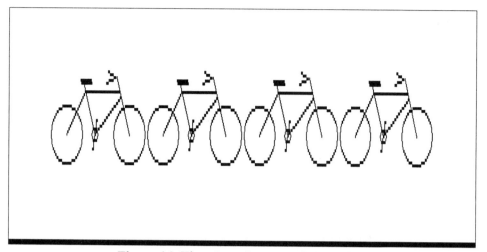

Figure 6.3. Time-lapsed output of BIKE.PAS

```
var
   BikePtr: pointer;              { Points to the image of the bike }

procedure DrawBike;
{ Draw a bicycle using calls to Circle and Line. Then capture
  the image of the bicycle with GetImage. }
begin
   Circle(50,100,25);             { Draw the wheels }
   Circle(150,100,25);
   Line(50,100,80,85);            { Draw part of the frame }
   Line(80,85,134,85);
   Line(77,82,95,100);
   Line(130,80,150,100);
   Line(128,80,113,82);           { Handlebars }
   Line(128,80,116,78);
   Line(72,81,89,81);             { Seat }
   Line(73,82,90,82);
   Circle(95,100,5);              { Draw the pedals }
   Line(92,105,98,95);
   Line(91,105,93,105);
   Line(97,95,99,95);
   Line(95,100,136,87);

   GetMem(BikePtr,ImageSize(25,75,175,125));  { Allocate image}
   GetImage(25,75,175,125,BikePtr^);          { Capture image of }
end;                                           { the bicycle }

procedure MoveBike;
{ Move bike across the screen in increments of Step }
var
   I, Times: integer;
begin
```

```
    Times := (GetMaxX-180) div Step;
    for I := 0 to Times do begin
      PutImage(25+I*Step,75,BikePtr^,XorPut);       { Erase bike }
      PutImage(25+(I+1)*Step,75,BikePtr^,XorPut);   { Display bike }
    end;
  end;

begin
  InitGraph(GDriver,GMode,'\tp\bgi');
  DrawBike;
  MoveBike;
  ReadLn;
  CloseGraph;
end.
```

The original image of the bicycle is created by a series of calls to **Line** and **Circle** in the routine **DrawBike**. Next, memory space is allocated to the pointer **BikePtr** to hold the screen image of the bicycle and then the image is retrieved by a call to **GetImage**. Here are the two statements that perform these operations:

```
GetMem(BikePtr,ImageSize(25,75,175,125));
GetImage(25,75,175,125,BikePtr^);
```

Next, the routine **MoveBike** is called to move the bicycle image in **BikePtr** across the screen. In this example, the image is moved from the coordinate (25,75) to (GetMaxX-180,75) in steps of 5 pixels. The movement is accomplished by the **for** loop in **MoveBike**, which is:

```
Times := (GetMaxX-180) div Step;
for I := 0 to Times do begin
  PutImage(25+I*Step,75,BikePtr^,XorPut);       { Erase bike }
  PutImage(25+(I+1)*Step,75,BikePtr^,XorPut);   { Display bike }
end;
```

As you can see, the **for** loop calls **PutImage** twice. The first erases the current image of the bicycle by exclusive-ORing **BikePtr** to the screen. The second displays the bicycle image at its next location using the **XorPut** option.

We can improve our example by rotating the bicycle's pedals as it moves. The basic idea is to create several images of the pedals at different orientations and then sequence through them to make it look like the pedals are turning. There are two ways of accomplishing this. For instance, we could make several images of the whole bicycle with the pedals at different orientations and then sequence through them or we could have one complete image of the bicycle and a series of smaller images that just show the pedals at various positions. With the second technique, we must overlay the pedal images with the bicycle image to create the motion.

You may be wondering why we would want to have two sets of images, one for the bicycle and one for animating the pedals. One important reason, which isn't critical for this example, is that for large pictures we can speed up the animation process and save memory by swapping images of only the regions that must be changed. In addition, several images of the whole bicycle can consume a lot more memory than a single image of the bicycle and a companion set of smaller images. For example, in high-resolution graphics modes, it is very easy to consume an excessive amount of memory.

Now let's return to the task of animating the bicycle pedals. The following program animates the bicycle by moving it across the screen as well as rotating its pedals. The program accomplishes this by creating four different images of the bicycle, each with different pedal orientations, and sequencing through them.

```
program Bike2;
{ BIKE2.PAS: Uses the BGI's GetImage and PutImage procedures to animate
  a bicycle across the screen. The program creates four images of a bike,
  each with the pedals in a different orientation, so that when the images
  are played back it looks like the pedals are moving as the bicycle is
  moved across the screen. }
uses
  Graph, Crt;
const
  Step: integer = 5;                      { Amount to move bicycle }
  GDriver: integer = CGA;                 { Use CGA high-resolution mode }
  GMode: integer = CGAHI;
var
  BikePtr1, BikePtr2,                     { The images of the bicycle }
  BikePtr3, BikePtr4: pointer;

procedure DrawBike;
{ Create four images of the bicycle. Each one will have a different
  pedal orientation so that when they are shown in sequence it
  appears like the pedals are turning. }
var
  Pedals: pointer;                        { Temporary image used to }
  Size: word;                             { draw bicycle }
begin
  Circle(50,100,25);                      { Draw wheels }
  Circle(150,100,25);
  Line(50,100,80,85);                     { Draw part of frame }
  Line(80,85,134,85);
  Line(77,82,95,100);
  Line(130,80,150,100);
  Line(128,80,113,82);                    { Handlebars }
  Line(128,80,116,78);
  Line(72,81,89,81);                      { Seat }
  Line(73,82,90,82);
  GetMem(BikePtr1,ImageSize(25,75,175,125));
```

```pascal
    GetMem(BikePtr2,ImageSize(25,75,175,125));
    GetMem(BikePtr3,ImageSize(25,75,175,125));
    GetMem(BikePtr4,ImageSize(25,75,175,125));
    Size := ImageSize(85,90,110,110);
    GetMem(Pedals,Size);
    Circle(95,100,5);                          { Draw base of pedals }
    Line(95,100,136,87);
    GetImage(85,90,110,110,Pedals^);           { Save screen of pedals }
    Line(86,100,104,100);                      { Draw pedals in }
    Line(85,100,87,100);                       { first position }
    Line(103,100,105,100);
    GetImage(25,75,175,125,BikePtr1^);
    PutImage(85,90,Pedals^,CopyPut);           { Restore pedal area }
    Line(88,96,102,104);                       { Draw pedals in second }
    Line(87,96,89,96);                         { position }
    Line(101,104,103,104);
    GetImage(25,75,175,125,BikePtr2^);

    PutImage(85,90,Pedals^,CopyPut);           { Restore pedal area }
    Line(95,95,95,105);                        { Draw pedals in third }
    Line(94,95,96,95);                         { position }
    Line(94,105,96,105);
    GetImage(25,75,175,125,BikePtr3^);

    PutImage(85,90,Pedals^,CopyPut);           { Restore pedal area }
    Line(102,96,88,104);                       { Draw pedals in forth }
    Line(101,96,103,96);                       { position }
    Line(87,104,89,104);
    GetImage(25,75,175,125,BikePtr4^);
    FreeMem(Pedals,Size);
end;

procedure MoveBikeAndPedals;
{ Sequences through the four images of the bicycle in order to move
  the bicycle across the screen }
var
  I, Times: integer;
begin
  Times := (GetMaxX-175) div Step;
  for I := 0 to Times-1 do begin
    case I mod 4 of
      0: begin
        PutImage(25+I*Step,75,BikePtr4^,XorPut);
        PutImage(25+(I+1)*Step,75,BikePtr1^,XorPut);
        end;
      1: begin
        PutImage(25+I*Step,75,BikePtr1^,XorPut);
        PutImage(25+(I+1)*Step,75,BikePtr2^,XorPut);
        end;
      2: begin
        PutImage(25+I*Step,75,BikePtr2^,XorPut);
        PutImage(25+(I+1)*Step,75,BikePtr3^,XorPut);
        end;
```

```
      3: begin
           PutImage(25+I*Step,75,BikePtr3^,XorPut);
           PutImage(25+(I+1)*Step,75,BikePtr4^,XorPut);
           end;
      end;
    Delay(10);              { This delay controls the speed of the bicycle }
  end
end;

begin
  InitGraph(GDriver,GMode,'\tp\bgi');
  DrawBike;
  MoveBikeAndPedals;
  ReadLn;
  CloseGraph;
end.
```

Animating Objects on a Backdrop

Thus far we have used **GetImage** and **PutImage** only to move objects across a plain background. Unfortunately, this does not represent the typical situation. In most animation programs, you'll probably want to place several objects in the background to make the screen more interesting. For example, we could use a country scene as the backdrop of our bicycle animation program. Unfortunately, if we put objects on the screen that our bicycle must cross over, the bicycle might change its color as the two objects overlap. The reason is that the animated object and the screen are exclusive-ORed together. Therefore, wherever the image being animated contains a bit value of 1, copying the image to the screen will change its corresponding pixel color if the screen is also a 1 at that location. Fortunately, there is a way around this problem. The solution is to use two slightly different images for the animated object. These two special masks will be combined so that the animated object will not change color as it passes over the background.

The method uses one mask that is ANDed with the screen and a second mask that is XORed over the first. When these two masks are combined in this manner, the object will appear on the screen in its normal colors. To remove the object, we'll need to save the screen image beneath the region where it is to be displayed so that we can later restore the screen by copying back the saved screen to the display. Table 6.1 shows how the bits in the AND and the XOR mask can be combined to select particular colors on the screen. By chosing appropriate values in each of the masks you can set each screen bit to 0, 1, keep it the same value, or invert it.

Unfortunately, this technique of animation can be slow. The problem is that there are several screen images that we must deal with. First, we must save the

Table 6.1. Using an AND and XOR mask

AND Mask Value	XOR Mask Value	Resulting Screen Bit
0	0	0
0	1	1
1	0	Unchanged
1	1	Inverted

screen, then AND an image, followed by XORing an image, and finally restore the screen to its original state by copying back the saved screen image. This can take a great deal of time—especially when the size of the object being animated is large. In fact, the bicycle image that we have been working with is too large to effectively animate with this approach.

Therefore, the next sample program will move only a small ball across the screen that has a backdrop as shown in Figure 6.4. The ball is drawn to the screen using two masks as outlined earlier. Actually, the ball is made from two small circles filled with different colors. This should give you a good idea of how the dual-mask approach works.

The two masks that are combined to make up the ball are shown in Figure 6.5. In the program, these two masks are accessed through the pointers **AndMask** and **XorMask**. A third pointer, **Covered**, is used to save the portion of the screen that is covered by the masks at any given time. Therefore, the process of moving the ball across the screen is encapsulated in the following four statements in the procedure **MoveBall**:

```
PutImage(35+Move,85,Covered^,CopyPut);
GetImage(35+Step+Move,85,65+Step+Move,115,Covered^);
PutImage(35+Step+Move,85,Andmask^,AndPut);
PutImage(35+Step+Move,85,XorMask^,XorPut);
```

The first statement overwrites the current position of the ball. The next statement saves the screen where the ball will next appear. And the last two statements write the two masks to the screen and draw the ball.

```
program Ball;
{ BALL.PAS: Demonstrates how figures can be moved across the screen
  without disturbing what is already on the screen. It uses an AND
  mask and an XOR mask to accomplish this. This program is written to
  work in CGA medium-resolution mode only. }
```

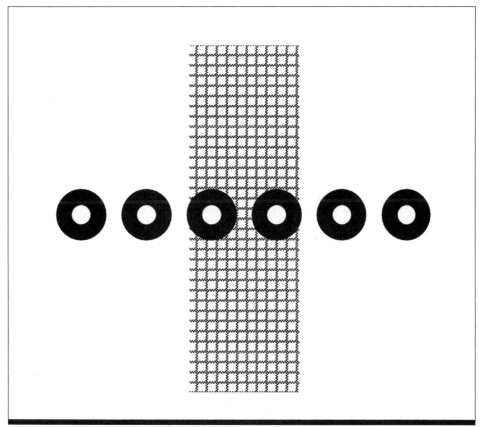

Figure 6.4. Time-lapsed output of BALL.PAS

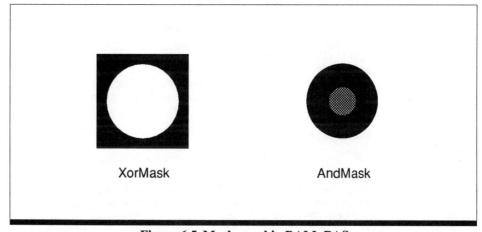

Figure 6.5. Masks used in BALL.PAS

```
uses
  Graph, Crt;
const
  Step = 2;
  DelayTime = 50;
  GDriver: integer = CGA;                { Written for CGA mode }
  GMode: integer = CGAC3;
var
  XorMask, AndMask, Covered: pointer;

procedure DrawBall;
begin
  GetMem(Covered,ImageSize(35,85,65,115));
  GetMem(XorMask,ImageSize(35,85,65,115));
  GetMem(AndMask,ImageSize(35,85,65,115));
  GetImage(35,85,65,115,Covered^);

  { Create the AND mask first }
  SetFillStyle(SolidFill,GetMaxColor);
  Bar(35,85,65,115);
  SetColor(0);
  SetFillStyle(SolidFill,0);
  PieSlice(50,100,0,360,12);
  GetImage(35,85,65,115,AndMask^);

  { Create the XOR mask }
  PutImage(35,85,Covered^,CopyPut);
  SetColor(GetMaxColor);
  SetFillStyle(SolidFill,GetMaxColor);
  PieSlice(50,100,0,360,12);
  SetFillStyle(SolidFill,1);
  SetColor(1);
  Circle(50,100,4);
  FloodFill(50,100,1);
  GetImage(35,85,65,115,XorMask^);

  { Erase ball and make the backdrop }
  PutImage(35,85,Covered^,CopyPut);
  SetFillStyle(HatchFill,2);
  Bar3D(100,10,150,199,0,False);
  { Redraw the ball on the screen by saving the screen area to
    be overwritten, using the AND mask and then the XOR mask }
  GetImage(35,85,65,115,Covered^);
  PutImage(35,85,AndMask^,AndPut);
  PutImage(35,85,XorMask^,XorPut);
end;

procedure MoveBall;
{ Move the ball across the screen by first overwriting the currently
  displayed ball and then moving it to the next location by using the
  AND and XOR masks. }
var
  I, Move: integer;
```

```
begin
  for I := 0 to 150 do begin
    Move := I * Step;
    PutImage(35+Move,85,Covered^,CopyPut);
    GetImage(35+Step+Move,85,65+Step+Move,115,Covered^);
    PutImage(35+Step+Move,85,Andmask^,AndPut);
    PutImage(35+Step+Move,85,XorMask^,XorPut);
    Delay(DelayTime);
  end
end;

begin
  InitGraph(GDriver,GMode,'\tp\bgi');
  DrawBall;
  MoveBall;
  repeat until KeyPressed;
  CloseGraph;
end.
```

Animating Multiple Objects

We can easily extend our program so that it will animate more than one object at a time. The major change that we need to make to the program is to supply more than one image or sequences of images to the screen to be moved. Then by sequencing through the list of animated objects as well as the images, we can easily create a scene with multiple moving objects.

Limitations of GetImage and PutImage

Using **GetImage** and **PutImage** to animate objects has several limitations that may restrict their usefulness. First, they can use up a lot of memory—particularly as the size of the image increases. In addition, as the image to save or write gets larger the speed at which **GetImage** and **PutImage** operate deteriorates.

However, when dealing with animation, one of the biggest drawbacks to using these two routines is that they do not allow for the bitmap image to be scaled or rotated. You could write routines to perform these operations yourself, but the bitmap patterns that the BGI uses are different for many of the modes. Therefore, you would have to write routines to handle each of the modes. This is a tedious task and one that we won't tackle here. Despite these issues, **GetImage** and **PutImage** provide a powerful, yet simple way of moving objects around the graphics screen.

Animation Using the Palette

Typically animation is created by drawing an object as it moves across the screen or copying the image of an object and moving it across the screen. However, an alternative method of animation that is sometimes quite dramatic and simple uses the palette to produce animation. The basic idea is to draw objects on the screen using different colors. Then the colors in the palette are changed. When this is done, all of the objects on the screen immediately change their colors and it appears as if all the objects were redrawn to new locations. By ordering objects so that their colors reflect the series of color changes, animation can be created.

Unfortunately, not all the graphics adapters support palette manipulation equally. In fact, the EGA and VGA are the most powerful in terms of this feature. With either graphics adapter you can use the **SetPalette** procedure to alter the colors in the palette. As mentioned earlier, by switching the colors in the palette, you can make objects appear to move.

A common example of animation using the color palette displays a mountain scene with flowing water. Actually, the water motion is induced by a series of changes to the palette. Since it would take a great deal of time and programming to create a good looking mountain scene, we'll use a simpler programming example.

The program that we'll look at is called FIREWORK.PAS and is listed at the end of this section. The program continually displays a series of color bursts that look like fireworks on the screen. Three images of random pixels are saved in memory and rapidly drawn to the screen using **PutImage** to create an expanding explosion pattern. The trick in the program is to use changes in the palette in order to achieve a wide variety of burst colors. This saves us from having to save many different burst patterns, each with a different color.

The program is written to operate on either an EGA or VGA system. The program won't run in a CGA mode because we'll be changing the palette and this technique doesn't work quite the same way as it does on an EGA or VGA.

Now let's take a closer look at the code. The fireworks burst pattern is generated by randomly plotting pixels on the screen. This is accomplished by the **for** loop:

```
for I := 0 to BlastSize * 3 div 2 - 1 do
  PutPixel(Random(BlastSize),Random(YRange),1);
```

which plots some number of white pixels in a region bounded by (0,0) and (**BlastSize,YRange**). The bottom-right coordinate pair of this region is dependent on the **BlastSize**. In this case it is 200 pixels wide. The variable **YRange** is simply **BlastSize**, which is scaled by the aspect ratio of the screen. After this **for** loop finishes, a square region on the top right of the screen will be filled with randomly placed pixels. Of course, we want a circular burst pattern—not square one. Therefore, the following statements are used to extract a circle of pixels.

```
Circle(BlastSize div 2,YRange div 2,BlastSize div 2 - 10);
Rectangle(0,0,BlastSize,YRange);
FloodFill(1,1,GetMaxColor);
SetFillStyle(SolidFill,0);
FloodFill(1,1,0);
{ Capture the burst pattern }
GetImage(0,0,BlastSize,YRange,Blast3^);
```

These statements use the **FloodFill** routine to erase all of the pixels between a circle (drawn to the size of the burst pattern desired) and a square encompassing the block of pixels. The first statement draws a circle that will define the burst pattern size. Next, the bounding rectangle is drawn by **Rectangle**. Then **FloodFill** is used to fill the region between the circle and rectangle with white. Note, black is not used because the background already contains it; therefore **FloodFill** would think that it has filled the region after encountering a few of the background pixels. Continuing to the next statement, the code refills the region between the circle and rectangle by another call to **FloodFill**. This time, however, the region is filled with black. Now the only thing remaining on the screen is the circular burst pattern. The final statement, therefore, is a call to **GetImage** to capture the image of the burst pattern. A similar process is performed in order to generate two smaller burst patterns, which are stored in **Blast2** and **Blast1**. Later, by sequencing through these images, it will appear that the burst pattern is expanding.

Of course, a good fireworks display would not be complete without a rocket to launch the fireworks from. The image for such a rocket is created by the next several lines. The rocket is drawn using **Bar**, **PutPixel**, and two calls to **Line**. The image of the rocket is saved to a pointer called **Rocket**.

The **while** loop that follows is used to continually draw a series of fireworks explosions until a key is pressed. The location of the explosion is randomly calculated by the lines:

```
X := Random(GetMaxX-BlastSize);
Y := Random(GetMaxY div 3);
```

The (**X,Y**) coordinate pair mark the top-left corner of the burst pattern images that will be written to the screen to create the fireworks effect. The **X** value is kept between 0 and **GetMaxX - BlastSize** so that the burst images will not extend off the edge of the screen and be clipped. The **Y** coordinate is restricted to one-third of the maximum y range, which you'll later see corresponds to the top portion of the screen.

The rocket is launched by the **for** loop after the two statements listed earlier. Its starting location and ending coordinates are calculated so that the rocket will steer to the middle of the burst pattern that is to be written to the screen. The call to **SetPalette** before the **for** loop is to ensure that the rocket is drawn white.

The statements after the **for** loop display the burst patterns in **Blast1**, **Blast2**, and **Blast3**. The burst images are displayed on the screen much as we have already described; so we will not look at them in detail. The unique part of the code, however, is the calls to the **SetPalette** routine. These are used to change the color of the fireworks. For instance, the line:

```
SetPalette(GetMaxColor,Random(15)+1);
```

randomly changes the palette color to one of the 16 possible colors in the current video mode (see Chapter 2 for a list of these). This is the color used for the fireworks. In order to avoid a lot of color changes, the color of the second burst pattern, **Blast2**, is designed so that it may or may not be changed, depending on whether the **Random** statement in the **if** statement, which follows, returns a 0 value or not (remember **Random** returns a value between 0 and n-1):

```
if Random(2) > 0 then SetPalette(GetMaxColor,Random(15)+1);
```

Similarly, the **if** statement surrounding the **PutImage** statement used to draw **Blast3** randomly restricts when the third blast pattern is drawn. By doing this, the program will generate two different-sized fireworks patterns.

You may have noticed a number of calls to the Turbo Pascal **Delay** procedure in FIREWORK.PAS. Each of these statements is used to give the fireworks program an aesthetic appeal. They control the speed of the rocket as well as how long any fireworks burst is displayed. Because different machines may be able to display the burst patterns faster than others, you may want to adjust the delay based on which computer is being used.

The only remaining part of the program involves the pointer **Covered**, which is used to save the screen before any of the burst patterns are generated or displayed. It is used to remove the fireworks from the screen and restore it to its original state.

```
program FireWork;
{ FIREWORK.PAS: Simulates a fireworks display by using the GetImage and
  PutImage procedures as well as palette animation. Press any key
  to quit. }
uses
  Graph, Crt;
const
  BlastSize: integer = 200;        { Size of fireworks in pixels }
  RocketHeight: integer = 7;       { Rocket is 7 pixels tall }
  RocketWidth: integer = 4;        { and 4 pixels wide }
  RocketStep: integer = 2;         { Rocket moves 2 pixels at a time }
  GDriver: integer = EGA;          { Use EGA and EGALo or VGA and VGALo }
```

```
      GMode: integer = EGALo;          { These are 640 x 200 modes that }
                                        { produce reasonably fast animation }
  var                                   { and do not require any extra }
    X, Y: integer;                      { modifications to this program to }
    I: integer;                         { draw correctly proportioned figures }
    StepTimes: integer;
    XAsp, YAsp: word;
    YRange: integer;
    Color: integer;
    Ry: integer;
    AspectRatio: real;
    Covered: pointer;                   { Holds screen under fire burst }
    Blast1, Blast2, Blast3: pointer;    { Three burst patterns }
    Rocket: pointer;                    { The fire rocket }
    Size: word;

begin
  InitGraph(GDriver,GMode,'\tp\bgi');
  if (GDriver <> EGA) and (GDriver <> VGA) then begin
    CloseGraph;
    WriteLn('This program requires an EGA or VGA graphics adapter.');
  end;
  Randomize;
  GetAspectRatio(XAsp,YAsp);
  AspectRatio := XAsp / YAsp;
  YRange := Round(BlastSize * AspectRatio);
  Size := ImageSize(0,0,BlastSize,YRange);
  GetMem(Blast1,Size);
  GetMem(Blast2,Size);
  GetMem(Blast3,Size);
  GetMem(Covered,Size);
  GetImage(0,0,BlastSize,YRange,Covered^);

  { Make the burst pattern by randomly filling a square with pixels }
  for I := 0 to BlastSize * 3 div 2 do
    PutPixel(Random(BlastSize),Random(YRange),GetMaxColor);
  { Then convert the square pixel pattern into a circle by erasing
    all of the pixels outside of a circle. Use a floodfill to
    perform this operation. Repeat this process three times, each
    with a smaller circle and after each time capture the circular
    burst pattern in Burst1, Burst2, or Burst3. }
  Circle(BlastSize div 2,YRange div 2,BlastSize div 2 - 10);
  Rectangle(0,0,BlastSize,YRange);
  FloodFill(1,1,GetMaxColor);
  SetFillStyle(SolidFill,0);
  FloodFill(1,1,0);

  { Capture the burst pattern }
  GetImage(0,0,BlastSize,YRange,Blast3^);
  SetFillStyle(SolidFill,GetMaxColor);      { Make smaller pattern }
  Circle(BlastSize div 2,YRange div 2,BlastSize div 4 + 10);
  Rectangle(0,0,BlastSize,YRange);
  FloodFill(1,1,GetMaxColor);
```

```
SetFillStyle(SolidFill,0);
FloodFill(1,1,0);
{ Capture the middle burst pattern }
GetImage(0,0,BlastSize,YRange,Blast2^);

Setfillstyle(SolidFill,GetMaxColor);        { Make smallest burst }
Circle(BlastSize div 2,YRange div 2,20);
Rectangle(0,0,BlastSize,YRange);
FloodFill(1,1,GetMaxColor);
SetFillStyle(SolidFill,0);
FloodFill(1,1,0);
GetImage(0,0,BlastSize,YRange,Blast1^);     { Get small burst }
PutImage(0,0,Covered^,CopyPut);             { Erase burst pattern }

{ Create the rocket }
Size := ImageSize(0,0,RocketWidth,RocketHeight);
GetMem(Rocket,Size);
SetFillStyle(SolidFill,GetMaxColor);
Bar(1,2,RocketWidth-1,RocketHeight-1);
PutPixel(2,1,GetMaxColor);
Line(0,RocketHeight-2,0,RocketHeight);
Line(RocketWidth,RocketHeight-2,RocketWidth,RocketHeight);
GetImage(0,0,RocketWidth,RocketHeight,Rocket^); { Rocket }
PutImage(0,0,Rocket^,XorPut);               { Erase rocket image }

{ Draw fireworks until a key is pressed }
while KeyPressed <> True do begin
  { Randomly decide where the rocket should explode. Use the upper
    half of the screen and avoid the edges of the screen. (x,y)
    corresponds to the top-left corner of the blast images. }
  X := Random(GetMaxX - BlastSize);
  Y := Random(GetMaxY div 3);

  SetPalette(GetMaxColor,15);               { Make rocket white }
  Ry := GetMaxY - RocketHeight;
  StepTimes := (Ry - YRange) div RocketStep;

  { Blast rocket off the ground }
  for I := 0 to StepTimes do begin
    Putimage(X+BlastSize div 2,Ry-I*RocketStep,Rocket^,XorPut);
    Delay(20);
    Putimage(X+BlastSize div 2,Ry-I*RocketStep,Rocket^,XorPut);
  end;
  SetPalette(GetMaxColor,Random(15)+1);  { Randomly select burst color }
  GetImage(X,Y,X+BlastSize,Y+YRange,Covered^);  { Save screen }
  PutImage(X,Y,Blast1^,CopyPut);      { Draw smallest burst }
  Delay(100);                          { Keep it on screen for a while }

  PutImage(X,Y,Blast2^,CopyPut);               { Show second burst }
  { Maybe change color }
  if Random(2) > 0 then SetPalette(GetMaxColor,Random(15)+1);
  Delay(100);
```

```
    if Random(2) > 0 then begin              { Randomly decide to }
      PutImage(X,Y,Blast3^,CopyPut);         { show third burst }
      if Random(2) > 0 then SetPalette(GetMaxColor,Random(15)+1);
    end;
    Delay(400 + Random(750));                { Wait for a while }
    PutImage(X,Y,Covered^,CopyPut);          { Erase burst }
    Delay(Random(3000));                     { Wait for next rocket }
  end;
  CloseGraph;
end.
```

A slight variation on the palette animation is to use it to make objects immediately appear on the screen. For instance, we can add a bolt of lightning to our fractal program in Chapter 1 that will immediately appear on the screen, yet is really there all of the time. The trick is to draw the lightning bolt the same color as the background color, using a different palette index. Then to make the lightning appear for a short time, the palette index color is changed to the lightning color and then restored to the background. Swapping the palette colors produces the effect that the lightning bolt is drawn to the screen; however, since it really is already there it saves the drawing time and makes for a very fast animation technique.

Using Multiple Screen Pages

Another animation technique that can produce fast animation effects uses multiple memory pages. This method takes advantage of the graphics hardware that provides several independent sections, or pages, of memory that you can draw in and display. However, like the palette trick, this approach is only possible on some graphics adapters (i.e., Hercules, EGA, and VGA). The basic idea is to have several partial or complete images of the screen ready to be displayed and then swap between them. By doing this animation can be created. The number of pages available depends on the graphics mode being used. For a complete list of the graphics modes and the pages that they have, refer to the sidebar "Working with Graphics Hardware" on page 29.

The BGI routine **SetActivePage** is used to select where the graphics operations will be written. The procedure **SetActivePage** is defined in the unit **Graph** as:

```
procedure SetActivePage(Page: word);
```

where **Page** is the page number to be used. Note that the active page does not have to be the page currently being displayed. In fact, the visual page is selected by the routine **SetVisualPage**. It is defined as:

```
procedure SetVisualPage(Page: word);
```

Another way to use multiple memory pages is as a scratch pad. The idea is to use one of the nonvisible pages as a working area to combine masks or create images of objects that can later be copied over to the visual page rapidly using **GetImage** and **PutImage**. In this manner, you can avoid having to display everything. For example, in the last program, we needed to create the pixel pattern for fireworks. This was done on the screen; however, if other memory pages had been available, we could have hidden these operations by doing them on a nonvisible page.

Creating Mouse Tools

One of the major benefits of using an object-oriented language such as Turbo Pascal 6.0 is that you can build powerful collections of objects that can be used as "black boxes" or to create other more powerful objects. In fact, the more you work with objects, the more you'll discover that this building block approach to programming goes the extra mile in helping you create tools that can easily be reused and extended.

In this chapter, we have two important goals. First, we'll develop an object type called **MouseObj** that houses all the basic routines and data needed to interface a mouse to a graphics program. This package will be the first of a number of interactive graphics tools that we'll be developing in Chapters 7 through 10 and putting to use in several drawing applications in subsequent chapters. The second goal is to show you how to use OOP techniques, such as *inheritance*, to derive one object type from another. In this case, we'll derive from **MouseObj** an object type that allows you to use the keyboard to emulate the functions of a mouse. Inheritance is an important property that we'll be using throughout the remainder of this book so we can build our programs in stages and later expand on what we've built.

Starting with the Mouse

Although the keyboard is an invaluable input device, it's not always best suited for interactive graphics programs. Even with useful positioning features such as cursor keys, the keyboard lacks speed and the ability to randomly select locations on the screen. These operations are typically required in an interactive graphics environment. What is needed is an interactive pointing device such as a light pen, joystick, or mouse. Because the mouse is more common on PCs than the other devices, we'll be selecting it as our primary input device. Although we'll try to support the keyboard as much as possible along the way, we'll design all our input routines around the mouse.

This chapter will show you how you can access a mouse from within your own graphics programs. We'll construct a mouse object type, called **MouseObj**, which contains numerous methods for performing such operations as initializing the mouse, determining the status and position of the mouse, and controlling its movement within a program. In addition, we'll be developing an object type called **KbdMouseObj** to support the keyboard if a mouse is not present. This object type is derived from **MouseObj** and contains methods for emulating the features of the mouse. These mouse and keyboard objects are implemented in the files MOUSEPAC.PAS and KBDMOUSE.PAS (see Listings 7.1 and 7.2). Because of the object-oriented nature of our mouse tools, you'll see that we can easily emulate the mouse with the keyboard—a task that is usually hard and messy to program.

Mouse Overview

Before we start coding up the mouse and keyboard objects, we'll need to cover the basics of how the mouse hardware and software works. If you have never written code to control the mouse, it might come as a surprise that the mouse is easy to support. In fact, only a few basic functions are required to initialize the mouse, obtain its cursor location, and move its cursor. As we work with the mouse, keep in mind that our code is designed to work with a Microsoft-compatible mouse, which happens to be the most common mouse standard for the PC. If you are using a different type of mouse, you may want to consult the user's manual for your mouse hardware and make the necessary changes to the code that we present so that your mouse will operate properly.

A mouse system consists of two essential elements: the mouse mechanism and a memory resident program called a *mouse driver*. The mouse driver provides all the low-level support needed to communicate with the mouse. In addition, it is responsible for automatically maintaining the mouse's cursor position and detecting any button presses.

Normally, the mouse driver is loaded into memory at power-up by a statement in your AUTOEXEC.BAT file. Once the driver is loaded, the mouse becomes available to any program that is subsequently executed.

A mouse is surprisingly simple to use in an application program. There are, however, some minor differences between text and graphics programs using the mouse, so consequently we'll be focusing on the mouse in graphics mode only.

The Mouse Functions

The mouse driver includes more than 20 mouse functions, most of which are listed in Table 7.1. We won't be using all these functions, but they are listed here for your reference. If you are interested in exploring the mouse further, you should refer to the *Microsoft Mouse Programmer's Guide*.

Although we could build our mouse toolkit using traditional programming techniques, we'll instead take our first true steps into the world of OOP. Why are we utilizing OOP here? Take a minute to examine Listing 7.1 (MOUSEPAC.PAS); you'll see that the technique of *encapsulation* is exploited to hide all of the data and coding details of the mouse-processing operations within the body of the object type, **MouseObj**. By creating a mouse object we are able to place all of the mouse-specific coding details under one roof and hide the low-level details of supporting the mouse hardware. Therefore, the application program that uses the mouse object doesn't have to know the intimate details of how the mouse works.

In addition, OOP enables us to go one step further. We can use *inheritance* to build on our **MouseObj** object type. In particular, **MouseObj** will serve as our *base type* from which we can derive the keyboard object type, **KbdMouseObj**, that emulates the mouse using the keyboard. But first, we need to return to the details of communicating with a mouse.

Accessing the Mouse Driver

We'll access the various features of the mouse and mouse-driver through the PC software interrupt 33h. The mouse-driver services calls to this interrupt location by redirecting them to its built-in low-level mouse functions. The specific function selected depends on the value in the AX register at the time of the interrupt. Three other registers, BX, CX, and DX, are used to pass parameters to the mouse routines. Similarly, the mouse functions use these four registers to return such things to the calling routine as the mouse location and the status of the mouse buttons. Figure 7.1 shows how a program uses interrupt 33h to invoke a mouse function.

Interrupt 33h can be invoked by Turbo Pascal's special procedure **Intr**. It provides direct access to the interrupt capabilities of the microprocessor and is typically of the form:

```
Intr(InterruptNumber,Registers);
```

where the first parameter is the interrupt vector to be used and the second is a record containing the processor's register values. The definition for this record's type is defined in the unit **Dos**.

Table 7.1. The mouse driver functions

Function Number (placed in AX)	Description
0	Resets the mouse and returns its status
1	Shows the mouse cursor on the screen
2	Removes the mouse cursor from the screen
3	Retrieves the current status of the buttons and the mouse position
4	Moves the mouse cursor to virtual location (x,y)
5	Retrieves the number of times a button was pressed since the last call
6	Retrieves the number of times a button was released since the last call
7	Sets the horizontal limits of the cursor
8	Sets the vertical limits of the cursor
9	Defines the cursor used in graphics mode
10	Sets the cursor used in text mode
11	Reads mouse movement counters
12	Sets up an interrupt routine
13	Turns light pen emulation on
14	Turns light pen emulation off
15	Sets mickey/pixel ratio, which is the ratio of the mouse movement to the cursor movement
16	Hides the mouse if it is within a region
19	Sets the parameters to allow faster mouse movement
20	Swaps interrupt routines
21	Retrieves mouse driver status
22	Saves mouse driver status
23	Restores mouse driver status
29	Sets CRT page number used by mouse cursor
30	Gets CRT page number used by mouse cursor

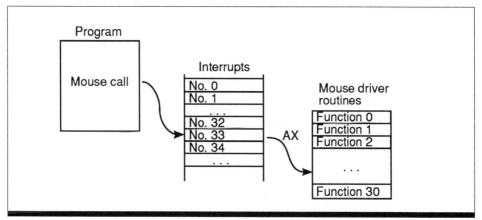

Figure 7.1. Sequence of invoking a mouse function

The core mouse method in **MouseObj** that we'll use to interact with the mouse driver is built around the **Intr** procedure. The method, **MSIntr**, simply loads the various registers with the parameters passed to it, calls the interrupt, and then copies the register values back into the parameters. The values contained in the arguments passed to **MSIntr** select the particular mouse function that is executed. Therefore, it is up to the caller of **MSIntr** to ensure that the correct values are provided. Throughout our program, we'll refer to the four mouse arguments as **M1, M2, M3,** and **M4.** They correspond to the registers AX, BX, CX, and DX, respectively. Here is the method **MSIntr**:

```
procedure MouseObj.MSIntr(var M1, M2, M3, M4: word);
{ This method provides the communication between the mouse driver and
  an application program. There are several predefined mouse functions
  supported by the Microsoft mouse--see accompanying text. Parameters
  are sent back and forth to the mouse driver through the AX, BX, CX,
  and DX registers. }
var
  Regs: Registers;
begin
  Regs.AX := M1;   Regs.BX := M2;
  Regs.CX := M3;   Regs.DX := M4;
  Intr($33,Regs);
  M1 := Regs.AX;   M2 := Regs.BX;
  M3 := Regs.CX;   M4 := Regs.DX;
end;
```

By setting the arguments **M1, M2, M3,** and **M4** to different values we can easily perform various operations such as initializing the mouse, reading the current position of the mouse, or determining the state of the mouse buttons. In the next section several of these operations are discussed.

Mouse Initialization

Before using the mouse, we must initialize it. This is done by invoking the mouse driver's function number 0. It resets the mouse driver to various default values and returns a –1 in AX if the mouse hardware and driver are detected. Otherwise, the function returns a 0. Therefore, by using the reset function **0**, we are able to verify that a mouse is present. We have built our own reset method around the mouse driver's as shown here:

```
function MouseObj.Reset: boolean;
{ Resets the mouse cursor to: screen center, mouse hidden, using arrow
  cursor and with minimum and maximum ranges set to full virtual screen
  dimensions. If a mouse driver exists, this function returns a True,
  otherwise it returns a False. }
var
  M1, M2, M3, M4: word;
begin
  M1 := ResetMouse;
  MSIntr(M1,M2,M3,M4);
  if M1 <> 0 then Reset := True     { Test for not equal to 0 }
    else Reset := False
end;
```

The **ResetMouse** term is a constant for function **0**, which is defined at the top of MOUSEPAC.PAS. We'll define similar constants for the other mouse functions that we'll be discussing in later sections.

Note that the **Reset** method does little more than load **M1** with the function number, make a call to **MSIntr**, and then return the status flag held in **M1**. The variables **M2**, **M3**, and **M4** are ignored in this case. Most other mouse methods will be similar in form.

Although **Reset** provides the basic mouse reset function, we need a higher-level routine to handle the complete task of initializing the mouse. We'll call this method **Setup**. Among other things, it calls **Reset** and sets **MouseExists** to **True** if **Reset** is successful. Otherwise, **MouseExists** is left **False** (it is initialized to **False** in the constructor **Init**). Later, we'll see that the variable **MouseExists** is used in all our mouse methods so that we can avoid making calls to the mouse driver if it hasn't been detected. In fact, when **MouseExists** is **False** we'll switch to the keyboard for input. We'll explore this feature in an upcoming section.

```
function MouseObj.Setup: boolean;
{ Call this method at the beginning of your program, but after the
  graphics adapter has been initialized. It will initialize the
  mouse and display the mouse cursor at the middle of the screen.
  Returns False if a mouse is not detected. }
```

```
var
  GMode: integer;
begin
  { Test whether the display being used is a Hercules monochrome
    display, if it is, patch the video BIOS location 40H:49H with 6. }
  GMode := GetGraphMode;
  if GMode = HERCMONOHI then
    Mem[$0040:$0049] := $06;
  if Reset then begin        { If mouse reset okay, assume mouse exists }
    MouseExists := True;     { Set mouse exists flag }
    Show;                    { Show the mouse }
    Setup := True;           { Return a success flag }
  end
  else
    Setup := False;          { Return initialization failure }
end;
```

The **Setup** method also makes the display of the mouse cursor visible by a call to another of **MouseObj**'s methods, **Show**. We'll look at this method later.

One oddity of the **Setup** method is the call to the BGI routine **GetGraphMode**. It is used to test whether your program is running on a Hercules card. If it is, you must write a value of six to the video BIOS location 40h:49h. This is a peculiarity of the Hercules board and is not needed for any other graphics adapter.

More Mouse Methods

Thus far we have covered the mouse initialization and reset methods. Now we'll examine the routines that actually put the mouse to use. The complete list of mouse-specific methods that we'll include in MOUSEPAC.PAS is shown in Table 7.2. The last two methods **GetInput** and **WaitForInput** are designed to work with both the mouse and the keyboard. We'll examine these two methods when we discuss the keyboard object later in this chapter.

We'll begin by writing these methods assuming that a mouse is present. Later we'll derive the **KbdMouseObj** object type to support the keyboard when a mouse isn't detected. An interesting aspect about our approach is that we'll be able to use the methods in **MouseObj** to create the keyboard processing object.

The Mouse Cursor

The next methods that we'll look at control the display of the mouse cursor. We saw in **Setup** that there is a method called **Show** that turns on the display of the mouse cursor. There is also a complementary method, **Hide**, that removes the mouse

Table 7.2. Mouse processing methods in MOUSEPAC.PAS

Function	Description
MSIntr	The interface for low-level mouse calls
Init	Initialize the mouse object
Setup	Set up the mouse
Reset	Reset the mouse and return its status
Move	Move the mouse to location (x,y)
Show	Display the mouse cursor
Hide	Remove the mouse cursor from the screen
GetCoords	Get the coordinates of the mouse cursor
ButtonPressed	Test whether a mouse button has been pressed since the last call
ButtonReleased	Test whether a mouse button has been released since the last call
TestButton	Internal routine to test the buttons
InBox	Check whether the mouse is in a region of the screen
GetInput	Check if a mouse button has been pressed and released or whether a key has been pressed
WaitForInput	Loop until a button has been pressed or until a key has been pressed

cursor from the screen. One important thing to note here is that both of these methods affect the display of the mouse cursor only. In other words, no matter what the display status of the mouse cursor is, the mouse driver will always update and maintain the cursor's position.

The **Show** and **Hide** methods use mouse functions **1** and **2** respectively. They do not require any parameters or return any values. Both methods are straightforward and are included in the MOUSEPAC.PAS source file shown in Listing 7.2.

It's easy to imagine that there are times when it is necessary to turn the mouse cursor on or off by using **Show** and **Hide**. However, their use is probably more important than you first thought. It turns out that whenever you *read or write anything* to the screen while using the mouse, you must always turn the mouse off first by a call to **Hide**. After you are done accessing the screen, you can restore the mouse display by calling **Show**. Why? Because the mouse cursor image is actually combined into the screen image. Therefore, whenever you access the screen when the mouse cursor is on, you run the risk of accessing the mouse cursor image or at least incorrectly modifying whatever is under the mouse cursor. Only by using **Hide** and **Show** before and after accessing the screen can you guarantee that the mouse will not interfere with what is on the screen.

One additional caution: you should not call **Hide** if the mouse is not already displayed. Further, you must accompany every subsequent call to **Hide** with a companion call to **Show**. This is required because of the way the mouse driver internally determines when to display the mouse cursor.

The Default Mouse Cursor

In graphics mode, the default mouse cursor is displayed as an arrow symbol as shown in Figure 7.2. Although it is possible to change the type of cursor displayed by calling function **9**, we won't take advantage of this feature in the mouse driver. (Refer to the *Microsoft Mouse Programmer's Reference Guide* if you would like to explore this further.)

Mouse Position

In the previous sections we learned how the mouse driver controls the display of the mouse cursor image. Now let's see how we can access and control the position of the mouse cursor through the driver.

Part of the responsibility of the mouse driver is to maintain the position of the mouse cursor. In addition, we can query the mouse driver to return the coordinates of the mouse by calling function **3**. Our mouse object includes a method called **GetCoords** that performs this operation.

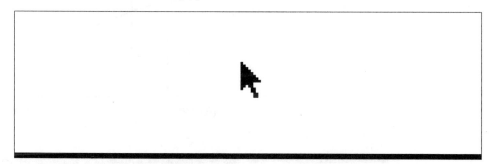

Figure 7.2. The graphics mouse cursor

Function **3** does not expect any arguments to be passed to it, and it returns the x and y coordinates of the mouse in **M3** and **M4**. Actually, mouse function **3** does more than just return the mouse coordinates. It also returns the current status of the buttons in **M2**; however, we'll be ignoring this aspect of the function.

The coordinates that function **3** returns will, in most cases, correspond to the screen coordinates of the mouse. Note, however, that we say "in most cases." It turns out that the mouse driver refers to all mouse coordinates in a virtual coordinate system and not in screen coordinates. Usually, these two coordinate systems are identical in graphics mode. However, whenever the screen is in a mode with 320 columns, for instance, the virtual coordinates in the x direction are not identical. The adjustment is fairly simple. In these situations, the real-screen coordinates are always one-half the virtual coordinates. Therefore, the x coordinate to the mouse driver need only be divided by two whenever the current graphics mode has 320 columns. Figure 7.3 shows the relationship between the coordinate systems for a 320-column graphics mode. For now our **GetCoords** method becomes:

```
procedure MouseObj.GetCoords(var X, Y: integer);
{ Get the current location of the mouse cursor }
var
  M1, M2: word;
begin
  M1 := GetMouseStatus;
  MSIntr(M1,M2,word(X),word(Y));
  if GetMaxX = 319 then X := X div 2;  { Adjust for virtual coordinates }
end;                                    { of the mouse }
```

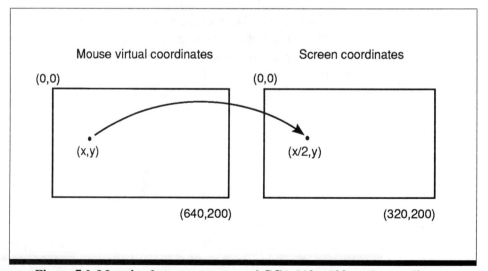

Figure 7.3. Mapping between mouse and CGA 320 x 200 mode coordinates

Mouse Buttons

The Microsoft mouse also provides two buttons that can be accessed through the mouse driver. Note that although other mice may have more buttons, usually these can be handled as a superset of the Microsoft mouse.

There are three ways to test the mouse buttons. For each button you can check its current state, whether it has been pressed, and whether it has been released. We'll use the last two methods of testing buttons in our programs and avoid testing the current status of the buttons, since it is possible that with it we may not be fast enough to catch all of the button presses.

Mouse functions **5** and **6** are used to determine the number of times that one of the mouse buttons has been pressed or released since the last check or mouse initialization. Both functions can test either of the buttons. Which particular button is tested depends on the value in parameter **M2** at the time of the function call. If **M2** is zero, then the left button is checked; if **M2** is one, then the right button is tested. The number of button actions (e.g., number of button presses for function **5**) is returned in **M2**. In addition, these functions return the location of the last button action in **M3** and **M4** (**M3** is the x coordinate and **M4** is the y coordinate). Note that the left and right buttons' status information is maintained separately.

Our mouse object uses functions **5** and **6** in the methods **ButtonPressed** and **ButtonReleased** to test the status of the mouse buttons. Both are Boolean functions accepting a single argument that specifies which button is to be tested. This argument can take on one of three values defined in the unit **MousePac** as **LeftButton**, **RightButton**, and **EitherButton**. In the case of **ButtonPressed**, the method returns a True value if the button indicated has been pressed since the last call to **ButtonPressed**. Otherwise, the method returns False. Similarly, **ButtonReleased** returns a True value only if the button specified in its parameter list has been released since the last time it was invoked.

Therefore, assuming we have declared a **MouseObj** called **Mouse**, we can write the following loop that waits until either of the buttons is pressed:

```
while not Mouse.ButtonPressed(EitherButton) do ;
```

Actually, the low-level mouse functions do not allow us to ask whether either button has been pressed. We have to test the left and right buttons individually. However, this is easy to do.

Since there is a lot of similarity between the button pressed and button released methods, we have combined their code into a method called **TestButton**. This method also returns a Boolean value; however, it takes two parameters. They are the action to test for (whether it is a button press or release) and which button to check. The method is:

```
function MouseObj.TestButton(TestType, WhichButton: integer): boolean;
{ Called by ButtonPressed and ButtonReleased to explicitly
  test the mouse button states. The function returns True if the
  specified mouse button (in WhichButton) performed the specified
  action (as indicated by TestType). Otherwise the function returns
  False, which means that the action tested for did not occur. }
var
  M1, M2, M3, M4: word;
begin
  M1 := TestType;
  TestButton := False;          { Return False as a catchall }
  if (WhichButton = LeftButton) or (WhichButton = EitherButton) then begin
    M2 := LeftButton;
    MSIntr(M1,M2,M3,M4);
    if M2 <> 0
      then TestButton := True;  { Return True if the action occurred }
    Exit;
  end;
  end;
  if (WhichButton = RightButton) or (WhichButton = EitherButton) then begin
    M1 := TestType;
    M2 := RightButton;
    MSIntr(M1,M2,M3,M4);
    if M2 <> 0
      then TestButton := True;  { Return True if the action occurred }
  end;
end;
```

Note that the mouse function number, which is loaded into **M1**, is passed as the parameter **TestType**. In addition, the mouse variable **M2** is loaded from the parameter **WhichButton** in order to select between the left and right buttons. Remember, this variable can take on one of these values: **LeftButton**, **RightButton**, or **EitherButton**. Note, however, that if the user specifies **EitherButton** both buttons must be individually checked.

After **TestButton** calls the mouse driver via **MSIntr**, **M2** contains the number of button actions for the button specified in **WhichButton**. Since we are concerned only with whether the button has been pressed or released, not how many times it has occurred, **TestButton** simply returns **True** if **M2** indicates that there was one or more button presses. Otherwise, **TestButton** returns **False**.

The function **TestButton** ignores two pieces of information that you may find valuable. First, it throws away the number of button actions that have taken place since the last test. You may find this information useful; although in tight loops of code it is very rare that you'd be able to click fast enough to register more than one button press or release.

Also, both functions **5** and **6** return the coordinates of the last button action in **M3** and **M4**. We'll ignore these and use **GetCoords** instead to retrieve the location of the mouse after a button action; however, the delay between the button detection and the call to **GetCoords** can be significant. Therefore, you may want to try to integrate the coordinates returned in **M3** and **M4** to your code to avoid this situation.

Mouse in a Box

When using the mouse, we'll often want to be able to test whether the mouse cursor is within a particular region on the screen. In order to accomplish this, a method called **InBox** is included in the mouse object. The method **InBox** checks to see whether the mouse cursor coordinates provided it are within a rectangular region bounded by a pair of screen coordinates as shown in Figure 7.4. The screen coordinates correspond to the upper-left and lower-right corners of the region being checked. If the mouse is in the rectangle, **InBox** will return **True**; otherwise it will return **False**. The method is:

```
function MouseObj.InBox(Left, Top, Right, Bottom, X, Y: integer): boolean;
{ Test if the mouse cursor is within the box specified. Returns True
  if the mouse is in the box; otherwise the function returns False. }
begin
  InBox := (X >= Left) and (X <= Right) and (Y >= Top) and (Y <= Bottom);
end;
```

More Mouse Control

Our mouse control routines are rounded out by the **Move** method. This method uses mouse function **4** to move the mouse cursor to a particular (x,y) screen loca-

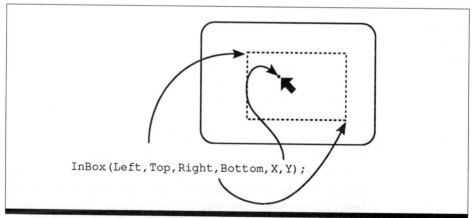

Figure 7.4. Testing whether the mouse within a region is done with InBox

tion. Note that in **Move** the screen coordinates passed to it must be adjusted into virtual coordinates when the graphics adapter is in a 320-column mode. This is done by the line:

```
if GetMaxX = 319 then X := X * 2;
```

Adding Keyboard Input

Although the mouse is an excellent input device in the graphics world, sometimes it is useful to be able to use the keyboard. For instance, there are times when it's easier for the user to select a function by typing a quick key combination rather than using the mouse. Therefore, we're going to need some new routines for processing the keyboard.

If you take a close look at **MouseObj**, you'll see that we've included two methods for processing the keyboard—**GetInput** and **WaitForInput**. These methods are both designed to work with the keyboard and the mouse. They are written so that they first check the keyboard buffer to see if any keys have been pressed. If so, these methods immediately return the first character in the keyboard buffer. Otherwise, the methods test the appropriate mouse buttons to see whether they have been pressed or released. Actually, **WaitForInput** does nothing more than call **GetInput** in a loop until a button has been pressed or the user has typed a character.

The keyboard buffer is checked by the Turbo Pascal function **KeyPressed**. If it returns a **False**, no key has been pressed, and **GetInput** proceeds to test whether the mouse buttons have been pressed. If they have been, then **GetInput** returns a -1. Otherwise, if a key has been pressed, **GetInput** returns the value of the keypress.

Emulating a Mouse

Thus far we have been talking about using the mouse almost exclusively. However, not everyone has a mouse and the reality of the situation is that a good program must accommodate nonmouse systems. Although you could use **GetInput** and **WaitForInput** provided with the **MouseObj** object type to help support both the keyboard and the mouse, you would have to integrate the keyboard support into your application programs. This can get very messy.

We'll be able to provide a better solution by deriving the **KbdMouseObj** object type. Because **KbdMouseObj** is derived from the **MouseObj** object type, it inherits all the mouse object's data and methods. To support the keyboard, we can then modify some of the inherited methods such as **Setup** and add new ones that are specifically designed to work with the keyboard to control an emulated mouse. That is, we'll be able to use our new object whether or not there actually is a mouse connected. We'll use the cursor keys to move the emulated mouse cursor around the screen and the Ins and Del keys to simulate the mouse buttons. This approach allows us to take advantage of code that we have already written instead of having to reinvent the wheel in order to support a new input device.

The new methods introduced by **KbdMouseObj** arc listed in Table 7.3. They are responsible for supporting the keyboard only. The other methods provided are designed to integrate both the mouse and the keyboard. If you examine the object definition in Listing 7.2 (KBDMOUSE.PAS), you'll see that the methods that support both devices are declared with the **virtual** keyword. For example, note that the declaration of the **Setup** method is:

```
function Setup: boolean; virtual;
```

These methods are actually inherited from **MouseObj** and they are declared as **virtual** here because we will be overriding them so that they can perform different operations. To see how this technique is used, let's take a close look at the **Setup** method.

Initializing a Keyboard Object

To support the keyboard, you'll need to create an object using the **KbdMouseObj** object type. And before a keyboard object is used, you must remember to call the

Table 7.3. Keyboard input methods in KbdMouseObj

Method	Description
GetKbInteraction	Updates the location of the cursor when an arrow key is pressed or sets the button pressed flag if a button key is pressed.
GetKb	Performs a low-level keyboard read of some of the extended key codes
InitCursor	Initializes the keyboard object so that it simulates a mouse
ToggleCursor	Turns the simulated mouse cursor on and off
DrawCursor	Draws a simulated mouse cursor

Using Inheritance

How many times have you written a useful Turbo Pascal routine to perform a certain task, such as converting a character string, only to later realize that you would have to rewrite the function to use it in a different context? The problem with most structured languages is that they don't provide a mechanism for enabling you to extend code that you've previously written. Turbo Pascal, however, because of its object-oriented nature, provides a feature called inheritance that allows you to derive new object types from existing ones. Such a derived object type incorporates all the members (data and methods) of an existing object type. That is, it *inherits* the members, and it can also add new members of its own.

To see how inheritance works, let's define an object type and derive a new one from the original type. Our first object, which we'll call **Cursor**, updates a cursor's position, which is internally maintained by the instance variables **X** and **Y**:

```
Cursor = object
  X, Y: integer;
  constructor Init;
  procedure UpdateXY(Xi, Yi: integer); virtual;
end;

constructor Cursor.Init;
begin
{ Constructors are required for objects with virtual methods }
  X := 0;  Y := 0;
end;

procedure Cursor.UpdateXY(Xi, Yi: integer);
begin
  X := Xi;  Y := Yi;
end;
```

Now suppose we wanted another object to update the position of the cursor and display its new position. Instead of changing the original object type, we can derive a new one using the original:

```
PosCursor = object(Cursor)
  procedure UpdateXY(Xi, Yi: integer); virtual;
end;

procedure PosCursor.UpdateXY(Xi, Yi: integer);
begin
  Cursor.UpdateXY(Xi,Yi);
  WriteLn('The cursor''s new position is ',X,Y);
end;
```

The syntax **PosCursor = object(Cursor)** instructs the compiler that **PosCursor** uses all of the members in the **Cursor** type. Therefore, a **PosCursor** object would inherit the **X** and **Y** variables and **Init** method from the **Cursor** object type so that it will initialize the **X** and **Y** variables to 0. However, the **PosCursor** object type goes a step further. It redefines the **UpdateXY** method so that if the **PosCursor** type were used, it would call **Cursor**'s **UpdateXY** method to update the variables **X** and **Y** and then display the cursor's position.

As you're looking over the definition of both of these object types note that the keyword **virtual** is used to define each of the **UpdateXY** methods. Because of this, **UpdateXY** is considered to be a *virtual method*. Virtual methods are treated differently from other methods. When a routine related to an object is called, it is usually linked up to the object at compile time. With virtual methods, this binding doesn't take place until run time, and it is called *late binding*. As a result, we can have more than one procedure with the same name, in this case two **UpdateXY** procedures; of course, they belong to different objects so the compiler can still keep them straight. You can look at it as if the object is telling the program which routine to use. Procedures and functions like this are said to be *overloaded*.

Note that in Turbo Pascal, object types that contain virtual functions must have a constructor also. As mentioned in Chapter 1, a constructor is a special method that initializes the object. Without one, the object will not work properly.

Init constructor and the **Setup** method. An object's constructor must always be called before using the object if it has one, in order to set up internal tables that are used to manage the object's virtual methods. (Note that **KbdMouseObj**'s **Init** constructor is inherited from **MouseObj**.) The **Setup** method is slightly different from any other method we've written because it makes a call to another **Setup** method—the one defined in the **MouseObj** type. To see how this works, let's examine the complete **Setup** method for **KbdMouseObj**:

```
function KbdMouseObj.Setup;
{ Call this function at the beginning of your program, after the graphics
  adapter has been initialized. It will initialize the mouse and display
  the mouse cursor at the middle of the screen. If a mouse is not
  present it will cause the emulated mouse to appear and the keyboard
  will be used to move the "mouse" cursor. }
begin
  if not MouseObj.Setup then begin { No mouse found--emulate the mouse }
    CInc := 1; CMinX := 0;           { The functionality is the }
    CMaxX := GetMaxX - 1;            { same as the real thing }
    CMaxY := GetMaxY - 1;            { Therefore, set the emulated }
    CMinX := 0; CMinY := 0;          { cursor to the top left of the }
    CDeltaX := 0; CDeltaY := 0;      { screen, set its bounds to the }
    Cx := CMaxX div 2;
    Cy := CMaxY div 2;               { full screen and initialize its }
    LButtonPress := False;           { mouse movement counters, and }
    RButtonPress := False;           { initialize all button states }
```

```
      NumLPress := 0;              { to false }
      NumRPress := 0;              { Set simulated mouse button }
      NumLRelease := 0;           { press and release counters to }
      NumRRelease := 0;           { zero }
      InitCursor;                 { Create cursor image }
      CursorOn := False;
      Show;                       { Call Show to display it }
      Setup := False;             { return a no mouse found flag }
    end
    else
      Setup := True;
end;
```

The first code statement in the method gives away the secret of how this initialization works:

```
if not MouseObj.Setup then begin
```

The code checks to see if a mouse is installed by calling the **Setup** method associated with the **MouseObj** object type. Because of inheritance, we can access any of the methods in the **MouseObj** type from our keyboard object if the **MouseObj** name is placed before the method call as shown. If a mouse is found, our new **Setup** keyboard method skips over the necessary code to set up the mouse emulation.

Note that emulating the mouse requires several new variables to be set and methods to be called. First, an emulated cursor must be created, and variables must be initialized to keep track of the location of the mouse cursor as well as the status of its buttons. Because all of the data needed to process the keyboard is hidden in the **KbdMouseObj** type, you don't have to worry about keeping track of this information. Needless to say, the approach that we've taken greatly simplifies the work of adding the keyboard to an interactive graphics application. In fact, the only decision you have to make is whether or not you want to add the keyboard. If you want to use the mouse only, create an object such as:

```
Mouse1: MouseObj;
```

However, if you want to use the mouse if one is present, or the keyboard if one is not, use the **KbdMouseObj** type:

```
InpDev: KbdMouseObj;
```

Whatever object you use, the initialization process is the same. Simply remember to call the **Init** constructor, and then the **Setup** method at the beginning of your program after the graphics adapter has been initialized.

Emulated Mouse Cursor

We'll now look at how we can emulate the mouse cursor. The basic idea is to use **GetImage** and **PutImage** to move the image of an emulated mouse cursor about the screen. We'll create the simulated cursor image in a new method called **InitCursor**. A pointer, private to the **KbdMouseObj** type, called **Cursor** will point to the cursor image that we'll actually draw in the method **DrawCursor**. The space for the cursor image is allocated in **InitCursor**. In addition, memory is allocated in **InitCursor** so that another private pointer, called **UnderCursor**, can be used to save the portion of the screen currently covered by the emulated mouse cursor. Moving the emulated cursor on the screen then becomes a three-step process:

1. Remove the current cursor image from the screen by overwriting it with the previously saved image in **UnderCursor**.
2. Use **GetImage** to save the screen region in **UnderCursor** where the cursor is next to appear.
3. Use **PutImage** to draw the cursor at its new location.

Creating the original cursor image in **InitCursor** follows this same process. First, the screen area where the cursor image is to be created is saved in **UnderCursor**. Then an arrow-shaped cursor is drawn by the method **DrawCursor** using a series of calls to **Line**. Next, the cursor image is saved in **Cursor** by a call to **GetImage** so that it can later be copied to the screen. Finally, the screen is restored to its original state, by overwriting the cursor with the image in **UnderCursor**. This removes the cursor image and restores the screen to its original state.

If you'd like to experiment with the type of cursor used in the emulated mode you need only change the method **DrawCursor**. The actual size of the cursor is declared by the constants **CursHeight** and **CursWidth** in **KbdMouse** to be 8 pixels high and 8 pixels wide.

Emulated Mouse Position

The position of the emulated mouse cursor is maintained in the variables **Cx** and **Cy**. Consequently, a call to **GetCoords** does nothing more than return these values when the emulated cursor is used. The variables **Cx** and **Cy** are updated whenever the program calls **GetInput** and the user has pressed one of the arrow keys on the keypad. This latter change involves an extensive portion of code in a new method called **GetKbInteraction**. Essentially, this routine checks to see if any keyboard action has taken place. If so, it calls **GetKb** to retrieve the input (which may be an extended scan code). Next, the input is matched against a list of codes that correspond to various key combinations. If one of the arrow keys was pressed the method updates **Cx** and **Cy**. Note that the emulated cursor position is also clipped to the coordinates **CMinX**, **CMinY**, **CMaxX**, and **CMaxY**. Although we do not use these clipping parameters, they can be used to mimic mouse functions **7** and **8**, which can be used to restrict the movement of the mouse cursor to a rectangular region on the screen. Finally, note that **GetKbInteraction** returns zero whenever it adjusts the position of the emulated cursor. This is equivalent to telling the calling function that no action need be taken, or in other words, that no key was pressed or no emulated button was pressed.

Emulated Mouse Buttons

The mouse buttons are emulated by the Ins and Del keys on the keypad. The **case** statement in **GetKbInteraction** tests to see whether either of these keys has been pressed and sets either the **LButtonPress** or **RButtonPress** flag if one has been pressed. These flags are **True** if the left and right buttons have been pressed, respectively. In addition, the two counters **NumLPress** and **NumRPress** are incremented each time there is a button press. These values are used by the routines **ButtonPressed** and **ButtonReleased** to detect any button presses and report the fact to the user.

Detecting button presses is easy using this technique. However, emulating button releases is another matter. To solve this problem we'll count every other press of the Ins or Del keys as a button release. Therefore, whenever **LButtonPress** or **RButtonPress** is **True** and the Ins or Del key is pressed, it is considered a button release and the special counters **NumLRelease** and **NumRRelease** are incremented to keep track of the number of button releases. As before, these values are used by the simulated button routines to detect any button releases and report the fact to the user.

Putting Your Mouse to the Test

Listing 7.3 presents a program that will partially test your mouse code. The program does nothing more than set your system into graphics mode and then initialize the mouse. If a mouse is detected, it is displayed and you can move the mouse cursor around. The program will continue until you press one of the buttons on the mouse.

If a mouse is not detected, the emulated mouse will appear. You can move it around the screen using the arrow keys. Use the gray + and – keys to change the amount that the emulated mouse cursor is moved. The program will continue until you press either the Ins or Del keys (these are the emulated mouse buttons).

Note that an object called **Mouse** is declared to be of type **KbdMouseObj**. This variable is used to access all the features of the mouse toolkits. Also, note the call to the mouse object's constructor in the statement:

```
Mouse.Init;
```

You'll need similar statements in your applications. Since this program uses the units in **MousePac** and **KbdMouse**, these units are listed in the uses clause of MOUSETST.PAS.

• Listing 7.1. MOUSEPAC.PAS

```
unit MousePac;
{ MOUSEPAC.PAS: Routines to support a Microsoft-compatible mouse.
  Mouse support is divided into two classes. The first,
  MouseObj, provides most of the functions you'll need to control
  the mouse. The other, KbdMouseObj, is a class derived from
  MouseObj that overrides the mouse functions so that they are
  emulated by the keyboard. This class is used when a mouse does
  not exist. Both classes assume they are running in graphics mode.
  To move the emulated cursor, use the arrow keys on the keyboard
  and the Ins and Del keys as the left and right mouse buttons,
  respectively. The gray + and - keys can be used to change the
  amount the emulated mouse cursor is moved. }
interface
uses
  Graph;
const
  LeftButton: integer = 0;        { Use left mouse button }
  RightButton: integer = 1;       { Use right mouse button }
  EitherButton: integer = 2;      { Use either mouse button }
type
MouseObjPtr = ^MouseObj;
MouseObj = object
  MouseExists: boolean; { Internal variable set True if a mouse driver is
                          detected during initialization. This variable
                          is used to select between the mouse code (if a
                          mouse exists) and the keyboard emulated mouse. }
  constructor Init;
  function Setup: boolean; virtual;
  procedure MSIntr(var M1, M2, M3, M4: word);
  function Reset: boolean; virtual;
```

```pascal
    procedure Hide; virtual;
    procedure Show; virtual;
    procedure Move(X, Y: integer); virtual;
    procedure GetCoords(var X, Y: integer); virtual;
    function ButtonReleased(WhichButton: integer): boolean; virtual;
    function ButtonPressed(WhichButton: integer): boolean; virtual;
    function TestButton(TestType, WhichButton: integer): boolean;
    function InBox(Left, Top, Right, Bottom, X, Y: integer): boolean;
    function GetInput(WhichButton: integer): integer; virtual;
    function WaitForInput(WhichButton: integer): integer;
  end;

implementation
uses
  Dos, Crt;
const
  ResetMouse = 0;          { Mouse function to reset the mouse }
  ShowMouse = 1;           { Mouse function to show the mouse cursor }
  HideMouse = 2;           { Mouse function to display the mouse cursor }
  GetMouseStatus = 3;      { Function to get the mouse's status }
  SetMouseCoord = 4;       { Function to set the mouse's coordinates }
  CheckButtonPress = 5;    { Not used here }
  CheckButtonRelease = 6;  { Not used here }
  GetMouseMovement = 11;   { Not used here }

constructor MouseObj.Init;
{ The MouseObj type must have a constructor since it has virtual
  methods. This constructor merely sets the MouseExists flag to False. }
begin
  MouseExists := False;
end;

function MouseObj.Setup: boolean;
{ Call this method at the beginning of your program, but after the
  graphics adapter has been initialized. It will initialize the
  mouse and display the mouse cursor at the middle of the screen.
  Returns False if a mouse is not detected. }
var
  GMode: integer;
begin
  { Test whether the display being used is a Hercules monochrome
    display, if it is, patch the video BIOS location 40H:49H with 6. }
  GMode := GetGraphMode;
  if GMode = HERCMONOHI then
    Mem[$0040:$0049] := $06;
  if Reset then begin      { If mouse reset okay, assume mouse exists }
    MouseExists := True;   { Set mouse exists flag }
    Show;                  { Show the mouse }
    Setup := True;         { Return a success flag }
  end
  else
    Setup := False;        { Return initialization failure }
end;
```

```
procedure MouseObj.MSIntr(var M1, M2, M3, M4: word);
{ This method provides the communication between the mouse driver and
  an application program. There are several predefined mouse functions
  supported by the Microsoft mouse--see accompanying text. Parameters
  are sent back and forth to the mouse driver through the AX, BX, CX,
  and DX registers. }
var
  Regs: Registers;
begin
  Regs.AX := M1;    Regs.BX := M2;
  Regs.CX := M3;    Regs.DX := M4;
  Intr($33,Regs);
  M1 := Regs.AX;    M2 := Regs.BX;
  M3 := Regs.CX;    M4 := Regs.DX;
end;

function MouseObj.Reset: boolean;
{ Resets the mouse cursor to: screen center, mouse hidden, using arrow
  cursor and with minimum and maximum ranges set to full virtual screen
  dimensions. If a mouse driver exists, this function returns a True
  otherwise it returns a False. }
var
  M1, M2, M3, M4: word;
begin
  M1 := ResetMouse;
  MSIntr(M1,M2,M3,M4);
  if M1 <> 0 then Reset := True    { Test for not equal to 0 }
    else Reset := False
end;

procedure MouseObj.Move(X, Y: integer);
{ Moves the mouse to the location (X,Y) }
var
  M1, M2: word;
begin
  M1 := SetMouseCoord;
  if GetMaxX = 319 then X := X * 2;  { Adjust between virtual and actual }
  MSIntr(M1,M2,word(X),word(Y));     { coordinates if necessary }
end;

procedure MouseObj.Hide;
{ Removes the mouse cursor from the screen. Call this function before you
  write or draw anything to the screen. It is also a good idea to turn off
  the mouse at the end of a program. Use Show to restore the mouse
  on the screen. The mouse movement will be maintained while the mouse is
  not visible. Due to a peculiarity of the mouse driver, make sure you
  don't call Hide if the mouse is not already visible. See text
  discussion for more on this. }
var
  M1, M2, M3, M4: word;
begin
  M1 := HideMouse;                   { Invoke the hide mouse function }
  MSIntr(M1,M2,M3,M4);
end;
```

```pascal
procedure MouseObj.Show;
{ Display the mouse cursor. Normally, you should not call this
  function if the mouse is already visible. The keyboard mouse
  is clipped to the minimum and maximum ranges in this routine. }
var
  M1, M2, M3, M4: word;
begin
  M1 := ShowMouse;
  MSIntr(M1,M2,M3,M4);              { Display the mouse cursor }
end;

procedure MouseObj.GetCoords(var X, Y: integer);
{ Get the current location of the mouse cursor }
var
  M1, M2: word;
begin
  M1 := GetMouseStatus;
  MSIntr(M1,M2,word(X),word(Y));
  if GetMaxX = 319 then X := X div 2;  { Adjust for virtual coordinates }
end;                                   { of the mouse }

function MouseObj.ButtonReleased(WhichButton: integer): boolean;
{ Test if a button has been released since the last call to this
  function. If so, return True, otherwise return False. }
begin
  ButtonReleased := TestButton(CheckButtonRelease,WhichButton);
end;

function MouseObj.ButtonPressed(WhichButton: integer): boolean;
{ Return True if the mouse button specified has been pressed since the
  last check with this function. If the button has not been pressed,
  return False. }
begin
  ButtonPressed := TestButton(CheckButtonPress,WhichButton);
end;

function MouseObj.TestButton(TestType, WhichButton: integer): boolean;
{ Called by ButtonPressed and ButtonReleased to explicitly
  test the mouse button states. The function returns True if the
  specified mouse button (in WhichButton) performed the specified
  action (as indicated by TestType). Otherwise the function returns
  False, which means that the action tested for did not occur. }
var
  M1, M2, M3, M4: word;
begin
  M1 := TestType;
  TestButton := False;              { Return False as a catchall }
  if (WhichButton = LeftButton) or (WhichButton = EitherButton) then begin
    M2 := LeftButton;
    MSIntr(M1,M2,M3,M4);
    if M2 <> 0
```

```
        then TestButton := True;  { Return True if the action occurred }
      Exit;
    end;
    if (WhichButton = RightButton) or (WhichButton = EitherButton) then begin
      M1 := TestType;
      M2 := RightButton;
      MSIntr(M1,M2,M3,M4);
      if M2 <> 0
        then TestButton := True;  { Return True if the action occurred }
    end;
end;

function MouseObj.InBox(Left, Top, Right, Bottom, X, Y: integer): boolean;
{ Test if the mouse cursor is within the box specified. Returns True
  if the mouse is in the box; otherwise the function returns False. }
begin
  InBox := (X >= Left) and (X <= Right) and (Y >= Top) and (Y <= Bottom);
end;

function MouseObj.GetInput(WhichButton: integer): integer;
{ Returns a character if a key has been pressed, or -1 if a mouse
  button has been pressed, or a zero if none of the above. If a
  mouse exists, this routine favors any keyboard action. }
begin
  if KeyPressed then                     { Check if a key has been pressed }
    GetInput := Ord(ReadKey)             { Return the character }
  else begin
    if ButtonPressed(WhichButton) then begin
      while not ButtonReleased(WhichButton) do ;
      GetInput := -1;
    end
    else if ButtonReleased(WhichButton) then
      GetInput := -1
    else
      GetInput := 0;
  end
end;

function MouseObj.WaitForInput(WhichButton: integer): integer;
{ Continue to call GetInput until a button or key has been pressed }
var
  C: integer;
begin
  repeat
    C := GetInput(WhichButton);
  until C <> 0;
  WaitForInput := C;
end;

begin
end.
```

• Listing 7.2. KBDMOUSE.PAS

```pascal
unit KbdMouse;
{ KBDMOUSE.PAS: Routines to emulate a mouse with a keyboard.
  To move the emulated cursor use the arrow keys on the keyboard
  and the INS and DEL keys as the left- and right-mouse buttons,
  respectively. The gray + and - keys can be used to change the
  amount the emulated mouse cursor is moved. Note that the routines
  will call the MouseObj methods if a mouse exists. }
interface
uses MousePac;
const
  MaxInc: integer = 32; { Largest amount emulated mouse cursor can move }
  CursWidth: integer = 8;  { The emulated cursor is 8 }
  CursHeight: integer = 8; { pixels by 8 pixels }
type
{ The keyboard mouse is derived from the MouseObj object type }
KbdMouseObj = object(MouseObj)
  Cx, Cy: integer;        { Internal variables used to maintain }
                          { the cursor location when the mouse is not used }
  CInc: integer;          { Internal variable used to increment }
                          { amount of the nonmouse cursor }
  Cursor: pointer;        { Points to image of the emulated mouse }
  UnderCursor: pointer;   { Area saved under emulated mouse }
  CursorOn: boolean;      { True if cursor currently visible }
  CMinX, CMaxX,           { Minimum, maximum x coordinates for cursor }
  CMinY, CMaxY: integer;  { Minimum, maximum y coordinates for cursor }
  LButtonPress,           { True if simulated left or right }
  RButtonPress: boolean;  { button is pressed }
  NumLPress: integer;     { Count the number of button presses }
  NumRPress: integer;
  NumLRelease: integer;   { Count the number of button releases }
  NumRRelease: integer;
  CDeltaX, CDeltaY: integer; { Keeps track of emulated mouse's movements }
  function Setup: boolean; virtual;
  procedure Hide; virtual;
  procedure Show; virtual;
  procedure Move(X, Y: integer); virtual;
  procedure GetCoords(var X, Y: integer); virtual;
  function ButtonReleased(WhichButton: integer): boolean; virtual;
  function ButtonPressed(WhichButton: integer): boolean; virtual;
  function GetInput(WhichButton: integer): integer; virtual;
  function GetKbInteraction(WhichButton: integer): integer; virtual;
  function GetKb: integer;
  procedure InitCursor;
  procedure ToggleCursor;
  procedure DrawCursor(X, Y: integer);
end;

implementation
uses
  Graph, Crt;
```

```
function KbdMouseObj.Setup;
{ Call this function at the beginning of your program, after the graphics
  adapter has been initialized. It will initialize the mouse and display
  the mouse cursor at the middle of the screen. If a mouse is not
  present it will cause the emulated mouse to appear and the keyboard
  will be used to move the "mouse" cursor. }
begin
  if not MouseObj.Setup then begin { No mouse found--emulate the mouse }
    CInc := 1; CMinX := 0;          { The functionality is the }
    CMaxX := GetMaxX - 1;           { same as the real thing }
    CMaxY := GetMaxY - 1;           { Therefore, set the emulated }
    CMinX := 0; CMinY := 0;         { cursor to the top left of the }
    CDeltaX := 0; CDeltaY := 0;     { screen, set its bounds to the }
    Cx := CMaxX div 2;
    Cy := CMaxY div 2;              { full screen and initialize its }
    LButtonPress := False;          { mouse movement counters, and }
    RButtonPress := False;          { initialize all button states }
    NumLPress := 0;                 { to false }
    NumRPress := 0;                 { Set simulated mouse button }
    NumLRelease := 0;               { press and release counters to }
    NumRRelease := 0;               { zero }
    InitCursor;                     { Create cursor image }
    CursorOn := False;
    Show;                           { Call Show to display it }
    Setup := False;                 { return a no mouse found flag }
  end
  else
    Setup := True;
end;


procedure KbdMouseObj.Move(X, Y: integer);
{ Moves the mouse to the location (x,y) }
begin
  if MouseExists then
    MouseObj.Move(x,y)
  else begin
    Hide;                           { Erase the current mouse cursor }
    Cx := X;  Cy := Y;              { Update the mouse cursor's location }
    Show;                           { Display mouse at the new location }
    CDeltaX := 0;  CDeltaY := 0; { Reset the mouse movement variables }
  end;
end;


procedure KbdMouseObj.Hide;
{ Removes the mouse cursor from the screen. Call Hide before writing or
  drawing to the screen. It is also a good idea to turn off the mouse at
  the end of a program. Use Show to restore the mouse on the screen. The
  mouse movement will be maintained while the mouse is not visible. Due to
  a peculiarity of the mouse driver, make sure you don't call Hide if
  the mouse is not already visible. See text discussion for more on this. }
begin
  if MouseExists then
    MouseObj.Hide
```

```pascal
    else                                 { Mouse doesn't exist, so turn }
      ToggleCursor;                      { off the emulated cursor }
  end;

procedure KbdMouseObj.Show;
{ Display the mouse cursor. Normally, you should not call this
  function if the mouse is already visible. The keyboard mouse
  is clipped to the minimum and maximum ranges in this routine. }
begin
  if MouseExists then
    MouseObj.Show                        { If the mouse doesn't exist, }
  else
    ToggleCursor;                        { turn on the emulated cursor }
end;

procedure KbdMouseObj.GetCoords(var x, y: integer);
{ Get the current location of the mouse cursor }
begin
  if MouseExists then
    MouseObj.GetCoords(x,y)
  else begin
    x := Cx; y := Cy;                    { The position of the emulated }
  end                                    { mouse is given by Cx and Cy }
end;

function KbdMouseObj.ButtonReleased(WhichButton: integer): boolean;
begin
  if MouseExists then
    ButtonReleased := MouseObj.ButtonReleased(WhichButton)
  else begin
    if ((WhichButton = LeftButton) or (WhichButton = EitherButton)) and
                                  (NumLRelease > 0) then begin
      Dec(NumLRelease);
      ButtonReleased := True;
    end
    else if ((WhichButton = RightButton) or (WhichButton = EitherButton))
                      and (NumRRelease > 0) then begin
      Dec(NumRRelease);
      ButtonReleased := True;
    end
    { If there isn't already a button released, check and see if
      the user just released one, and if so repeat the tests above. }
    else if (GetKbInteraction(WhichButton) < 0) then begin
      if (WhichButton = LeftButton) or (WhichButton = EitherButton) then
        ButtonReleased := True
      else if (WhichButton = RightButton) or
              (WhichButton = EitherButton) then
        ButtonReleased := True
    end
    else
      ButtonReleased := False; { Return a value that the button was not
                                 pressed }
  end
end;
```

```
function KbdMouseObj.ButtonPressed(WhichButton: integer): boolean;
{ Return a 1 if the mouse button specified has been pressed since the
  last check with this function. If the button has not been pressed,
  return a 0. }
begin
  if MouseExists then
    ButtonPressed := MouseObj.ButtonPressed(WhichButton)
  else begin
    if ((WhichButton = LeftButton) or (WhichButton = EitherButton)) and
                  (NumLPress > 0) then begin
      Dec(NumLPress);
      ButtonPressed := True;
    end
    else if ((Whichbutton = RightButton) or (WhichButton = EitherButton))
                        and (NumRPress > 0) then begin
      Dec(NumRPress);
      ButtonPressed := True;
    end
    { If there isn't already a button pressed, check and see if
      the user just pressed one, and if so repeat the tests above. }
    else if GetKbInteraction(WhichButton) < 0 then begin
      if (WhichButton = LeftButton) or (WhichButton = EitherButton) then
        ButtonPressed := True
      else if (WhichButton = RightButton) or
              (WhichButton = EitherButton) then
        ButtonPressed := True;
    end
    else
      ButtonPressed := False;  { Return a value that the button was not
pressed }
  end
end;

function KbdMouseObj.GetInput(WhichButton: integer): integer;
{ Returns a character if a key has been pressed, or -1 if an emulated
  mouse button has been pressed, or a zero if none of the above. If a
  mouse exists, this function calls the mouse routines. }
begin
  if MouseExists then
    GetInput := MouseObj.GetInput(WhichButton)
  else
    GetInput := GetKbInteraction(WhichButton)
end;

function KbdMouseObj.GetKbInteraction(WhichButton: integer): integer;
{ This routine is used only if the mouse does not exist. It updates
  the location of the cursor whenever an arrow key is pressed or
  will set the button pressed flags if a button key is pressed. In
  addition, it will change the cursor increment amount if the plus or
  minus keys are pressed. If the "button" specified is pressed or was
  already pressed, the function returns -1. If an arrow key is pressed
  then a 0 is returned, which means that the caller does not have to
  perform any action. Finally, if some other key is pressed, then its
```

```pascal
        value is returned. }
var
  C: integer;
begin
  if KeyPressed then begin
    C := GetKb;
    Hide;                           { Emulated mouse may be moved }
    case C of
      $5200 : begin                 { INS key--Emulate left mouse button press }
        if not LButtonPress then LButtonPress := True
          else LButtonPress := False;
        Show;
        if ((WhichButton = LeftButton) or (WhichButton = EitherButton))
          then begin
          GetKbInteraction := -1;   { Return mouse button click signal }
          Exit;
        end;
        if LButtonPress then Inc(NumLPress)
          else Inc(NumLRelease);
        GetKbInteraction := 0;      { Wrong mouse "button" pressed }
        Exit;
      end;
      $5300 : begin                 { DEL key emulates right mouse button }
        Show;
        if RButtonPress then RButtonPress := False
          else RButtonPress := True;
        if ((WhichButton = RightButton) or
            (WhichButton = EitherButton)) then begin
          GetKbInteraction := -1;   { Return mouse button signal }
          Exit;
        end;
        if RButtonPress then Inc(NumRPress)
          else Inc(NumRRelease);
        GetKbInteraction := 0; { Wrong mouse "button" pressed }
        Exit;
      end;
      $002B : begin              { '+' key: increase the mouse movement amount }
        if CInc < MaxInc then Inc(CInc,6)
          else CInc := MaxInc;
      end;
      $002D : begin              { '-' key: decrease the mouse movement amount }
        if CInc > 1 + 6 then Dec(CInc,6)
          else CInc := 1;
      end;
      $4800 : begin                 { Up key moves the cursor up by the }
        Dec(Cy,CInc);
        if Cy < CMinY then Cy := CMinY;
        Dec(CDeltaY,CInc);  { increment amount and clip; also }
      end;                          { decrement movement amount }
      $5000 : begin                 { Down key }
        Inc(Cy,CInc);
        if Cy > CMaxY then Cy := CMaxY;
        Inc(CDeltaY,CInc);
```

```
            end;
        $4B00 : begin           { Left key }
          Dec(Cx,CInc);
          if Cx < CMinX then Cx := CMinX;
          Dec(CDeltaX,CInc);
          end;
        $4D00 : begin           { Right key }
          Inc(Cx,CInc);
          if Cx > CMaxX then Cx := CMaxX;
          Inc(CDeltaX,CInc);
          end;
        $4700 : begin           { Home key }
          Dec(Cy,CInc);
          if Cy < CMinY then Cy := CMinY;
          Dec(Cx,CInc);
          if Cx < CMinX then Cx := CMinX;
          Dec(CDeltaX,CInc);   Dec(CDeltaY,CInc);
          end;
        $4900 : begin           { PgUp key }
          Dec(Cy,CInc);
          if Cy < CMinY then Cy := CMinY;
          Inc(Cx,CInc);
          if Cx > CMaxX then Cx := CMaxX;
          Inc(CDeltaX,CInc);  Dec(CDeltaY,CInc);
          end;
        $4F00 : begin           { End key }
          Inc(Cy,CInc);
          if Cy > CMaxY then Cy := CMaxY;
          Dec(Cx,CInc);
          if Cx < CMinX then Cx := CMinX;
          Dec(CDeltaX,CInc);  Inc(CDeltaY,CInc);
          end;
        $5100 : begin           { PgDn key }
          Inc(Cy,CInc);
          if Cy > CMaxY then Cy := CMaxY;
          Inc(Cx,CInc);
          if Cx > CMaxX then Cx := CMaxX;
          Inc(CDeltaX,CInc);  Inc(CDeltaY,CInc);
          end;
        else begin Show; GetKbInteraction := C; Exit; end;
      end;
      Show;                     { Restore mouse to possibly new position }
    end;
  GetKbInteraction := 0;   { Tell caller not to take any action }
end;


function KbdMouseObj.GetKb: integer;
{ Low-level keyboard input that retrieves some of the extended
  codes produced by the arrow keys and gray keys. This function does
  not support all of the extended key codes. }
var
  Ch1, Ch2: integer;
begin
```

```
      Ch1 := Ord(ReadKey);
      if Ch1 = 0 then begin            { Arrow keys have two character sequences }
        Ch2 := Ord(ReadKey);           { where the first character is a zero }
        Ch2 := Ch2 shl 8;              { Combine these two characters into one }
        Ch2 := Ch2 or Ch1;            { and return the value }
        GetKb := Ch2;
      end
      else
        GetKb := Ch1;
    end;

    procedure KbdMouseObj.InitCursor;
    { Creates the image of the simulated mouse. It calls DrawCursor,
      which is a routine that you must supply to actually draw the cursor.
      Note: A DrawCursor routine that draws an arrow is provided below. }
    begin
      { Allocate space for the emulated mouse cursor and for the space
        below it. If not enough memory, quit the program. }
      GetMem(Cursor,ImageSize(0,0,CursWidth,CursHeight));
      GetMem(UnderCursor,ImageSize(0,0,CursWidth,CursHeight));
      if (Cursor = Nil) or (UnderCursor = Nil) then begin
        CloseGraph;
        WriteLn('Not enough memory for program.');
        Halt(1);
      end;
      { Save the image of the screen where the cursor image will be
        created. Clear this space and call DrawCursor to draw cursor. }
      GetImage(Cx,Cy,Cx+CursWidth,Cy+CursHeight,UnderCursor^);
      SetLineStyle(SolidLn,0,0);
      SetFillStyle(SolidFill,0);
      Bar(Cx,Cy,Cx+CursWidth,Cy+CursHeight);
      DrawCursor(Cx,Cy);
      { Save the image of the cursor and overwrite the screen area
        where the cursor is with the original screen image. }
      GetImage(Cx,Cy,Cx+CursWidth,Cy+CursHeight,Cursor^);
      PutImage(Cx,Cy,UnderCursor^,CopyPut);
    end;

    procedure KbdMouseObj.ToggleCursor;
    { Used by the simulated mouse to turn the mouse cursor on and off.
      The viewport settings may have changed so temporarily reset them
      to the full screen while the cursor image is displayed or erased. }
    var
      Vp: ViewPortType;
      OldX, OldY: integer;
    begin
      GetViewSettings(Vp);                              { Save view settings }
      OldX := GetX;   OldY := GetY;                     { and current position }
      SetViewPort(0,0,GetMaxX,GetMaxy,True);
      if CursorOn then begin                            { To erase the cursor, }
        PutImage(Cx,Cy,UnderCursor^,CopyPut);           { overwrite it with }
        CursorOn := False;                              { the saved image of }
      end                                               { the screen }
```

```pascal
      else begin                        { To draw the cursor first }
        GetImage(Cx,Cy,Cx+CursWidth,Cy+CursHeight,UnderCursor^);
        PutImage(Cx,Cy,Cursor^,CopyPut); { save the area where the cursor }
        CursorOn := True;               { will be and then display the cursor }
      end;
      { Reset the viewport settings and its current position }
      SetViewPort(Vp.x1,Vp.y1,Vp.x2,Vp.y2,True);
      MoveTo(OldX,OldY);
  end;

procedure KbdMouseObj.DrawCursor(X, Y: integer);
{ This function draws a cursor if a mouse does not exist. It draws
  a small arrow. If you want a different cursor, just change this
  routine. CursWidth and CursHeight define the dimensions of cursor. }
begin
  SetColor(GetMaxColor);
  Line(x+1,y+1,x+CursWidth-1,y+CursHeight-1);
  Line(x+2,y+1,x+CursWidth-1,y+CursHeight-2);
  Line(x+1,y+2,x+CursWidth-2,y+CursHeight-1);
  Line(x+2,y+1,x+2,y+5);
  Line(x+1,y+1,x+1,y+5);
  Line(x+1,y+1,x+5,y+1);
  Line(x+1,y+2,x+5,y+2);
end;


begin
end.
```

• Listing 7.3. MOUSETST.PAS

```pascal
program MouseTst;
{ MOUSETST.PAS: This program partially tests MOUSEPAC.PAS and
  KBDMOUSE.PAS. It displays a mouse cursor and lets you move it
  around the screen until a mouse button is pressed. If no mouse is
  detected, the keyboard emulated mouse is used. Use the arrow keys
  to move this mouse and the Ins or Del keys as the mouse buttons
  in order to quit the program. }
uses
  Graph, MousePac, KbdMouse;
const
  GDriver: integer = Detect;              { Use autodetect }
var
  GMode, GErr, C: integer;
  Mouse: KbdMouseObj;
begin
  InitGraph(GDriver,GMode,'\tp\bgi');     { Initialize the screen }
  GErr := GraphResult;
  if GErr <> grOk then begin
    WriteLn('Graphics error: ',GraphErrorMsg(GErr));
    Halt;
  end;
```

```
{ You must call MouseObj's constructor after initializing the
   graphics system and before using any of MouseObj's methods. }
Mouse.Init;
if not Mouse.Setup then begin
   Mouse.Hide;                              { Always turn off the mouse cursor }
   OutTextXY(0,0,'No mouse detected'); { before writing to the screen }
   OutTextXY(0,20,'Press Ins or Del key to quit');
   Mouse.Show;                              { When done display mouse }
end
else begin
   Mouse.Hide;                              { Mouse exists. Use it }
   OutTextXY(0,10,'Press a mouse button to quit');
   Mouse.Show;
end;                                        { Wait until the mouse routine }
repeat                                      { returns a negative value. This }
   C := Mouse.WaitForInput(EitherButton); { indicates a button was
                                              pressed }
until C < 0;
{ It's generally a good idea to turn the mouse off when done }
Mouse.Hide;
CloseGraph;                                 { Exit graphics mode }
end.
```

8

Working with Icons

In Chapter 7 we learned how to use the mouse in a graphics environment. Part of its attraction is that a mouse can play an integral role in building extremely intuitive user interfaces. For instance, in later chapters we'll see how the mouse can be used to easily draw figures on the screen. However, another way to use the mouse is as a pointing device for selecting commands from the screen. Icons are one popular means of representing commands while in graphics mode. If you've ever used a PC graphics application, such as a painting program, you should already be aware of the benefits icons provide.

In this chapter, we'll take a close look at icons and expand our set of graphics programming tools as we develop a standalone icon editor that we'll use to create, save, and edit icons. In addition, we'll present several sample icon patterns that we'll use in developing custom graphics programs in Chapters 11 and 12.

Why Icons?

Icons are used in many graphics-based applications, such as CAD and paint programs, because they can represent complex commands as small symbols or pictures. As a result, extremely intuitive and easy to use graphics interfaces can be designed around them. Instead of having to type a command or select one from a list of often ambiguous menus, the mouse can be used to point and click on an icon to invoke the command.

Our goal here is to develop a program that allows us to create icons interactively. Although we could design our icons by hand, the interactive nature of this program simplifies the process of drawing and editing icons. The program can also be used as a tool to help us experiment with different icon designs.

The **IconEd** program, shown in Listing 8.1, closely resembles the fill pattern editor that we created in Chapter 2. One key difference is that we'll be using the **MouseObj** and **KbdMouseObj** object types, developed in Chapter 7, to give us access to the mouse; this will improve user interaction. But before we get into any further details of the **IconEd** program, let's discuss how the icons will be represented.

Representing Icons

Icons can be represented in various ways. Our primary concern here is to develop icons that look good when displayed with the different graphics modes supported by the BGI. An icon drawn in one mode may appear different in another mode because of the varying screen resolutions that exist. In general, it is nearly impossible to create one icon pattern that looks the same in all graphics modes.

Writing Device-Independent Graphics Programs

One issue that comes up again and again in graphics programming is whether a particular program can run in different graphics modes. A program that accomplishes this is said to be device independent. Clearly, this is an admirable goal, because an application that is not tied to a particular graphics standard would be the most useful. However, there are so many different graphics "standards" that achieving a device-independent application can be a real challenge. Essentially, there are three issues you must deal with:

- Screen resolution
- Colors
- Aspect ratio

The problems relating to screen resolution and aspect ratio overlap somewhat. Generally, you want to try to avoid writing statements that display graphics figures at specific screen coordinates. For example, a program that draws a square with the upper-left coordinate at (0,0) and the bottom-right coordinate at (240,240) will work in VGA's high-resolution mode but not in CGA, because the CGA does not have 240 rows available. One way to get around this is to scale all of your calculations based on the dimensions of the screen. Therefore, in this case, it would be better to use the coordinates (0,0) and (240,GetMaxY div 2).

Unfortunately, if you follow this approach, your figures may still not display equally well in different modes. The reason is that different modes have different pixel aspect ratios. For instance, in 320 by 200 CGA mode, pixels are twice as tall as they are wide. However, in a VGA high-resolution mode, pixels are about the same in both dimensions. You can adjust for the difference in the aspect ratio by scaling

We'll standardize our icons so that they are all 16 by 16 pixels. This size seems to work well in most cases (at least in the graphics modes that we'll be using). Nevertheless, we'll need to compensate for the aspect ratio of the screens in order to make the icons look proportionally correct when displayed with different graphics modes. However, we won't be compensating for the size of the icons, so the icons will appear in different sizes and slightly different shapes in each of the graphics modes. For more on this issue refer to the sidebar "Writing Device-Independent Graphics Programs."

Internally, an icon pattern is represented in our icon editor as a two-dimensional array of bytes. Here's the declaration for this array:

```
const
  IconWidth   = 16;   { An icon is a 16 by 16 pattern }
  IconHeight  = 16;
var
  Icon: array[1..IconHeight,1..IconWidth] of byte;
```

your figures using a ratio calculated from the values returned by the BGI function **GetAspectRatio**. You have two choices here. You can either stretch the figure in the x direction to compensate for the screen resolution difference, or you can compress the y values. In trying to draw a good square, let's take the latter approach. Our example can be improved by first calculating the screen's aspect ratio:

```
GetAspectRatio(Xasp,Yasp);
AspectRatio := Xasp / Yasp;
```

and then multiplying each y dimension by **AspectRatio**. Therefore, the square's top-left and bottom-right coordinates become (0,0) and (240,240*AspectRatio). Now the square will truly appear as a square. (Note that in the icon editor, we stretch the x values rather than compress the y values; therefore, the aspect ratio calculated is inverted from what is shown here.) This example still forces the size to a specific value, but you can get around this with the scaling technique shown earlier.

Compensating for the various colors is another matter. Generally, if you use only the EGA or VGA standard palette, you shouldn't have a problem when going between these two graphics adapters. However, if you try to use the same program in a CGA mode or on a monochrome system, you'll have only a few "colors" available and the same display may not look the way you intended it to. Some of this can be avoided by planning ahead and with clever choices of colors and fill patterns. One technique you might try is to create a *logical palette* that all of your code accesses to select colors and which is assigned a set of colors from those available. Of course, this doesn't add colors to modes where they don't exist, but it will help you program with the color settings in mind. When you run across a mode where your program doesn't look good, it's often a simple matter of changing the values in the logical palette for that particular mode.

The constants **IconHeight** and **IconWidth** specify the height and width of the icon, respectively, and are declared to be 16. Consequently, each location in the icon array represents one pixel in the icon pattern. We'll be using only black and white icons, so these byte locations will take on only a 1 or 0 value. If the value is 1, the corresponding icon pixel is drawn in white; otherwise, it is left as the background color by reserving other values to represent additional colors. If you desire, you can add color to your icons; however, keep in mind that not all of the graphic modes can produce the same colors.

Saving Icons

To simplify our application programs and make our icons easier to maintain, we'll save each icon pattern in its own file. In addition, we'll store the icons in text format so that they can be easily inspected.

The format of the icon files consists of two major parts—a header and a body. The header is located at the top of the file and is a single line that specifies the icon's width and height. Since all our icons are 16 by 16 pixels, the first line will always start with these two numbers. The rest of the file contains the icon pattern, which is organized so that each row of the icon is on a separate line. Therefore a 16-by-16-pixel icon has 16 numbers per line where each pixel of the icon image is represented by either a 0 or a 1. Figure 8.1 shows a sample icon and the file that is used to store this icon. If you compare the two, you'll see that there is a one-to-one correspondence between each pixel set in the icon and each value of 1 in the file.

While we are discussing the format of an icon file, let's look at the **SaveIcon** routine, which is used to write an icon pattern to disk. To simplify user input, **SaveIcon** assumes that it is called while the program is in text mode. It first prompts you to enter the filename of the icon file to be written. It then calls **Assign** and **Rewrite** to open the file and prepare for reading. If the file cannot be opened or created the Turbo Pascal error flag, **IOResult**, is nonzero and the routine immediately returns without performing any other actions. However, if the file is opened, **SaveIcon** writes the icon pattern stored in the array **Icon** to the file using the following statements:

```
WriteLn(IconFile,IconWidth,' ',IconHeight); { Write header }
for J := 1 to IconHeight do begin           { Write icon pattern }
  for I := 1 to IconWidth do                { to file one row at a }
    Write(IconFile,Icon[J][I],' ');         { time }
  WriteLn(IconFile);
end;
Close(IconFile);
```

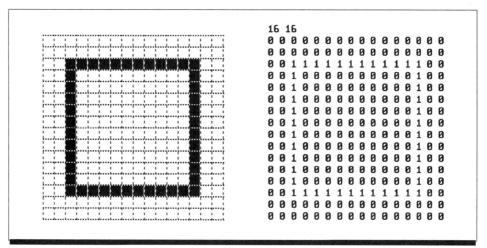

Figure 8.1. An icon and the file that represents it

The first **WriteLn** in this code writes the header data containing the width and height of the icon to the file. The nested **for** loops that follow copy the icon pattern to the file by writing each row of the icon pattern on a separate line. After the icon pattern is completely written, the file is closed with a call to **Close**.

Reading an Icon File

The process of reading an icon file into the icon editor is similar to that of writing a file and is performed by the routine **ReadIcon**. Like **SaveIcon**, this routine is designed to run in text mode in order to simplify the text input.

The routine begins by initializing an icon pattern so that it contains all zeros:

```
for J := 1 to IconHeight do begin    { Initialize the icon }
  for I := 1 to IconWidth do          { array to all blanks }
    Icon[J][I] := 0;
end;
```

This technique ensures that the icon pattern starts as a completely black icon. The **ReadIcon** routine then continues by displaying a program banner and asking you if you wish to edit an existing icon file. If your response is *yes* (any character but the letter n), **ReadIcon** assumes you want to edit an existing icon and asks you for the name of the file where it is stored. Remember that during this process, the data entry operations are performed in text mode in order to simplify the code. You can, however, try to integrate the GTEXT.PAS text processing utilities developed in

Chapter 3 in the routine, in order to avoid having to switch between graphics and text modes.

Once the filename is determined, **ReadIcon** attempts to open it for reading. If this operation is successful, the first line of the file, which contains the header, is read. As long as this line consists of two values equivalent to **IconWidth** and **IconHeight**, **ReadIcon** continues. If any other numbers are found, then the file is invalid and **ReadIcon** terminates.

The icon pattern is read from the file into the array **Icon** by two **for** loops like those used in **SaveIcon** to write the icon data to a file. The difference is that here the **ReadLn** routine is used to read the icon pattern from the file. Once the icon pattern has been read into the array **Icon**, we can display it. We'll look at how this is done a bit later.

The Interactive Editor

Now that we know how to read and write icon files, we're ready to look at the icon editor itself. Figure 8.2 shows the icon editor while it is being used to edit an icon. Notice that there are two primary regions in the display. On the left side of the screen is an enlarged representation of the icon being edited. All editing is actually performed within this window. On the right side of the screen is the current state of the icon pattern shown in its actual size.

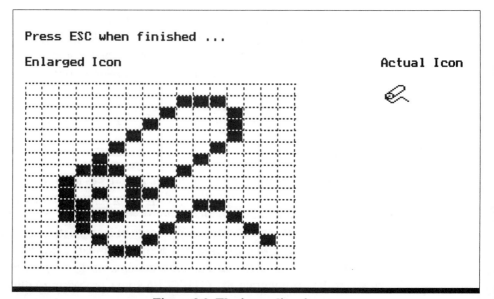

Figure 8.2. The icon editor in use

You can edit an icon by clicking the mouse on any of the big icon bits of the enlarged icon pattern. Each time you click the mouse while it is over one of these big pixels, the pixel's state is toggled from white to black or black to white. In addition, after every mouse action, the current state of the icon is updated on the right side of the screen.

You can use the icon editor by toggling the various pixels you want to change in the enlarged icon pattern until you are satisfied with how the normal-sized icon looks. To exit the editing process, you select the Esc key. Once this is done, the screen is cleared and you are asked if you want to save the icon pattern currently in the editor to a file of your choice. If so, you will be prompted to enter the filename and then the program will save the icon pattern and terminate. Otherwise, the program simply ends. Let's examine the different components of the icon editor program.

Creating the Screen

The first 10 statements in the **IconEd** program initialize various aspects of the icon editor. The process begins by reading an icon file (if necessary), initializing the graphics mode, initializing the mouse, generating the enlarged icon pattern, and displaying the initial state of the icon pattern. The routine calls used are as follows:

```
ReadIcon;                  { If a person wants an icon file to }
InitGraphics;              { be read, read it, otherwise }
Mouse.Init;                { simply initialize the screen }
T := Mouse.Setup;          { with an empty big icon pattern }
DrawEnlargedIcon;
ShowIcon;                  { Draw the icon to start with }
```

These statements must be called in this order. In particular, we want to keep the **ReadIcon** routine in text mode (before graphics initialization) in order to simplify user interaction. In addition, the call to the **Mouse** object's **Setup** method must come after graphics initialization since it checks which graphics mode is being used. But this isn't done until the **Mouse** object's constructor **Init** is called because it initializes the internal state of the **Mouse** object. The ordering of the last two statements is probably a little more obvious. We'll look at these two routines later in this section.

The next five statements are used to print a series of banners to the screen by calling the **OutTextXY** routine. Note that a pair of **Mouse.Hide** and **Mouse.Show** calls surround the screen output statements. They are needed to ensure that the mouse cursor is off while the screen is being written to.

Creating an Enlarged Icon

The routine **DrawEnlargedIcon** generates a grid on the left side of the screen in which the enlarged icon pattern is edited. The grid consists of 17 horizontal and vertical dotted lines which mark out a 16 by 16 grid for the icon pattern as shown in Figure 8.3. These are drawn by the following two **for** loops:

```
Mouse.Hide;                      { Draw vertical and horizontal dashed }
for I := 0 to IconHeight do    { lines to make big icon pattern }
  Line(BigIconLeft,BigIconTop+I*(BigBitSize+NormWidth),
      Right,BigIconTop+I*(BigBitSize+NormWidth));
for I := 0 to IconWidth do
  Line(BigIconLeft+Aspect*(I*(BigBitSize+NormWidth)),BigIconTop,
      BigIconLeft+Aspect*(I*(BigBitSize+NormWidth)),Bottom);
Mouse.Show;
```

Once again, note that before anything is written to the screen, the mouse is first turned off by a call to **Mouse.Hide** and later restored by a call to **Mouse.Show**.

You have probably noticed by now that **DrawEnlargedIcon** relies on numerous constants. A list of these constants along with a description of their meanings is shown in Table 8.1. You may want to refer to this table to help you understand the **DrawEnlargedIcon** routine.

The last line in **DrawEnlargedIcon** is a call to the routine **InitBigBit**, which creates an image of an enlarged icon pixel. To toggle the icon pixels in the enlarged icon pattern, we'll exclusive-OR the image created by **InitBigBit** to the rectangular regions within the enlarged icon pattern. Let's look at this routine.

The image of one of the enlarged bits is created at the beginning of **InitBigBit** by the following nested **for** loops:

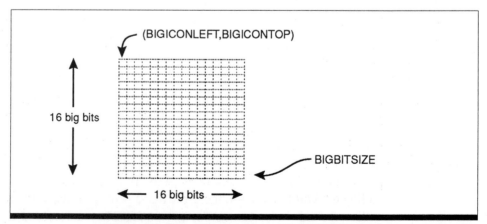

Figure 8.3. The editing grid used in ICONED.PAS

Table 8.1. Constants used in drawing the enlarged icon pattern

Constant	Description
BigIconLeft	The column where the big icon pattern begins
BigIconTop	The top row of the big icon pattern
BigBitSize	Size of the big pixels in the enlarged icon pattern
IconWidth	Width of an icon
IconHeight	Height of an icon
DottedLn	From Graph, specifies the line type
NormWidth	From Graph, pixel width of lines

```
for J := Bby+1 to Bby+BigBitSize do           { Draw big bit }
  for I := Bbx+1 to Bbx+Aspect*BigBitSize do   { one pixel at a }
    PutPixel(I,J,GetMaxColor);                 { time }
```

These two loops paint a block of pixels in the top-left corner of the enlarged icon pattern the size of **BigBitSize**. Actually, the width of the enlarged icon, **BigBitSize**, is adjusted by the aspect ratio of the screen by multiplying it by the screen's aspect ratio, which is contained in the variable **Aspect**. This variable is calculated in **InitGraphics** by the statements:

```
GetAspectRatio(Xasp,Yasp);
Aspect := Round(Yasp / Xasp);
```

We do this to adjust for the aspect ratios of the different graphics modes in which the icon editor might be used.

Once the enlarged icon pixel image is created, it is copied into **BigBit**. First, however, space for this image must be allocated by a call to **GetMem**. After storage is allocated, **GetImage** is called to copy the image of the big pixel as shown here:

```
GetMem(BigBit,ImageSize(Bbx,Bby,Bbx+Aspect*BigBitSize, Bby+BigBitSize));
GetImage(Bbx+1,Bby+1,Bbx+Aspect*BigBitSize,Bby+BigBitSize, BigBit^);
```

Later, when we want to toggle one of the enlarged icon pixels while editing, we'll need only to exclusive-OR an image of this pixel pattern, stored in **BigBit**, over the appropriate location in the grid. Of course, now we have a big pixel in the top-left corner of the enlarged icon pixel that we must remove. We do this by a call to **PutImage** using the **XorPut** replacement as shown:

```
PutImage(Bbx+1,Bby+1,BigBit^,XorPut);
```

After accomplishing these operations, the mouse cursor is finally restored by a call to **Mouse.Show** and **InitBigBit** ends.

Displaying the Original Icon

The next step in the screen initialization process consists of displaying the icon pattern that was read in at the beginning of the program. Remember, if an icon file is not read in, then the icon array is initialized to all zeros in **ReadIcon**. The routine **ShowIcon** is used to display the current state of the icon pattern. This routine consists of two nested **for** loops that sequence through the array **Icon**. For each byte location that stores a 1, a corresponding big bit is toggled in the enlarged icon and the small icon pattern is updated as well. Setting one of the big icon pixels is a matter of exclusive-ORing the image of the big icon pixel (discussed earlier in this chapter) at the appropriate locations. The **PutImage** routine located within the inner **for** loop performs this step.

The call to **ToggleIconsBit** is required in order to turn on the appropriate pixel in the small icon pattern. The routine accepts as parameters the logical indexes of a pixel in the **Icon** array, and checks the pixel corresponding to the **Icon** array indexes by testing whether it is equal to the background color. Depending on its current value, the small icon's pixels are toggled. The small icon is displayed at the column indicated by **IconLeft**. Its top row coincides with **BigIconTop**. You will notice that although the icon is represented as a 16 by 16 pattern, the small icon may be drawn wider. This may occur because we are multiplying the width of the icon by the aspect ratio of the screen. Recall that this technique is used to adjust for the varying aspect ratios of the graphics modes we'll be using.

Interacting with the User

After the screen is initialized, the icon editor is ready for business. While editing an icon, there are two types of input that are acceptable:

- Pressing the left mouse button—which toggles the current icon pixel that is pointed at, if there is one
- Pressing Esc—which exits the program

The **while** loop in the mainline supports this user interaction:

```
C := Mouse.WaitForInput(LeftButton); { Get input from mouse/keyboard }
while C <> 27 do begin      { if input is Esc, quit program }
  if C < 0 then begin       { if input is less than zero then a mouse }
    Mouse.GetCoords(X,Y); { button has been pressed; get current }
    ToggleBigBit(X,Y);      { coordinates and toggle big bit }
  end;
  C := Mouse.WaitForInput(LeftButton);
end;                        { Loop until user types Esc }
```

The loop centers around the use of the **Mouse** object's **WaitForInput** method. This function returns a negative value if the button specified, in this case the left mouse button, is pressed, or it returns the value of a key pressed. The **while** loop is written so that the program will continue until the Esc key is pressed. If the left mouse button is pressed, the routine will progress to the **if** statement. At this point, **GetCoords** retrieves the current location of the mouse cursor and passes it along to the routine **ToggleBigBit**, which changes the setting of the icon pixel that the mouse is pointing to.

Toggling an Icon Pixel

Toggling a pixel in an icon that is being edited involves the following three operations:

> 1. The pixel's value in the icon array must be changed.
> 2. The big pixel image in the enlarged icon pattern must be toggled.
> 3. The icon's pixel in the small icon pattern must be updated.

Each of these actions is set in motion by a call to **ToggleBigBit**. This routine takes two parameters that correspond to the screen coordinates of the enlarged icon bit that is to be changed. This screen coordinate is determined from the location of the mouse cursor at the time of the button press. The mouse coordinates come from the **Mouse** method **GetCoords**.

The bulk of **ToggleBigBit**, which follows, is involved in determining which icon bit should be toggled, if any.

```
for J := 1 to IconHeight do begin
  Line1 := BigIconTop+(J-1)*(BigBitSize+NormWidth);
  Line2 := BigIconTop+J*(BigBitSize+NormWidth);
  if (Line1 <= Y) and (Y < Line2) then begin
    for I := 1 to IconWidth do begin
      Col1 := BigIconLeft+Aspect*((I-1)*(BigBitSize+NormWidth));
      Col2 := BigIconLeft+Aspect*(I*(BigBitSize+NormWidth));
```

```
        if (Col1 <= X) and (X < col2) then begin
          Mouse.Hide;                          { Toggle the big bit using }
          PutImage(Col1+1,Line1+1,BigBit^,XorPut); { the XOR }
          Mouse.Show;                          { feature of PutImage }
          { Toggle the corresponding pixel in the small icon }
          ToggleIconsBit(I,J);
        end
      end
    end
end
```

This is accomplished by the two **for** loops in the routine. They sequence through the locations of the big icon pattern and test whether the coordinates passed to **ToggleBigBit** fall within any of the rows or columns in the big icon pattern. If so, the **PutImage** routine is used to exclusive-OR an image of the **BigBit** image made earlier over the current location in the icon pattern. This takes care of toggling the icon pixel in the large icon pattern. Now we need to change the corresponding bit in the small icon pattern. Fortunately, the routine is designed so that the line number and column number determined by the **for** loops will correspond to the indexes that can access the same bit in the icon array. These values, stored in the variables **I** and **J**, are passed to the **ToggleIconsBit** routine to actually change the **Icon** array value and update the small icon on the screen. This routine was presented earlier in this chapter.

Exiting the Icon Editor

The **while** loop discussed earlier that controls user interaction continues until the Esc key is pressed. Once this is done, the mouse cursor is disabled, the screen is returned to text mode, and you are prompted to save the icon currently in the icon editor. If you respond with anything other than the letter n, the program enters the **SaveIcon** routine and you will be prompted for the filename in which to store the icon. The **SaveIcon** routine was also discussed earlier in this chapter.

Sample Icons

The icons in Figure 8.4 were all developed with the icon editor in this chapter. We will be using many of these icon patterns in our later programs. To minimize any confusion, we have provided specific filenames for these icons that you should also use. This should guarantee the greatest compatibility with any code we will be developing later.

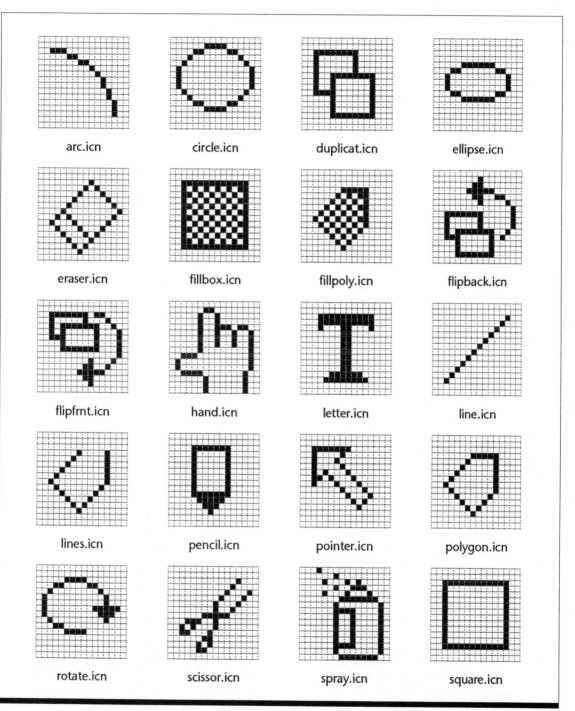

arc.icn   circle.icn   duplicat.icn   ellipse.icn

eraser.icn   fillbox.icn   fillpoly.icn   flipback.icn

flipfrnt.icn   hand.icn   letter.icn   line.icn

lines.icn   pencil.icn   pointer.icn   polygon.icn

rotate.icn   scissor.icn   spray.icn   square.icn

Figure 8.4. Sample icons

Compiling the Program

In order to compile the icon editor program you'll need the following files:

Source file	Chapter
MOUSEPAC.PAS	7
KBDMOUSE.PAS	7
ICONED.PAS	8

• Listing 8.1. ICONED.PAS

```
program IconEditor;
{ ICONED.PAS: This program will enable you to interactively create icons
  that can be used in a graphics program. It enables you to create an
  icon, edit an existing one, or save an icon pattern to a file. The
  program supports both keyboard and mouse interaction. The icon files
  are of the form:
                    IconWidth IconHeight
                    one row of icon pattern
                    next row of icon pattern
                         .  .  .
                    last row of icon pattern }
uses
  Graph, Crt, MousePac, KbdMouse;
const
  BigIconLeft = 20;    { Left side of the big icon pattern }
  BigIconTop  = 50;    { Top side of the big icon pattern }
  BigBitSize  = 8;     { Big bits are 8 pixels in size }
  IconWidth   = 16;    { An icon is a 16 by 16 pattern }
  IconHeight  = 16;
  IconLeft    = 400;   { Small icon pattern is located here }
var
  BigBit: pointer;     { Points to image of a big bit }
  { Holds the 16x16 icon pattern }
  Icon: array[1..IconHeight,1..IconWidth] of byte;
  X, Y, C, Aspect: integer;
  Ch: char;
  T: boolean;
  Mouse: KbdMouseObj;

procedure InitBigBit;
{ Create the image of a single big bit. This image will be used to toggle
  the big bits later in the program whenever the user clicks on the big
  icon pattern. }
var
  Bbx, Bby, I, J: integer;
```

```
begin
  Bbx := BigIconLeft;     { Create the big bit image at top-left }
  Bby := BigIconTop;      { corner of the big icon already drawn }
  Mouse.Hide;             { Hide mouse before drawing to screen }
  for J := Bby+1 to Bby+BigBitSize do        { Draw big bit }
    for I := Bbx+1 to Bbx+Aspect*BigBitSize do  { one pixel at a }
      PutPixel(I,J,GetMaxColor);               { time }
  { Set aside enough memory for the big bit image and then use
    GetImage to capture its image }
  GetMem(BigBit,ImageSize(Bbx,Bby,Bbx+Aspect*BigBitSize,
                                    Bby+BigBitSize));
  GetImage(Bbx+1,Bby+1,Bbx+Aspect*BigBitSize,Bby+BigBitSize,
                                    BigBit^);
  { Erase the big bit by exclusive ORing it with itself }
  PutImage(Bbx+1,Bby+1,BigBit^,XorPut);
  Mouse.Show;                          { Turn mouse back on }
end;

procedure DrawEnlargedIcon;
{ This routine draws an enlarged view of the icon pattern being edited.
  Click on the big bits in this pattern to toggle the corresponding icon's
  pixels on and off. The enlarged icon is drawn from BigIconLeft,
  BigIconTop, to Right, Bottom. }
var
  I, Right, Bottom: integer;
begin
  SetLineStyle(DottedLn,0,NormWidth);
  Right := BigIconLeft + IconWidth * Aspect * (BigBitSize + NormWidth);
  Bottom := BigIconTop + IconHeight * (BigBitSize + NormWidth);
  Mouse.Hide;                     { Draw vertical and horizontal dashed }
  for I := 0 to IconHeight do     { lines to make big icon pattern }
    Line(BigIconLeft,BigIconTop+I*(BigBitSize+NormWidth),
         Right,BigIconTop+I*(BigBitSize+NormWidth));
  for I := 0 to IconWidth do
    Line(BigIconLeft+Aspect*(I*(BigBitSize+NormWidth)),BigIconTop,
         BigIconLeft+Aspect*(I*(BigBitSize+NormWidth)),Bottom);
  Mouse.Show;
  InitBigBit;                     { Create the big bit image }
end;

procedure ToggleIconsBit(X, Y: integer);
{ This routine toggles a single pixel in the icon pattern. It changes the
  pixel's color and its value in the icon pattern array. The arguments x
  and y are between 0 and IconWidth or IconHeight. The array icon saves
  the icon pattern. If one of its locations is 1, then the corresponding
  pixel in the icon is to be drawn on. }
var
  I: integer;
begin
  Mouse.Hide;
  if GetPixel(Aspect*X+IconLeft,BigIconTop+y) <> Black then begin
    for I := 0 to Aspect-1 do
      PutPixel(Aspect*X+I+IconLeft,BigIconTop+Y,Black);
```

```
      Icon[Y][X] := 0;
    end
  else begin
    for I := 0 to Aspect-1 do
      PutPixel(Aspect*X+I+IconLeft,BigIconTop+Y,GetMaxColor);
    Icon[Y][X] := 1;
  end;
  Mouse.Show;
end;

procedure ToggleBigBit(X, Y: integer);
{ When the user clicks on the big icon pattern, toggle the appropriate big
  bit and the corresponding pixel in the icon pattern. This routine accepts
  screen coordinates specifying where the mouse button was pressed. The
  two for loops test to see which logical bit in the icon pattern must
  be toggled. Use PutImage to toggle the BigBit. Call ToggleIconsBit to
  toggle the appropriate pixel in the icon pattern. }
var
  I, J, Line1, Line2, Col1, Col2: integer;
begin
  for J := 1 to IconHeight do begin
    Line1 := BigIconTop+(J-1)*(BigBitSize+NormWidth);
    Line2 := BigIconTop+J*(BigBitSize+NormWidth);
    if (Line1 <= Y) and (Y < Line2) then begin
      for I := 1 to IconWidth do begin
        Col1 := BigIconLeft+Aspect*((I-1)*(BigBitSize+NormWidth));
        Col2 := BigIconLeft+Aspect*(I*(BigBitSize+NormWidth));
        if (Col1 <= X) and (X < col2) then begin
          Mouse.Hide;                        { Toggle the big bit using }
          PutImage(Col1+1,Line1+1,BigBit^,XorPut); { the XOR }
          Mouse.Show;                        { feature of PutImage }
          { Toggle the corresponding pixel in the small icon }
          ToggleIconsBit(I,J);
        end
      end
    end
  end
end;

procedure SaveIcon;
{ Writes the icon pattern to a file. The user is prompted for the file-
  name. The format of the file is given at the top of the program. }
var
  FileName: string[80];
  IconFile: text;
  I, J: integer;
begin
  WriteLn;
  Write('Enter the name of the file you want to');
  Write(' store the icon in: ');
  ReadLn(FileName);
  {$I-} Assign(IconFile,FileName);
  Rewrite(IconFile);   {$I+}
```

```
    if not (IOResult = 0) then begin
      CloseGraph;
      WriteLn('Cannot open file.');
      Halt(1);
    end
    else begin
      WriteLn(IconFile,IconWidth,' ',IconHeight); { Write header }
      for J := 1 to IconHeight do begin            { Write icon pattern }
        for I := 1 to IconWidth do                 { to file one row at a }
          Write(IconFile,Icon[J][I],' ');          { time }
        WriteLn(IconFile);
      end;
      Close(IconFile);
    end;
end;

procedure ReadIcon;
{ This routine reads an icon file into the icon pattern array and calls
  ShowIcon to turn on the appropriate pixels. If the header of the file
  does not match the IconWidth and IconHeight values, then the file is
  invalid and no icon will be read in. }
var
  FileName: string[80];
  Ch: char;
  IconFile: text;
  I, J, Width, Height: integer;
begin
  for J := 1 to IconHeight do begin    { Initialize the icon }
    for I := 1 to IconWidth do          { array to all blanks }
      Icon[J][I] := 0;
  end;
  WriteLn;
  WriteLn;
  WriteLn('———  ICON EDITOR ———');
  WriteLn;
  Write('Do you want to edit an existing icon? (y) ');
  Ch := ReadKey;
  if Ch <> 'n' then begin
    WriteLn;
    Write('Enter the name of the file to read the icon from: ');
    ReadLn(FileName);
    {$I-}  Assign(IconFile,FileName);
    Reset(IconFile); {$I+}
    if not (IOResult = 0) then begin
      CloseGraph;
      WriteLn('Cannot open file.');
      Halt(1);
    end;
    { Read the first line of the icon file. It should contain two
      numbers that are equal to IconWidth and IconHeight. }
    Readln(IconFile,Width,Height);
    if (Width <> IconWidth) or (Height <> IconHeight) then begin
      WriteLn('Incompatible icon file.');
```

```pascal
      Halt(1);
    end
    else begin
      for J := 1 to IconHeight do
        for I := 1 to IconWidth do
          Read(Iconfile,Icon[J][I]);
      Close(IconFile);
    end
  end
end;

procedure InitGraphics;
const
  GDriver: integer = Detect;
var
  GMode, GError: integer;
  Xasp, Yasp: word;
begin
  InitGraph(GDriver,GMode,'\tp\bgi');
  GError := GraphResult;
  if GError < 0 then begin
    WriteLn('Initialization error: GError= ',GraphErrorMsg(GError));
    Halt(1);
  end;
  GetAspectRatio(Xasp,Yasp);
  Aspect := Round(Yasp / Xasp);
end;

procedure ShowIcon;
{ Show the icon pattern that is in the icon array }
var
  X, Y: integer;
begin
  for Y := 1 to IconHeight do
    for X := 1 to IconWidth do
      if Icon[Y][X] = 1 then begin        { Display each icon bit in }
        PutImage(BigIconLeft+Aspect*((X-1)*(BigBitSize+NormWidth))+1,
        BigIconTop+(Y-1)*(BigBitSize+NormWidth)+1,BigBit^,XorPut);
        ToggleIconsBit(X,Y);               { the big and small icons }
      end
end;

begin
  ReadIcon;                 { If user wants an icon file to }
  InitGraphics;             { be read, read it, otherwise }
  Mouse.Init;               { simply initialize the screen }
  T := Mouse.Setup;         { with an empty big icon pattern }
  DrawEnlargedIcon;
  ShowIcon;                 { Draw the icon to start with }
  { When using the mouse, first turn it off before writing anything
    to the screen }
  Mouse.Hide;
  OutTextXY(BigIconLeft,10,'Press Esc when finished ...');
```

```
    OutTextXY(BigIconLeft,BigIconTop-20,'Enlarged Icon');
    OutTextXY(IconLeft,BigIconTop-20,'Actual Icon');
    Mouse.Show;                  { Redraws mouse to the screen }
    C := Mouse.WaitForInput(LeftButton); { Get input from mouse/keyboard }
    while C <> 27 do begin     { if input is Esc, quit program }
      if C < 0 then begin      { if input is less than zero then a mouse }
        Mouse.GetCoords(X,Y);  { button has been pressed; get current }
        ToggleBigBit(X,Y);     { coordinates and toggle big bit }
      end;
      C := Mouse.WaitForInput(LeftButton);
    end;                         { Loop until user types Esc }
    Mouse.Hide;                  { Turn mouse off and then get out }
    CloseGraph;                  { of graphics mode to make user }
                                 { input easier }
    Write('Do you want to save this icon to a file? (y) ');
    Ch := ReadKey;
    if Ch <> 'n' then            { Save the icon to a file if the }
      SaveIcon;                  { user types anything except 'n' }
  end.
```

9

Pop-Up Windows in Graphics

This chapter presents another useful feature often found in interactive graphics environments—pop-up windows. Like the icons we explored in Chapter 8, pop-up windows have become popular over the past several years. They are attractive because they can be used to tile messages, create pull-down menus, and enhance other forms of program input/output.

Our goal in this chapter is to develop a pop-up window package that we can use in any of the graphics modes supported by the BGI. This window unit, which we'll call GPOPPAC.PAS (see Listing 9.1), allows us to pop up and remove windows in graphics mode with two simple commands. The window tools that we develop here will be used with the programs in Chapters 11, 12, and 13.

The Basic Approach

With the help of the low-level BGI screen tools, pop-up windows are easy to support in Turbo Pascal. In this section we'll show you the steps involved in both creating and removing a pop-up window.

What's most unique about the window system that we'll be developing is that it is object oriented. (For a discussion of how to divide an application into objects, refer to the sidebar "How to Select an Object.") The main building block of the system is the object type **GWindows**. This object type contains its own window stack for managing how windows are displayed and removed, a set of variables for storing the data needed to process graphics windows, and a set of special-purpose methods for creating, displaying, and removing pop-up windows.

By using an object-oriented design we'll be able to keep all of our window details hidden under one roof, thereby making the window package easier to use and modify. Of course, you could argue that a Turbo Pascal **unit** can do the same job. But remember, an object type can also be extended by deriving new object types from existing ones, whereas units can't. Therefore, an OOP approach can offer more in the long term. And finally, although it's not important here, keep in mind that you can declare multiple instances of an object, but you can use only *one* instance of a unit.

Introducing the GWindows Object Type

Since the heart of our window system is the **GWindows** type, let's examine it first:

```
GWindows = object
  WStack: array [1..NumWindows] of GraphicsWindowPtr;  { Window stack }
  GWindowPtr: integer;              { Points to next free stack location }
  constructor Init;
  function GPopup(Left, Top, Right, Bottom, BorderType, BorderColor,
                  BackFill, FillColor: integer): boolean;
  function GUnpop: boolean;
  procedure UnpopAllWindows;
  procedure PaintWindow(Left, Top, Right, Bottom: integer); virtual;
  function SaveWindow(Left, Top, Right, Bottom: integer): boolean;
end;
```

The top of the **GWindows** definition includes the two variables **WStack** and **GWindowPtr** that are used to represent the window stack. The rest of the object type includes the support routines for manipulating the stack and painting pop-up windows on the screen.

The first routine listed in **GWindows** is the constructor, **Init**, which is used to initialize a windows object. It performs one important task—setting the stack pointer, **GWindowPtr**, so that it points to the bottom of the stack. The **GPopup** method comes next. It is responsible for storing information about the window on the stack and calling the **SaveWindow** method to save the screen where the pop-up window is to be displayed. To actually draw a window, **PaintWindow** is provided. The counterpart to **GPopup** is **GUnpop**, which deallocates memory for a window and removes it from the screen. And finally, to remove all the windows that are currently displayed, the **UnpopAllWindows** method is included in **GWindows**.

How to Select an Object

One important issue that comes up when programming with Turbo Pascal's OOP features involves the process of determining which program components should be represented as objects. Essentially, you want to design your code so that you can take advantage of the three key properties of OOP: *encapsulation, inheritance,* and *polymorphism.* Here are some guidelines you can follow that will help you get started designing your object-oriented applications:

1. Most traditional dynamic data structures such as linked lists, trees, queues, stacks, buffers, and so on are good candidates for objects. Why? The object structure allows you to encapsulate the operations needed to process the data structure with the data stored in the structure itself. The advantage here is that the program that uses the data structure (object) doesn't really need to know how the data structure is processed.

2. User-interface components such as windows, menus, buttons, and dialog boxes are also good candidates for objects. These types of components can really benefit from the property of inheritance. For example, you can define a window object to work in text mode and then use that object to derive a window that works in graphics mode. The base window object type could also be used to derive a menu object or an interactive button object, and so on.

3. Components used in your programs that model real-world objects or events such as gauges, graphs, charts, people, countries, and planets, should be considered as objects.

4. Hardware components such as the mouse, keyboard, and the screen also make useful objects. When working with these types of objects you might want to back up a level and define a general input and output device object and then use it to define more specific I/O objects to support the mouse, keyboard, and screen.

5. There are situations where the code that is usually placed in your main program can itself be represented as an object.

6. There are also situations where algorithms can be represented as objects. For example, you could create a search object to encapsulate different search algorithms or a compression object to encapsulate compression algorithms. You could even represent a general parser as an object and derive different parsers from the general parser object to handle different languages.

Creating Pop-Up Windows

The process of creating a pop-up window is outlined in Figure 9.1. As shown in the figure, the basic idea is to save the region of the screen that is to be overlayed by the pop-up window as well as any screen and drawing parameters that might be changed. Later this information can be used to restore the screen to its state before the pop-up window was created. We'll save this information on a stack so that we can build up layers of pop-up windows.

Unfortunately, the stack approach does limit access to the windows. That is, the windows will have to be removed in the reverse order from which they were created. Therefore, we won't be able to arbitrarily bring a window that is covered by several other windows to the front of the screen. Actually, this feature can be added, but to keep the code simple it is left out. To remove a pop-up window from the screen, all we need do is perform two steps.

1. Overwrite the pop-up window with the stored image of the screen by popping it from the stack.

2. Restore the screen parameters that were saved on the stack.

After this process, the screen will appear as if the pop-up window never existed.

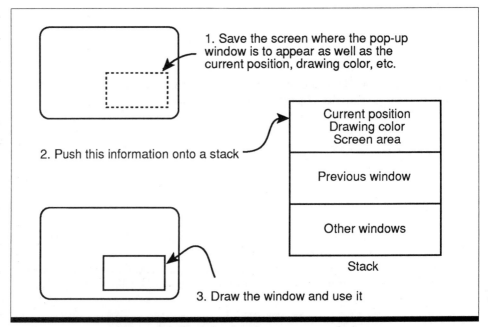

Figure 9.1. Steps in creating a pop-up window

We'll save and restore the screen image using the BGI's **GetImage** and **PutImage** routines. Since these procedures work in all graphics modes supported by the BGI, our pop-up windows will also. The screen parameters that we'll save include such attributes as the current drawing position and the drawing colors. We need to save these attributes because the pop-up windows may change them.

Working with a Stack

The main data structure that we'll be using to maintain the pop-up windows is a stack. In order to keep things simple, our stack is implemented as a single-dimensioned array, as shown in Figure 9.2, where each element in the array stores the information discussed earlier for a single pop-up window. Note that the stack pointer is essentially the index of the array and normally points to the next available location on the stack. It is incremented by one each time a new window is pushed on the stack. Therefore, if there are four items on the stack, the stack pointer will point to the fifth element (the array starts at index 1).

Each element points to a record of type **GraphicsWindow**, which is used to save the viewport settings, the current position, the drawing parameters, and the region of the screen that is below the window. This record is defined in GPOPPAC.PAS as:

```
GraphicsWindowPtr = ^GraphicsWindow;
GraphicsWindow = record              { Record to save graphics settings }
  VLeft,VTop,VRight,VBottom: integer; { Parent window boundaries }
  Cpx,Cpy: integer;                  { Current position in parent window }
  SaveArea1, SaveArea2: pointer;     { Pointers to the saved region }
  DrawColor: word;                   { Current drawing color }
  Bt,Bc,Bft,Bfc: word;               { Border type and color. Back- }
end;                                 { ground type and color. }
```

Each record in the stack is used to save any of the things that may be changed when a window is popped up. These attributes are then used to restore the screen settings to their original states when the pop-up window is removed from the screen. Beginning at the top of the record, **VLeft, VTop, VRight,** and **VBottom** save the current viewport boundaries at the time the pop-up window is created. Similarly, **Cpx** and **Cpy** save the coordinate of the current position. The **SaveArea1** and **SaveArea2** variables are pointers to the screen area to be saved. The memory storage for saving the screen is allocated just before the window is written. In addition, the current drawing color is saved in the field **DrawColor**. Finally, the window's border style, fill settings, and colors are stored in the variables **Bt, Bc, Bft,** and **Bfc**.

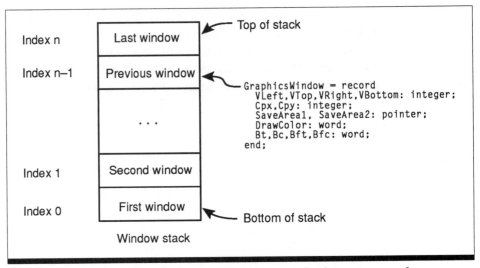

Figure 9.2. The window stack is an array of pointers to records

Recall that our stack, which is an array of pointers to records of type **GraphicsWindow**, is defined in the **GWindows** object type as:

```
WStack: array [1..NumWindows] of GraphicsWindowPtr;  { Window stack }
```

We'll wait to allocate space for these records until we need them. In this manner we won't be wasting memory that is never used. Also, note that we have declared a stack large enough to hold 10 records (**NumWindows** is a constant set to 10). This means that we'll only be able to have 10 pop-up windows at a time. For most applications, this should be more than enough. If you develop an application program that needs more windows open at once, then you should increase this number appropriately.

The stack pointer, **GWindowPtr**, is an index into the **WStack** array. Remember, **GWindowPtr** is also defined in the **GWindows** object type. Figure 9.3 shows how the stack changes as a new window is added to the screen.

Initializing the Windows Package

Like many of the other tools in this book, we need an initialization routine before using any of the pop-up window routines. As we've seen, the window initialization routine in **GWindows** is the constructor **Init**. It is responsible for initializing the stack pointer to the first element of the stack array as:

```
GWindowPtr := 1;
```

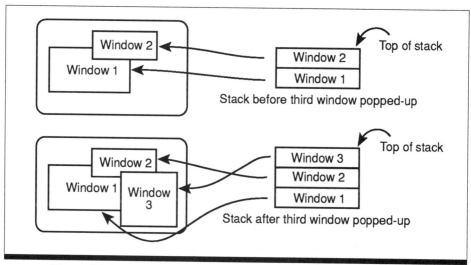

Figure 9.3. The stack changes when a window is added to the screen

Remember, an additional purpose of the **GWindows** constructor is to initialize the internal state of each **GWindows** object. Its constructor must be called before using any of its other methods.

The Pop-Up Routine

Now let's take a look at the method **GPopup** that we'll use to pop up a window. It is declared in the unit GPOPPAC.PAS as:

```
function GPopup(Left, Top, Right, Bottom, BorderType,
            BorderColor, BackFill, FillColor: integer): boolean;
```

As you can see, **GPopup** takes a hefty eight parameters. The first four specify two opposing corners of the pop-up window and must be in full-screen coordinates, not the coordinates of the current window. The other four parameters define the graphics parameters to be used in the pop-up window. These are shown in Table 9.1.

Finally, the **GPopup** method returns True if the window is successfully created; otherwise, it returns False indicating a failure in popping up the window.

Now let's see how to pop up a window with **GPopup** that stretches from the top left of the screen to its middle, has a solid border, and a solid fill pattern. Assuming we have declared a **GWindows** object called **WinObj**, you can use the line:

```
WinObj.GPopup(0,0,GetMaxX div 2,GetMaxY div 2,SolidLn,White,
            SolidFill,White);
```

Table 9.1. Drawing parameters used by GPopup

Parameter	Description
BorderType	Defines the line style used to draw the border of the pop-up window
BorderColor	Sets the drawing color to be used to draw the border
BackFill	Defines the fill pattern used to fill the pop-up window
FillColor	Sets the color to be used by the fill pattern

A Closer Look at GPopup

Now that we have a functional description of the pop-up window routine, let's take a closer look at how it works. In this section, we'll be examining portions of the **GPopup** method, but for a complete listing of the routine refer to the GPOPPAC.PAS source code (Listing 9.1).

The first thing that is done in **GPopup** is to test whether the stack is full. Since we are using an array to implement the stack, this is simply a matter of testing whether or not the stack pointer, **GWindowPtr**, has reached the end of the array **WStack**. If it has, then **GPopup** returns False indicating that it cannot pop up the window. Remember that the stack pointer normally points to the next available location in the stack; therefore, the test for whether or not the stack is full is:

```
if GWindowPtr > NumWindows then
  GPopup := False                    { Stack is full }
```

Once we know that there is enough room on the stack for another window, we must allocate space for one of the **GraphicsWindow** records used to hold the current state of the screen. This is accomplished by the lines:

```
GetMem(WStack[GWindowPtr],Sizeof(GraphicsWindow));
if WStack[GWindowPtr] = Nil then begin
  GPopup := False;            { Out of memory }
  Exit;
end;
```

The next step in the process is to save the viewport and drawing parameters, because these may be changed when we pop up the window. This is done in the lines immediately following the allocation of the **GraphicsWindow** record.

Next we'll save the region of the screen that is to be overwritten by the pop-up window by calling the method **SaveWindow** (discussed in the next section). However, first the viewport settings are set to the full screen since our pop-up window coordinates are given relative to the full screen and not the current viewport. This allows us to specify locations for pop-up windows anywhere on the screen, no matter what view settings are currently active. The **if** statement in **GPopup** makes the call to **SaveWindow** to save the region of the screen to be overwritten. If **SaveWindow** returns False, then the operation has failed so the pop-up window should not be created. If this is the case, the viewport settings must be restored (because they were changed before the call to **SaveWindow**) and the **GraphicsWindow** record that was allocated must be freed. Once these are done the **GPopup** routine reports a failure by returning False. The code that performs these operations is:

```
if not SaveWindow(Left,Top,Right,Bottom) then begin
  { Save screen failed, restore viewport settings and current position }
  SetViewPort(OldView.X1,OldView.Y1,OldView.X2,OldView.Y2,True);
  MoveTo(OldX,OldY);
  FreeMem(WStack[GWindowPtr],Sizeof(WStack[GWindowPtr]));
  GPopup := False;              { Return failure flag }
end
```

In a short while, we'll see what happens if **GPopup** succeeds, but first let's take a close look at what the **SaveWindow** routine does.

Saving the Screen

The **SaveWindow** method is called to save the region of the screen that is to be overwritten by the pop-up window. We'll use **GetImage** to capture a copy of this screen image. Actually, we'll divide the screen region to be copied into two equal sections and use *two* calls to **GetImage**—one for each region. These regions will be pointed to by the fields **SaveArea1** and **SaveArea2**. We'll save the screen region in two parts because in some high-resolution modes, it may require too much memory (more than 64K) to save a screen image if we use only a single call to **GetImage**.

Of course, before we call **GetImage** we must allocate memory to hold the screen images. This is done using the following statements in **SaveWindow**:

```
HalfPoint := (Top + Bottom) div 2;
Size := ImageSize(Left,Top,Right,HalfPoint);
GetMem(WStack[GWindowPtr]^.SaveArea1,Size);
Size := ImageSize(Left,HalfPoint+1,Right,Bottom);
```

```
GetMem(WStack[GWindowPtr]^.SaveArea2,Size);
if (WStack[GWindowPtr]^.SaveArea1 = Nil) or
   (WStack[GWindowPtr]^.SaveArea2 = Nil) then
  SaveWindow := False    { Not enough memory to save screen }
```

There is the possibility that the memory allocation will fail. Normally, Turbo Pascal would abruptly abort the program if this were to happen. But since our programs are running in graphics mode, we don't want this to occur. We at least want to restore the screen to its original mode before exiting. In order to do this, we must redirect Turbo Pascal's built-in heap error handling function to use a customized version. This special function, which we've called **HeapFunc** and defined in GPOPPAC.PAS, simply returns a 1. However, the value of 1 has a special meaning. It signals Turbo Pascal that it should return **Nil** whenever a memory allocation failure occurs, rather than abort the program as it normally does. By doing this, we can trap for **Nil** pointers and handle the memory failure more gracefully. Our custom function is installed using the following statement located in **GPopPac**'s initialization section:

```
HeapError := @HeapFunc;
```

It redirects Turbo Pascal's **HeapError** function to our custom routine. Note that programs that use GPOPPAC.PAS will now have this new feature.

In terms of the code previously listed, if **GetMem** fails, **SaveArea1** or **SaveArea2** will be **Nil** and **SaveWindow** will return immediately with a value of False. It will be up to the application program to handle the error. Otherwise, the routine continues and makes two calls to **GetImage** to save the screen and then returns a True value indicating that **SaveWindow** was successful.

```
GetImage(Left,Top,Right,HalfPoint,WStack[GWindowPtr]^.SaveArea1^);
GetImage(Left,HalfPoint+1,Right,Bottom,WStack[GWindowPtr]^.SaveArea2^);
SaveWindow := True;    { Return a success flag }
```

Generally, the pop-up window routine will fail if you try to save a window that is too large. The maximum area that it can handle is 64k in size. This may seem like a lot of memory, but the higher-resolution modes on the EGA and VGA can easily surpass this. As a rule, as long as you do not allocate windows that are more than about two-thirds the size of the screen you should be okay.

Creating the Pop-Up Window

Now let's return to our discussion of the **GPopup** routine. We left it at the point where it had just made a call to **SaveWindow** to save the screen image. Next, the drawing parameters that are used to draw the pop-up window are temporarily saved on the stack. Then the pop-up window is drawn by a call to the **PaintWindow** method. It in turn calls **Bar3D** to draw most of the window rather than **Bar** or **Rectangle** because it supports both line styles for its border as well as the full range of fill patterns. As before, we use a depth of zero for **Bar3D** so that it draws a rectangular region.

There are two basic window styles supported. One draws a three-dimensional window where the pop-up window looks as if it is in relief. This window style is selected when the border type, **Bt**, is set to **ThreeD**. It appears to best advantage in an EGA or VGA mode. The other window style is drawn with a single border and filled interior. It is selected as long as **Bt** is not set to **ThreeD** (a value of 10). Instead, **Bt** can be set to one of the line styles provided in the BGI. This line style is then used to draw the window's border.

Note that **PaintWindow** is defined as a virtual method. We did this because we wanted to make it easy for you to override it. Currently, **PaintWindow** supports two types of windows: those with simple borders, and three-dimensional-looking windows. Since **PaintWindow** is virtual, you can readily derive a new object type derived from **GWindows** that overrides **PaintWindow** to provide a customized window style.

After a window is drawn, the current state of the drawing parameters that were previously saved in temporary variables are copied into the current **WStack** record. In addition, the fill style, line style, and drawing color are restored to their values before the window was drawn. Then the stack pointer is incremented so that it points to the next location on the stack and **GPopup** returns True as a success flag.

Removing a Pop-Up Window

Removing a pop-up window from the screen is handled by the method **GUnpop**. It is responsible for restoring the original screen image that is overwritten by the pop-up window and for resetting the various screen parameters.

The **GUnpop** method does not take any parameters and will only remove an element from the stack if one exists. If it succeeds in removing a pop-up window it returns True. Otherwise, if the stack is empty, meaning there aren't any windows left to remove, **GUnpop** takes no action and returns False.

The next step in the removal of the pop-up window is to decrement the stack pointer. Since it normally points to the next free location on the stack, decrementing the stack pointer forces it to the topmost window displayed. The pointer to the record for this window is then copied into **W**, a temporary pointer that will be used to refer to the record.

Now we have access to the window record that contains the state of the screen before the window was created. First, we'll restore the screen image by two calls to **PutImage** using **CopyPut**. (Remember we are saving the screen in *two* buffers, **SaveArea1** and **SaveArea2**.)

```
PutImage(0,0,W^.SaveArea1^,CopyPut);
PutImage(0,(CurrView.Y2-CurrView.Y1) div 2 + 1,W^.SaveArea2^,CopyPut);
```

Note that the top-left coordinate of the current window is used as the location to place the **SaveArea1** image. The other screen image, **SaveArea2,** is placed half-way down the current window, since it saved the lower portion of the screen where the pop-up window was placed.

The next several lines of **GUnpop** reset the viewport, current position, and various drawing parameters before the pop-up window was created. Finally, the memory for the screen images and the window structure that were allocated in **GPopup** and **SaveWindow** are freed and **GUnpop** returns True indicating that the removal of the pop-up window was successful.

Removing All Windows

Sometimes it is handy to remove all the pop-up windows at once. For this purpose the **UnpopAllWindows** method is included in **GWindows**. It contains the single line:

```
while GWindowPtr > 1 do T := GUnpop;
```

This will loop until **GUnpop** has removed all of the pop-up windows from the screen at which time it will return False.

Using the Windows Package

Now that we have dispensed with all of the preliminaries, let's go over the details of how the windows package can be used in an application. It's a very simple process. First, place the **GPopPac** unit in the list of units being used by your program. You'll also need to declare a window object of type **GWindows** in your application that you'll use to access the window package's features. Remember, as with all objects that have virtual methods (as **GWindows** does), you must call its constructor **Init** before calling any of the object's methods. Whenever you want to pop up a window, call **GPopup** as discussed earlier in the chapter. Remember that the pop-up window coordinates are specified relative to the whole screen and not to the current viewport. This gives you the greatest control over the placement of the pop-up window. To remove the window, make a call to **GUnpop**. You must use one call to **GUnpop** for every window that you have created.

Also, keep in mind that the pop-up windows are maintained on a stack. Therefore, when you call **GUnpop** the most recent window will always be unpopped first.

Once a pop-up window is created, the viewport settings will be changed to reflect the new window. As Figure 9.4 illustrates, the top-left corner of the new pop-up window will correspond to location (0,0), the current position will be set to this point, and clipping will be set on.

Test Program

Before we end this chapter, let's present a test program that will put our graphics window package through its paces. It will also demonstrate how to put the pop-up windows package to work. The test program, POPTEST.PAS (see Listing 9.2), creates three pop-up windows (as shown in Figure 9.5) and then removes them from the screen. After each window is displayed or removed you must press a key in order to proceed with the program.

As written, the program uses the default mode available on your video adapter. If you want to try a specific graphics mode, change the values assigned to **GDriver** and **GMode**. In addition, note that the window object used is called **Win** and that all the pop-up routines are accessed through it.

Finally, check how the program accesses the coordinates in each of the windows. For instance, in the first pop-up window a circle is drawn at its center. In order to determine the center point of the window, **GetViewSettings** must be called and then the center of the window is calculated from the view settings. This simply

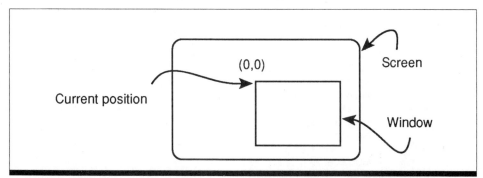

Figure 9.4. The location of the current position after a window is popped up

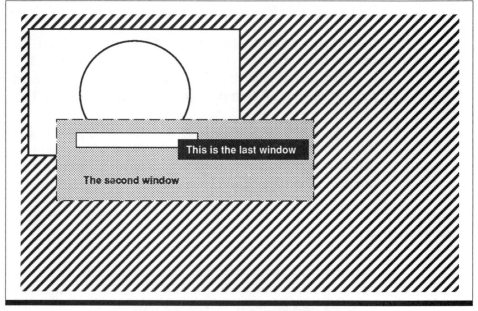

Figure 9.5. Output of POPTEST.PAS

demonstrates that the coordinates in the windows are accessed relative to the current pop-up window.

```
{ The view settings are now equal to the pop-up window boundaries }
GetViewSettings(View);
{ Draw a circle in the window }
Circle((View.X2-View.X1) div 2,(View.Y2-View.Y1) div 2,
     (View.X1+View.X2) div 4);
```

• Listing 9.1. GPOPPAC.PAS

```
unit GPopPac;
{$R+}
{ A set of utilities for pop-up windows in graphics mode. The routines use
  Turbo Pascal's BGI tools to simplify the code. Most of the graphics
  settings are saved before a new window is put up and they are restored
  when the window is closed. This window data is saved on a stack. The
  stack is implemented as an array in order to simplify things. Note
  that an object is used to encapsulate the features of the window
  package. }

interface
uses
 Graph;
```

```
const
  NumWindows = 10;                     { Allow for 10 pop-up windows }
  ThreeD = 10;                         { Selects three-dimensional windows }
type
GraphicsWindow = record               { Record to save graphics settings }
  VLeft,VTop,VRight,VBottom: integer; { Parent window boundaries }
  Cpx,Cpy: integer;                   { Current position in parent window }
  SaveArea1, SaveArea2: pointer;      { Pointers to the saved region }
  DrawColor: word;                    { Current drawing color }
  Bt,Bc,Bft,Bfc: word;                { Border type and color. Back- }
end;                                  { ground type and color. }

GraphicsWindowPtr = ^GraphicsWindow;
GWindows = object
  WStack: array [1..NumWindows] of GraphicsWindowPtr;  { Window stack }
  GWindowPtr: integer;                { Points to next free stack location }
  constructor Init;
  function GPopup(Left, Top, Right, Bottom, BorderType, BorderColor,
               BackFill, FillColor: integer): boolean;
  function GUnpop: boolean;
  procedure UnpopAllWindows;
  procedure PaintWindow(Left, Top, Right, Bottom: integer); virtual;
  function SaveWindow(Left, Top, Right, Bottom: integer): boolean;
end;

implementation
{$F+}      { Force a far call }
function HeapFunc(Size: word): integer;
{ Function to modify the heap error handler so that New and GetMem
  return Nil pointers when they fail rather than exiting the program. }
begin
  HeapFunc := 1;
end;
{$F-}

constructor GWindows.Init;
{ The constructor initializes the window stack pointer }
begin
  GWindowPtr := 1;
end;

function GWindows.SaveWindow(Left, Top, Right, Bottom: integer): boolean;
{ Pushes the graphics window onto the window stack. This is an internal
  routine that saves the area where the window is supposed to appear. This
  routine will return True if successful and False if not. The latter case
  may occur if there isn't enough memory to save the screen area or the
  stack is full. Note that the saved region is divided into two sections
  so that you can save large-screen regions in high-resolution modes. }
var
  Size: word;
  HalfPoint: integer;
begin
  { Divide the screen region to be saved into two parts }
```

```
          HalfPoint := (Top + Bottom) div 2;
          Size := ImageSize(Left,Top,Right,HalfPoint);
          GetMem(WStack[GWindowPtr]^.SaveArea1,Size);
          Size := ImageSize(Left,HalfPoint+1,Right,Bottom);
          GetMem(WStack[GWindowPtr]^.SaveArea2,Size);
          if (WStack[GWindowPtr]^.SaveArea1 = Nil) or
            (WStack[GWindowPtr]^.SaveArea2 = Nil) then
            SaveWindow := False     { Not enough memory to save screen }
          else begin
            { Save the screen image where the window is to appear. }
            GetImage(Left,Top,Right,HalfPoint,WStack[GWindowPtr]^.SaveArea1^);
            GetImage(Left,HalfPoint+1,Right,Bottom,WStack[GWindowPtr]^.SaveArea2^);
            SaveWindow := True;     { Return a success flag }
          end
        end;

      function GWindows.GPopup(Left, Top, Right, Bottom, BorderType,
                  BorderColor, BackFill, FillColor: integer): boolean;
      { Call this function to pop up a window in graphics mode. It returns
        True if successful and False if not. The routine may not be able to
        pop up a window if it requires too much memory. This may occur
        in some high-resolution modes. }
      var
        OldView: ViewPortType;
        OldX, OldY, SaveColor: integer;
        SaveLine: LineSettingsType;
        SaveFill: FillSettingsType;
      begin
        if GWindowPtr > NumWindows then
          GPopup := False               { Stack is full }
        else begin
          { Allocate a new window record on the stack }
          GetMem(WStack[GWindowPtr],Sizeof(GraphicsWindow));
          if WStack[GWindowPtr] = Nil then begin
            GPopup := False;            { Out of memory }
            Exit;
          end;
          GetViewSettings(OldView);   { Save the view settings and current }
          OldX := GetX;               { position so we can temporarily switch }
          OldY := GetY;               { viewport to the full screen }
          SetViewPort(0,0,GetMaxX,GetMaxY,True);
          { Save current drawing parameters before drawing window. This does not
            support user-defined line styles or user-defined fill patterns. }
          GetLineSettings(SaveLine);
          SaveColor := GetColor;
          GetFillSettings(SaveFill);
          if not SaveWindow(Left,Top,Right,Bottom) then begin
            { Save screen failed, restore viewport settings and current
              position }
            SetViewPort(OldView.X1,OldView.Y1,OldView.X2,OldView.Y2,True);
            MoveTo(OldX,OldY);
            FreeMem(WStack[GWindowPtr],Sizeof(WStack[GWindowPtr]));
```

```
      GPopup := False;              { Return failure flag }
    end
  else begin
    WStack[GWindowPtr]^.Bc := BorderColor;
    WStack[GWindowPtr]^.Bt := BorderType;
    WStack[GWindowPtr]^.Bft := BackFill;
    WStack[GWindowPtr]^.Bfc := FillColor;
    PaintWindow(Left,Top,Right,Bottom);
    SetViewPort(Left,Top,Right,Bottom,True);  { Set viewport to window }
    { Save the current state of all settings on the stack }
    WStack[GWindowPtr]^.VLeft := OldView.X1;
    WStack[GWindowPtr]^.VTop := OldView.Y1;
    WStack[GWindowPtr]^.VRight := OldView.X2;
    WStack[GWindowPtr]^.VBottom := OldView.Y2;
    WStack[GWindowPtr]^.Cpx := OldX;
    WStack[GWindowPtr]^.Cpy := OldY;
    WStack[GWindowPtr]^.DrawColor := SaveColor;
    { Restore drawing parameters }
    SetLineStyle(SaveLine.LineStyle,SaveLine.Pattern,SaveLine.Thickness);
    SetColor(SaveColor);
    SetFillStyle(SaveFill.Pattern,SaveFill.Color);
    Inc(GWindowPtr);                          { Increment the stack pointer }
    GPopup := True;                           { Return success flag }
  end
 end
end;

procedure GWindows.PaintWindow(Left, Top, Right, Bottom: integer);
{ Draw the window using the styles specified. This method is virtual
  so that you can override it to define your own window styles. }
var
  I: integer;
begin
  if WStack[GWindowPtr]^.Bt = ThreeD then begin
    { Bottom and left edge are dark gray. Top and left sides
      are drawn white. }
    for I := 0 to 2 do begin
      SetColor(EgaDarkgray);
      Line(Right-I,Top+I,Right-I,Bottom-I);
      Line(Left+I,Bottom-I,Right-I,Bottom-I);
      { Left and top are white }
      SetColor(EgaWhite);
      Line(Left+I,Top+I,Right-I,Top+I);
      Line(Left+I,Top+I,Left+I,Bottom-I);
    end;
    SetColor(WStack[GWindowPtr]^.Bfc);
    SetLineStyle(SolidLn,0,NormWidth);
    { Fill in the window }
    SetFillStyle(WStack[GWindowPtr]^.Bft,WStack[GWindowPtr]^.Bfc);
    Bar3d(Left+3,Top+3,Right-3,Bottom-3,0,False);
  end
  else begin
```

```
      { Set the graphics parameters for the pop-up window to be displayed.
        Then create the window. Use Bar3d so that there will be a border. }
      SetColor(WStack[GWindowPtr]^.Bc);
      SetLineStyle(WStack[GWindowPtr]^.Bt,0,NormWidth);
      SetFillStyle(WStack[GWindowPtr]^.Bft,WStack[GWindowPtr]^.Bfc);
      Bar3d(Left,Top,Right,Bottom,0,False);
    end;
end;

function GWindows.GUnpop: boolean;
{ Remove the current graphics window from the screen }
var
  W: GraphicsWindowPtr;
  CurrView: ViewPortType;
begin
  if GWindowPtr > 1 then begin        { Make sure the stack is not empty }
    Dec(GWindowPtr);                  { Access the most recent window }
    W := WStack[GWindowPtr];          { Get the topmost window }
    { Restore the screen image }
    GetViewSettings(CurrView);
    PutImage(0,0,W^.SaveArea1^,CopyPut);
    PutImage(0,(CurrView.Y2-CurrView.Y1) div 2 + 1,W^.SaveArea2^,CopyPut);
    { Restore the view settings to those before the window was created }
    SetViewPort(W^.VLeft,W^.VTop,W^.VRight,W^.VBottom,True);
    MoveTo(W^.Cpx,W^.Cpy);
    SetColor(W^.DrawColor);
    { Free stack structure and screen }
    FreeMem(W^.SaveArea1,Sizeof(W^.SaveArea1));
    FreeMem(W^.SaveArea2,Sizeof(W^.SaveArea2));
    FreeMem(W,Sizeof(W));
    GUnpop := True;
  end
  else GUnpop := False;
end;

procedure GWindows.UnpopAllWindows;
{ Unpop all windows that currently exist. This is a handy routine to
  clean up the screen in certain situations. }
var
  T: boolean;
begin
  while GWindowPtr > 1 do T := GUnpop;
end;

begin
{ Modify the heap error handler so that it returns Nil rather than
  aborting the program when a memory allocation error occurs. }
  HeapError := @HeapFunc;
end.
```

• Listing 9.2. POPTEST.PAS

```
program PopTest;
{ Tests the graphics pop-up window routines. This program displays three
  overlapping pop-up windows on a patterned background. The windows are
  drawn one at a time and then removed one at a time. Press any key to
  step through the various phases of this demo. This program demonstrates
  how the screen is saved and the use of the screen coordinates in a
  pop-up window. }
uses
  Graph, Crt, GPopPac;
const
  GDriver: integer = Detect;    { Use a graphics mode with several colors }
  Message: string[25] = ' This is the last window ';
var
  GMode: integer;
  View: ViewPortType;
  HalfWidth, Height: integer;
  Ch: char;
  Win: GWindows;
  T: boolean;

procedure WindowError;
begin
  CloseGraph;
  WriteLn('Failed to open window');
  Halt(1);
end;

begin
  InitGraph(GDriver,GMode,'\tp\bgi');
  Win.Init;                         { Initialize the window system }
  SetFillStyle(SlashFill,Blue);     { Draw a background that }
  SetLineStyle(DashedLn,0,White);   { covers the whole screen }
  Bar(0,0,GetMaxX,GetMaxY);
  { Pop up a window in the top-left portion of the screen. Use a solid
    line border in the maximum color and fill the pop-up window with
    color 0. }
  if not Win.GPopup(10,10,GetMaxX div 2,100,SolidLn,
                GetMaxColor,SolidFill,0) then
    WindowError;
  { The view settings are now equal to the pop-up window boundaries }
  GetViewSettings(View);
  { Draw a circle in the window }
  Circle((View.X2-View.X1) div 2,(View.Y2-View.Y1) div 2,
    (View.X1+View.X2) div 4);
  Ch := ReadKey;                            { Wait until a key is pressed }
  { Draw a second pop-up window with a dashed border drawn with
    color 1 and the window's background set to color 2 }
  if not Win.GPopup(50,75,GetMaxX*2 div 3,GetMaxY*2 div 3,ThreeD,1,
                HatchFill,EgaLightGray) then
    WindowError;
```

```
      SetFillStyle(WideDotFill,Black);
      Bar3D(30,10,200,20,0,False);              { Draw a box in the window }
      SetColor(GetMaxColor);
      OutTextXY(40,40,'The second window');     { This text might clip }
      Ch := ReadKey;                            { Wait for a key to be pressed }
      { The last pop-up window displays a message at the center of the screen.
        This type of pop-up window is good for displaying error messages in
        graphics mode. }
      HalfWidth := TextWidth(Message) div 2;    { Calculate size of the }
      Height := TextHeight(Message);            { window based on string }
      if not Win.GPopup(GetMaxX div 2-HalfWidth,GetMaxY div 2-Height,
        GetMaxX div 2+HalfWidth,GetMaxY div 2+Height,SolidLn,1,SolidFill,2)
        then WindowError;
      SetColor(0);
      SetTextJustify(CenterText,CenterText);    { Center message and }
      GetViewSettings(View);                    { Write it to the screen }
      OutTextXY((View.X2-View.X1) div 2,(View.Y2-View.Y1) div 2,Message);
      Ch := ReadKey;                            { Wait for a key to be pressed }
      T := Win.GUnpop;                          { Remove the last window }
      Ch := ReadKey;                            { Wait until a key is pressed }
      T := Win.GUnpop;                          { Remove the middle window }
      Ch := ReadKey;                            { Wait until a key is pressed }
      T := Win.GUnpop;                          { Remove the first window }
      CloseGraph;                               { Exit graphics mode }
    end.
```

10

Interactive Drawing Tools

It's simple enough to draw figures using the BGI by placing drawing functions in a program. However, in a paint or CAD application we need to *interactively* draw figures using the mouse or keyboard. As you've seen, the BGI does not include interactive drawing routines so we must create our own. Therefore, in this chapter we'll take the time to construct a set of object types that provide rubber-banding lines, a spray painting effect, polygon drawing, text entry, and more.

These objects will become the primary drawing tools we'll use in the paint and CAD programs in Chapters 11 and 12. However, you'll find that these interactive drawing tools are general enough to be useful in other interactive graphics applications that you create on your own.

We'll accomplish this flexibility by building the tools using the resources of object-oriented programming. In particular, each drawing tool will be implemented as a separate object type. As the details of the various object types unfold, you'll see how OOP can be a powerful means of sharing code and a great way of leaving the door open for extending a toolkit—which is exactly what we'll be doing in the CAD program in Chapter 12.

An Interactive Graphics Package

The interactive drawing package we'll develop includes 13 drawing tools, where each tool is implemented as a separate object (see Table 10.1). All of the tools share a common ancestor—the **DrawingTool** object type. The object hierarchy is shown in Figure 10.1.

Table 10.1. Interactive drawing objects included in DRAW.PAS

Object type	Description
DrawingTool	Base type for all interactive drawing objects
PencilTool	Supports freehand drawing
EraserTool	Erases a portion of the screen
SpraycanTool	Provides a spray painting effect
LineTool	Draws lines interactively
RectangleTool	Draws rectangles interactively
FillRectangleTool	Draws filled rectangles interactively
PolygonTool	Draws polygons interactively
FillPolygonTool	Allows user to draw filled polygons
CircleTool	Draws circles interactively
EllipseTool	Draws ellipses interactively
ArcTool	Draws arcs interactively
TextTool	Supports text entry
ClearWindowTool	Clears the drawing window

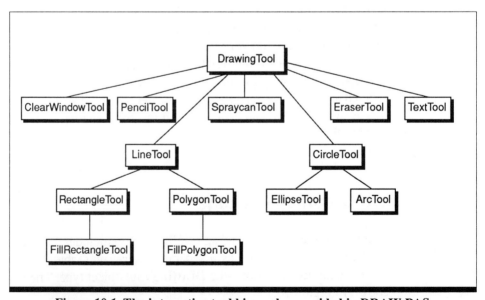

Figure 10.1. The interactive tool hierarchy provided in DRAW.PAS

At first, this number of object types may seem a bit overwhelming. However, as you explore the code you'll see that most of these objects are rather small and build upon others in simple, manageable steps.

The **DrawingTool** type outlines the basic flow of the user interaction and provides a common programming interface for the drawing routines. Since all of the tools are built from the same *base type*, **DrawingTool**, we'll be able to fully take advantage of the OOP technique called *polymorphism* in our application programs. We'll see this technique in action many times in the paint and CAD programs in Chapters 11 and 12.

The source code for the drawing object types are included in the unit DRAW.PAS shown in Listing 10.1.

Drawing Conventions

Each of the interactive drawing objects adheres to several conventions. First, they assume that the mouse object types developed in Chapter 7 will be used. Since our mouse methods support both the mouse and the keyboard, the drawing methods will work with either input device. You'll find, however, that the mouse provides the best performance.

Second, there are a series of global variables that are used by the drawing tools. These variables must be defined and assigned appropriate values in your applications. A list of these variables is found in Table 10.2. You must assign values in your application program to all of the global drawing variables listed in Table 10.2 before you call any of the interactive drawing functions in DRAW.PAS.

In particular, the drawing functions restrict their output to a predefined window. Therefore, whenever one of the drawing methods is called, the current viewport is set to the drawing window and clipping is enabled. When the drawing action ends, the viewport is restored to the full screen. The boundaries of the drawing window, therefore, must be initialized in the application program by setting the four global variables **Wl**, **Wt**, **Wr**, and **Wb** to the left, top, right, and bottom sides of the drawing window desired.

In addition, there are five global variables that must be set to initialize the drawing parameters that are used by the drawing methods. The five global variables listed in Table 10.2 that follow the window size variables specify various drawing parameters. They should be set to the appropriate macro constants defined in the unit **Graph**. For example, **GlobalFillStyle** can take on values of **SolidFill**, **EmptyFill**, or any of the other acceptable fill pattern values defined in **Graph**.

Lastly, the drawing package DRAW.PAS assumes that you have defined a **KbdMouseObj** object called **Mouse** in your application. Recall that the

Table 10.2. Global variables defined in an application program using DRAW.PAS

Variable	Description
Wl	Left column of drawing window
Wt	Top of drawing window
Wr	Right side of drawing window
Wb	Bottom of drawing window
GlobalDrawColor	Defines the drawing color to be used in any of the drawing methods
GlobalFillColor	Defines the fill color to use
GlobalFillStyle	Defines the fill style to use
GlobalLineStyle	Defines the line style to use
GlobalTextStyle	Defines the text style to use
MaxX	Rightmost coordinate of screen
MaxY	Bottom-most coordinate of screen
Mouse	Mouse object used in DRAW.PAS

KbdMouseObj type is defined in the keyboard and mouse packages developed in Chapter 7 and uses the mouse if one is present or the keyboard if one isn't.

A Close Look at the DRAW.PAS Tools

Now we're ready to walk through the hierarchy of interactive drawing object types supplied in DRAW.PAS. Some of these types are similar to others, so we won't give all of them the same attention; however, we'll provide a short description of how to use each one.

The **DrawingTool** type provides the basic shell that prescribes the programming interface we'll use with the drawing tools. Here's its definition:

```
DrawingTool = object
  X, Y, OldX, OldY: integer;          { Current and last mouse positions }
  Left, Top, Right, Bottom: integer;  { Bounds of the figure }
  DrawColor: integer;                 { Color to be used in figure }
  constructor Init;
  procedure Draw; virtual;            { High-level drawing function }
  procedure PerformDraw; virtual;     { Defines user interaction }
  procedure StartDrawing; virtual;    { Sets up for drawing }
```

```
   procedure UpdateDrawing; virtual;    { Interactively draws figure }
   procedure FinishDrawing; virtual;    { Finalizes drawing }
   procedure Hide; virtual;             { Removes figure from screen }
   procedure Show; virtual;             { Displays or updates figure }
   { The following routines will be defined in the CAD program }
   procedure Display; virtual;
   procedure GetBounds(var L, T, R, B: integer); virtual;
   procedure Translate(Transx, Transy: real); virtual;
   procedure Rotate(Angle: real); virtual;
   function Dup: DrawingToolPtr; virtual;
end;
```

The **DrawingTool** object type starts with the four instance variables **X**, **Y**, **OldX**, and **OldY**, which keep track of the current and previous location of the mouse. These variables will be updated when events such as button presses occur.

Now let's step through each of the methods in **DrawingTool** to better understand how they are used. The topmost method, **Draw**, is the high-level routine that we'll call when we want to interactively draw a figure. We'll assume that this is the method called when a specific drawing function has been selected.

If you look at the code, however, you'll notice that **Draw** does very little. It merely sets the viewport coordinates and enables clipping to the size of the drawing window, calls **PerformDraw**, and then restores the viewport coordinates to the full screen. You might now be wondering whether **PerformDraw** does the actual drawing. Not quite. But it does give us a better clue as to how the user interaction is managed within **DrawingTool**. Let's take a look.

The **PerformDraw** method is built around an infinite **while** loop that waits for the user to press the left mouse button:

```
while not Mouse.ButtonPressed(LeftButton) do ;
```

Once the left button is pressed, the mouse coordinates are retrieved by a call to **Mouse.GetCoords**. These coordinates, which are saved in the instance variables **X** and **Y**, are checked against the drawing viewport to see if the user has clicked outside of the drawing window. If so, **PerformDraw** terminates via the **Exit** statement:

```
Mouse.GetCoords(X,Y);      { Get location where button was pressed }
if (X < Wl) or (Y < Wt) or (Y > Wb) or (X > Wr) then Exit;
                                          { Exit drawing }
StartDrawing;              { Set up for the drawing }
UpdateDrawing;             { Do the drawing }
FinishDrawing;             { Clean up drawing as needed }
```

Otherwise, the method continues by calling the trio of methods **StartDrawing**, **UpdateDrawing**, and **FinishDrawing**. These latter three methods are actually the ones where the drawing takes place.

Why is the drawing process split between three routines? Because we'll be deriving drawing tools from one another, we need our base type to be as flexible as possible so that we can override only those portions of the code that need to be modified. In this way we'll be able to share the greatest amount of code and have to modify only small blocks of code in our derived object types.

Let's examine each of these three new methods. The first, **StartDrawing**, is responsible for setting up any variables for the drawing process. For example, when drawing a line, **StartDrawing** will move the current position to the location where the mouse was pressed.

In a similar fashion, **FinishDrawing** performs any cleanup actions that need to be done after the figure has been drawn. For instance, it might fill the interior of a polygon after its exterior has been sketched out. The base type, however, leaves this function empty. Derived object types can override it as necessary.

The **UpdateDrawing** method, if you haven't already guessed, is the workhorse. It's where the real interaction takes place. Here's its code:

```
procedure DrawingTool.UpdateDrawing;
begin
  while not Mouse.ButtonReleased(LeftButton) do begin
    { Button must have been pressed already }
    Mouse.GetCoords(X,Y);                { Get current location of mouse }
    if (X <> OldX) or (Y <> OldY) then begin
      { Update figure only if the mouse has moved }
      Hide;                              { Remove part or all of the figure }
      Show;                              { Draw the figure }
      OldX := X;  OldY := Y;             { Update saved position of mouse }
    end;
  end;
end;
```

This routine is also built around a **while** loop, but this time the loop continues as long as the left mouse button is pressed. (Recall that the drawing process began in **PerformDraw** once the mouse button was initially pressed.) In other words, drawing a figure continues as long as the mouse button is pressed. However, to avoid unnecessary screen writing, **UpdateDrawing** proceeds with a drawing only if the mouse's position has changed. This prevents the screen from flickering when nothing really needs to be updated. This is regulated by the **if** statement that compares the mouse's most recent position with its last recorded location. The pieces are beginning to fall together.

But where is the drawing done? For this we need to turn to the **Show** and **Hide** methods, which are called in **UpdateDrawing**. These methods are used to draw and erase a figure from the drawing window.

The **Show** method is probably self-explanatory, but what about **Hide**? Remember that in interactive drawing, the user can change the size of the figure. As a result, the **Hide** function is used to erase the old figure so that **Show** can come along and repaint the figure with its new dimensions. This is where the **if** statement, shown earlier, comes in. If the location of the mouse has not changed, then the figure's size hasn't changed so we bypass **Hide** and **Show**. The instance variables **OldX** and **OldY** keep track of the last location of the mouse, and hence the last position and size of the figure. The initial values of **OldX** and **OldY** are set in **StartDrawing**, and then are updated each time through the while loop in **UpdateDrawing**.

Recall that **OldX** and **OldY** give the last location of the mouse and are initialized in **StartDrawing** and updated in **UpdateDrawing**.

Drawing with a Pencil

Now that we've pulled apart the components of the **DrawingTool** object type, let's see how the type is used to derive a specific drawing tool. We'll begin with the **PencilTool** object type, which is used to draw freehand figures like those shown in Figure 10.2.

With **PencilTool**, you can draw a continuous curve as long as the left mouse button is pressed. Whenever the mouse button is released, the drawing stops. To resume drawing, you simply hold down the left button again. To finish using the tool, you click the left mouse button outside the drawing window. Presumably, this will be to select another drawing function. We'll see how this technique works in Chapter 11 when we develop our paint program.

Deriving a tool, like **PencilTool** from **DrawingTool**, is a matter of overriding those methods where we need to replace the inherited object's routines or supplement them. We'll start at the highest level and work our way down, adding as we go. The **PencilTool** object definition, therefore, indicates which functions we have overridden to implement the pencil tool. Here's its definition:

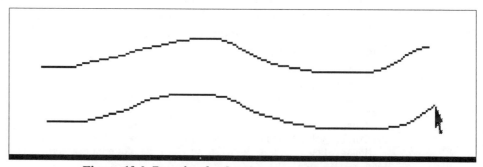

Figure 10.2. Drawing freehand curves with the PencilTool

```
PencilToolPtr = ^PencilTool;
PencilTool = object(DrawingTool)          { A curve-drawing object type }
  procedure Draw; virtual;
  procedure StartDrawing; virtual;
  procedure Show; virtual;
end;
```

The **Draw** method needs to be overridden first so that we can set the drawing color and line style to be used in the pencil drawing operation. These values must be reset to the proper global variables listed in Table 10.2 because they may have been changed by another function in the application program. We'll override **Draw** in the other object types for a similar reason. Once the drawing parameters are reset, the **Draw** method inherited from **DrawingTool** is called to proceed with the drawing:

```
procedure PencilTool.Draw;
{ Use the global drawing color for drawing with the PencilTool type }
begin
  SetColor(GlobalDrawColor);        { Switch to the global drawing color }
  DrawingTool.Draw;                 { Draw with the pencil }
end;
```

Next, **StartDrawing** is overridden to initiate the drawing action. (Recall that this method is invoked when the left mouse button has been pressed.) The freehand curves are created by drawing a line from the mouse's current location to its previous position. Therefore, as the mouse moves, the line grows. To start this process, then, **StartDrawing** calls **MoveTo** to set the current position to the location of the mouse given by the instance variables **X** and **Y**.

```
MoveTo(X-Wl,Y-Wt);
```

Note that the coordinates passed to **MoveTo** and **LineTo** are adjusted by the left and top boundaries of the drawing viewport. This must be done since **MoveTo** uses coordinates that are relative to the current viewport; the drawing window and the mouse coordinates, **X** and **Y**, are always given in full-screen coordinates.

Finally, the **Show** method is overridden to complete the line drawing by making a call to **LineTo**:

```
procedure PencilTool.Show;
{ Draw a line from the last position of the mouse to its current position }
begin
  Mouse.Hide;                       { Hide mouse before drawing }
  LineTo(X-Wl,Y-Wt);                { Draw a line from last position }
  Mouse.Show;                       { Restore the mouse cursor }
end;
```

As this code illustrates, calls to **Mouse.Hide** and **Mouse.Show** surround **LineTo** in order to prevent the mouse cursor from interfering with the screen.

Erasing

Now that we've learned how to draw figures, let's see how we can erase them. For this, we'll introduce the object type **EraserTool** which is designed to set a rectangular screen region below the mouse cursor to the background color. By holding down the left mouse button and moving the mouse around, you can erase any area of the drawing window that you'd like.

The **EraserTool** type is similar to **PencilTool** except that it draws small bars filled with the background color to the screen rather than a series of lines. In order to generate these small erasing blocks, the fill style is set to **SolidFill** and the fill and drawing colors are set to the background color. This is accomplished by overriding **Draw** as we did with **PencilTool** and inserting the following statements before the inherited **Draw** method is called:

```
SetColor(GetBkColor);                { Use the background color }
SetFillStyle(SolidFill,GetBkColor);  { to erase the screen }
```

The routine draws these small solid-filled bars wherever the mouse cursor is located while the mouse button is pressed. The pixel dimensions of the eraser bar are specified by **EraserSize**, which is a constant defined at the top of DRAW.PAS:

```
const
  EraserSize = 5;                    { Half the size of the eraser }
```

You might try making the eraser size a variable so that the user can interactively change the size of the eraser.

The erasing action then occurs in **Show** by using the BGI's **Bar** procedure:

```
Bar(X-Wl,Y-Wt,X-Wl+EraserSize,Y-Wt+EraserSize);  { Erase region }
```

Spray Painting Effect

The function **SpraycanTool** provides a simple spray painting effect by randomly setting pixels within a rectangular region to the current drawing color.

While the left mouse button is pressed, the spray painting action will occur as shown in Figure 10.3. The longer you hold the mouse in one position, the more

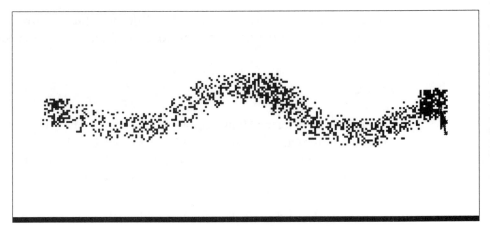

Figure 10.3. Using the SpraycanTool

that screen location will be filled in. To temporarily stop the spray painting, you release the left mouse button. To finish using the spray painting tool, you move the mouse outside the drawing viewport and click the left button.

Since the spray painting effect continually paints while the mouse button is pressed—even when the mouse is not being moved—we need to override **UpdateDrawing**. Recall that the implementation of **DrawingTool**'s **UpdateDrawing** calls **Hide** and **Show** only if the mouse has been moved.

The spray painting effect is produced by two **for** loops in the overridden method **Show**:

```
for I := 0 to 7 do                 { Randomly draw eight pixels }
  PutPixel(X-Random(SpraySize)+5-Wl,
           Y-Random(SpraySize)+5-Wt,GlobalDrawColor);
for I := 0 to 7 do                 { Randomly draw another eight pixels }
  PutPixel(X-Random(SpraySize-2)+3-Wl,
           Y-Random(SpraySize-2)+3-Wt,GlobalDrawColor);
```

Each of the **for** loops is responsible for plotting 8 pixels in a rectangular region around the mouse cursor. The first **for** loop plots pixels away from the mouse cursor while the second **for** loop plots pixels closer. Note that the particular pixel that is painted by each iteration of the **for** loops is randomly selected using the Turbo Pascal function **Random**. This distributes the pixels evenly. The size of the spray region is partly determined by the constant **SpraySize** declared in **SpraycanTool**. However, the other integer values in the two **for** loops affect the distribution and location of the spray painting as well. You may want to experiment with other spray patterns.

Drawing Lines

The **LineTool** object type is used to draw line segments. It lets you draw a single line by pointing to where the line is to begin, pressing and holding down the left mouse button, and then dragging the mouse to the desired endpoint. When the button is released, the line is frozen. However, while the button is pressed, **LineTool** continues to draw the line from the initial location of the mouse, where the button was pressed, to the mouse's current position. Therefore, as the mouse is moved around the screen, the line will shrink and stretch as needed. This procedure for drawing lines is shown in Figure 10.4. This type of line is called a *rubber-banding* line because the line segment appears to be flexible like a rubber-band. To draw more lines you just repeat this simple process.

As you might expect, **LineTool** is similar to the previously discussed functions. The first thing **LineTool** does is override **Draw** in order to set the drawing color and line style:

```
SetLineStyle(GlobalLineStyle,0,NormWidth);
SetColor(GlobalDrawColor);
```

Note that the line width is restricted to **NormWidth**. This is done to simplify the code. You may want to modify DRAW.PAS so that the line width is a variable like **GlobalLineStyle** and **GlobalDrawColor**.

An important aspect of **LineTool** is the rubber-banding line effect. The technique uses the exclusive-ORing feature provided by the BGI **SetWriteMode** procedure (Chapter 6) to allow us to draw and move a line around the screen without permanently affecting what it overwrites. Once the exclusive-OR mode is set,

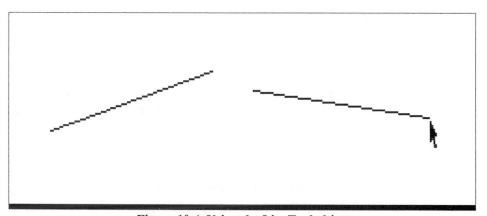

Figure 10.4. Using the LineTool object

lines can be erased from the screen by writing over them with another line. The exclusive-OR feature is turned on in **StartDrawing** after the left button is pressed by the line:

```
SetWriteMode(XorPut);
```

After this point, all lines are drawn by exclusive-ORing them to the screen. Sometimes you will see the effects of the exclusive-ORing as the line changes color as it crosses over other figures on the screen. It is restored to its normal mode in **FinishDrawing** by calling **SetWriteMode** with the argument **CopyPut**.

When you press the left mouse button while inside the drawing window, the exclusive-ORing mode is set as described earlier and the first line is drawn, although at this time it is merely a point. While the mouse button is pressed, the code remains in the **while** loop in **UpdateDrawing**.

Within this loop, you can see that the line drawing is performed by the calls to **Hide** and **Show**, which are almost identical. Notice that **Hide** calls **Line** using the fixed coordinate (**X1,Y1**) and the last mouse location (**OldX,OldY**)

```
Line(X1-Wl,Y1-Wt,OldX-Wl,OldY-Wt); { Erase the line }
```

whereas **Show** uses the same fixed point but the mouse's new location given by (**X,Y**):

```
Line(X1-Wl,Y1-Wt,X-Wl,Y-Wt); { Draw the line }
```

Since the exclusive-ORing mode is on, the first time **Line** is called, by calling **Hide**, the old line is erased and the second call to **Line**, by the method **Show**, draws the line at the new position. Notice that the first coordinate pair in each call to **Line** corresponds to the position on the screen where the user first pressed the mouse button. This point does not change. The only endpoint of the line that does change is the one you drag around the screen with the mouse. These two lines create the rubber-banding effect.

When the left mouse button is released, the **FinishDrawing** method is called. It has been overridden to redraw the line using the following statements:

```
SetWriteMode(CopyPut);
Hide;
```

The line is redrawn with **SetWriteMode** taken out of the exclusive-OR mode, so that the line is drawn in its proper color. Remember that a figure exclusive-ORed with an object on the screen may change its color.

Drawing Polygons

There are two object types in our toolkit that allow you to draw polygons—**PolygonTool** and **FillPolygonTool**. The first allows you to draw a series of lines connected at their endpoints. The second object type, **FillPolygonTool**, is capable of drawing closed polygons using any of the predefined fill patterns.

In effect, **PolygonTool** is nothing more than a variation of **LineTool**; therefore **PolygonTool** is derived from **LineTool**. Similarly, **FillPolygonTool** operates just like **PolygonTool**, except for the fact that it draws filled polygons; consequently, it is derived from **PolygonTool**. Now you can see where our object hierarchy is really paying off since we are able to share the code in the inherited methods.

Both polygon object types operate in a similar manner although the way they work is slightly different from the object types previously discussed. As before, they begin their drawing after the first click of the mouse's left button. Next, they draw a rubber-banding line as the mouse is moved around the screen, which defines one side of the polygon, until the left button is pressed again. The current line then becomes frozen and a new rubber-banding line is drawn starting from the current mouse location. This process (shown in Figure 10.5) can be repeated to create additional sides to the polygon. When you want to close off the polygon, however, simply press the right mouse button and the closing side of the polygon is drawn. If **FillPolygonTool** is used, the interior of the polygon is filled.

Since the user interaction is different, we have overridden **UpdateDrawing** so that we can replace the **while** loop we were using earlier with a **do** loop that waits for the closing signal—a right button press. To refresh your memory, the **while**

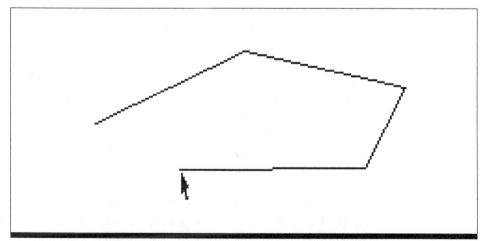

Figure 10.5. Drawing a polygon with PolygonTool

loop was used to draw a figure as long as the left mouse button was pressed. In **PolygonTool**, the **do** loop is used to test for a right button press. In addition, an **if** statement has been added inside the **do** loop that tests for the left button. If any left button presses occur, the mouse coordinates are saved, the current rubber-banding line is frozen, and a new rubber-banding line is started at the previous line's end-point. If, on the other hand, the right button is pressed, the polygon is closed off by tying it back to the first coordinate in **FinishDrawing**.

Again, the exclusive-ORing technique is used to create the rubber-banding effect by a call to **SetWriteMode** with **XorPut**. So that the correct colors will be displayed, the complete polygon must then be redrawn with the write mode set to **CopyPut** after the user has closed off a polygon. For this reason, a polygon object keeps track of the screen coordinates that are used to draw the polygon. These coordinates are saved in the **Poly** array included in the **PolygonTool** type. For simplicity, the **Poly** array is declared to be of type **PCArray**, which is defined in MATRIX.PAS to be large enough to hold 30 coordinates.

Drawing Rectangles

We'll now develop two companion object types to interactively draw a rectangle and a filled rectangle—**RectangleTool** and **FillRectangleTool**. These tools are built around the BGI's **Rectangle** and **Bar3D** commands, respectively.

Once again we'll use the BGI's exclusive-OR feature to create a rubber-banding effect. But, how does this work with the filled rectangle version of the tool? Since **Bar3D** is not affected by the **SetWriteMode** option, we'll use a dashed empty rectangle to size the rectangle and then fill it when the size is set by calling **Bar3D**. (Remember from Chapter 2 that **Bar3D** can draw a filled square if its depth is set to zero.) This suggests that **FillRectangleTool** should be derived from **RectangleTool**, and that's exactly what we'll do. In addition, we'll derive **RectangleTool** from **LineTool** so that we can take advantage of its user interaction and the code that sets the line styles appropriately. Because of this, the only methods we need to override in the **RectangleTool** object type are **Show** and **Hide**. They both call **Rectangle** to draw a rectangle; however, **Hide** uses the previous location of the mouse specified by (**OldX,OldY**) and **Show** uses the new mouse location (**X,Y**). Remember we're using the exclusive-OR feature here to toggle between drawing the line and erasing it.

To draw filled rectangles we need to add only a little more code. First, **Draw** and **StartDrawing** are overridden in order to set the fill settings and the line style to dashed lines. (Remember we'll use a dashed rectangle until the rectangle is the desired size.) Second, we'll override **FinishDrawing** so that once the rectangle's size has been set—when the left mouse button is released—we'll paint over the outline rectangle with the filled rectangle. This is done using the call to **Bar3D**:

```
Bar3D(X1-W1,Y1-Wt,X-W1,Y-Wt,0,0);   { Draw the filled rectangle }
```

As before, drawing does not begin until the left button is pressed. In addition, the only way to exit the drawing method is to click the mouse outside of the drawing window.

Drawing Circles

The next object type to derive is **CircleTool**, which allows us to interactively draw a circle as shown in Figure 10.6. Drawing a circle with **CircleTool** begins by specifying the center point of the circle. This is done by moving the mouse to the desired location and pressing the left mouse button. Then while holding down the left mouse button, you can drag the mouse to the left and right to change the size of the circle.

You may be wondering how we create a rubber-banding circle; after all, the BGI's **Circle** procedure is not affected by **SetWriteMode**. There are a couple approaches we could take. For instance, we could write our own **Circle** routine that does support exclusive-ORing; as shown in the sidebar "Creating Rubber-Banding Circles." We won't take this approach, however.

Instead, we'll use **GetImage** and **PutImage** to help us create the rubber-banding effect needed to draw circles. This is done by saving the screen image where the circle is to be drawn, so that later we can remove it from the screen by copying the saved image back to the screen with **PutImage**. In effect, we are doing nothing

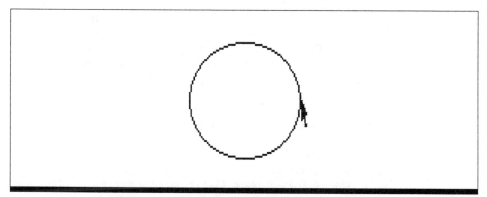

Figure 10.6. Using the CircleTool to draw circles

more than popping up a window with the figure inside it. Let's begin by taking a closer look at **CircleTool**.

The first thing you'll notice about **CircleTool** is that it is much longer and probably more intimidating than any of the prior object types. However, taken piece by piece, this type is pretty much similar to those discussed earlier.

There are two basic reasons why the code in **CircleTool** is more complex than what we've seen before. First, as we just described we'll be simulating the rubber-banding effect by using **GetImage** and **PutImage**. But because of this, we'll need to make sure the images these routines use don't extend beyond the drawing window. Second, using **GetImage** and **PutImage** is a challenge in higher-resolution modes. Because many of these modes require more than 64K to save the whole drawing window, we can't use a single call to **GetImage**. Instead, we'll split the

---

Creating Rubber-Banding Circles

One way to create a rubber-banding circle is to write your own circle routine. We could do this from scratch, but another approach is to draw a circle using a series of very small lines using the BGI's **Line** procedure. A **Circle** routine that does this is shown next.

The arguments to the custom routine, **Circle2**, are the same as the BGI's, except that it accepts one additional argument that specifies the number of line segments to be used to draw the circle. The larger this number, the smoother the circle, although there's really not much reason to make the number larger than about 100.

The **Circle2** procedure works by rotating a line segment so that its endpoints fall on the perimeter of a circle. As long as the line segments are very short in relation to the size of the circle, you'll get a good approximation of a circle by drawing the rotated segments. The length of the line segment, and the smoothness of the circle, depends on the number of divisions you request in the variable **NumSides**.

The **for** loop calculates the rotation for each line segment specified. The calculations in the **for** loop should look familiar. They're the same calculations introduced in Chapter 5 for rotating two-dimensional figures.

The **Circle2** procedure also adjusts for the screen's aspect ratio in the call to **Line** by multiplying the y coordinate by the **AspectRatio** value calculated previously. This is particularly important in some modes. Otherwise, the circle drawn will look more like an ellipse.

In case you're wondering, the same approach can be applied to drawing ellipses. All you need to do is multiply the radius in the x and y directions by some scale factor.

```
program NewCircle;
{ CIRCLE2.PAS: Draws a circle using a series of line segments. }
uses
  Graph;
```

area to save into two regions as shown in Figure 10.7 and save each independently. The screen regions are saved into the two blocks of memory pointed to by **Covered1** and **Covered2**, which are new instance variables declared in **CircleTool**.

The **Draw** method is overridden so that we can allocate and deallocate the memory required to save the screen. Notice that we are setting aside enough memory here to save the whole drawing window. Once the memory is allocated, the inherited **Draw** method is called to perform the drawing operation. Then after the drawing is finished, the memory claimed by **Covered1** and **Covered2** is freed.

If there isn't enough memory to save the screen image, the procedure **MallocError** is called. Currently, **MallocError** aborts the program. You might want to modify this error handler to make the program more user-friendly.

```
var
  AspectRatio: real;
  GDriver, GMode, Xasp, Yasp;

procedure Circle2(X, Y, Radius, NumSides: integer);
{ Draws a circle as a series of line segments. The center of the
  circle is specified by (x,y). The variable NumSides determines
  how many line segments the circle will be divided into. }
const
var
  I: integer;
  X0, Y0, Xi, Yi, Tinc, Ct: real;
begin
  Tinc := Pi * 2.0 / NumSides;
  Ct := Cos(Tinc);  Ct := Sin(Tinc);
  X0 := Radius;  Y0 := 0.0;
  for I := 0 to NumSides-1 do begin
    Xi := X0 * Ct - Y0 * St;
    Yi := X0 * St + Y0 * Ct;
    Line(X0+X,Y0*AspectRatio+Y,Xi+X,Yi*AspectRatio+Y);
    X0 := Xi;  Y0 := Yi;
  end
end;

begin
  GDriver := Detect;
  InitGraph(GDriver,GMode,'\tp\bgi');
  GetAspectRatio(Xasp,Yasp);
  AspectRatio = Xasp / Yasp;
  { Draw a circle using the function below }
  Circle2(100,100,50,40);
  Getch;
  CloseGraph;
end.
```

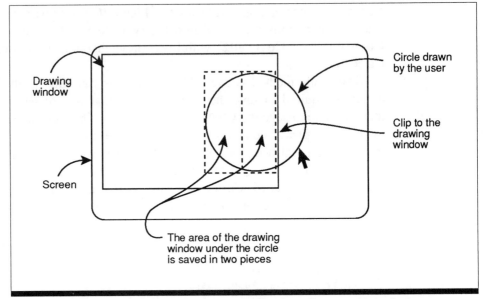

Figure 10.7. The clipping performed for rubber-banding circles

The drawing process begins in the **StartDrawing** method. Note that it calls **GetImage** twice to save the screen located at the cursor. Although it is effectively saving only a point, this will begin our rubber-banding process.

Drawing a circle is regulated by the **UpdateDrawing** method. As the mouse is moved, the radius of the circle is continually calculated by taking the absolute value of the difference between the center x coordinate of the circle and the mouse's current position:

```
AbsRadiusx := Abs(CenterX - X);
```

The **AbsRadiusx** result is used later as the radius argument in the call to the BGI **Circle** procedure in the method **Show**.

The rest of the complexity of **UpdateDrawing** is due to clipping the bounds of the screen region used by **GetImage** and **PutImage**. Keep in mind that these two functions do not clip their images relative to the current viewport. This means that we must perform the clipping ourselves.

The clipping is accomplished with four **if-else** statements in **UpdateDrawing** that check to see if the circle extends beyond the edge of the drawing window. Since the aspect ratio of the screen may be different in the x and y directions, this method may wind up saving too much of the drawing window, particularly in the y direction. However, this is not much of a problem.

One other point to note about **CircleTool** is that it does not draw the circle if the radius is zero. This is necessary because the BGI procedure **Circle** will draw a circle of radius zero with a 1-pixel radius. Because this is not what we want, we avoid drawing such circles in **Show** by checking whether the **AbsRadiusx** variable has a value of zero. We'll have to do the same type of tests for the **Ellipse** and **Arc** procedures too.

Drawing Ellipses

Drawing an ellipse is accomplished by the **EllipseTool** object type, which is very similar to **CircleTool**. The primary difference between the two is that **EllipseTool** allows you to change both the x and y radius of the ellipse. As with **CircleTool**, the x radius is changed by dragging the mouse left and right, but now the y radius can also be changed by dragging the mouse up and down.

Because of the similarity between them, we've derived **EllipseTool** from **CircleTool**. This way we'll inherit the code from **CircleTool** that allocates and deallocates the memory required to save the screen. However, we'll still need to override **UpdateDrawing** so that we can keep track of the changes in the y coordinate of the ellipse. Similarly, **Show** is overridden so that we can draw an ellipse rather than a circle.

Drawing Arcs

The **ArcTool** object type allows us to interactively draw a series of arcs. Unfortunately, the BGI **Arc** procedure is not well suited for an interactive arc drawing routine. The main difficulty is that it is cumbersome to come up with a way to interactively specify all the parameters needed by the **Arc** procedure, such as the center point, the radius and the sweep angle. We'll sidestep the problem and create an extremely simple method to draw arcs.

Our object type, **ArcTool**, always begins drawing arcs at the 3 o'clock position, but it allows you to change the sweep angle of the arc and alter the radius of the arc. These components, used to draw an arc, are shown in Figure 10.8. The center point of the arc is selected when the left mouse button is first pressed. Then by dragging the mouse right and left, with the left button pressed, the radius of the arc is increased and decreased, respectively. In addition, by moving the mouse down the angle that the arc sweeps is increased. Similarly, when the mouse is moved up while the left button is pressed, the angle swept by the arc is decreased. The procedure for drawing an arc is illustrated in Figure 10.9.

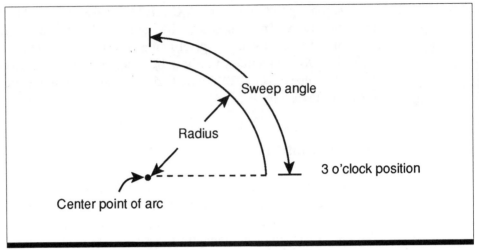

Figure 10.8. The components of an arc

As with **CircleTool** and **EllipseTool**, we'll track the mouse movement by calculating the absolute value of the difference between the mouse's current position and the center point of the arc. In addition, **GetImage** and **PutImage** are used to produce the exclusive-OR, rubber-banding effect that we used in some of the other drawing routines. The **ArcTool** object type saves a rectangular region large enough to contain the full 360-degree arc. These features are available to **ArcTool** by deriving **ArcTool** from **CircleTool**.

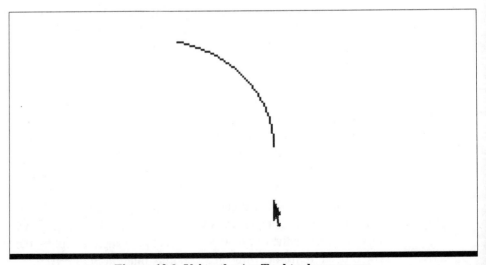

Figure 10.9. Using the ArcTool to draw an arc

Miscellaneous Drawing Support

We've covered all of the drawing object types included in DRAW.PAS, but we're not finished yet. The toolkit includes two additional object types: **TextTool** and **ClearWindowTool**.

The first object type, **TextTool**, allows you to enter text in the drawing window. To use **TextTool** you click the left mouse button where you want to begin entering text. Then a vertical bar will appear as the cursor. At this point as you type in text it will be displayed left-to-right starting from the vertical bar. When you are finished entering a block of text you must click the left mouse button again.

The vertical cursor is made by drawing an exclusive-ORed line the height of the text. The cursor is drawn, for instance, for the first time in **StartDrawing**, by the statements:

```
SetWriteMode(XorPut);
Mouse.Hide;     { Exclusive-OR in a cursor where mouse was pressed }
Line(X-W1,Y-Wt,X-W1,Y+TextHeight('S')-Wt);
Mouse.Show;
SetWriteMode(CopyPut);
```

For the most part, entering the text is handled by the **UpdateDrawing** method. As characters are typed in, the text cursor position is updated and the character is added to **Str**, an instance variable added to **DrawingTool**, so that the text can later be used by an application program.

The object type **TextTool** also allows you to enter a series of carriage returns by pressing the Enter key. The test for this feature can be found in the **while** loop in **UpdateDrawing**. It tests for a carriage return value, **CR**, and then simulates the carriage return by the statements:

```
if C = CR then begin         { If input is a carriage return }
  Inc(Y,TextHeight('S')+2);  { then move to another line and }
  X := Leftx;                { insert a newline character into }
  MoveTo(X-W1,Y-Wt);         { the string array. }
  if Len < MaxString-1 then begin
    Str[Len+1] := Char(CR);  { Add a carriage return to the }
    Inc(Len);                { string }
  end;
end
```

If a carriage return is detected, the text cursor is moved down by the height of the text and the current position is set to the original x location, **Leftx**, and the new calculated height, given by **Y**.

Currently **TextTool** does not support backspacing, vertical text, or many of the other powerful text features of the BGI. You might consider adding these.

The **ClearWindowTool** object type is also a supplemental drawing tool. It is used to erase the whole drawing window. It accomplishes this by setting the viewport to the drawing window and then calling **ClearViewPort**. Although it wasn't necessary to encapsulate this operation in an object, we did it anyway so that it would have a consistent program interface with the other drawing functions. This will be important in our application programs.

• Listing 10.1. DRAW.PAS

```pascal
unit Draw;
{$R+}
{ DRAW.PAS: Interactive drawing tools used in the Paint and CAD programs. }
interface
uses
  Graph, MousePac, KbdMouse, Matrix;
const
  CR = 13;                    { Carriage return value }
  EraserSize = 5;             { Half the size of the eraser }
  SpraySize = 15;             { Size of the spray area }
  MaxPolySize = 40;           { Can have this many edges }
  MaxString = 80;             { A string can be this long }
var
{ The fill parameters, drawing colors, and so forth are all kept as global
  variables. From time to time the current drawing, fill, and line
  styles may be changed, so before calling any drawing routines make sure
  the various drawing parameters are reset to these global values. }
GlobalFillStyle: integer; { The fill style that should be used }
GlobalFillColor: integer; { Holds the fill color that should be used }
GlobalDrawColor: integer; { Holds the drawing color to use }
GlobalLineStyle: integer; { Holds the line style that should be used }
GlobalTextStyle: integer; { Specifies the text font to use }
Wl, Wt, Wr, Wb: integer;  { Window bounds where drawing is to be done }
MaxX, MaxY: integer;      { Maximum dimensions of the screen }
Mouse: KbdMouseObj;       { A keyboard mouse is used for interaction }

type
{ The base type that defines the basic format of the drawing tools }
DrawingToolPtr = ^DrawingTool;
DrawingTool = object
  X, Y, OldX, OldY: integer;              { Current and last mouse positions }
  Left, Top, Right, Bottom: integer;      { Bounds of the figure }
  DrawColor: integer;                     { Color to be used in figure }
  constructor Init;
  procedure Draw; virtual;                { High-level drawing function }
  procedure PerformDraw; virtual;         { Defines user interaction }
  procedure StartDrawing; virtual;        { Sets up for drawing }
  procedure UpdateDrawing; virtual;       { Interactively draws figure }
  procedure FinishDrawing; virtual;       { Finalizes drawing }
  procedure Hide; virtual;                { Removes figure from screen }
```

```
      procedure Show; virtual;                  { Displays or updates figure }
      { The following routines will be defined in the CAD program }
      procedure Display; virtual;
      procedure GetBounds(var L, T, R, B: integer); virtual;
      procedure Translate(Transx, Transy: real); virtual;
      procedure Rotate(Angle: real); virtual;
      function Dup: DrawingToolPtr; virtual;
   end;

PencilToolPtr = ^PencilTool;
PencilTool = object(DrawingTool)       { A curve-drawing object type }
   procedure Draw; virtual;
   procedure StartDrawing; virtual;
   procedure Show; virtual;
end;

EraserToolPtr = ^EraserTool;
EraserTool = object(DrawingTool)       { An eraser object type }
   procedure Draw; virtual;
   procedure StartDrawing; virtual;
   procedure Show; virtual;
end;

SpraycanToolPtr = ^SpraycanTool;
SpraycanTool = object(DrawingTool)     { A spraycan object type }
   procedure Draw; virtual;
   procedure UpdateDrawing; virtual;
   procedure Show; virtual;
end;

LineToolPtr = ^LineTool;
LineTool = object(DrawingTool)         { Draws single lines }
   X1, Y1, X2, Y2: integer;            { Endpoints of line drawn }
   LineStyle: integer;                 { Line style used for lines }
   procedure Draw; virtual;
   procedure StartDrawing; virtual;
   procedure FinishDrawing; virtual;
   procedure Hide; virtual;
   procedure Show; virtual;
end;

RectangleToolPtr = ^RectangleTool;
RectangleTool = object(LineTool)       { Draws a rectangle }
   procedure Hide; virtual;
   procedure Show; virtual;
end;

FillRectangleToolPtr = ^FillRectangleTool;
FillRectangleTool = object(RectangleTool) { A filled rectangle }
   FillStyle: integer;                 { Fill pattern used in rectangle }
   FillColor: integer;                 { Color used in fill pattern }
   procedure Draw; virtual;
   procedure StartDrawing; virtual;
```

```
      procedure FinishDrawing; virtual;
   end;

   PolygonToolPtr = ^PolygonTool;
   PolygonTool = object(LineTool)          { Draws a polygon }
      Poly: PCArray;
      NumPts: integer;
      FillStyle: integer;                  { Fill pattern used }
      FillColor: integer;                  { Color used in fill pattern }
      procedure StartDrawing; virtual;
      procedure UpdateDrawing; virtual;
      procedure FinishDrawing; virtual;
   end;

   FillPolygonToolPtr = ^FillPolygonTool;
   FillPolygonTool = object(PolygonTool) { Draws filled polygon }
      procedure StartDrawing; virtual;
      procedure FinishDrawing; virtual;
   end;

   CircleToolPtr = ^CircleTool;
   CircleTool = object(DrawingTool)        { Draws a circle }
      Halfx, OldRight: integer;            { These variables are used to }
      Covered1, Covered2: pointer;         { save an image where circle is drawn }
      Size1, Size2: word;
      CLeft, CRight,
      CBottom, CTop: integer;              { Clipped figure }
      CenterX, CenterY, AbsRadiusx,
      OldLeft, OldTop: integer;            { Figure's dimensions }
      procedure Draw; virtual;
      procedure StartDrawing; virtual;
      procedure UpdateDrawing; virtual;
      procedure Hide; virtual;
      procedure Show; virtual;
   end;

   EllipseToolPtr = ^EllipseTool;
   EllipseTool = object(CircleTool)        { Draws an ellipse }
      AbsRadiusy: integer;                 { The y radius of ellipse. The }
      procedure UpdateDrawing; virtual;    { x radius is inherited from }
      procedure Show; virtual;             { the CircleTool object type. }
   end;

   ArcToolPtr = ^ArcTool;
   ArcTool = object(CircleTool)            { Draws an arc }
      Radius, Angle: integer;              { Radius and sweep angle of arc }
      procedure UpdateDrawing; virtual;
      procedure Show; virtual;
   end;

   TextToolPtr = ^TextTool;
   TextTool = object(DrawingTool)          { Text entry object type }
      Leftx, Lefty: integer;              { Top left location of text }
```

```
    Str: string[MaxString];                { String entered }
    Len: integer;                          { Length of string }
    TextStyle: integer;                    { Font used }
    procedure Draw; virtual;
    procedure StartDrawing; virtual;
    procedure UpdateDrawing; virtual;
    procedure FinishDrawing; virtual;
  end;

  ClearWindowToolPtr = ^ClearWindowTool;
  ClearWindowTool = object(DrawingTool)
    procedure Draw; virtual;               { Erases drawing window }
  end;

  procedure MallocError;  { Function called if memory allocation fails }

implementation
{ Although this constructor doesn't do anything, it is necessary
  because the DrawingTool object type has virtual methods. }
constructor DrawingTool.Init;  begin  end;

procedure DrawingTool.Draw;
{ The high-level method that is called to draw a figure. It sets
  the viewport to the drawing FinishDrawing, calls PerformDraw to
  perform the drawing action, and then restores the viewport to
  the full screen. }
var
  View: ViewPortType;
begin
  GetViewSettings(View);           { Save the viewport coordinates }
  SetViewPort(Wl,Wt,Wr,Wb,True); { Set viewport to drawing window }
  DrawColor := GlobalDrawColor;  { Save the drawing color }
  PerformDraw;                     { Draw the figure }
  { Restore viewport coordinates to those saved earlier }
  SetViewPort(View.X1,View.Y1,View.X2,View.Y2,View.Clip);
end;

procedure DrawingTool.PerformDraw;
{ Drawing begins when the left mouse button is pressed. Then the
  coordinates of the mouse are checked to see if the mouse was pressed
  outside of the drawing window. If so, the drawing routine ends.
  Otherwise, the actual drawing begins by calling StartDrawing. }
begin
  while True do begin           { Wait for button press }
    while not Mouse.ButtonPressed(LeftButton) do ;
    Mouse.GetCoords(X,Y);       { Get location where button was pressed }
    if (X < Wl) or (Y < Wt) or (Y > Wb) or (X > Wr) then Exit;
                                        { Exit drawing }
    StartDrawing;                { Set up for the drawing }
    UpdateDrawing;               { Do the drawing }
    FinishDrawing;               { Clean up drawing as needed }
  end;
end;
```

```
procedure DrawingTool.StartDrawing;
{ Initializes the drawing style and various variables used by the
  drawing function. By default it saves the last location of the mouse. }
begin
  OldX := X;  OldY := Y;
end;

procedure DrawingTool.UpdateDrawing;
{ Complete the figure being drawn. Most of the derived types will
  draw while the left mouse button is pressed. Note: The figure is not
  updated if the mouse has not been moved. }
begin
  while not Mouse.ButtonReleased(LeftButton) do begin
    { Button must have been pressed already }
    Mouse.GetCoords(X,Y);                 { Get current location of mouse }
    if (X <> OldX) or (Y <> OldY) then begin
      { Update figure only if the mouse has moved }
      Hide;                               { Remove part or all of the figure }
      Show;                               { Draw the figure }
      OldX := X;  OldY := Y;              { Update saved position of mouse }
    end;
  end;
end;

{ Perform any final operations that must be made to finish the drawing.
  For instance, figures that are drawn with exclusive-OR lines must
  be redrawn with the exclusive-OR feature disabled so that the figure's
  color will come out correctly. By default, do nothing. }
procedure DrawingTool.FinishDrawing;  begin  end;

{ The following methods in DrawingTool do nothing or very little.
  They are used exlusively in the CAD program and are provided here
  in the DrawingTool object type in order to define the core set of
  routines that will later be overridden so that polymorphism can be
  exploited. }
procedure DrawingTool.Hide; begin end;
procedure DrawingTool.Show; begin end;
procedure DrawingTool.Display; begin end;
procedure DrawingTool.GetBounds(var L, T, R, B: integer); begin end;
procedure DrawingTool.Translate(Transx, Transy: real); begin end;
procedure DrawingTool.Rotate(Angle: real); begin end;
function DrawingTool.Dup: DrawingToolPtr; begin Dup := @Self; end;

procedure PencilTool.Draw;
{ Use the global drawing color for drawing with the PencilTool type }
begin
  SetColor(GlobalDrawColor);      { Switch to the global drawing color }
  DrawingTool.Draw;               { Draw with the pencil }
end;

procedure PencilTool.StartDrawing;
{ Initialize drawing with pencil by moving the current position to
  the current location of the mouse. Adjust for the fact that the
```

```
    mouse coordinates are given with respect to the whole screen and
    the pencil tool's coordinates are relative to the drawing window. }
begin
  DrawingTool.StartDrawing;        { Call DrawingTool's StartDrawing }
  MoveTo(X-Wl,Y-Wt);               { Set the current position }
end;

procedure PencilTool.Show;
{ Draw a line from the last position of the mouse to its current position }
begin
  Mouse.Hide;                      { Hide mouse before drawing }
  LineTo(X-Wl,Y-Wt);               { Draw a line from last position }
  Mouse.Show;                      { Restore the mouse cursor }
end;

procedure EraserTool.Draw;
{ Use a solid background color to erase a region of the screen }
begin
  SetColor(GetBkColor);                    { Use the background color }
  SetFillStyle(SolidFill,GetBkColor);  { to erase the screen }
  DrawingTool.Draw;                        { Draw with the eraser }
end;

procedure EraserTool.StartDrawing;
{ Erase the spot pointed to when the left mouse button is pressed }
begin
  DrawingTool.StartDrawing;
  Show;
end;

procedure EraserTool.Show;
{ Erase a rectangular region of the screen where the mouse is located }
begin
  Mouse.Hide;                              { Remove the mouse from screen }
  Bar(X-Wl,Y-Wt,X-Wl+EraserSize,Y-Wt+EraserSize);  { Erase region }
  Mouse.Show;                              { Restore the mouse cursor }
end;

procedure SpraycanTool.Draw;
{ Initialize the Random function to be used by the spraycan tool
  before performing the spray painting }
begin
  Randomize;                               { Initializes Random function }
  DrawingTool.Draw;                        { Use spraycan }
end;

procedure SpraycanTool.UpdateDrawing;
{ Override DrawingTool's UpdateDrawing method so that the spraycan
  paints as long as the left mouse button is pressed--even if the
  mouse has not been moved. }
begin
  while not Mouse.ButtonReleased(LeftButton) do begin
    Mouse.GetCoords(X,Y);                  { Get current mouse location }
```

```
    Show;                                      { Spray paint }
  end;
end;

procedure SpraycanTool.Show;
{ Spray a small region of the screen. Two separate for loops are
  used to Randomly paint a series of pixels using the global
  drawing color. }
var
  I: integer;
begin
  Mouse.Hide;    { Remove the mouse before painting on the screen }
  for I := 0 to 7 do              { Randomly draw eight pixels }
    PutPixel(X-Random(SpraySize)+5-Wl,
             Y-Random(SpraySize)+5-Wt,GlobalDrawColor);
  for I := 0 to 7 do              { Randomly draw another eight pixels }
    PutPixel(X-Random(SpraySize-2)+3-Wl,
             Y-Random(SpraySize-2)+3-Wt,GlobalDrawColor);
  Mouse.Show;    { Restore the mouse cursor to the screen }
end;

procedure LineTool.Draw;
{ Set the line styles and color before drawing }
begin
  SetLineStyle(GlobalLineStyle,0,NormWidth);  { Use global line style }
  SetColor(GlobalDrawColor);                  { Use global draw color }
  LineStyle := GlobalLineStyle;               { Save line style used }
  DrawingTool.Draw;                           { Draw one or more lines }
end;

procedure LineTool.StartDrawing;
{ Use exclusive-ORed lines while the line is initially drawn }
begin
  DrawingTool.StartDrawing;
  SetWriteMode(XorPut);        { Use exclusive-OR lines while drawing }
  X1 := X;  Y1 := Y;    { This will be the stationary point of the line }
end;

procedure LineTool.Show;
{ Draw a line from fixed point where the mouse was pressed (which
  was saved in StartDrawing) to its current location. Save the
  current location of the mouse in (X2,Y2). }
begin
  Mouse.Hide;                    { Hide the mouse before drawing }
  Line(X1-Wl,Y1-Wt,X-Wl,Y-Wt); { Draw the line }
  Mouse.Show;                    { Restore the mouse to the screen }
  X2 := X;  Y2 := Y;             { Save the line's other endpoint }
end;

procedure LineTool.Hide;
{ Erase the line by drawing it again. This works since the exclusive-OR
  mode is being used. }
begin
```

```
    Mouse.Hide;                          { Hide the mouse cursor }
    Line(X1-Wl,Y1-Wt,OldX-Wl,OldY-Wt);  { Erase the line }
    Mouse.Show;                          { Restore the mouse cursor }
end;

procedure LineTool.FinishDrawing;
{ The size of the line has been fixed, so switch out of exclusive-OR
  mode and draw the line in permanently by drawing it again. }
begin
    SetWriteMode(CopyPut);               { Get out of exclusive-OR mode }
    Show;                                { Draw the line in permanently }
end;

procedure RectangleTool.Show;
{ Drawing a rectangle is similar to drawing a line, except that
  Rectangle is called rather than line }
begin
    Mouse.Hide;                          { Hide the mouse cursor }
    Rectangle(X1-Wl,Y1-Wt,X-Wl,Y-Wt);    { Draw the rectangle }
    Mouse.Show;                          { Show the mouse cursor }
end;

procedure RectangleTool.Hide;
{ Remove the current rectangle by drawing it again. This method
  assumes that the exclusive-OR feature is being used. }
begin
    Mouse.Hide;                          { Hide the mouse cursor }
    Rectangle(X1-Wl,Y1-Wt,OldX-Wl,OldY-Wt); { Erase the rectangle }
    Mouse.Show;                          { Show the mouse cursor }
end;

procedure FillRectangleTool.Draw;
{ Set up for drawing a filled rectangle by selecting fill settings
  before performing the drawing operation }
begin
    SetFillStyle(GlobalFillStyle,GlobalFillColor);
    RectangleTool.Draw;
end;

procedure FillRectangleTool.StartDrawing;
{ This routine is overridden so a dashed rectangle style is used while
  the user interactively sets the size of a filled rectangle }
begin
    SetLineStyle(DashedLn,0,NormWidth);
    RectangleTool.StartDrawing;
end;

procedure FillRectangleTool.FinishDrawing;
{ Draw the filled rectangle }
begin
    SetLineStyle(GlobalLineStyle,0,NormWidth);
    SetWriteMode(CopyPut);               { Switch out of exclusive-OR mode }
    Mouse.Hide;
```

```
      Bar3D(X1-W1,Y1-Wt,X-W1,Y-Wt,0,False);   { Draw the filled rectangle }
      Mouse.Show;
    end;

procedure PolygonTool.StartDrawing;
{ Save the starting location of the polygon. These coordinates are
  saved in the same array, Poly. }
begin
    LineTool.StartDrawing;
    FillColor := GlobalFillColor;  FillStyle := GlobalFillStyle;
    Poly[0].X := X-W1; Poly[0].Y := Y-Wt;  { Save current location of mouse }
    NumPts := 1;                        { One coordinate pair is saved }
end;

procedure PolygonTool.UpdateDrawing;
{ Override UpdateDrawing so that the left mouse button is used to
  specify the location of vertices and the right mouse button ends
  the drawing of the polygon. }
var
    T: boolean;
begin
    repeat
      Mouse.GetCoords(X,Y);             { Get current location of mouse }
      if (X <> OldX) or (Y <> OldY) then begin
        Hide;                           { If mouse hasn't moved, update }
        Show;                           { current edge of polygon }
        OldX := X;  OldY := Y;          { Remember last location of edge }
      end;
      if Mouse.ButtonReleased(LeftButton) then begin
        T := Mouse.ButtonPressed(LeftButton);
        SetWriteMode(CopyPut);          { Draw line in permanently }
        Show;
        SetWriteMode(XorPut);           { Switch back to exlusive-OR mode }
        X1 := X;   Y1 := Y;             { Save the new vertice of the line }
        Poly[NumPts].X := X-W1;  Poly[NumPts].Y := Y-Wt;
        Inc(NumPts);
      end;
      { End drawing when right mouse button is pressed }
    until Mouse.ButtonPressed(RightButton);
end;

procedure PolygonTool.FinishDrawing;
{ Close off polygon by drawing a line back to its beginning }
begin
    Poly[NumPts].X := X - W1;
    Poly[NumPts].Y := Y - Wt;       Inc(NumPts);
    Poly[NumPts].X := Poly[0].X;
    Poly[NumPts].Y := Poly[0].Y;  Inc(NumPts);
    SetWriteMode(CopyPut);              { Draw line in permanently }
    Mouse.Hide;
    Line(X1-W1,Y1-Wt,X-W1,Y-Wt);
    Line(x-W1,y-Wt,Poly[0].X,Poly[0].Y); { Close polygon }
```

```
    Mouse.Show;
end;

procedure FillPolygonTool.StartDrawing;
{ Prepare for drawing a filled polygon }
begin
  SetFillStyle(GlobalFillStyle,GlobalFillColor);
  PolygonTool.StartDrawing;
end;

procedure FillPolygonTool.FinishDrawing;
{ Draw a filled polygon }
begin
  Poly[NumPts].X := X - Wl;
  Poly[NumPts].Y := Y - Wt;        Inc(NumPts);
  Poly[NumPts].X := Poly[0].X;
  Poly[NumPts].Y := Poly[0].Y;     Inc(NumPts);
  SetWriteMode(CopyPut);           { Draw line in permanently }
  Mouse.Hide;                      { Hide the mouse cursor }
  FillPoly(NumPts,Poly);           { Draw the filled polygon }
  Mouse.Show;                      { Show the mouse cursor }
end;

procedure CircleTool.Draw;
{ The GetImage and PutImage routines are used to create a rubber-
  banding circle effect by popping up a "window" with a circle in it.
  This method allocates and frees the memory used to save the screen
  where the circle is displayed. Since some high-resolution modes
  consume more than 64K, the drawing window is saved in two pieces,
  Covered1 and Covered2. }
begin
  HalfX := (Wr + Wl) div 2;        { Split drawing window into two }
  Size1 := ImageSize(Wl,Wt,HalfX,Wb);
  Size2 := ImageSize(HalfX,Wt,Wr,Wb);
  GetMem(Covered1,Size1);          { Allocate memory }
  GetMem(Covered2,Size2);
  if (Covered1 = Nil) or (Covered2 = Nil) then MallocError;
  SetColor(GlobalDrawColor);  { Prepare for drawing }
  DrawingTool.Draw;                { Draw one or more circles }
  FreeMem(Covered2,Size2);    { Free the memory allocated earlier }
  FreeMem(Covered1,Size1);
end;

procedure CircleTool.StartDrawing;
{ Start drawing by saving the point where the mouse cursor is located }
begin
  DrawingTool.StartDrawing;
  CenterX := X;  CenterY := Y;
  OldLeft := X;  OldTop := Y;  OldRight := X;
  Mouse.Hide;
  GetImage(OldLeft-Wl,OldTop-Wt,OldLeft-Wl,OldTop-Wt,Covered1^);
  GetImage(OldLeft-Wl,OldTop-Wt,OldLeft-Wl,OldTop-Wt,Covered2^);
  Mouse.Show;
end;
```

```
procedure CircleTool.UpdateDrawing;
{ Draw a circle while the left mouse button is pressed. Need to
  calculate the bounds of the drawing window to be saved. These
  values are stored in CLeft, CRight, CTop, and CBottom. The radius
  of the circle is changed as the mouse is moved left and right. }
begin
  while not Mouse.ButtonReleased(LeftButton) do begin
    Mouse.GetCoords(X,Y);
    if X <> OldX then begin
      { If the size of the circle has changed, redraw it }
      AbsRadiusx := Abs(CenterX - X);   { Calculate new radius of circle }
      { Clip the region that must be saved below the circle
        to the boundaries of the drawing window }
      if CenterX-AbsRadiusx < Wl then CLeft := Wl
        else CLeft := CenterX - AbsRadiusx;
      if CenterX+AbsRadiusx > Wr then CRight := Wr
        else CRight := CenterX + AbsRadiusx;
      if CenterY-AbsRadiusx < Wt then CTop := Wt
        else CTop := CenterY - AbsRadiusx;
      if CenterY+AbsRadiusx > Wb then CBottom := Wb
        else CBottom := CenterY + AbsRadiusx;
      Hide;  Show; { Erase old circle and draw a new one }
      OldLeft := CLeft;  OldTop := CTop;  OldX := X;  OldRight := CRight;
    end
  end
end;

procedure CircleTool.Hide;
{ Remove the current circle by OverWriting it with the stored screen
  image that was saved before the circle was drawn }
begin
  Mouse.Hide;
  PutImage(OldLeft-Wl,OldTop-Wt,Covered1^,CopyPut);{ OverWrite the circle }
  PutImage((OldLeft+OldRight) div 2-Wl,OldTop-Wt,Covered2^,CopyPut);
  Mouse.Show;
end;

procedure CircleTool.Show;
{ Draw the circle, but first save the screen region where the circle
  will be drawn. This screen image is used in Hide to erase the circle. }
begin
  Mouse.Hide;
  GetImage(CLeft-Wl,CTop-Wt,(CLeft+CRight) div 2-Wl,CBottom-Wt,Covered1^);
  GetImage((CLeft+CRight) div 2-Wl,CTop-Wt,CRight-Wl,CBottom-Wt,Covered2^);
  if AbsRadiusx <> 0 then        { Draw circle if its radius is not zero }
    Circle(CenterX-Wl,CenterY-Wt,AbsRadiusx);   { Draw circle }
  Mouse.Show;
end;

procedure EllipseTool.UpdateDrawing;
{ Drawing an ellipse is similar to drawing a circle except that
  when the mouse is moved up and down it also changes the vertical
  height of the figure }
```

```
begin
  while not Mouse.ButtonReleased(LeftButton) do begin
    Mouse.GetCoords(X,Y);
    AbsRadiusx := abs(CenterX - X);
    AbsRadiusy := abs(CenterY - Y);
    { Clip the region that must be saved below the ellipse
      to the boundaries of the drawing window }
    if CenterX-AbsRadiusx < Wl then CLeft := Wl
      else CLeft := CenterX - AbsRadiusx;
    if CenterX+AbsRadiusx > Wr then CRight := Wr
      else CRight := CenterX + AbsRadiusx;
    if CenterY-AbsRadiusy < Wt then CTop := Wt
      else CTop := CenterY - AbsRadiusy;
    if CenterY+AbsRadiusy > Wb then CBottom := Wb
      else CBottom := CenterY + AbsRadiusy;
    { If the size of the ellipse has changed, redraw it }
    if (X <> OldX) or (Y <> OldY) then begin
      Hide; Show;
      OldLeft := CLeft;        OldTop := CTop;
      OldX := X;  OldY := Y;   OldRight := CRight;
    end
  end
end;

procedure EllipseTool.Show;
{ Display the ellipse, but first save the screen region where the
  ellipse is to be drawn so that the ellipse can later be erased
  by overwriting the screen with these saved images. }
begin
  Mouse.Hide;
  GetImage(CLeft-Wl,CTop-Wt,(CLeft+CRight) div 2-Wl,CBottom-Wt,Covered1^);
  GetImage((CLeft+CRight) div 2-Wl,CTop-Wt,CRight-Wl,CBottom-Wt,Covered2^);
  if (AbsRadiusx <> 0) and (AbsRadiusy <> 0) then    { Draw ellipse }
    Ellipse(CenterX-Wl,CenterY-Wt,0,360,AbsRadiusx,AbsRadiusy);
  Mouse.Show;
end;

procedure ArcTool.UpdateDrawing;
{ The radius is changed by moving the mouse left and right. The
  sweep angle of the arc changes as the mouse is moved up and down. }
begin
  while not Mouse.ButtonReleased(LeftButton) do begin
    Mouse.GetCoords(X,Y);
    Radius := abs(CenterX - X);
    Angle := abs(CenterY - Y);
    if CenterX-Radius < Wl then CLeft := Wl
      else CLeft := CenterX - Radius;
    if CenterX+Radius > Wr then CRight := Wr
      else CRight := CenterX + Radius;
    if CenterY-Radius < Wt then CTop := Wt
      else CTop := CenterY - Radius;
    if CenterY+Radius > Wb then CBottom := Wb
      else CBottom := CenterY + Radius;
```

```
                    { If the size of the ellipse has changed, redraw it }
                    if (X <> OldX) or (Y <> OldY) then begin
                      Hide;    Show;
                      OldLeft := CLeft;        OldTop := CTop;
                      OldX := X;  OldY := Y; OldRight := CRight;
                    end
                end
            end;

procedure ArcTool.Show;
{ Draw the arc using the current radius and angle. See the
  discussions of similar methods in CircleTool and EllipseTool
  for how this function works. }
begin
  Mouse.Hide;
  GetImage(CLeft-Wl,CTop-Wt,(CLeft+CRight) div 2-Wl,CBottom-Wt,Covered1^);
  GetImage((CLeft+CRight) div 2-Wl,CTop-Wt,CRight-Wl,CBottom-Wt,Covered2^);
  if (Radius > 0) and (Angle > 0) then
    Arc(CenterX-Wl,CenterY-Wt,0,Angle,Radius);   { Draw the arc }
  Mouse.Show;
end;

procedure TextTool.Draw;
{ Writes text to the drawing window. A vertical line is used as a cursor.
  The text is saved in the field "string." Use the global drawing
  color as the color of the text. }
begin
  SetColor(GlobalDrawColor);          { Use this color for text }
  SetTextJustify(LeftText,TopText); { Set the text justification }
  TextStyle := GlobalTextStyle;       { Remember which font is being used }
  DrawingTool.Draw;
end;

procedure TextTool.StartDrawing;
begin
  while not Mouse.ButtonReleased(LeftButton) do ;
  DrawingTool.StartDrawing;
  SetWriteMode(XorPut);
  Mouse.Hide;       { Exclusive-OR in a cursor where mouse was pressed }
  Line(X-Wl,Y-Wt,X-Wl,Y+TextHeight('S')-Wt);
  Mouse.Show;
  SetWriteMode(CopyPut);        { Make sure to use the right mode when }
  MoveTo(X-Wl,Y-Wt);            { displaying text }
  Leftx := X;    Lefty := Y;  { Save starting location of text }
  Len := 0;                     { Initialize length of string }
end;

procedure TextTool.UpdateDrawing;
{ Main routine to enter text. This method displays characters
  entered until the left mouse button is pressed. }
var
  C: integer;
  Buff: string[2];
```

```
begin
  while True do begin
    C := Mouse.Waitforinput(LeftButton);
    if C < 0 then Exit;           { Left button pressed, so quit }
    Mouse.Hide;
    SetWriteMode(XorPut);         { Erase the cursor }
    Line(X-Wl,Y-Wt,X-Wl,Y+TextHeight('S')-Wt);
    SetWriteMode(CopyPut);
    Mouse.Show;
    if C = CR then begin          { If input is a carriage return }
      Inc(Y,TextHeight('S')+2);   { then move to another line and }
      X := Leftx;                 { insert a newline character into }
      MoveTo(X-Wl,Y-Wt);          { the string array. }
      if Len < MaxString-1 then begin
        Str[Len+1] := Char(CR);   { Add a carriage return to the }
        Inc(Len);                 { string }
      end;
    end
    else begin                    { Show the character just entered }
      Buff[0] := #1;  Buff[1] := Char(C);
      Mouse.Hide;
      OutText(Buff);              { Display the new character }
      Mouse.Show;
      Inc(x,TextWidth(buff));     { Keep track of the cursor location }
      if Len < MaxString-1 then begin
        Str[Len+1] := Char(C);    { Add character to string }
        Inc(Len);
      end;
    end;
    SetWriteMode(XorPut);         { Write a new cursor }
    Mouse.Hide;
    Line(X-Wl,Y-Wt,X-Wl,Y+TextHeight('S')-Wt); { Display new cursor }
    Mouse.Show;
    SetWriteMode(CopyPut);
  end
end;

procedure TextTool.FinishDrawing;
{ Finish the text input routine by erasing the cursor and setting
  the length of the string that is stored in the first byte of the string }
begin
  SetWriteMode(XorPut);           { Erase the cursor }
  Mouse.Hide;
  Line(X-Wl,Y-Wt,X-Wl,Y+TextHeight('S')-Wt);
  Mouse.Show;
  SetWriteMode(CopyPut);
  Str[0] := Char(Len);            { Set length of string }
end;

procedure ClearWindowTool.Draw;
{ Erase the drawing window }
var
  Vp: ViewPortType;
```

```
begin
  GetViewSettings(Vp);
  SetViewPort(Wl,Wt,Wr,Wb,True); { Set viewport to drawing window }
  Mouse.Hide;
  ClearViewPort;                   { Erase the drawing window }
  Mouse.Show;
  SetViewPort(Vp.X1,Vp.Y1,Vp.X2,Vp.Y2,True); { Restore viewport settings }
end;

procedure MallocError;
{ If an error occurs in memory allocation call this routine and
  an error message will be displayed and the program will quit }
begin
  CloseGraph;
  WriteLn('Not enough memory to run program.');
  Halt(1);
end;

begin
end.
```

11

A Paint Program

This chapter has two interconnected goals. First, it will show you how to create the paint program for which we have been developing tools in earlier chapters, and second it will serve as the user's guide for the paint program. By now, you should be armed with a powerful package of graphics programming tools, and, because building a useful paint program is not a trivial task, we'll be relying heavily on these tools to simplify the process. Before we complete this chapter, we'll also discuss several enhancements that you might try implementing so that you can create your own customized version of the paint program.

Overview of the Paint Program

Although our paint program uses many tools that we have developed throughout this book, we'll still need to develop more code in this chapter to create the program. The missing ingredients are handled by a series of files. The first, USERTOOL.PAS (Listing 11.1), provides a handful of additional interactive tools that we'll need in the paint program, including object types to display pull-down menus, a set of fill patterns, and a palette. The second file we'll construct, INTERACT.PAS (Listing 11.2), ties together the tools in DRAW.PAS and USERTOOL.PAS with the icons and menu options on the screen. The last file we'll build is called PAINT.PAS (Listing 11.3). It is responsible for drawing the paint program's environment by arranging the icons, providing the pull-down menus, and segmenting off a portion of the screen for the drawing window. It also initiates the loop that responds to any user input.

Using Screen Objects

Figure 11.1 shows the screen view of the paint program's environment. As indicated, a large portion of the screen is reserved for the drawing window, but what's of more interest right now are the other components of the drawing environment. The left side of the screen is reserved for the icons that represent the commands supported by the program. The top of the screen contains several keywords that are used to pull down various menus or select additional functions. At the bottom of the screen is a list of the fill patterns and the colors that are accessible in the current video mode.

One important thing to realize is that each item described so far is designed to be handled as a separate graphics object that is managed by the INTERACT.PAS file. As a result, each of these screen objects (icons, words, and so on) has a predefined functionality that can be accessed by clicking on it with the mouse. For instance, when you click on the spraycan icon, the **SpraycanTool** can be used to spray paint inside the drawing window. So before we continue, we need to build the INTERACT.PAS package that ties together these screen objects and their operations.

The INTERACT.PAS source file contains three new object types, listed in Table 11.1. The first type, **InteractObj**, ties together a screen object with a particular drawing tool. Here's its definition:

```
InteractObjPtr = ^InteractObj;
InteractObj = object
```

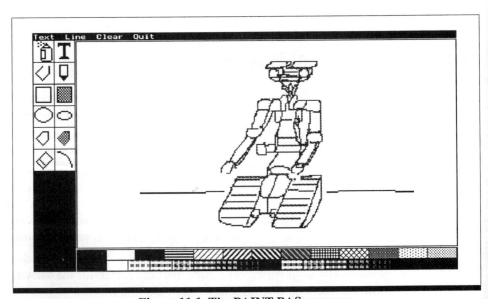

Figure 11.1. The PAINT.PAS program

Table 11.1. Object types in INTERACT.PAS

Object type	Description
InteractObj	Ties together a screen object and an action
UserInteract	Derived from Interact and does everything that Interact does except modify the screen when a screen object is selected
ToolSet	An array of Interact tools and the code to select and process them

```
    Cmd: integer;                   { Letter command that selects the object }
    Left, Right: integer;           { Screen region where command is displayed }
    Top, Bottom: integer;
    ITool: DrawingToolPtr;
    constructor Init(C, L, T, R, B: integer; ToolPtr: DrawingToolPtr);
    procedure Select; virtual;
    procedure Highlight; virtual;
end;
```

The first instance variable in **InteractObj** specifies a code or letter that can be used, in addition to the mouse, for selecting the drawing object. The next four variables, **Left**, **Right**, **Top**, and **Bottom**, define the screen region where the screen object resides. This region contains an icon or menu option that the user can click on to select a drawing tool. Next lies the pointer, **ITool**, which is set to the **DrawingTool** object that is to be executed when the **InteractObj** object is selected. Note that a pointer is used here so that we can fully exploit polymorphism to invoke any of the methods in the hierarchy of drawing tools we created in Chapter 10.

The **InteractObj** type also contains three methods. The first is a constructor that is used to initialize a particular **InteractObj** object. It is passed the bounds of the screen region that contains the screen object, and a pointer to the drawing tool to be used when the screen object is selected. We'll need to create one **InteractObj** object for each drawing tool used in the paint and CAD programs.

The **Select** method, which follows, is included in **InteractObj** to invoke the **DrawingTool** object that it contains:

```
procedure InteractObj.Select;
begin
  Highlight;             { Show that the option has been selected }
  ITool^.Draw;           { Do the function selected }
  Highlight;             { Restore the option to its normal state }
end;
```

It now becomes the method that we must call when we want to select a particular drawing function. Recall that the **Draw** procedure is the high-level method that is to be used to initiate the action of a **DrawingTool**. The calls to **Highlight** that are included in **Select** are provided to highlight the screen object that the user has selected.

Currently, **Highlight** merely reverses the image of the screen object. Therefore, the first call reverses the colors in an icon or menu option, while the second call restores the screen object to its original image.

The **InteractObj** type provides everything we need to encapsulate a screen object with a drawing tool. But there are cases, as with the palette, where we don't want the screen object to be reversed when it is selected. For this reason, the **Interact** unit also includes the derived type **UserInteract**. It inherits everything in **InteractObj**, except that it overrides **Select** so that only the nested **DrawingTool**'s **Draw** method is called and the highlighting action does not take place:

```
procedure UserInteract.Select;
begin
  ITool^.Draw;
end;
```

You'll find this statement in the object declaration of **UserInteract** in INTERACT.PAS.

Now that we have an object hierarchy that allows us to select drawing tools from the screen, we need to build an object type that ties a set of these together into one package. This is the job of the **ToolSet** type in INTERACT.PAS. As shown next, **ToolSet** contains an array of pointers to **InteractObj** objects, called **Tool**, and a set of three methods that manage this array:

```
ToolSetPtr = ^ToolSet;
ToolSet = object
  Tool: array[0..MaxTools] of InteractObjPtr;    { List of tools }
  NumTools: integer;                      { Number of tools in list }
  constructor Init;
  procedure AddTool(ToolPtr: InteractObjPtr);
  procedure AnyToProcess(C: integer);
end;
```

Note that we have allocated space for only 21 interactive objects by using the integer constant **MaxTools**. This is just big enough for the paint and CAD programs we'll be developing.

The **NumTools** variable in **ToolSet** keeps track of the number of objects currently in the **Tool** array. It is initialized to zero in the **ToolSet** constructor. So how do objects get placed in the **Tool** array? This is the job of the **AddTool** method, shown next:

```
procedure ToolSet.AddTool(ToolPtr: InteractObjPtr);
begin
  if NumTools > MaxTools then Exit;  { No more room in list }
  Tool[NumTools] := ToolPtr;  Inc(NumTools);
end;
```

We must call **AddTool** for every interactive tool we want included in an application program. For example, let's say we want to add a spraycan object and its icon that spans from (4,10) to (36,42) to the list of drawing tools. First, we must declare a pointer to a **DrawingTool** object that we'll use to point to our spraycan tool:

```
var
  Spraycan: DrawingToolPtr;
```

Then we must call **New** to allocate and initialize the spraycan tool:

```
Spraycan := New(SpraycanToolPtr,Init);
```

Finally, we can call **AddTool** to add the spraycan tool to the list maintained by **ToolSet**:

```
Tools.AddTool(New(InteractObjPtr(Ord('s'),4,10,36,42,Spraycan)));
```

The last method in **ToolSet**, **AnyToProcess**, is used in an application program to determine which drawing tool has been selected, if any, and then execute it. The method is broken into two cases that are built around an **if-then-else** statement. Which part of the **if** statement gets executed depends on the value of **C** passed into **AnyToProcess**. This variable is either a keyboard or mouse event code that was presumably returned from **WaitForInput**, which we developed in the mouse tools in Chapter 7. If **C** is greater than zero, then a keyboard event has occurred; if it's less than zero, then a mouse button was pressed; if it equals zero then it means that no event has taken place, so nothing should be done.

The top part of **AnyToProcess** handles the situation where a user has entered a character code to select an object. The second, which is quite similar, is used when a mouse action has occurred. It retrieves the current coordinates of the mouse and then searches through the tool array to find if any screen object was located where the mouse was pressed. If there was one, then that tool's corresponding **Select** method is executed:

```
else if C < 0 then begin            { Mouse button pressed }
  Mouse.GetCoords(X,Y);             { Find which region was selected }
  for I := 0 to NumTools do begin
    if Mouse.InBox(Tool[I]^.Left,Tool[I]^.Top,
              Tool[I]^.Right,Tool[I]^.Bottom,X,Y) then begin
```

```
        Tool[I]^.Select;                    { Execute the function }
        Exit;
      end
    end
end
```

For more on how polymorphism is used to manage the array of drawing tools used in the paint program refer to the sidebar entitled "Polymorphism with Pointers."

Setting Up the Environment

All the components discussed in the last section are created in the function **SetupScreen**, which can be found in PAINT.PAS. Although this is a long routine, it is easy to follow if broken up into manageable segments.

Part of **SetupScreen** is responsible for setting up the main menu bar at the top of the screen, which is drawn by the following two statements:

```
H := TextHeight('H') + 2;
if GetMaxColor = 1 then SetFillStyle(SolidFill,0)
  else SetFillStyle(SolidFill,EgaBlue);
Bar3D(0,0,MaxX,H,0,False);
OutTextXY(2,2,'Text  Line  Clear  Quit');
```

The processing of the menu bar is created in the lines that follow these two statements. The succeeding lines add each of the menu bar commands (*Text*, *Line*, *Clear*, and *Quit*) to the list of objects that are on the screen. This is accomplished by using the object-oriented utility, INTERACT.PAS, discussed in the last section. Here we're using a **ToolSet** object called **Tools**. It's declared in INTERACT.PAS. Adding an object to the **Tools** list is simply a matter of calling the **AddTool** method.

Later we'll write routines to pull down the appropriate menu when one of these text icons is selected. Note that the location under these words is saved in a pair of global variables in **SetupScreen** so that we'll know where to place the pull-down menus. For example, in the case of the **Text** option, the pull-down menu appears at **TextWindowX** and **TextWindowY**. These variables are defined in USERTOOL.PAS.

The next sequence of statements displays a series of icons on the left side of the screen and appends the corresponding drawing objects to the **Tools** object. Each of these icons is located in a separate file and follows the naming convention that we introduced when we developed the icon editor in Chapter 8.

Displaying an icon is a two-step process. First, the icon is read from its file and displayed (this is accomplished in **ReadIcon**, a procedure included in

---

Polymorphism with Pointers

We've already seen how inheritance can be used so that we can construct objects out of other objects and share common code. We did this, for example, in our interactive drawing toolkit by deriving the object types **PencilTool** and **LineTool** from the generic **DrawingTool** object type. It's fairly easy to see how we can declare objects of each of these derived types, but how can we handle arrays of **DrawingTool** objects where each array element is a different type, like **PencilTool**, **LineTool**, and so on? Don't forget, we want to exploit polymorphism to call each object in the array with the same invocation—no matter what type it is.

To get the job done, we must resort to using *pointers* to the objects; furthermore, these pointers must be declared as the base type. For example, to construct an array of ten **DrawingTools** we could use the array declaration

```
ToolList: array[1..10] of DrawingToolPtr;
```

and assign a tool to each array element using a statement like:

```
ToolList[1] := New(PencilToolPtr, Init);
```

Following this, we can access any of the methods that the various tools in the array **Tool** inherited from the **DrawingTool** object type using the same notation—polymorphism at work. For instance, to call each of the **Draw** methods in the **Tool** array one after another we could use:

```
for I := 1 to 10 do
  ToolList[I]^.Draw;
```

This is the same approach that we use in the paint and CAD programs, although we'll be building a list of pointers to **InteractObj** objects instead of **DrawingTools**.

USERTOOL.PAS). Next, the icon is added to the list of objects on the screen by calls to **AddTool**. These icons are used to invoke one of the drawing functions that we created in Chapter 10.

The next block of code in **SetupScreen** creates the fill patterns and color palette at the bottom of the screen. In order to keep our environment as consistent as possible, the fill patterns and palette are used by activating one of two new object types that are derived from **DrawingTool**. These types, called **ChangeFillPatternTool** and **ChangeFillColorTool**, are located in USERTOOL.PAS.

We'll add these objects to our tool list as we did earlier with the icon and menu objects and we'll activate them by calling their **Draw** methods. If you look at the definition of each of their objects, in fact, you'll find that all we're doing is overriding **DrawingTool**'s **Draw** and replacing it with code with which to select a fill pattern and a color from the palette.

Because the size of the screen may vary according to the graphics mode in use, the **Draw** method in these object types is slightly more complicated than it would need to be otherwise. The primary thing to note is that each routine first calculates how wide each cell (for example, a single fill pattern) needs to be in order for all of the cells to fit across the screen. A **for** loop is then used to sequence through each of the patterns or colors until all of them have been displayed. Note also that we are not adding each cell individually to our list of objects; instead we add the complete block of fill patterns and the block of colors as two individual objects.

To the left of these fill styles in the paint program's environment is a rectangular region that displays the current fill pattern and color. This region is also added as an object, called **ChangeDrawColorTool**, and it serves as a platform for us to change the drawing color. For example, whenever you click on this region, the current fill color will become the current drawing color. As was true with the fill pattern and palette tools, this action is performed by the **Draw** method in **ChangeDrawColorTool**.

One last operation that **SetupScreen** performs is to calculate and draw the boundaries of the drawing window. As per the requirements of our DRAW.PAS, these boundaries are saved in the global variables **Wl**, **Wt**, **Wr**, and **Wb**.

The Paint Routines

Although we have the basic form of the paint program under control, there are a handful of functions that we still need to flesh out. These will all be packaged in USERTOOL.PAS. We've already touched on some of them briefly, like **ChangeFillPatternTool** and **ChangeFillColorTool**, but there are details in these and other methods in the **UserTool** unit that we need to cover.

Table 11.2 is a list of the support object types in **UserTool**. We'll start by examining the routine associated with the *Quit* option in the main menu bar and then we'll proceed to the others. Remember, the drawing tools corresponding to the icons, the text entry option, and the clear window function have already been taken care of by using the object types in the DRAW.PAS package from Chapter 10.

Quitting the Program

The **QuitTool** object type provides the only path out of the paint program. When it is selected, it simply exits graphics mode and terminates the program by calling

Table 11.2. Paint program support routines in USERTOOL.PAS

Routine	Description
QuitTool	Terminates the paint program
ChangeFontTool	Selects a new font style
ChangeLineStyleTool	Selects a new line style
ChangeFillPatternTool	Selects a new fill pattern
ChangeFillColorTool	Selects a new fill color
ChangeDrawColorTool	Sets the drawing color to the fill color

Halt. It is implemented in **UserTool** as a derived **DrawingTool** type so that we can add it to our list of drawing operations and select it in the same way as all the other tools. Of course, **QuitTool** doesn't do any drawing; instead, **Draw** is overridden to execute the statements that terminate the program.

The Pull-Down Menus

As we stated earlier, the paint program uses pull-down menus for changing the text and line style. We could develop a general menu package to support pull-down menus, but this would lead to even more groundwork and would only delay our efforts to build a working paint program. Instead, we'll use a rather hard-coded approach in order to simplify the task of adding pull-down menus to our program.

The pull-down menus for the text and line styles are accessed by clicking on the words *Text* or *Line*. When one of these options is selected, either the object type **ChangeFontTool** or **ChangeLineStyleTool** is invoked through our object-oriented utility, INTERACT.PAS.

The **Draw** methods in both of these object types are overridden to supply the user interaction in the pull-down menus. At the beginning of each of these routines are several statements that create the pull-down menus. The process begins by using **GPopup** to pop up the window for the menu. Note that USERTOOL.PAS declares a global window object, called **Win**, for it to use.

Next, a **for** loop is used to fill the window with the appropriate selections. For instance, if the *Text* option is selected, the different font styles are displayed so that you can select one. Similarly, if the line pull-down menu is chosen, a set of available line styles is shown. Figure 11.2 shows the paint environment with the *Line* pull-down menu visible.

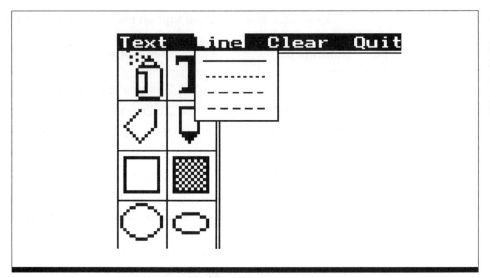

Figure 11.2. The Line pull-down menu

The positions of the pull-down menu options are hard-coded and defined within the methods **ChangeFontTool.Draw** and **ChangeLineStyleTool.Draw**. Therefore, when you click on one of the font styles (in the case of the text menu) or one of the line segments (in the case of the line pull-down menu), the program can determine which option has been selected and take the appropriate action.

Determining which menu selection has been chosen is performed by the second **for** loop in **ChangeFontTool.Draw** and **ChangeLineStyleTool.Draw**. However, both of the methods wait for you to click the left mouse button with the statement:

```
while not Mouse.ButtonPressed(LeftButton) do ;
```

Once the button is pressed, the mouse coordinates are retrieved and compared against the possible choices within the menu to see if one has been selected. If so, the appropriate text style or line style is changed and the routine returns. If the mouse coordinates do not correspond to a menu selection then **Draw** returns without performing any action.

Changing the Fill Style

At the bottom of the screen are a series of fill patterns and colors that can be used in the paint program. To easily integrate these utilities into our existing packages, the fill patterns and the color palette are added to the object list as two objects and not as a series of smaller objects. Therefore, if you click the mouse within one of the fill patterns, no matter which one has been selected, the **ChangeFillPatternTool** object type is used. Alternatively, if you select one of the color boxes, **ChangeFillColorTool** is used.

These types operate much like **ChangeFontTool** and **ChangeLineStyleTool** in that they compare the mouse coordinates at the time of the button press with the locations of each of the regions. If the mouse has selected one of the boxes, the fill pattern or color from that box is used to set either **GlobalFillStyle** or **GlobalFillColor**, which are two of the global drawing parameters defined in DRAW.PAS.

User Interaction

The code used to process and control the user's input to the paint program is placed in the **repeat** loop at the bottom of the mainline in the PAINT.PAS. This infinite loop calls the mouse method **WaitForInput** to get any user input, and then subsequently invokes **AnyToProcess** to perform the appropriate action, if any.

```
repeat
  C := Mouse.WaitForInput(LeftButton);   { Get user input }
  Tools.AnyToProcess(C);                  { If tool selected, use it }
until False;
```

The **WaitForInput** method is found in the files MOUSEPAC.PAS and KBDMOUSE.PAS that we developed in Chapter 7. As written, this function waits for either the left mouse button to be pressed or a key to be struck before it returns. The value of the action is assigned to the integer variable **C**.

The input value is passed to **AnyToProcess**, which is a method of **ToolSet** that we defined in INTERACT.PAS. It steps through the list of objects and tests whether the user has clicked in the region bounding an object or has pressed its quick access key. If either is True, the method invokes the appropriate routine associated with it.

Note that the **repeat** loop in the main body of PAINT.PAS is an infinite loop. The infinite loop functions as what is commonly called an event-driven loop. (An event can be a mouse click or a keyboard action.) That is, the loop repeats as it waits for an event to occur. Remember that the **QuitTool** object type provides a path for exiting the program. Therefore, one of the events that can occur is that the user can select the *Quit* option or type in the letter q, which in turn calls **QuitTool.Draw**.

Compiling the Paint Program

As mentioned before, our paint program uses several of the tools that we developed in earlier chapters. A listing of these files and the chapters in which they are discussed is shown in Table 11.3. You will need to have access to each of these files; the best thing to do is to have them in the same directory as the PAINT.PAS file.

Using the Paint Program

Once you have a compiled version of the paint program you are ready to try it out. After invoking the program, the first thing you should see is the environment as it was shown in Figure 11.1. If you have any difficulty, make sure you have all of the icon files and graphics libraries in their appropriate location.

The program is easy to run. You can use the mouse or keyboard as outlined in Chapter 7 to move the cursor around the screen. The drawing functions should all work as described in Chapter 10. Most of the other functions that we have added have been described earlier in this chapter. The only one remaining is how to change the drawing color.

Remember that the palette on the bottom of the screen is used to change the fill color directly. To change the drawing color, you need to click on the box just to the left of the fill patterns, which shows the current fill settings. By clicking on this

Table 11.3. Description of files used in paint program

Source file	Chapter	Description
GTEXT.PAS	3	Graphics mode text utilities
MATRIX.PAS	5	Provides array declaration for polygons
MOUSEPAC.PAS	7	Mouse utilities
KBDMOUSE.PAS	7	Keyboard-emulated mouse
GPOPPAC.PAS	9	Pop-up window package
DRAW.PAS	10	Interactive drawing utilities
INTERACT.PAS	11	Object-oriented utilities
USERTOOL.PAS	11	Miscellaneous environment tools
PAINT.PAS	11	The main paint program

box, which also was added as an object in **SetupScreen**, you will force the drawing color to be changed to the drawing color currently displayed within it.

Enhancing the Paint Program

Although the complete paint program is large, there are many features you might want to add. If you have some ideas, you should not have too much difficulty in carrying them out; in fact, the program was designed so that additions could easily be made.

First, let's look at what you need to do to add a new function that would be accessible through an icon. Let's say you want to add a routine that will use the flood fill operation to fill selected regions:

1. Create an icon that reflects the functionality of the new feature using the icon editor from Chapter 8.

2. Derive an object type from **DrawingTool** that implements the desired feature.

3. Add a call to **Tools.AddTool** within **SetupScreen** to install your new object.

Ideas to Experiment With

Probably the most useful addition you might make to the paint program would be to add functions to save the image of the current drawing window to disk and similarly read an image from disk. This way you can work on various pictures intermittently and begin to archive your work. To add this feature, you will need to write a routine that captures the screen and writes it to disk and a companion routine to read the saved screen image and display it. In addition, you must supply a function that can acquire from the user the name of the file from which the disk is supposed to be written or read. For this you could try expanding on the **GReadStr** function included in GTEXT.PAS and combining it with the pop-up window function. In this way you you could create a pop-up window that supports user interaction while in graphics mode.

Another possibility is to expand some of the existing methods. For instance, you could modify **TextTool** so that the user can use the backspace key. In addition, you could modify **TextTool** so that it can type vertical text or text automatically scaled or justified. Each of these can be added with a minimal amount of effort.

A final idea is to add a routine that allows the user to cut out a portion of the image and move it elsewhere. This feature could be implemented by letting the user mark off a rectangular region of the drawing window and then use **GetImage** and **PutImage** to move it to another location.

• Listing 11.1. USERTOOL.PAS

```
unit UserTool;
{$R+}
{ USERTOOL.PAS: User interface tools used in the paint program. }
interface
uses
  Graph, Draw, MousePac, KbdMouse, GPopPac, GText;
const
  IconWd = 16;              { Icons are defined as 16 x 16- }
  IconHt = 16;              { pixel patterns }
  FillHeight = 16;          { All 12 of the BGI fill patterns }
  NumFillsWide = 12;        { are 16 pixels high in size }
  Border = 2;               { 2-pixel border is used }
  WindowLines = 5;          { Size of line menu }
  LineHeight = 10;          { A line menu entry is this many pixels high }
  LineWidth = 40;           { A line menu entry is this many pixels wide }
  MaxLineStyles = 4;        { The line menu has this many entries }
type
QuitToolPtr = ^QuitTool;
QuitTool = object(DrawingTool)
  procedure Draw; virtual;
end;

{ User has selected one of the fill patterns--find which one it is
  and set GlobalFillStyle to this type }
ChangeFillPatternToolPtr = ^ChangeFillPatternTool;
ChangeFillPatternTool = object(DrawingTool)
  procedure Draw; virtual;
end;

{ User has selected one of the fill colors--find which one it is
  and set GlobalFillColor to this value }
ChangeFillColorToolPtr = ^ChangeFillColorTool;
ChangeFillColorTool = object(DrawingTool)
  procedure Draw; virtual;
end;

{ User has selected the DrawColor block. Change GlobalDrawColor
  to the color used by GlobalFillColor, which is the current color
  in the DrawColor block. }
ChangeDrawColorToolPtr = ^ChangeDrawColorTool;
ChangeDrawColorTool = object(DrawingTool)
  procedure Draw; virtual;
end;
```

```
{ User has selected text main menu option. Pull down the text menu
  and let user select one of the fonts. Load this new font, if
  any is selected. }
ChangeFontToolPtr = ^ChangeFontTool;
ChangeFontTool = object(DrawingTool)
  procedure Draw; virtual;
end;

{ Pull-down line style menu. Change GlobalLineStyle to the line type
  selected from the menu, if any. }
ChangeLineStyleToolPtr = ^ChangeLineStyleTool;
ChangeLineStyleTool = object(DrawingTool)
  procedure Draw; virtual;
end;

var
TextWindowX: integer;        { Global values that specify where the }
TextWindowY: integer;        { font pull-down menu should appear }
LineWindowX: integer;        { Specifies where the line pull-down menu }
LineWindowY: integer;        { should appear }
Win: GWindows;   { Declare a window object to be used in the pop-up menus }
{ Holds an icon pattern read from a file }
Icon: array [0..IconWd-1,0..IconHt-1] of byte;

{ This routine is accessible to programs that use the UserTool unit }
procedure ReadIcon(X, Y: integer; Filename: string);

implementation
procedure QuitTool.Draw;
begin
  CloseGraph;
  Halt(0);
end;

procedure ChangeFillPatternTool.Draw;
{ Allows the user to interactively select a fill pattern to be used
  from a palette of fill pattern styles }
var
  J, I, FillWidth, FillType, Mx, My: integer;
begin
  FillWidth := (GetMaxx-1-IconWd*4+2) div (NumFillsWide+1);
  FillType := 0;
  J := IconWd * 4 + 2 + FillWidth;
  for I := 0 to NumFillsWide-1 do begin
    Mouse.GetCoords(Mx,My);
    if Mouse.InBox(J,GetMaxy-FillHeight*2,J+FillWidth,
                   GetMaxy-FillHeight,Mx,My) then begin
      GlobalFillStyle := FillType;
      SetFillStyle(GlobalFillStyle,GlobalFillColor);
      SetLineStyle(SolidLn,0,ThickWidth);
      Mouse.Hide;
```

```
      { Show the new fill style }
      Bar3D(IconWd*4+2+2,GetMaxY-FillHeight*2+2,
            IconWd*4+2+FillWidth-2,GetMaxY-2,0,False);
      SetLineStyle(SolidLn,0,NormWidth);
      Mouse.Show;
      Exit;
    end;
    Inc(FillType);  Inc(J,FillWidth);
  end;
end;

procedure ChangeFillColorTool.Draw;
{ User has selected one of the fill colors--find which one it is
  and set GlobalFillColor to this value }
var
  MaxColors, ColorWidth, FillColor, FillWidth, I, J, Mx, My: integer;
begin
  FillWidth := (GetMaxX-1-IconWd*4+2) div (NumFillsWide+1);
  MaxColors := GetMaxColor;
  ColorWidth := (GetMaxX-1-IconWd*4+2-FillWidth) div (MaxColors + 1);
  FillColor := 0;
  J := IconWd * 4 + 2 + FillWidth;
  for I := 0 to MaxColors do begin
    Mouse.GetCoords(Mx,My);
    if Mouse.InBox(J,GetMaxY-FillHeight,
                   J+ColorWidth,GetMaxY,Mx,My) then begin
      GlobalFillColor := FillColor;
      SetFillStyle(GlobalFillStyle,GlobalFillColor);
      SetLineStyle(SolidLn,0,ThickWidth);
      Mouse.Hide;
      { Show the new fill color }
      Bar3D(IconWd*4+2+2,GetMaxY-FillHeight*2+2,
            IconWd*4+2+FillWidth-2,GetMaxY-2,0,False);
      SetLineStyle(SolidLn,0,NormWidth);
      Mouse.Show;
      Exit;
    end;
    Inc(FillColor);
    Inc(J,ColorWidth);
  end
end;

procedure ChangeDrawColorTool.Draw;
{ User has selected the DrawColor block. Change GlobalDrawColor
  to the color used by GlobalFillColor, which is the current color
  in the DrawColor block. }
var
  FillWidth: integer;
begin
  FillWidth := (GetMaxX-1-IconWd*4+2) div (NumFillsWide+1);
  GlobalDrawColor := GlobalFillColor;
  SetFillStyle(GlobalFillStyle,GlobalFillColor);
```

```
    SetLineStyle(SolidLn,0,ThickWidth);
    SetColor(GlobalDrawColor);
    Mouse.Hide;
    Bar3D(IconWd*4+2+2,GetMaxY-FillHeight*2+2,          { Show new color as }
          IconWd*4+2+FillWidth-2,GetMaxY-2,0,False); { border to the block }
    SetLineStyle(SolidLn,0,NormWidth);
    Mouse.Show;
  end;

procedure ChangeFontTool.Draw;
{ User has selected text main menu option. Pull down the text menu
  and let user select one of the fonts. Load this new font, if
  any is selected. }
const
  FontStr: array[0..WindowLines-1] of string = ('Default', 'Triplex',
      'Small', 'Sans Serif', 'Gothic');
var
  SaveText: TextSettingsType;
  T: boolean;
  WindowWidth, WindowHeight, Offset, I, Mx, My: integer;
begin
  GetTextSettings(SaveText);
  SetTextStyle(DefaultFont,HorizDir,1);
  WindowWidth := TextWidth('Sans Serif') + Border;
  WindowHeight := (TextHeight('S')+2) * WindowLines + 3 * Border;
  SetTextStyle(SaveText.Font,SaveText.Direction,SaveText.CharSize);
  Mouse.Hide;
  T := Win.GPopup(TextWindowX,TextWindowY,TextWindowX+WindowWidth+Border,
                  TextWindowY+WindowHeight,SolidLn,GetMaxColor,
                  SolidFill,Black);
  SetTextJustify(LeftText,TopText);
  SetTextStyle(DefaultFont,HorizDir,1);
  SetColor(GetMaxColor);
  Offset := Border;
  for I := 0 to WindowLines-1 do begin
    OutTextXY(Border,Offset,FontStr[I]);
    Inc(Offset,TextHeight(FontStr[I])+2);
  end;
  Mouse.Show;
  while not Mouse.ButtonPressed(LeftButton) do ;
  Mouse.GetCoords(Mx,My);
  Offset := Border;
  for I := 0 to WindowLines-1 do begin
    if (Mouse.InBox(TextWindowX+Border,Offset,
        TextWindowX+TextWidth(FontStr[I]),
        TextWindowY+Offset+TextHeight(FontStr[I])+2,Mx,My)) then begin
      Mouse.Hide;
      T := Win.GUnpop;
      Mouse.Show;
      SetTextStyle(I,HorizDir,1);
      GlobalTextStyle := I;
      while not Mouse.ButtonReleased(LeftButton) do ;
```

```
      Exit;
    end;
    Inc(Offset,TextHeight(FontStr[I])+2);
  end;
  Mouse.Hide;
  T := Win.GUnpop;
  Mouse.Show;
end;

procedure ChangeLineStyleTool.Draw;
{ Pull-down line style menu. Change GlobalLineStyle to the line type
  selected from the menu, if any. }
var
  WindowWidth, WindowHeight, Offset, I, Mx, My: integer;
  T: boolean;
begin
  WindowWidth := LineWidth + Border * 6;
  WindowHeight := LineHeight * MaxLineStyles;
  Mouse.Hide;
  T := Win.GPopup(LineWindowX,LineWindowY,
                  LineWindowX+WindowWidth+Border,
                  LineWindowY+WindowHeight+LineHeight div 2,
                  SolidLn,GetMaxColor,SolidFill,Black);
  SetColor(GetMaxColor);
  Offset := Border;
  for I := 0 to MaxLineStyles-1 do begin
    SetLineStyle(I,0,NormWidth);
    Line(Border*3,Offset+LineHeight div 2,Border*3+LineWidth,
         Offset+LineHeight div 2);
    Inc(Offset,LineHeight);
  end;
  Mouse.Show;
  while not Mouse.ButtonPressed(LeftButton) do ;
  Mouse.GetCoords(Mx,My);
  Offset := Border;
  for I := 0 to MaxLineStyles-1 do begin
    if Mouse.InBox(LineWindowX+Border*3,Offset-LineHeight div 2,
                   LineWindowX+Border*3+LineWidth,
                   LineWindowY+Offset+LineHeight div 2,Mx,My) then begin
      Mouse.Hide;
      T := Win.GUnpop;
      Mouse.Show;
      SetLineStyle(I,0,NormWidth);
      GlobalLineStyle := I;
      while not Mouse.ButtonReleased(LeftButton) do ;
      Exit;
    end;
    Inc(Offset,LineHeight);
  end;
  Mouse.Hide;
  T := Win.GUnpop;
  Mouse.Show;
end;
```

```
procedure ReadIcon(X, Y: integer; Filename: string);
{ Read an icon from a file and display it. Program quits if
  the icon file cannot be found. }
var
  IconFile: text;
  I, J, Width, Height, IconPixel: integer;
begin
  {$I-}  Assign(IconFile,Filename);
  Reset(IconFile);  {$I+}
  if IOResult <> 0 then begin
    CloseGraph;
    WriteLn('Icon file not found: ',Filename);
    Halt(1);
  end;
  ReadLn(IconFile,Width,Height);
  if (Width <> IconWd) or (height <> IconHt) then begin
    CloseGraph;
    WriteLn('Incompatible icon file: ',Filename);
    Halt(1);
  end;
  { Double the size of the icon so that it is a good size }
  for J := 0 to IconHt-1 do begin
    for I := 0 to IconWd-1 do begin
      Read(IconFile,IconPixel);
      if IconPixel = 1 then begin
        PutPixel(2*I+X,Y+2*J,White);
        PutPixel(2*I+1+X,Y+2*J,White);
        PutPixel(2*I+X,Y+2*J+1,White);
        PutPixel(2*I+1+X,Y+2*J+1,White);
      end;
    end;
  end;
  Close(IconFile);
  Rectangle(X,Y,X+IconWd*2,Y+IconHt*2);
end;

begin
end.
```

• Listing 11.2. INTERACT.PAS

```
unit Interact;
{$R+}
{ INTERACT.PAS: Defines an object that ties together interface objects
  on the screen, such as icons and menu entries, with their operations. }
interface
uses
  Graph, MousePac, KbdMouse, Draw;
const
  MaxTools = 20;
type
```

```
{ The following object type ties together a drawing tool and the screen
  region that the user selects to activate the function }
InteractObjPtr = ^InteractObj;
InteractObj = object
  Cmd: integer;                    { Letter command that selects the object }
  Left, Right: integer;            { Screen region where command is displayed }
  Top, Bottom: integer;
  ITool: DrawingToolPtr;
  constructor Init(C, L, T, R, B: integer; ToolPtr: DrawingToolPtr);
  procedure Select; virtual;
  procedure Highlight; virtual;
end;

UserInteractPtr = ^UserInteract;
UserInteract = object(InteractObj)
  constructor Init(C, L, T, R, B: integer; Tl: DrawingToolPtr);
  procedure Select; virtual;
end;

{ The following is the primary object type used to provide the user-
  interaction tools for the environment. It ties together a drawing
  routine with menu options, icon, and so on. }
ToolSetPtr = ^ToolSet;
ToolSet = object
  Tool: array[0..MaxTools] of InteractObjPtr;    { List of tools }
  NumTools: integer;                             { Number of tools in list }
  constructor Init;
  procedure AddTool(ToolPtr: InteractObjPtr);
  procedure AnyToProcess(C: integer);
end;

var
  Tools: ToolSet;                            { Declare a list of tools }

implementation
constructor InteractObj.Init(C, L, T, R, B: integer;
                             ToolPtr: DrawingToolPtr);
{ Specify a code that can be used to select the object and a
  screen region that can be selected using the mouse to activate
  the DrawingTool passed in using ToolPtr }
begin
  Cmd := C;    ITool := ToolPtr;
  Left := L;  Top := T;  Right := R;  Bottom := B;
end;

procedure InteractObj.Select;
{ A particular DrawingTool has been selected using the mouse. Call
  its Highlight routine to show that it has been activated and
  then call its Draw method. }
begin
  Highlight;          { Show that the option has been selected }
  ITool^.Draw;        { Do the function selected }
  Highlight;          { Restore the option to its normal state }
end;
```

```
procedure InteractObj.Highlight;
{ Highlight the option on the screen by reversing the screen image
  where the option is placed. This action can be applied to both
  icons and menu options. }
var
  Region: pointer;
begin
  { Allocate memory to be used to reverse screen option }
  GetMem(Region,ImageSize(Left,Top,Right,Bottom));
  if Region = Nil then Exit;                 { Not enough memory }
  Mouse.Hide;
  GetImage(Left,Top,Right,Bottom,Region^); { Get the option's image }
  PutImage(Left,Top,Region^,NotPut);       { Reverse it }
  Mouse.Show;
  Dispose(Region);                         { Free the memory used }
end;

constructor UserInteract.Init(C, L, T, R, B: integer; Tl: DrawingToolPtr);
{ Note call to the base type constructor }
begin
  InteractObj.Init(C,L,T,R,B,Tl);
end;

procedure UserInteract.Select;
begin
  ITool^.Draw;
end;

constructor ToolSet.Init;
begin
  NumTools := 0;
end;

procedure ToolSet.AddTool(ToolPtr: InteractObjPtr);
{ This method is called to add an object to the user object list }
begin
  if NumTools > MaxTools then Exit; { No more room in list }
  Tool[NumTools] := ToolPtr;  Inc(NumTools);
end;

procedure ToolSet.AnyToProcess(C: integer);
{ After a button press, search the icon list to see if the mouse is
  positioned over an object. If an object is found, execute the function
  associated with the object. The argument C specifies what action has
  just taken place. If it is a letter, then the if-statement is executed
  and the list is checked to see if any of the objects have a Cmd code
  equal to C. If so, the function associated with that object is executed.
  The else part is executed when C<0, which occurs when a mouse button has
  been pressed. It is similar to the code described above except that it
  uses the mouse as the selector. }
var
  I, X, Y: integer;
begin
```

```
        if C > 0 then begin                { A letter command is supplied }
          for I := 0 to NumTools do begin  { Find which command the letter }
            if Tool[I]^.Cmd = C then begin  { corresponds to }
              Tool[I]^.Select;             { Execute the drawing function }
              Exit;
            end
          end
        end
        else if C < 0 then begin           { Mouse button pressed }
          Mouse.GetCoords(X,Y);            { Find which region was selected }
          for I := 0 to NumTools do begin
            if Mouse.InBox(Tool[I]^.Left,Tool[I]^.Top,
                        Tool[I]^.Right,Tool[I]^.Bottom,X,Y) then begin
              Tool[I]^.Select;             { Execute the function }
              Exit;
            end
          end
        end
      end;

      begin
      end.
```

• Listing 11.3. PAINT.PAS

```
program Paint;
{$R+}
{ PAINT.PAS: This is the main program file for the paint program
  discussed in Chapter 11. This program exploits many of the BGI
  functions to build a simple yet powerful paint program. Several
  of the tools built up earlier in the book are put to use in this
  program. The paint program will run without modification in most
  modes, although in some low-resolution modes you may want to make
  the icons smaller. The program uses MousePac and KbdMouse so that
  it supports either the mouse or the keyboard automatically. Most of
  the drawing tools used in PAINT.PAS are discussed in Chapter 10. }
uses
  Graph, MousePac, KbdMouse, GText, GPopPac, Draw, Interact, UserTool;
const
  GDriver: integer = Detect;
var
  C, ErrCode, GMode: integer;
  T: boolean;

procedure SetupScreen;
{ Set up the environment for the paint program }
var
  H, I, X, FillWidth, Offset, Space: integer;
  FillType, ColorWidth, MaxColors, FillColor: integer;
  { Declare a set of drawing tools. Note that late binding
    is used to get the power of polymorphism. }
```

```
      ChangeFont, ChangeLineStyle, ClearWorkArea, Quit, Pencil,
      Eraser, Spraycan, LineT1, Rect, FillRect, Poly, FillPoly,
      CircleT1, EllipseT1, ArcT1, TextT1, ChangeFillPattern,
      ChangeFillColor, ChangeDrawColor: DrawingToolPtr;
begin
   ChangeFont := New(ChangeFontToolPtr,Init);
   ChangeLineStyle := New(ChangeLineStyleToolPtr,Init);
   ClearWorkArea := New(ClearWindowToolPtr,Init);
   Quit := New(QuitToolPtr,Init);
   Pencil := New(PencilToolPtr,Init);
   Eraser := New(EraserToolPtr,Init);
   Spraycan := New(SpraycanToolPtr,Init);
   LineT1 := New(LineToolPtr,Init);
   Rect := New(RectangleToolPtr,Init);
   FillRect := New(FillRectangleToolPtr,Init);
   Poly := New(PolygonToolPtr,Init);
   FillPoly := New(FillPolygonToolPtr,Init);
   CircleT1 := New(CircleToolPtr,Init);
   EllipseT1 := New(EllipseToolPtr,Init);
   ArcT1 := New(ArcToolPtr,Init);
   TextT1 := New(TextToolPtr,Init);
   ChangeFillPattern := New(ChangeFillPatternToolPtr,Init);
   ChangeFillColor := New(ChangeFillColorToolPtr,Init);
   ChangeDrawColor := New(ChangeDrawColorToolPtr,Init);

   { Draw a main menu bar across the top of the screen. Each of the
     words in the menu bar will act as a user-interface object that
     can be selected. Some of the words, such as Text and Line, will
     cause pull-down menus to appear if the user clicks on them. }
   H := TextHeight('H') + 2;
   if GetMaxColor = 1 then SetFillStyle(SolidFill,0)
     else SetFillStyle(SolidFill,EgaBlue);
   Bar3D(0,0,MaxX,H,0,False);
   OutTextXY(2,2,'Text  Line  Clear  Quit');
   Space := TextWidth(' ');
   Offset := 2;

   Tools.AddTool(New(InteractObjPtr,Init(Ord('t'),Offset,0,
       Offset+TextWidth('Text'),TextHeight('Text'),ChangeFont)));
   TextWindowX := Offset;
   TextWindowY := TextHeight('Text') + Border;
   Inc(Offset,TextWidth('Text')+Space);
   Tools.AddTool(New(InteractObjPtr,Init(Ord('l'),Offset,0,
       Offset+TextWidth('Line'),TextHeight('Line'),ChangeLineStyle)));
   LineWindowX := Offset;
   LineWindowY := TextHeight('Line') + Border;
   Inc(Offset,TextWidth('Line')+Space);
   Tools.AddTool(New(InteractObjPtr,Init(Ord('c'),Offset,0,
       Offset+TextWidth('Clear'),TextHeight('Clear'),ClearWorkArea)));
   Inc(Offset,TextWidth('Clear')+Space);
   Tools.AddTool(New(InteractObjPtr,Init(Ord('q'),Offset,0,
       Offset+TextWidth('Quit'),TextHeight('Quit'),Quit)));
   { Now draw the icons on the left-hand side of the screen }
```

```
ReadIcon(0,H,'SPRAY.ICN');
Tools.AddTool(New(InteractObjPtr,Init(Ord('s'),0,H,IconWd*2,
    H+IconHt*2,Spraycan)));
ReadIcon(IconWd*2,H,'LETTER.ICN');
Tools.AddTool(New(InteractObjPtr,Init(Ord('c'),IconWd*2,H,
    IconWd*4,H+IconHt*2,TextT1)));
ReadIcon(0,H+IconHt*2,'LINE.ICN');
Tools.AddTool(New(InteractObjPtr,Init(Ord('d'),0,H+IconHt*2,
    IconWd*2,H+2*IconHt*2,LineT1)));
ReadIcon(IconWd*2,H+IconHt*2,'PENCIL.ICN');
Tools.AddTool(New(InteractObjPtr,Init(Ord('p'),IconWd*2,
    H+IconHt*2,IconWd*4,H+2*IconHt*2,Pencil)));
ReadIcon(0,H+2*IconHt*2,'SQUARE.ICN');
Tools.AddTool(New(InteractObjPtr,Init(Ord('s'),0,H+2*IconHt*2,
    IconWd*2,H+3*IconHt*2,Rect)));
ReadIcon(IconWd*2,H+2*IconHt*2,'FILLBOX.ICN');
Tools.AddTool(New(InteractObjPtr,Init(Ord('r'),IconWd*2,
    H+2*IconHt*2,IconWd*4,H+3*IconHt*2,FillRect)));
ReadIcon(0,H+3*IconHt*2,'CIRCLE.ICN');
Tools.AddTool(New(InteractObjPtr,Init(Ord('c'),0,H+3*IconHt*2,IconWd*2,
    H+4*IconHt*2,CircleT1)));
ReadIcon(IconWd*2,H+3*IconHt*2,'ELLIPSE.ICN');
Tools.AddTool(New(InteractObjPtr,Init(Ord('g'),IconWd*2,
    H+3*IconHt*2,IconWd*4,H+4*IconHt*2,EllipseT1)));
ReadIcon(0,H+4*IconHt*2,'POLYGON.ICN');
Tools.AddTool(New(InteractObjPtr,Init(Ord('p'),0,H+4*IconHt*2,
    IconWd*2,H+5*IconHt*2,Poly)));
ReadIcon(IconWd*2,H+4*IconHt*2,'FILLPOLY.ICN');
Tools.AddTool(New(InteractObjPtr,Init(Ord('x'),IconWd*2,H+4*IconHt*2,
    IconWd*4,H+5*IconHt*2,FillPoly)));
ReadIcon(0,H+5*IconHt*2,'ERASER.ICN');
Tools.AddTool(New(InteractObjPtr,Init(Ord('e'),0,H+5*IconHt*2,IconWd*2,
    H+6*IconHt*2,Eraser)));
ReadIcon(IconWd*2,H+5*IconHt*2,'ARC.ICN');
Tools.AddTool(New(InteractObjPtr,Init(Ord('a'),IconWd*2,
    H+5*IconHt*2,IconWd*4,H+6*IconHt*2,ArcT1)));

{ Draw a backdrop below the icons }
SetFillStyle(SolidFill,EgaBlue);
Bar3D(0,H+6*IconHt*2,IconWd*4,MaxY,0,False);

{ Create the fill pattern box. This will appear on the lower portion
  of the screen. }
FillWidth := (MaxX-1-IconWd*4+2) div (NumFillsWide+1);
GlobalFillColor := GetMaxColor;    { Start fill color at max color }
GlobalDrawColor := GlobalFillColor;
FillType := 0;
X := IconWd * 4 + 2 + FillWidth;
for I := 0 to NumFillsWide-1 do begin
  SetFillStyle(filltype,GlobalFillColor);
  Bar3D(X,MaxY-FillHeight*2,X+FillWidth,MaxY-FillHeight,0,False);
  Inc(FillType);
  Inc(X,FillWidth);
```

```
      end;
      Rectangle(IconWd*4+2,MaxY-FillHeight*2,MaxX,MaxY);
      Tools.AddTool(New(UserInteractPtr,Init(Ord('w'),IconWd*4+2+FillWidth,
            MaxY-FillHeight*2,MaxX,MaxY-FillHeight,ChangeFillPattern)));
      GlobalFillStyle := SolidFill;

      MaxColors := GetMaxColor;
      ColorWidth := (MaxX-1-IconWd*4+2-FillWidth) div (MaxColors + 1);
      FillColor := 0;
      X := IconWd * 4 + 2 + FillWidth;
      for I := 0 to MaxColors do begin
        SetFillStyle(SolidFill,FillColor);
        Bar3D(X,MaxY-FillHeight,X+ColorWidth,MaxY,0,False);
        Inc(FillColor);
        Inc(X,ColorWidth);
      end;
      Tools.AddTool(New(UserInteractPtr,Init(Ord('z'),IconWd*4+2+FillWidth,
            MaxY-FillHeight,MaxX,MaxY,ChangeFillColor)));
      SetLineStyle(SolidLn,0,ThickWidth);
      SetFillStyle(GlobalFillStyle,GlobalFillColor);
      Bar3D(IconWd*4+4,MaxY-FillHeight*2+2,IconWd*4+FillWidth,MaxY-2,0,False);
      Tools.AddTool(New(UserInteractPtr,Init(Ord('y'),IconWd*4+2,
            MaxY-FillHeight*2,IconWd*4+FillWidth+2,MaxY,ChangeDrawColor)));
      SetLineStyle(SolidLn,0,NormWidth);

      { Draw main draw area window }
      Wl := IconWd*4+2+1;    Wt := H+2+1;
      Wr := MaxX-1;
      Wb := MaxY-FillHeight*2-2-1;
      Rectangle(Wl-1,Wt-1,Wr+1,Wb+1);
      GlobalFillStyle := SolidFill;
      GlobalLineStyle := SolidLn;
      GlobalTextStyle := DefaultFont;
    end;

begin
    InitGraph(GDriver,GMode,'\tp\bgi');
    ErrCode := GraphResult;
    if Errcode <> grOk then begin
      WriteLn('Graphics error: ',GraphErrorMsg(ErrCode));
      Halt(1);                       { Return with error code }
    end;
    MaxX := GetMaxX;  MaxY := GetMaxY;
    Mouse.Init;                      { Call mouse's constructor }
    T := Mouse.Setup;                { Initialize the mouse }
    Win.Init;                        { Call window system's constructor }
    Tools.Init;                      { Call tool list's constructor }
    SetupScreen;                     { Set up the screen }
    repeat
      C := Mouse.WaitForInput(LeftButton);  { Get user input }
      Tools.AnyToProcess(C);                { If tool selected, use it }
    until False;
end.
```

12

A CAD Program

In Chapter 11 we developed a paint program that provides a graphics environment for drawing figures and shapes. In this chapter we'll extend the paint program so that it becomes a working CAD package. The differences between the two graphics programs may seem minor based on appearance; however, internally the two differ in several important ways. We'll explore these differences throughout this chapter as we discuss how the CAD program is written and how it functions. Finally, we'll end this chapter by outlining several enhancements that you might want to add to the CAD program to create your own custom version.

Painting versus Drafting

The environment for the CAD program is shown in Figure 12.1. Although the program looks like the paint program we developed in the last chapter, the two have significant differences. For instance, the paint program is designed to provide an environment for drawing pictures—much like an artist painting with watercolors. Once a scene has been painted, it's difficult to change it. The CAD program, on the other hand, is designed so that each of the scenes it displays is constructed from individual components that can readily be moved, rotated, or deleted.

The flexibility of the CAD program is due to the fact that it maintains a list of all the graphics objects that are in its drawing window. This list contains various attributes associated with each figure such as their sizes and locations. In addition, the dimensioning information is saved in world coordinates so that it can more easily match the specifications of a real-world object.

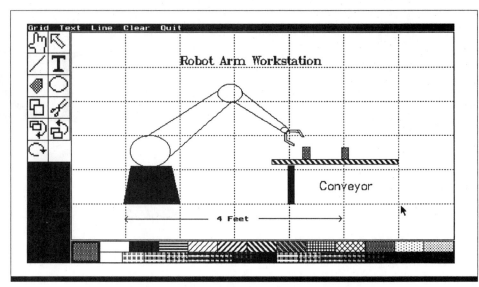

Figure 12.1. The environment of the CAD program

Each object in the drawing window is kept in an object list, which is similar to the technique we used in the paint program (Chapter 11) to process the icons and menu options. With this new object list we can easily access, manipulate, and move each of the graphics objects in the drawing window.

Here is a summary of the major enhancements included in the CAD program:

1. All objects are stored in real world coordinates.
2. Objects can be selected and moved.
3. Graphics figures are saved in an object list.
4. It supports a rotate and duplication feature.
5. It draws dimensioning lines.
6. An alignment grid is displayed.
7. The order in which objects are drawn can be changed.

In order to support each of these features, the CAD program will become rather large. Fortunately, we'll be able to exploit Turbo Pascal's inheritance capability and build on the code we used in the paint program. We will, however, have to develop seven new files that support the specialized functions for the CAD program. These files are listed in Table 12.1 along with a short description of each.

The file CAD.PAS is very similar to the main source file developed for the paint program in Chapter 11, so it won't be the primary focus of this chapter. In-

Table 12.1. Source files specific to the CAD program

Filename	Listing	Description
CAD.PAS	12.1	Contains the main function for the CAD program
GOBJLST.PAS	12.2	Maintains list of figures in the drawing window
GOBJECT.PAS	12.3	Provides the objects used to represent the figures in the drawing window
CADDRAW.PAS	12.4	Miscellaneous routines used by the CAD program
CADWINDW.PAS	12.5	Support routines for the drawing window

stead, we'll devote the majority of this chapter to discussions of GOBJLST.PAS and CADDRAW.PAS.

Because of the large size of the CAD program, only the line, polygon, circle, and text drawing functions are supported. These functions provide enough power to make a useful CAD package. However, you could easily modify the CAD program to include several of the other drawing functions found in the paint program.

In addition, the program is currently designed to work best in one of the higher-resolution modes on the EGA, VGA, or Hercules adapter. You may want to adjust the sizing of the icons or the size of the drawing window if you use other modes.

Setting Up the Screen

In Figure 12.1 you'll notice that the environment of the CAD program is slightly different from that of the paint program. There are several new icons and a grid pattern added to the drawing window. Each of these changes can be found in the **SetupScreen** procedure in CAD.PAS, which is used to create the environment of the CAD program.

Let's start by examining the new icon patterns and their corresponding functions. If you review CAD.PAS, you'll notice that several new or modified calls are being made to **AddTool** in **SetupScreen**. We are, however, using the same technique for maintaining a list of all the drawing tools. Therefore, the majority of **SetupScreen** involves adding the various drawing tools in the CAD program to the list of interactive tools that can be used.

A less visible change to **SetupScreen** is that the drawing window is set up to reflect real-world coordinates that are 7 units wide by 6 units high. (You can consider the units to be of any type—inches, feet, kilometers, etc.) This is done by the following two statements in **SetupScreen**:

```
Set_Window(0.0,0.0,7.0,6.0);
Set_ViewPort(Wl,Wt,Wr,Wb);
```

Both routines were introduced in Chapter 5. To refresh your memory, they are used to set the relationship between real-world coordinates and screen coordinates. The routine **Set_Window** defines the real-world coordinate bounds to be between (0.0,0.0) and (7.0,6.0). The **Set_ViewPort** procedure (different from the **SetViewPort** BGI procedure) defines the bounds of the drawing window for the MATRIX.PAS package.

A new feature added to the CAD program is the grid displayed in the drawing window. It is drawn by the **DrawGrid** procedure included in CADWINDW.PAS (Listing 12.5). You'll find a call to this routine in **SetupScreen** after the window and viewports are initialized. The grid is designed to help you align objects in the drawing window. It consists of a series of horizontal and vertical dashed lines, spaced one unit apart in real-world coordinates. After the line style is temporarily changed to dotted lines, the grid is drawn in **DrawGrid** with the two **for** loops as shown:

```
for J := 1 to 5 do begin        { Place same number here as that }
  WorldToPC(0.0,0.0+J,X,Y);     { used in Set_Window in SetupScreen }
  Line(Wl,Y,Wr,Y);
end;
for I := 1 to 6 do begin        { Use same number here as that }
  WorldToPC(0.0+I,0.0,X,Y);     { in SetupScreen }
  Line(X,Wt,X,Wb);
end;
```

The top **for** loop sequences through the horizontal lines extending across the screen and the second **for** loop draws the vertical lines. Notice that the index variables are added to real-world coordinates that are then converted to screen coordinates by **WorldToPC** and then drawn. This ensures that the lines are spaced according to the dimensions of the world coordinates. You may need to adjust the values passed to **Set_Window** and used in the **for** loops so that your grid pattern contains square-looking cells.

A Boolean global flag called **GridOn** (defined in CAD.PAS) controls whether the grid is displayed. If **GridOn** is True the grid is displayed; if it's set to False, however, the grid won't be displayed. To toggle the display of the grid you can select the word *Grid* in the main menu bar of the program.

Now that we've looked at the major changes that are visible in the environment, let's turn to the unique internal parts of the CAD program.

The Object List

One of the major differences between the paint program in Chapter 11 and the CAD program is that the CAD program maintains a list of all the objects in its drawing window. This list is much like the object-oriented list, found in INTERACT.PAS, that we used to tie together the icons, pop-up menus, and commands on the screen in the paint program with their operations.

As was the case in INTERACT.PAS, the list of objects is implemented as an object type that contains an array of pointers to objects. (We'll discuss these objects shortly.) Each figure on the screen will have an object associated with it in the list. The new object type that manages the list of graphics figures, **GObjList**, is defined in GOBJLST.PAS as:

```
{ Maximum number of figures that can be drawn on the screen }
const NumGObjects = 20;

{ This object type is used to maintain the list of figures currently
  displayed in the drawing window }
type
GObjList = object
  { List of graphics figures }
  GObjects: array[0..NumGObjects-1] of DrawingToolPtr;
  NextObj: integer;                        { Number of graphics objects }
  CurrentObj: integer;                     { Currently selected object }
  constructor Init;
  procedure AddObj(ObjPtr: DrawingToolPtr);
  procedure DeleteObj;
  procedure DeleteAll;
  procedure FlipToBack;
  procedure FlipToFront;
  procedure Duplicate;
  procedure Rotate;
  procedure Select;
  procedure Move;
  procedure Mark(Obj: integer);
  procedure DisplayAll;
end;
```

Table 12.2 provides a short description of each of the methods in **GObjList**. As this definition shows, a **GObjList** object contains a list of pointers to **DrawingTools** in the array **GObjects**. Are these the same **DrawingTools** we developed in Chapter 10 and used in the paint program? Not quite. The objects in **GObjects** are actually specialized versions of the drawing tools that we used in the paint program. In other words, these objects are derived from the **DrawingTool** objects we used in the paint program. We'll talk more about them in an upcoming section, but first let's get back to the details of **GObjList**. You'll

Table 12.2. Methods in GObjList

Method	Description
AddObj	Adds an object to the GObjects array
DeleteObj	Deletes the current object from the GObjects array and removes its figure from the screen
DeleteAll	Deletes all objects from the GObjects array and clears the screen
FlipToBack	Moves the current object to the back of the screen
FlipToFront	Moves the current object to the front of the screen
Duplicate	Duplicates the current object
Rotate	Rotates the current object by 45 degrees
Select	Enables user to specify which object is the current object
Move	Enables user to interactively move the current object
Mark	Displays a bounding box around the current object
DisplayAll	Displays all of the objects in GObjects array on the screen

notice that **GObjects** is declared to be large enough to hold **NumGObjects** −1 objects. **NumGObjects** is defined to be 20. You may want to increase this number if you want to have more than 20 graphics figures on the screen at a time. A global **GObjList** object, called **FigList**, is declared in CADDRAW.PAS and is used in the CAD program to access the features of the **GObjList** object type.

A graphics figure is added to the **GObjects** array by a call to the **GObjList** method **AddObj**. It simply appends a **DrawingTool** object passed into the method to the **GObjects** array if there is room. In addition, **AddObj** increments the **NextObj** variable that specifies the next free location in the **GObjects** array. At the same time, the variable **CurrentObj**, which points to the object in the array that is currently being manipulated, is set to the object just added.

The remaining methods in **GObjList** are also used to manipulate the graphics figures in the **GObjects** list. These methods manage which objects are displayed and in what order. For instance, there are methods to delete, duplicate, move, and select graphics objects on the screen. We'll look at these additional methods when we discuss the various operations supported in the CAD program.

Drawing Objects

The CAD program supports a limited set of drawing functions. These include a line drawing routine, a polygon function, a text routine, and a circle drawing function. Each of these routines uses the same code we used in the paint program to draw its figures. Recall that these drawing tools were implemented as object types that were derived from the base type **DrawingTool**. Actually, these tools won't be exactly the same. We've extended them by deriving a new set of tools so that they add the figures that they draw to a **GObjList** object (discussed in the last section). For instance, we've derived a **LineObj** type from the **LineTool** object type that we used in the last chapter. Figure 12.2 shows the new hierarchy we'll be using. The code for these new tools is included in GOBJECT.PAS (Listing 12.3).

So what do these new object types contain and how are they used? Here are some of the new features you'll find in them:

- They save the coordinates of their figures in world coordinates

- They provide methods to select, move, duplicate, translate, and rotate a particular figure

- They override the inherited **FinishDrawing** method so figures are added to the object list after they are drawn

One important point to note is that all the graphics objects are saved in world coordinates. This is done so that the objects can easily be manipulated in the program. If you examine the various methods in the derived **DrawingTool** object types you will see the conversions that are made between screen and world coordinates. In the next section we'll learn how objects are drawn and added to the graphics object list.

Working with Lines

The new line drawing object type, called **LineObj** (GOBJECT.PAS), is derived from the **LineTool** type (DRAW.PAS). We're overriding the original drawing tools so that we can add the new functionality outlined in the previous section. For instance, **FinishDrawing** is overridden so that after an object is drawn, which is the only time it is called, we can add the figure to the **GObjects** array. Therefore, the first thing our new **FinishDrawing** method does is call its inherited method:

```
LineTool.FinishDrawing;
```

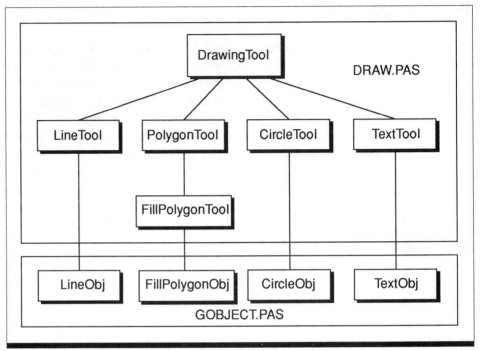

Figure 12.2. The CAD drawing tools are derived from those in DRAW.PAS

This will ensure that all the finishing touches on the figure are handled correctly. Next, a **LineObj** is created, called **Nl**, and the contents of the **LineTool** object, which was used to draw the figure, are copied to the **LineObj** object. Finally, the **LineObj** object is added to the **GObjects** array. These steps are performed by the following statements:

```
Nl := New(LineObjPtr,Init);    { Create a new line object }
GetBounds(Left,Top,Right,Bottom);
PCtoWorld(X1,Y1,Xw1,Yw1);      { Save endpoints in world }
PCtoWorld(X2,Y2,Xw2,Yw2);      { coordinates }
Nl^.Copy(@Self);               { Copy all settings to new object }
DrawArrows;                    { Draw arrows on new line }
FigList.AddObj(Nl);
```

It's important to note that the **LineObj** data is copied from the **LineTool** object and that its endpoints are converted to world coordinates by **PCToWorld** (MATRIX.PAS) and saved in world coordinates.

The **GetBounds** method, which is called in this sequence of statements, calculates the PC screen boundaries of the object and is used when determining which object the mouse has selected when one of its buttons is pressed. Note that the boundary values in **LineObj**'s **GetBounds** are offset by 3 pixels. This is done so that when the line is horizontal or vertical it appears slightly larger, and thus, easier to select.

Prior to the call to **AddObj** is the call to **AddArrows**, which is also a method in **LineObj**. This method appends arrowheads to the line segment if the user has selected this style. Three new line types have been added to the *Line* menu to support these arrows. The new pull-down menu for the *Line* menu option, which includes these new arrow line styles, is shown in Figure 12.3. Since two of the line styles are designed so that the arrow is on the leading or trailing edge of the line, it is important to maintain which side of the line the arrowhead is to be placed. Depending on the style of arrow selected, either **LeftArrow** or **RightArrow** or both are set to True. These are used in the routine **AddArrows** to select which arrows are displayed. The size of the arrow is specified by **ArrowSize** and is set in GOBJECT.PAS to be 4 pixels in width and height.

The one difficult part in dealing with arrows is that the arrowhead must be rotated so that it is oriented at the same angle as the line segment to which it is attached. These adjustments are done in **AddArrows**. Let's take a closer look at this.

The method **AddArrows** draws an arrow on the leading edge of the line segment, at (Xw1,Yw1), if **LeftArrow** is True and an arrow on the trailing edge of the line segment, at (Xw2, Yw2), if **RightArrow** is True. The arrowhead itself is made from two connected line segments joined to one of the ends of the line. The points describing this are contained in the array **Arrowhead**. The arrowhead figure is adjusted so that its angle matches that of the line segment, by first translating

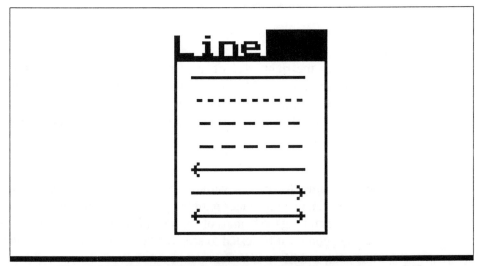

Figure 12.3. The line style pull-down menu includes arrow symbols

its center to the origin, rotating it, and then translating it back to the tip of the line segment. This process is performed by the lines:

```
PCTranslatePoly(3,Arrowhead,-XPC1+W1,-YPC1+Wt);
PCRotatePoly(3,Arrowhead,Angle);
PCTranslatePoly(3,Arrowhead,XPC1-W1,YPC1-Wt);
```

Finally, the arrow is drawn by the statement:

```
DrawPoly(3,Arrowhead);
```

Drawing Polygons and Circles

Displaying and managing figures of polygons and circles is handled by the object types **FillPolygonObj** and **CircleObj**. They are derived from the equivalent interactive drawing tools from DRAW.PAS. You'll find that they are quite similar to the **LineObj** type discussed in the last section; therefore, we'll focus on their differences.

You'll notice that the **GetBounds** methods for the two object types are quite different. The reason is that each object stores its figure information differently. For instance, we saw in **LineObj** that the endpoints readily gave us the dimensions of a bounding box. For a circle or polygon, however, the task is only slightly more complicated.

In the case of a circle, the bounding box is calculated by adding or subtracting the radius of the circle to its center. For example, the statement:

```
R := Centerx + AbsRadiusx;
```

calculates the right edge of the circle. Recall that **AbsRadiusx** was saved by **CircleTool** when the figure was drawn. Calculating the top and bottom of the circle is a little different. In these instances, we need to account for the screen's aspect ratio. To calculate the top of the circle, therefore, the following statement is used:

```
T := Centery - AbsRadiusx * AspectRatio;
```

where **AspectRatio** is a variable declared in MATRIX.PAS and calculated in CAD.PAS using the values returned by the BGI function **GetAspectRatio**.

Determining the bounds of the polygon is unique in that each of the vertices of the polygon must be tested to see whether it lies on the bounding box. The code, however, is fairly straightforward.

Text as a Graphics Object

In order to support text as a graphics object, a few changes have been made to the **TextTool** object type that appeared in the paint program. These changes appear in the derived type **TextObj** also included in GOBJECT.PAS. One modification is that **FinishDrawing** is overridden so that **AddObj** can be called to add the text string you type to the object list.

Recall that when **TextTool** is called to add a text object to the object list, the ASCII text is saved in the **Str** field of the object. The starting screen coordinates of the text are specified in **Leftx** and **Lefty**. These are converted to world coordinates and saved in the **Xw** and **Yw** fields of **TextObj**.

Displaying text stored in a **TextObj** is handled by the **Display** method. It is somewhat complicated by the fact that the text string may contain newline characters. Therefore, we must check whether a newline character is present and then skip to a new line by adjusting the current position (CP). In addition, recall that the first character of the **Str** string contains the length of the string and that the actual characters in the string are stored after it. The process of displaying a text string is handled by the **for** loop in **Display**:

```
for I := 1 to Length(Str) do begin
  if Str[I] = Char(CR) then begin    { Newline character }
    Inc(Lefty,TextHeight('S'));      { Skip to next line }
    MoveTo(Leftx-Wl,Lefty-Wt);       { Adjust current position }
  end
  else begin
    C[1] := Str[I];                  { Write out the next character }
    OutText(C);
  end;
end;
```

Displaying the Graphics Objects

Because the CAD program is designed so that you can modify the objects in the drawing window, it must have functions that are capable of redrawing the screen after the objects are changed. This is the purpose of many of the methods in the **GObjList** object type and the tools in GOBJECT.PAS that we have not touched on yet.

For instance, in the last section we saw how **TextObj**'s **Display** was used to display one or more lines of text stored in a string. There are comparable methods for the **LineObj**, **FillPolygonObj**, and **CircleObj** object types. In addition, the routine **DisplayAll** is included in **GObjList** to draw all the objects in the list. The heart of its action takes place in the **for** loop, which sequences through the

GObjects array—until the **NextObj** index is reached—and calls that object's **Display** method. Therefore, each graphics object draws itself:

```
for Obj := 0 to NextObj-1 do
  GObjects[Obj]^.Display;
```

Deleting a Graphics Object

Now let's take a look at how to remove an object from the drawing window. Deleting an object from the screen involves two steps: first, the object is deleted from the internal **GObjects** array; then, the whole screen is cleared and all remaining objects in **GObjects** are displayed.

The delete method in the GOBJLST.PAS source file is called **DeleteObj**. It removes the object indexed by the global variable **CurrentObj**. The routine starts by calling the destructor for the deleted **DrawingTool**:

```
Dispose(GObjects[CurrentObj]);
```

The array is rearranged so that the current object is moved to the end of the **GObjects** array and all objects that were above it are moved down one index location:

```
for I := CurrentObj to NextObj-2 do
  GObjects[I] := GObjects[I+1];
```

Next, the index **NextObj**, which points to the next available object location in **GObjects**, is decremented by one. In addition, a test is made to see if the last object is the one being deleted. If so, the **CurrentObj** index is also decremented. Finally, the screen is cleared and all the objects in the object list are redrawn by calling the functions:

```
ClearDrawingArea;
DisplayAll;
```

The procedure **ClearDrawingArea** clears the drawing window by using the BGI **ClearViewPort** procedure and, in addition, draws a grid if the flag **GridOn** is True. The second routine, **DisplayAll**, redraws all of the objects on the screen, except, of course, the object just deleted. Notice that after the delete operation, the **CurrentObj** normally becomes the next object in the array **GObjects**.

The Duplicate Routine

The CAD program also includes the routine **Duplicate**, which is used to duplicate objects in the object list. This method is included in **GObjList** and copies the object indexed by **CurrentObj** to the next free location in **GObjects** pointed to by the variable **NextObj**.

Actually, each **DrawingTool** object now has its own duplicate method, called **Dup**, that is called to have an object duplicate itself and return a pointer to the new object. Of course, simply duplicating all the information about an object will cause the new figure to be displayed over the original object. To avoid this, the **Dup** methods translate a figure's coordinates by 0.1 (in world coordinates) in the x and y directions. The translated copy of the current object, which now becomes the current object, is drawn at the end of **Duplicate** by the call to:

```
GObjects[CurrentObj]^.Display;
```

The Rotate Command

Another function provided by the CAD program allows you to rotate objects around their center. This is accomplished by the **GObjList** method **Rotate** and the **Rotate** methods in the new **DrawingTool** objects. Once again, **GObjList**'s method actually calls **DrawingTool**'s **Rotate** method to perform the rotation.

These **DrawingTool Rotate** methods use a series of calls to routines in MATRIX.PAS (Chapter 5) to rotate the current object clockwise by 45-degree increments around its center points.

If the object is a polygon or a line (circles and text cannot be rotated in the CAD program) then the object's center is translated to the origin, the object is rotated, and then it is translated back to its original location. Once the object is rotated, its new screen boundaries are determined by calling the **GetBounds**. Finally, the screen is cleared and all objects are redrawn using **DisplayAll**.

Changing the Drawing Order

Each time **DisplayAll** is called it draws each of the objects in the **GObjects** array, starting from the zero index and working toward the last location in the array, which is just before the index **NextObj**. Since this drawing order is always followed, objects at the beginning of the list are always drawn first. Consequently, if two objects overlap, the object closer to the beginning of the **GObjects** array is always drawn below the other.

The CAD program allows you to modify the order in which the objects are displayed by swapping the positions of objects in the **GObjects** array. For instance, to move an object behind all other objects, it is simply a matter of moving the object to the beginning of the list. This is what is done in the **GObjList** method **FlipToBack**. Similarly, the method **FlipToFront** moves an object from its current location to the tail of the list so that it will be displayed last and, therefore, on top of all of the other objects. Since they are similar, let's just look at **FlipToFront**.

The method begins by testing whether the object list is empty. This is the case if **NextObj** is zero. If so, the procedure simply returns with no action taken.

```
if NextObj = 0 then Exit;
```

Next, a temporary pointer, called **TempPtr**, is used to save the object pointed to by **CurrentObj**. This is the object that will be moved to the end of the **GObjects** array. Then each of the objects above **CurrentObj** are shifted down one position in the array by the **while** loop:

```
I := CurrentObj;
while I < NextObj-1 do begin
  GObjects[I] := GObjects[I+1];
  Inc(i);
end;
```

Finally, the object pointed to by **TempPtr** is copied to the end of the object list and the **CurrentObj** index is updated so it still points to the same object, even though it is now at the end of the list.

```
GObjects[I] := TempPtr;
CurrentObj = I;
```

Once the object list is modified, the drawing window is updated by clearing the screen and displaying all objects in **GObjects** by executing the two statements:

```
ClearDrawingArea;
DisplayAll;
```

This will cause the current object to be displayed on top of all the other graphics objects in the drawing window.

Now that we have learned how to duplicate, rotate, and flip an object in the object list, let's look at how we can select one and move it on the screen.

Selecting and Moving an Object

The CAD program allows you to select an object in the drawing window by moving the mouse to the object and clicking on it. When this is done, a dashed rectangle will appear around the figure and **CurrentObj** will be set to the index location of its corresponding object. Consequently, this object will become the object manipulated by any subsequent uses of functions like duplicate and rotate. If another object shares the same area on the screen as the currently selected object, it can be selected instead by clicking on the mouse again in the same region. Similarly, if there are several objects in the same area, you can sequence through them by clicking the mouse several times.

The **GObjList** method **Select** performs the actions described earlier. Rather than go through its code line by line, let's take a high-level view of it. Its main purpose is to change the **CurrentObj** index to the object pointed at by the mouse when the left mouse button is pressed. The **Select** method shows which object is the current object by calling **Mark**, which draws a rectangular box around it. The rectangle uses the **Left**, **Top**, **Right**, and **Bottom** components of the **DrawingTool** object type for the current object to determine its location. Note that **SetWriteMode** is set to **XorPut** so that the rectangle can be exclusive-ORed on the screen, and therefore, easily moved. When **Select** exits, the rectangle is erased by a final call to **Mark**.

Moving a selected object is done by clicking on the hand icon, moving the mouse to the object, and then pressing the left mouse button and dragging the object to its new location. When the mouse button is released, the whole screen is redrawn with the object at its new location.

This operation is performed in the method **Move**, which is also included in the **GObjList** type. Moving an object is accomplished by keeping track of the amount that the mouse has been moved in the variables **MoveX** and **MoveY**. This amount is then mapped into world coordinates and used to translate the object. Once it is translated, the screen is erased and completely redrawn to reflect the change.

Accessing Methods in GObjList

So far we have described several new operations that have been added to the CAD program. Most of these are included in the **GObjList** type. But how are its methods, such as **DeleteObj**, accessed from the environment? Remember that all of our other drawing operations are linked to a **DrawingTool** that is activated when an icon or some other screen object is selected. But since our **DeleteObj** procedure is a member of the **GObjList** object type, we can't simply add it to our list of

DrawingTool objects—it has the wrong base type. We have therefore defined a series of **DrawingTool** objects in CADDRAW.PAS that call the appropriate actions in **GObjList**. These object types serve as a bridge between the **DrawingTools** used in the environment and the methods in **GObjList**. The **DeleteObj** method, for example, is called within the object type **DeleteObjTool** that is derived from **DrawingTool**. The declaration of **DeleteObjTool** is:

```
DeleteObjToolPtr = ^DeleteObjTool;
DeleteObjTool = object(DrawingTool)
  procedure Draw; virtual;
end;
```

The **Draw** method is overridden because this is the method that gets called when the drawing tool is selected. In this case, we want **Draw** to simply call the **DeleteObj** method in the global list **FigList**:

```
procedure DeleteObjTool.Draw; begin FigList.DeleteObj; end;
```

This new "drawing tool" is added to our list of tools in the **SetupScreen** routine in CAD.PAS and is activated whenever its icon is clicked on. A similar technique is used to access the other methods in the **GObjList** type, such as **FlipToBack**, **Rotate**, and **Move**.

Extending the CAD Program

There are many ways to enhance the CAD program presented in this chapter. You might add routines to save the objects in the drawing window to a file, provide a facility to zoom in and out on the objects being displayed, or add the capability of grouping objects. Briefly, let's look at the first two suggestions.

If you want to be able to save the objects in the CAD program, all you'll need to do is save the **GObjects** array to a file. You could use the first line of the file to save the number of objects in the **GObjects** array and the index of the current object. The rest of the file can be used to save each of the **DrawingTool** structures in the **GObjects** array where each object would have a tag associated with it that identifies what type of object data is to follow. Reading this information from a file into the **GObjects** array is a very simple matter and would allow you to initialize the whole screen or read in selected objects.

Another feature you might want to add is the ability to zoom in and out on objects in the drawing window. The basic idea is to change the window size of the world coordinates that are displayed on the screen. For instance, to zoom in on objects in the drawing window you can set the window to between (0.0,0.0) and (3.0,3.0) as follows:

```
procedure ZoomIn;
begin
  Set_Window(0.0,0.0,3.0,3.0);
  Set_ViewPort(Wl,Wt,Wr,Wb);
  ClearDrawingArea;
  DisplayAll;
end;
```

Compiling the CAD Program

Table 12.3 lists the source files you'll need to compile the CAD program, and the chapters in which they are found.

Table 12.3. Files used to compile the CAD program

Filename	Chapter
GTEXT.PAS	3
MATRIX.PAS	5
MOUSEPAC.PAS	7
KBDMOUSE.PAS	7
GPOPPAC.PAS	9
DRAW.PAS	10
USERTOOL.PAS	11
INTERACT.PAS	11
CADDRAW.PAS	12
CADWINDW.PAS	12
GOBJECT.PAS	12
GOBJLST.PAS	12
CAD.PAS	12

• Listing 12.1. CAD.PAS

```
program CAD;
{ CAD.PAS: A simple CAD program built around many of the BGI's functions.
  Several of the tools built up earlier in the book are put to use in
  this program. The program will run on many of the graphics adapters
  supported by the BGI and supports many of their modes. However, it is
  currently configured so that it will look best if run on an EGA or
  VGA display. The program supports either the mouse or the keyboard
  automatically. }
uses
  Graph, MousePac, KbdMouse, UserTool, Interact, GText,
  GPopPac, Matrix, CADDraw, Draw, GObject, CADWindw;
const
  GDriver: integer = Detect;
var
  T: boolean;
  C, ErrCode, GMode: integer;
  Xasp, Yasp: word;

procedure SetupScreen;
{ Set up the environment for the CAD program }
var
  H, I, X, FillWidth, Offset, Space: integer;
  FillType, ColorWidth, MaxColors, FillColor: integer;
  { Declare a set of drawing tools. Note that late binding
    is used to get the power of polymorphism. }
  ToggleGridPtr, DeleteAllObjPtr, ChangeFontPtr, ChangeLineStylePtr,
  QuitPtr, LineTlPtr, FillPolyPtr, CircleTlPtr, TextPtr,
  ChangeFillPatternPtr, ChangeFillColorPtr, ChangeDrawColorPtr,
  MoveObjPtr, SelectObjPtr, DuplicateObjPtr, DeleteObjPtr, FlipToFrontPtr,
  FlipToBackPtr, RotateObjPtr: DrawingToolPtr;
begin
  ToggleGridPtr := New(ToggleGridToolPtr,Init);
  DeleteAllObjPtr := New(DeleteAllObjToolPtr,Init);
  ChangeFontPtr := New(ChangeFontToolPtr,Init);
  ChangeLineStylePtr := New(CADChangeLineStyleToolPtr,Init);
  QuitPtr := New(QuitToolPtr,Init);
  LineTlPtr := New(LineObjPtr,Init);
  FillPolyPtr := New(FillPolygonObjPtr,Init);
  CircleTlPtr := New(CircleObjPtr,Init);
  TextPtr := New(TextObjPtr,Init);
  ChangeFillPatternPtr := New(ChangeFillPatternToolPtr,Init);
  ChangeFillColorPtr := New(ChangeFillColorToolPtr,Init);
  ChangeDrawColorPtr := New(ChangeDrawColorToolPtr,Init);
  MoveObjPtr := New(MoveObjToolPtr,Init);
  SelectObjPtr := New(SelectObjToolPtr,Init);
  DuplicateObjPtr := New(DuplicateObjToolPtr,Init);
  DeleteObjPtr := New(DeleteObjToolPtr,Init);
  FlipToFrontPtr := New(FlipToFrontToolPtr,Init);
  FlipToBackPtr := New(FlipToBackToolPtr,Init);
  RotateObjPtr := New(RotateObjToolPtr,Init);
```

```
{ Draw a main menu bar across the top of the screen. Each of the words in
   the menu bar will act as a user-interface object that can be selected. }
H := TextHeight('H') + 2;
if GetMaxColor = 1 then SetFillStyle(SolidFill,0)
   else SetFillStyle(SolidFill,EgaBlue);
Bar3D(0,0,MaxX,H,0,False);
OutTextXY(2,2,'Grid  Text  Line  Clear  Quit');
Space := TextWidth(' ');
Offset := 2;

Tools.AddTool(New(InteractObjPtr,Init(Ord('g'),Offset,0,
             Offset+TextWidth('Grid'),TextHeight('Grid'),ToggleGridPtr)));
Inc(Offset,TextWidth('Grid')+Space);
Tools.AddTool(New(InteractObjPtr,Init(Ord('t'),Offset,0,
             Offset+TextWidth('Text'),TextWindowX := Offset;
TextWindowY := TextHeight('Text') + Border;
Inc(Offset,TextWidth('Text') + Space);
Tools.AddTool(New(InteractObjPtr,Init(Ord('l'),Offset,0,
         Offset+TextWidth('Line'),TextHeight('Line'),ChangeLineStylePtr)));
LineWindowX := Offset;
LineWindowY := TextHeight('Line') + Border;
Inc(Offset,TextWidth('Line') + Space);
Tools.AddTool(New(InteractObjPtr,Init(Ord('c'),Offset,0,
          Offset+TextWidth('Clear'),TextHeight('Clear'),DeleteAllObjPtr)));
Inc(Offset,TextWidth('Clear') + Space);
Tools.AddTool(New(InteractObjPtr,Init(Ord('q'),Offset,0,
             Offset+TextWidth('Quit'),TextHeight('Quit'),QuitPtr)));

{ Now draw the icons on the left-hand side of the screen }
ReadIcon(0,H,'hand.icn');
Tools.AddTool(New(InteractObjPtr,Init(Ord('s'),0,H,IconWd*2,
             h+IconHt*2,MoveObjPtr)));
ReadIcon(IconWd*2,H,'POINTER.ICN');
Tools.AddTool(New(InteractObjPtr,Init(Ord('c'),IconWd*2,H,IconWd*4,
             H+IconHt*2,SelectObjPtr)));
ReadIcon(0,H+IconHt*2,'LINE.ICN');
Tools.AddTool(New(InteractObjPtr,Init(Ord('d'),0,H+IconHt*2,IconWd*2,
             H+2*IconHt*2,LineT1Ptr)));
ReadIcon(IconWd*2,H+IconHt*2,'LETTER.ICN');
Tools.AddTool(New(InteractObjPtr,Init(Ord('p'),IconWd*2,
             H+IconHt*2,IconWd*4,H+2*IconHt*2,TextPtr)));
ReadIcon(0,H+2*IconHt*2,'FILLPOLY.ICN');
Tools.AddTool(New(InteractObjPtr,Init(Ord('s'),0,H+2*IconHt*2,IconWd*2,
             H+3*IconHt*2,FillPolyPtr)));
ReadIcon(IconWd*2,H+2*IconHt*2,'CIRCLE.ICN');
Tools.AddTool(New(InteractObjPtr,Init(Ord('r'),IconWd*2,
             H+2*IconHt*2,IconWd*4,H+3*IconHt*2,CircleT1Ptr)));
ReadIcon(0,H+3*IconHt*2,'DUPLICATE.ICN');
Tools.AddTool(New(InteractObjPtr,Init(Ord('p'),0,H+3*IconHt*2,IconWd*2,
             H+4*IconHt*2,DuplicateObjPtr)));
ReadIcon(IconWd*2,H+3*IconHt*2,'SCISSOR.ICN');
Tools.AddTool(New(InteractObjPtr,Init(Ord('x'),IconWd*2,
             H+3*IconHt*2,IconWd*4,H+4*IconHt*2,DeleteObjPtr)));
```

```
ReadIcon(0,H+4*IconHt*2,'FLIPFRNT.ICN');
Tools.AddTool(New(InteractObjPtr,Init(Ord('e'),0,H+4*IconHt*2,IconWd*2,
            H+5*IconHt*2,FlipToFrontPtr)));
ReadIcon(IconWd*2,H+4*IconHt*2,'FLIPBACK.ICN');
Tools.AddTool(New(InteractObjPtr,Init(Ord('x'),IconWd*2,
            H+4*IconHt*2,IconWd*4,H+5*IconHt*2,FlipToBackPtr)));
ReadIcon(0,H+5*IconHt*2,'ROTATE.ICN');
Tools.AddTool(New(InteractObjPtr,Init(Ord('e'),0,H+5*IconHt*2,IconWd*2,
            H+6*IconHt*2,RotateObjPtr)));
{ Draw a backdrop below the icons }
SetFillStyle(SolidFill,EgaBlue);
Bar3D(0,H+6*IconHt*2,IconWd*4,MaxY,0,False);

{ Create the fill pattern box. This will appear on the lower
  portion of the screen. }
FillWidth := Round((MaxX-1-IconWd*4+2) / (NumFillsWide+1));
GlobalFillColor := GetMaxColor;      { Start fill color at maximum color }
GlobalDrawColor := GlobalFillColor;
FillType := 0;
X := IconWd * 4 + 2 + FillWidth;
for I := 0 to NumFillsWide-1 do begin
  SetFillStyle(FillType,GlobalFillColor);
  Bar3D(X,MaxY-FillHeight*2,X+FillWidth,MaxY-FillHeight,0,False);
  Inc(FillType);
  Inc(X,FillWidth);
end;
Rectangle(IconWd*4+2,MaxY-FillHeight*2,MaxX,MaxY);
Tools.AddTool(New(UserInteractPtr,Init(Ord('w'),IconWd*4+2+FillWidth,
      MaxY-FillHeight*2,MaxX,MaxY-FillHeight,ChangeFillPatternPtr)));
GlobalFillStyle := SolidFill;
MaxColors := GetMaxColor;
ColorWidth := Round((MaxX-1-IconWd*4+2-FillWidth) / (MaxColors + 1));
FillColor := 0;
X := IconWd * 4 + 2 + FillWidth;
for I := 0 to MaxColors-1 do begin
  SetFillStyle(SolidFill,FillColor);
  Bar3D(X,MaxY-FillHeight,X+ColorWidth,MaxY,0,False);
  Inc(FillColor);
  Inc(X,ColorWidth);
end;
Tools.AddTool(New(UserInteractPtr,Init(Ord('z'),IconWd*4+2+FillWidth,
      MaxY-FillHeight,MaxX,MaxY,ChangeFillColorPtr)));
SetLineStyle(SolidLn,0,ThickWidth);
SetFillStyle(GlobalFillStyle,GlobalFillColor);
Bar3D(IconWd*4+2+2,MaxY-FillHeight*2+2,
      IconWd*4+2+FillWidth-2,MaxY-2,0,False);
Tools.AddTool(New(UserInteractPtr,Init(Ord('y'),IconWd*4+2+2,MaxY-
            FillHeight*2+2,IconWd*4+FillWidth-2,MaxY,ChangeDrawColorPtr)));
SetLineStyle(SolidLn,0,NormWidth);

{ Paint drawing window }
Wl := IconWd*4+2+1;    Wt := H+2+1;
Wr := MaxX-1;          Wb := MaxY-FillHeight*2-2-1;
Rectangle(Wl-1,Wt-1,Wr+1,Wb+1);
```

```
  { Set the world-to-screen coordinate relationship. If you change these
    values, change the corresponding ones in DrawGrid located in
    CADDRAW.PAS. Pick numbers that make the grid look square. These work
    well on a VGA. }
  Set_Window(0.0,7.0,0.0,6.0);
  Set_Viewport(Wl,Wr,Wt,Wb);

  GlobalFillStyle := SolidFill;
  GlobalLineStyle := SolidLn;
  GlobalTextStyle := DefaultFont;
  GridOn := True;
  DrawGrid;
  LeftArrow := False;  RightArrow := False;

  { Set the font here to what you want to use for the dimension labels.
    On the CGA in medium-resolution mode, small font is good. }
  SetTextStyle(GlobalTextStyle,HorizDir,1);
end;

begin
  InitGraph(GDriver,GMode,'\tp\bgi');
  ErrCode := GraphResult;
  if ErrCode <> grOk then begin
    WriteLn('Graphics error: ',GraphErrorMsg(ErrCode));
    Halt(1);                      { Return with error code }
  end;
  GetAspectRatio(Xasp,Yasp);
  AspectRatio := Xasp / Yasp;
  MaxX := GetMaxX;  MaxY := GetMaxY;
  Win.Init;        { Initialize the window tools }
  Tools.Init;      { Initialize the list of interactive tools }
  FigList.Init;    { Initialize the list of graphics objects on the screen }
  SetupScreen;
  Mouse.Init;
  T := Mouse.Setup;
  repeat
    C := Mouse.WaitForInput(LeftButton);
    Tools.AnyToProcess(C);
  until False;
end.
```

• Listing 12.2. GOBJLST.PAS

```
unit GObjLst;
{$R+}
{ GOBJLST.PAS: Contains the GObjList object type used to
  manage a list of GObject graphics objects. Recall that GObject
  objects represent individual graphics figures on the screen. }
interface
uses
  Graph, Matrix, MousePac, KbdMouse, Draw, CADWindw;
```

```
{ Maximum number of figures that can be drawn on the screen }
const NumGObjects = 20;

{ This object type is used to maintain the list of figures currently
  displayed in the drawing window }
type
GObjList = object
  { List of graphics figures }
  GObjects: array[0..NumGObjects-1] of DrawingToolPtr;
  NextObj: integer;                         { Number of graphics objects }
  CurrentObj: integer;                      { Currently selected object }
  constructor Init;
  procedure AddObj(ObjPtr: DrawingToolPtr);
  procedure DeleteObj;
  procedure DeleteAll;
  procedure FlipToBack;
  procedure FlipToFront;
  procedure Duplicate;
  procedure Rotate;
  procedure Select;
  procedure Move;
  procedure Mark(Obj: integer);
  procedure DisplayAll;
end;

implementation
constructor GObjList.Init;
{ Initializes the count of the number of objects in the list }
begin
  NextObj := 0;
end;

procedure GObjList.AddObj(ObjPtr: DrawingToolPtr);
{ Adds an object to the list of graphic objects in the drawing window }
begin
  if NextObj >= NumGObjects then Exit;  { List is full. Do nothing. }
  CurrentObj := NextObj;
  GObjects[NextObj] := ObjPtr;
  Inc(NextObj);
end;

procedure GObjList.DeleteObj;
{ Delete an object from the graphics object list. Make the next
  object in the GObjects array the CurrentObj. Update the screen
  after deleting object from the list by erasing it and then
  redrawing all remaining objects. }
var
  I: integer;
begin
  if NextObj = 0 then Exit;               { Empty list. No objects. }
  Dispose(GObjects[CurrentObj]);
  for I := CurrentObj to NextObj-2 do
    GObjects[I] := GObjects[I+1];
```

```pascal
      Dec(NextObj);
      if (CurrentObj >= NextObj) and (CurrentObj > 0) then
        Dec(CurrentObj);                      { Deleted last, but not first }
      ClearDrawingArea;
      DisplayAll;
    end;

procedure GObjList.DeleteAll;
{ Delete all objects in the object list }
var
    I: integer;
begin
    for I := 0 to NextObj-1 do Dispose(GObjects[I]);
    NextObj := 0;
    CurrentObj := 0;
    ClearDrawingArea;
end;

procedure GObjList.FlipToBack;
{ Move the current object to the back by copying it to the
  head of the object list. After the operation the same object
  is the current object. }
var
    I: integer;
    TempPtr: DrawingToolPtr;
begin
    if NextObj = 0 then Exit;
    TempPtr := GObjects[CurrentObj];
    for I := CurrentObj downto 1 do
      GObjects[I] := GObjects[I-1];
    GObjects[0] := TempPtr;
    CurrentObj := 0;
    ClearDrawingArea;
    DisplayAll;
end;

procedure GObjList.FlipToFront;
{ Move the object to the front by putting it at the end of the object
  list and redrawing all of the objects. After the operation the same
  object is the current object. }
var
    I: integer;
    TempPtr: DrawingToolPtr;
begin
    if NextObj = 0 then Exit;
    TempPtr := GObjects[CurrentObj];
    I := CurrentObj;
    while I < NextObj-1 do begin
      GObjects[I] := GObjects[I+1];
      Inc(i);
    end;
    GObjects[I] := TempPtr;
    CurrentObj := I;
```

```
    ClearDrawingArea;
    DisplayAll;
  end;

procedure GObjList.Duplicate;
{ Duplicate CurrentObj. Make a copy of the current object in the drawing
  window. New object appears offset from the original by translating it
  (.1,.1). Make sure the object is saved in world coordinates. }
begin
  if NextObj = 0 then Exit;                   { No objects in list }
  if NextObj >= NumGObjects then Exit;  { Object list is full }
  GObjects[NextObj] := GObjects[CurrentObj]^.Dup;
  CurrentObj := NextObj;  { New object becomes current object }
  Inc(NextObj);
  SetViewPort(Wl,Wt,Wr,Wb,True);
  GObjects[CurrentObj]^.Display;
  SetViewPort(0,0,GetMaxX,GetMaxY,True);
end;

procedure GObjList.Rotate;
{ Rotate the current object around its center point. The object is
  rotated in 45-degree increments. Note that only polygon and line
  rotations are supported. }
begin
  if NextObj = 0 then Exit;                   { No objects in list }
  GObjects[CurrentObj]^.Rotate(45);
  ClearDrawingArea;
  DisplayAll;                                 { Display updated objects }
end;

procedure GObjList.Move;
{ Interactively move the current object on the screen }
var
  X, Y, Oldx, Oldy, MoveX, MoveY, L, T, R, B: integer;
  Originalx, Originaly, TranslateX, TranslateY: real;
begin
  if NextObj = 0 then Exit;                   { No objects in list }
  SetViewPort(Wl,Wt,Wr,Wb,True);
  Mark(CurrentObj);
  while True do begin
    while not Mouse.ButtonPressed(LeftButton) do ;
    Mouse.GetCoords(X,Y);
    if (X <= Wl) or (Y <= Wt) or (Y > Wb) or (X > Wr) then begin
      Mark(CurrentObj);   { Unmark object. User clicked mouse outside }
      SetViewPort(0,0,GetMaxX,GetMaxY,True); { of the drawing window. }
      Exit;                                   { Quit move routine }
    end;
    L := GObjects[CurrentObj]^.Left;   T := GObjects[CurrentObj]^.Top;
    R := GObjects[CurrentObj]^.Right;  B := GObjects[CurrentObj]^.Bottom;
    if Mouse.InBox(L,T,R,B,X,Y) then begin
      Oldx := X;    Oldy := Y;
      while not Mouse.ButtonReleased(LeftButton) do begin
        Mouse.GetCoords(X,Y);
```

```
            MoveX := X - Oldx;    MoveY := Y - Oldy;
            if (MoveX <> 0) or (MoveY <> 0) then begin
              { The object is being moved. Update its position. }
              Mark(CurrentObj);              { Erase dashed box }
              Inc(GObjects[CurrentObj]^.Left,MoveX);
              Inc(GObjects[CurrentObj]^.Top,MoveY);
              Inc(GObjects[CurrentObj]^.Right,MoveX);
              Inc(GObjects[CurrentObj]^.Bottom,MoveY);
              Mark(CurrentObj);              { Draw dashed box }
              Oldx := X;    Oldy := Y;
            end;
          end;
          PCtoWorld(L,T,OriginalX,OriginalY);
          PCtoWorld(GObjects[CurrentObj]^.Left,
                  GObjects[CurrentObj]^.Top,TranslateX,TranslateY);
          TranslateX := TranslateX - OriginalX;
          TranslateY := TranslateY - OriginalY;
          GObjects[CurrentObj]^.Translate(TranslateX,TranslateY);
          ClearDrawingArea;
          DisplayAll;
          Mark(CurrentObj);
        end
        else
          while not Mouse.ButtonReleased(LeftButton) do ;
      end
    end;

procedure GObjList.Select;
{ Select an object by encompassing it with a rectangle. An object can
  be selected by pressing the left mouse button while over the object.
  To select another object in the same region, click the mouse button
  again. Upon exiting, the currently marked object becomes the
  CurrentObj, which is used in all succeeding operations. }
var
  X, Y, TestObj, LastObj: integer;
  Done: boolean;
begin
  if NextObj = 0 then Exit;          { No objects in list }
  SetViewPort(Wl,Wt,Wr,Wb,True);
  TestObj := CurrentObj + 1;
  if TestObj >= NextObj then TestObj := 0;
  Mark(CurrentObj);                  { Mark object }
  LastObj := CurrentObj;
  while True do begin
    while not Mouse.ButtonPressed(LeftButton) do ;
    Mouse.GetCoords(X,Y);
    if (X <= Wl) or (Y <= Wt) or (Y > Wb) or (X > Wr) then begin
      Mark(CurrentObj);                      { Unmark object }
      SetViewPort(0,0,GetMaxX,GetMaxY,True);
      Exit;
    end;
    while not Mouse.ButtonReleased(LeftButton) do ;
    Mouse.GetCoords(X,Y);
```

```
        Done := False;
        repeat
          if Mouse.InBox(GObjects[TestObj]^.Left,
             GObjects[TestObj]^.Top,GObjects[TestObj]^.Right,
             GObjects[TestObj]^.Bottom,x,y) then begin
            Mark(LastObj);    { Unmark object }
            Mark(TestObj);    { Mark object }
            LastObj := TestObj;
            CurrentObj := TestObj;
            Inc(TestObj);
            if TestObj >= NextObj then TestObj := 0;
            Done := True;
          end
          else begin
            Inc(TestObj);
            if TestObj >= NextObj then TestObj := 0;
          end;
        until (TestObj = CurrentObj) or Done;
    end
end;

procedure GObjList.DisplayAll;
{ Display all of the graphics objects in the drawing window }
var
  Obj: integer;
  Vp: ViewPortType;
begin
  GetViewSettings(Vp);                    { Save viewport settings }
  SetViewPort(Wl,Wt,Wr,Wb,True);          { Use drawing window }
  SetWriteMode(CopyPut);
  for Obj := 0 to NextObj-1 do
    GObjects[Obj]^.Display;
  SetViewPort(Vp.X1,Vp.Y1,Vp.X2,Vp.Y2,Vp.Clip);  { Restore viewport }
end;

procedure GObjList.Mark(Obj: integer);
{ Highlight an object by drawing a dashed rectangle around its border }
var
  SaveLine: LineSettingsType;
  SaveColor: integer;
  ObjPtr: DrawingToolPtr;
begin
  ObjPtr := GObjects[Obj];
  SaveColor := GetColor;
  GetLineSettings(SaveLine);
  SetWriteMode(XorPut);
  SetColor(GetMaxColor);
  SetLineStyle(DashedLn,0,NormWidth);
  Mouse.Hide;
  Rectangle(ObjPtr^.Left-Wl,ObjPtr^.Top-Wt,
            ObjPtr^.Right-Wl,ObjPtr^.Bottom-Wt);
  Mouse.Show;
  SetLineStyle(SaveLine.LineStyle,SaveLine.Pattern,SaveLine.Thickness);
```

```
  SetColor(SaveColor);
  SetWriteMode(CopyPut);
end;

begin
end.
```

• Listing 12.3. GOBJECT.PAS

```
unit GObject;
{$R+}
{ GOBJECT.PAS: Defines the functions used to support graphics figures
  as objects in the CAD program. The objects here are derived from the
  tools developed in DRAW.PAS in Chapter 10. These objects are maintained
  in a list by the type GObjList, defined in GOBJLST.PAS. }
interface
uses
  Graph, GObjLst, MousePac, KbdMouse, Matrix, GText, CADDraw, Draw;

type
{ Text object. The location of the text in real-world coordinates,
  its style and what it Displays are saved. Note that rotation of
  text is not supported. }
TextObjPtr = ^TextObj;
TextObj = object(TextTool)
  Xw, Yw: real;      { Top left of text in real-world coordinates }
  procedure Draw; virtual;
  procedure Copy(FigPtr: TextObjPtr); virtual;
  procedure Translate(TransX, TransY: real); virtual;
  procedure GetBounds(var L, T, R, B: integer); virtual;
  procedure Display; virtual;
  procedure FinishDrawing; virtual;
  function Dup: DrawingToolPtr; virtual;
end;

{ Line object }
const ArrowSize = 4;  { Size of arrow heads is 4 pixels }
type
LineObjPtr = ^LineObj;
LineObj = object(LineTool)
  Xw1, Yw1: real;    { Top left of text in real-world coordinates }
  Xw2, Yw2: real;    { Other endpoints of line }
  LeftArrow, RightArrow: boolean; { True if the line has an arrowhead }
  procedure Draw; virtual;
  procedure Translate(TransX, TransY: real); virtual;
  procedure GetBounds(var L, T, R, B: integer); virtual;
  procedure Copy(FigPtr: LineObjPtr); virtual;
  procedure Display; virtual;
  procedure FinishDrawing; virtual;
  procedure DrawArrows; virtual;
  function Dup: DrawingToolPtr; virtual;
```

```
      procedure Rotate(Angle: real); virtual;
    end;

    { Circle object }
    CircleObjPtr = ^CircleObj;
    CircleObj = object(CircleTool)
      CenterWx, CenterWy: real;  { Center of circle in world coordinates }
      procedure Draw; virtual;
      procedure GetBounds(var L, T, R, B: integer); virtual;
      procedure Copy(FigPtr: CircleObjPtr); virtual;
      procedure Translate(TransX, TransY: real); virtual;
      procedure Display; virtual;
      procedure FinishDrawing; virtual;
      function Dup: DrawingToolPtr; virtual;
    end;

    FillPolygonObjPtr = ^FillPolygonObj;
    FillPolygonObj = object(FillPolygonTool)
      PointsW: WorldArray;
      procedure Draw; virtual;
      procedure GetBounds(var L, T, R, B: integer); virtual;
      procedure Copy(FigPtr: FillPolygonObjPtr); virtual;
      procedure Display; virtual;
      procedure Translate(TransX, TransY: real); virtual;
      procedure FinishDrawing; virtual;
      function Dup: DrawingToolPtr; virtual;
      procedure Rotate(Angle: real); virtual;
    end;

implementation
procedure TextObj.Draw;
{ Override draw so it won't be called if the object list is full }
begin
  if FigList.NextObj < NumGObjects-1 then TextTool.Draw;
end;

function TextObj.Dup: DrawingToolPtr;
{ Create a new text object by making a copy of the current text
  object and then translating it in world coordinates by (0.1,0.1).
  Returns a pointer to the new object. }
var
  Nt: TextObjPtr;
begin
  Nt := New(TextObjPtr,Init);           { Create new text object }
  Nt^.Copy(@Self);                      { Copy itself to new object }
  Nt^.Xw := Nt^.Xw + 0.1;               { Translate new text by (0.1,0.1) }
  Nt^.Yw := Nt^.Yw + 0.1;               { in world coordinates }
  { Calculate screen position of duplicated text }
  WorldToPC(Nt^.Xw,Nt^.Yw,Nt^.Leftx,Nt^.Lefty);
  Nt^.GetBounds(Nt^.Left,Nt^.Top,Nt^.Right,Nt^.Bottom);
  Dup := Nt;                            { Return pointer to new object }
end;
```

```
procedure TextObj.Display;
{ Display the text in the text object. It accounts for newline
  characters included in the string. }
var
  I: integer;
  C: string;                           { Holds one character }
begin
  SetColor(DrawColor);                 { Use the stored drawing color }
  WorldToPC(Xw,Yw,Leftx,Lefty);        { Using the world coordinates saved }
  MoveTo(Leftx-Wl,Lefty-Wt);           { in the object, write the text out }
  SetTextStyle(TextStyle,HorizDir,1);
  C[0] := #1;
  Mouse.Hide;
  for I := 1 to Length(Str) do begin
    if Str[I] = Char(CR) then begin    { Newline character }
      Inc(Lefty,TextHeight('S'));      { Skip to next line }
      MoveTo(Leftx-Wl,Lefty-Wt);       { Adjust current position }
    end
    else begin
      C[1] := Str[I];                  { Write out the next character }
      OutText(C);
    end;
  end;
  Mouse.Show;
end;

procedure TextObj.GetBounds(var L, T, R, B: integer);
{ Get bounding box of text object in screen coordinates. Since text
  can stretch across multiple lines, check for the newline character
  to get the real text block's height, and to find its true width. }
var
  I, Linew, W, H, StartOfLine, Ptr: integer;
  Buff: string;
begin
  I := 0;  Linew := 0;  W := 0;  H := 0;  StartOfLine := 0;
  l := Leftx;  T := Lefty;
  for I := 1 to Length(Str) do begin
    Inc(Linew);                        { Increment line width }
    if Str[I] = Char(CR) then begin    { Newline encountered }
      Inc(H);                          { Increment height count }
      if Linew > W then begin          { Check whether this line is }
        W := Linew-1; Ptr := StartOfLine; { the longest line so far }
      end;
      Linew := 0;                      { Reset the line width counter }
      StartOfLine := I + 1;            { Remember where next line starts }
    end
  end;
  if Linew > W then begin              { Check whether last line is }
    W := Linew; Ptr := StartOfLine;    { the longest line }
  end;
  Buff := System.Copy(Str,Ptr,W);      { Copy the longest line to a string }
                                       { so it can be used to get the }
  R := Leftx + TextWidth(Buff);        { width of the widest line }
```

```
    B := Lefty + (TextHeight('C') + 2) * (H + 1);
  end;

procedure TextObj.Translate(TransX, TransY: real);
{ Move the top-left location of the text by the amount (TransX,TransY) }
begin
  Xw := Xw + TransX;    Yw := Yw + TransY;
end;

procedure TextObj.Copy(FigPtr: TextObjPtr);
{ Copy the text object pointed to by FigPtr to this object }
begin
  Left  := FigPtr^.Left;       Top := FigPtr^.Top;
  Right := FigPtr^.Right;      Bottom := FigPtr^.Bottom;
  Leftx := FigPtr^.Leftx;      Lefty := FigPtr^.Lefty;
  Xw := FigPtr^.Xw;            Yw := FigPtr^.Yw;
  DrawColor := FigPtr^.DrawColor;  TextStyle := FigPtr^.TextStyle;
  Len := FigPtr^.Len;
  Str := FigPtr^.Str;
end;

procedure TextObj.FinishDrawing;
{ After entering a text string, add it to the figure object list }
var
  N1: TextObjPtr;
begin
  TextTool.FinishDrawing;
  if Len = 0 then Exit;              { Don't add object if string is empty }
  N1 := New(TextObjPtr,Init);        { Create a new object to add }
  GetBounds(Left,Top,Right,Bottom);
  PCtoWorld(Leftx,Lefty,Xw,Yw);      { Save things in world coordinates }
  N1^.Copy(@Self);                   { Copy settings to new object }
  FigList.AddObj(N1);                { Add "this" to the list of objects }
end;

procedure LineObj.Draw;
{ Override draw so it won't be called if the object list is full }
begin
  if FigList.NextObj < NumGObjects-1 then LineTool.Draw;
end;

procedure LineObj.FinishDrawing;
{ After drawing a line, append it to the figure list }
var
  N1: LineObjPtr;
begin
  LineTool.FinishDrawing;            { Call inherited routine }
  LeftArrow := CADDRAW.LeftArrow;    { Remember the settings of }
  RightArrow := CADDRAW.RightArrow;  { the arrows }
  N1 := New(LineObjPtr,Init);        { Create a new line object }
  GetBounds(Left,Top,Right,Bottom);
  PCtoWorld(X1,Y1,Xw1,Yw1);          { Save endpoints in world }
```

```
    PCtoWorld(X2,Y2,Xw2,Yw2);          { coordinates }
    N1^.Copy(@Self);                   { Copy all settings to new object }
    DrawArrows;                        { Draw arrows on new line }
    FigList.AddObj(N1);                { Add the line to the figure list }
  end;

function LineObj.Dup: DrawingToolPtr;
{ Create a new line object by making a copy of the current line
  object. Translate the new line in world coordinates by (0.1,0.1)
  and then set its bounding box size. }
var
  N1: LineObjPtr;
begin
  N1 := New(LineObjPtr,Init);        { Create new line }
  N1^.Copy(@Self);                   { Copy current object to new object }
  N1^.Xw1 := N1^.Xw1 + 0.1;          { Translate the new line by }
  N1^.Yw1 := N1^.Yw1 + 0.1;          { (0.1,0.1) in world coordinates }
  N1^.Xw2 := N1^.Xw2 + 0.1;
  N1^.Yw2 := N1^.Yw2 + 0.1;
  WorldToPC(N1^.Xw1,N1^.Yw1,N1^.X1,N1^.Y1);   { Calculate new line's }
  WorldToPC(N1^.Xw2,N1^.Yw2,N1^.X2,N1^.Y2);   { screen position }
  N1^.GetBounds(N1^.Left,N1^.Top,N1^.Right,N1^.Bottom);
  Dup := N1;
end;

procedure LineObj.Copy(FigPtr: LineObjPtr);
{ Copy the line object passed in to this line's object }
begin
  Left := FigPtr^.Left;           Top := FigPtr^.Top;
  Right := FigPtr^.Right;         Bottom := FigPtr^.Bottom;
  X1 := FigPtr^.X1;               Y1 := FigPtr^.Y1;
  X2 := FigPtr^.X2;               Y2 := FigPtr^.Y2;
  Xw1 := FigPtr^.Xw1;             Yw1 := FigPtr^.Yw1;
  Xw2 := FigPtr^.Xw2;             Yw2 := FigPtr^.Yw2;
  DrawColor := FigPtr^.DrawColor; LineStyle := FigPtr^.LineStyle;
  LeftArrow := FigPtr^.LeftArrow; RightArrow := FigPtr^.RightArrow;
end;

procedure LineObj.Display;
{ Display the line in the line object }
var
  XPC1, YPC1, XPC2, YPC2: integer;
begin
  SetColor(DrawColor);
  SetLineStyle(LineStyle,0,NormWidth);
  WorldToPC(Xw1,Yw1,XPC1,YPC1);
  WorldToPC(Xw2,Yw2,XPC2,YPC2);
  Mouse.Hide;
  Line(XPC1-W1,YPC1-Wt,XPC2-W1,YPC2-Wt);
  Mouse.Show;
  DrawArrows;
end;
```

```pascal
procedure LineObj.Translate(TransX, TransY: real);
{ Translate the line in world coordinates by the (TransX,TransY) }
begin
  Xw1 := Xw1 + TransX;  Yw1 := Yw1 + TransY;
  Xw2 := Xw2 + TransX;  Yw2 := Yw2 + TransY;
end;

procedure LineObj.GetBounds(var L, T, R, B: integer);
{ Get the bounding box for a line object. Note that the bounding box
  is expanded by 3 pixels to make it easier to select a line. }
begin
  if X1 <= X2 then begin
    L := X1 - 3;    R := X2 + 3;
  end
  else begin
    L := X2 - 3;    R := X1 + 3;
  end;
  if Y1 <= Y2 then begin
    T := Y1 - 3;    B := Y2 + 3;
  end
  else begin
    T := Y2 - 3;    B := Y1 + 3;
  end
end;

procedure LineObj.Rotate(Angle: real);
{ Rotate a line }
var
  Cx, Cy, NumPoints: integer;
  PCPoints: PCArray;
  Points: WorldArray;
  Cwx, Cwy: real;
begin
  NumPoints := 2;
  Cx := (Left + Right) div 2;                  { Get the center of the line }
  Cy := (Top + Bottom) div 2;
  PCtoWorld(Cx,Cy,Cwx,Cwy);                    { Translate to world coordinates }
  Points[0].X := Xw1;  Points[0].Y := Yw1;   { Store line endpoints in an }
  Points[1].X := Xw2;  Points[1].Y := Yw2;   { array }
  WorldTranslatePoly(NumPoints,Points,-Cwx,-Cwy);
  WorldRotatePoly(NumPoints,Points,Angle);
  WorldTranslatePoly(NumPoints,Points,Cwx,Cwy);
  WorldPolyToPCPoly(NumPoints,Points,PCPoints);
  Xw1 := Points[0].X;   Yw1 := Points[0].Y;
  Xw2 := Points[1].X;   Yw2 := Points[1].Y;
  X1 := PCPoints[0].X;  Y1 := PCPoints[0].Y;
  X2 := PCPoints[1].X;  Y2 := PCPoints[1].Y;
  GetBounds(Left,Top,Right,Bottom);        { Calculate new bounding box }
end;

procedure LineObj.DrawArrows;
{ Draw arrows to the line if needed. The mouse is already hidden when this
  routine is called. The arrows are displayed as an open-ended polygon. }
```

```
var
  Arrowhead: PCArray;    { An arrow is made from two lines offset }
                         { 45 degrees on each side of the line }
  Angle: real;           { Calculated slope of line }
  XPC1, XPC2, YPC1, YPC2: integer;

  function ArcTan2(y, x: integer): real;
  { Returns the arctan of y/x }
  begin
    if x = 0 then begin
      if y < 0 then ArcTan2 := -Pi / 2.0
        else ArcTan2 := Pi / 2.0
    end
    else if x < 0 then ArcTan2 := ArcTan(y/x) + Pi
      else ArcTan2 := ArcTan(y/x);
  end;

begin
  WorldToPC(Xw1,Yw1,XPC1,YPC1);
  WorldToPC(Xw2,Yw2,XPC2,YPC2);
  if LeftArrow then begin          { Draw an arrow at the start of the line }
    Arrowhead[0].X := XPC1 + ArrowSize - Wl;
    Arrowhead[0].Y := YPC1 - ArrowSize - Wt;
    Arrowhead[1].X := XPC1 - Wl;
    Arrowhead[1].Y := YPC1 - Wt;
    Arrowhead[2].X := XPC1 + ArrowSize - Wl;
    Arrowhead[2].Y := YPC1 + ArrowSize - Wt;
    Angle := ArcTan2((YPC2-YPC1) / ((XPC2-XPC1) * 180.0 / Pi));
    PCTranslatePoly(3,Arrowhead,-XPC1+Wl,-YPC1+Wt);
    PCRotatePoly(3,Arrowhead,Angle);
    PCTranslatePoly(3,Arrowhead,XPC1-Wl,YPC1-Wt);
    Mouse.Hide;
    DrawPoly(3,Arrowhead);         { Draw the arrow }
    Mouse.Show;
  end;
  if RightArrow then begin         { Draw an arrow at the end of the line }
    Arrowhead[0].X := XPC2 - ArrowSize - Wl;
    Arrowhead[0].Y := YPC2 - ArrowSize - Wt;
    Arrowhead[1].X := XPC2 - Wl;
    Arrowhead[1].Y := YPC2 - Wt;
    Arrowhead[2].X := XPC2 - ArrowSize - Wl;
    Arrowhead[2].Y := YPC2 + ArrowSize - Wt;
    Angle := ArcTan2((YPC2-YPC1) / ((XPC2-XPC1) * 180.0 / Pi));
    PCTranslatePoly(3,Arrowhead,-XPC2+Wl,-YPC2+Wt);
    PCRotatePoly(3,Arrowhead,Angle);
    PCTranslatePoly(3,Arrowhead,XPC2-Wl,YPC2-Wt);
    Mouse.Hide;
    DrawPoly(3,Arrowhead);                    { Draw the arrow }
    Mouse.Show;
  end;
end;
```

```pascal
procedure CircleObj.Draw;
{ Override draw so it won't be called if the object list is full }
begin
  if FigList.NextObj < NumGObjects-1 then CircleTool.Draw;
end;

procedure CircleObj.GetBounds(var L, T, R, B: integer);
{ Get the bounding box of a circle object }
begin
  WorldToPC(CenterWx,CenterWy,CenterX,CenterY);
  L := CenterX - AbsRadiusx;                              { Centerx - Radius }
  T := Round(CenterY - AbsRadiusx * AspectRatio);   { Centery - Radius }
  R := CenterX + AbsRadiusx;                              { Centerx + Radius }
  B := Round(CenterY + AbsRadiusx * AspectRatio);   { Centery + Radius }
end;

function CircleObj.Dup: DrawingToolPtr;
{ Make a copy of a circle object. The new circle is the same as
  this circle object, except it is translated by (0.1,0.1). Returns
  pointer to new circle object. }
var
  Nc: CircleObjPtr;
begin
  Nc := New(CircleObjPtr,Init);                  { Create a new circle object }
  Nc^.Copy(@Self);                               { Copy the circle settings }
  Nc^.CenterWx := Nc^.CenterWx + 0.1;  { Translate the center (0.1,0.1) }
  Nc^.CenterWy := Nc^.CenterWy + 0.1;
  { Calculate position and bounds of new circle }
  WorldToPC(Nc^.CenterWx,Nc^.CenterWy,Nc^.CenterX,Nc^.CenterY);
  Nc^.GetBounds(Nc^.Left,Nc^.Top,Nc^.Right,Nc^.Bottom);
  Dup := Nc;                                { Return pointer to new circle }
end;

procedure CircleObj.Copy(FigPtr: CircleObjPtr);
{ Copy the settings of the object pointed to by FigPtr into this
  circle object }
begin
  CenterWx := FigPtr^.CenterWx;
  CenterWy := FigPtr^.CenterWy;
  Centerx := FigPtr^.Centerx;
  Centery := FigPtr^.Centery;
  Left := FigPtr^.Left;
  Top := FigPtr^.Top;
  Right := FigPtr^.Right;
  Bottom := FigPtr^.Bottom;
  AbsRadiusx := FigPtr^.AbsRadiusx;
  DrawColor := FigPtr^.DrawColor;
end;

procedure CircleObj.Display;
{ Display the circle object }
begin
  SetColor(DrawColor);
```

```
    WorldToPC(CenterWx,CenterWy,Centerx,Centery);
    Mouse.Hide;
    Circle(Centerx-Wl,Centery-Wt,AbsRadiusx);        { Draw the circle }
    Mouse.Show;
end;

procedure CircleObj.FinishDrawing;
{ After drawing a circle, append an object for it to the list of
  graphics figures on the screen }
var
  Nc: CircleObjPtr;
begin
  CircleTool.FinishDrawing;              { Call the inherited routine }
  Nc := New(CircleObjPtr,Init);          { Create a new circle object }
  PCtoWorld(Centerx,Centery,CenterWx,CenterWy); { Use world coordinates }
  GetBounds(Left,Top,Right,Bottom);      { Save bounding box of circle }
  Nc^.Copy(@Self);                       { Copy settings to new object }
  FigList.AddObj(Nc);                    { Add object to figure list }
end;

procedure CircleObj.Translate(TransX, TransY: real);
{ Translate a circle in world coordinates }
begin
  CenterWx := CenterWx + TransX;    CenterWy := CenterWy + TransY;
end;

procedure FillPolygonObj.Draw;
begin
  if FigList.NextObj < NumGObjects-1 then FillPolygonTool.Draw;
end;

function FillPolygonObj.Dup: DrawingToolPtr;
{ Duplicate the current polygon object by creating an identical
  polygon except that it is translated by (0.1,0.1). A pointer
  to the new object is returned. }
var
  Np: FillPolygonObjPtr;
begin
  Np := New(FillPolygonObjPtr,Init);      { Create new polygon object }
  Np^.Copy(@Self);                        { Copy settings to new object }
  WorldTranslatePoly(Np^.NumPts,Np^.PointsW,0.1,0.1);
  WorldPolyToPCPoly(Np^.NumPts,Np^.PointsW,Np^.Poly);
  Np^.GetBounds(Np^.Left,Np^.Top,Np^.Right,Np^.Bottom);
  Dup := Np;                              { Return pointer to new object }
end;

procedure FillPolygonObj.FinishDrawing;
{ After drawing a polygon, add an object for it to the list of
  figures. Copy the polygon's settings that were used to draw
  the figure to the new object. }
var
  Np: FillPolygonObjPtr;
begin
```

```
  FillPolygonTool.FinishDrawing;
  Np := New(FillPolygonObjPtr,Init);              { Create a polygon object }
  PCPolyToWorldPoly(NumPts,Poly,PointsW);         { Use world coordinates }
  GetBounds(Left,Top,Right,Bottom);               { Get bounds of polygon }
  Np^.Copy(@Self);                                { Copy settings }
  FigList.AddObj(Np);                             { Add polygon object }
end;

procedure FillPolygonObj.Copy(FigPtr: FillPolygonObjPtr);
{ Copy the polygon pointed to by FigPtr to the polygon's "self" }
var
  I: integer;
begin
  Left := FigPtr^.Left;        Top := FigPtr^.Top;
  Right := FigPtr^.Right;      Bottom := FigPtr^.Bottom;
  NumPts := FigPtr^.NumPts;
  { Note: Poly is an array of type PCArray (defined in MATRIX.PAS)
    and therefore cannot have any more edge points than are
    specified by MaxPoint, which is also defined in MATRIX.PAS }
  for I := 0 to NumPts-1 do begin              { Copy PC points }
    Poly[I].X := FigPtr^.Poly[I].X;
    Poly[I].Y := FigPtr^.Poly[I].Y;
  end;
  CopyWorldPoly(FigPtr^.NumPts,FigPtr^.PointsW,PointsW);
  DrawColor := FigPtr^.DrawColor;
  LineStyle := FigPtr^.LineStyle;
  FillColor := FigPtr^.FillColor;
  FillStyle := FigPtr^.FillStyle;
end;

procedure FillPolygonObj.Display;
{ Display a polygon }
begin
  SetColor(DrawColor);
  SetLineStyle(LineStyle,0,NormWidth);
  SetFillStyle(FillStyle,FillColor);
  WorldPolyToPCPoly(NumPts,PointsW,Poly);
  Mouse.Hide;
  FillPoly(NumPts,Poly);
  Mouse.Show;
end;

procedure FillPolygonObj.GetBounds(var L, T, R, B: integer);
{ Get bounding box of polygon object in screen coordinates }
var
  I: integer;
begin
  L := GetMaxX;  T := GetMaxY;
  R := 0;        B := 0;
  WorldPolyToPCPoly(NumPts,PointsW,Poly);
  for I := 0 to NumPts-1 do begin
    if Poly[I].X < L then L := Poly[I].X;
    if Poly[I].X > R then R := Poly[I].X;
```

```
      if Poly[I].Y < T then T := Poly[I].Y;
      if Poly[I].Y > B then B := Poly[I].Y;
    end;
    Inc(L,Wl);  Inc(R,Wl);  Inc(T,Wt);  Inc(B,Wt);
  end;

procedure FillPolygonObj.Translate(TransX, TransY: real);
{ Translate a polygon in world coordinates }
begin
  WorldTranslatePoly(NumPts,PointsW,TransX,TransY);
end;

procedure FillPolygonObj.Rotate(Angle: real);
{ Rotate a polygon by the amount in "angle" }
var
  I, Cx, Cy: integer;
begin
  Cx := (Left + Right) div 2 - Wl;
  Cy := (Top + Bottom) div 2 - Wt;
  WorldPolyToPCPoly(NumPts,PointsW,Poly);
  PCTranslatePoly(NumPts,Poly,-Cx,-Cy);
  PCRotatePoly(NumPts,Poly,Angle);
  PCTranslatePoly(NumPts,Poly,Cx,Cy);
  for I := 0 to NumPts-1 do
    PCtoWorld(Poly[I].X,Poly[I].Y,PointsW[I].X,PointsW[I].Y);
  GetBounds(Left,Top,Right,Bottom);
end;

begin
end.
```

• Listing 12.4. CADDRAW.PAS

```
unit CADDraw;
{ CADDRAW.PAS: Drawing and object support routines for the CAD program. }
interface
uses
  Graph, Draw, GObjLst, GPopPac, CADWindw, MousePac, KbdMouse,
  Matrix, UserTool;
const
  LineHeight: integer  = 8;     { Vertical spacing between lines in menu }
  LineWidth: integer = 40;      { Width of a line in the pop-up menu }
  MaxLineStyles: integer = 7;   { Number of line styles in the menu }
  Border = 2;                   { Two-pixel borders are used }
type
{ Provides the routine to pop up a menu of different line styles }
CADChangeLineStyleToolPtr = ^CADChangeLineStyleTool;
CADChangeLineStyleTool = object(DrawingTool)
  procedure Draw; virtual;
end;
```

```
{ The following object types are provided so that we can have
  access to various functions in the environment through the
  same drawing tool object list we created in Chapter 11 for
  the paint program }
ToggleGridToolPtr = ^ToggleGridTool;
ToggleGridTool = object(DrawingTool)
  procedure Draw; virtual;
end;

DeleteAllObjToolPtr = ^DeleteAllObjTool;
DeleteAllObjTool = object(DrawingTool)
  procedure Draw; virtual;
end;

MoveObjToolPtr = ^MoveObjTool;
MoveObjTool = object(DrawingTool)
  procedure Draw; virtual;
end;

SelectObjToolPtr = ^SelectObjTool;
SelectObjTool = object(DrawingTool)
  procedure Draw; virtual;
end;

DuplicateObjToolPtr = ^DuplicateObjTool;
DuplicateObjTool = object(DrawingTool)
  procedure Draw; virtual;
end;

DeleteObjToolPtr = ^DeleteObjTool;
DeleteObjTool = object(DrawingTool)
  procedure Draw; virtual;
end;

FlipToFrontToolPtr = ^FlipToFrontTool;
FlipToFrontTool = object(DrawingTool)
  procedure Draw; virtual;
end;

FlipToBackToolPtr = ^FlipToBackTool;
FlipToBackTool = object(DrawingTool)
  procedure Draw; virtual;
end;

RotateObjToolPtr = ^RotateObjTool;
RotateObjTool = object(DrawingTool)
  procedure Draw; virtual;
end;

var
  FigList: GObjList;         { Globally define a list of screen figures }
  LeftArrow, RightArrow: boolean; { Specifies whether arrowheads should }
                            { be placed on the ends of line segments }
```

```
implementation
{ Used to interface the environment to the move function }
procedure MoveObjTool.Draw; begin  FigList.Move;  end;

{ Used to interface the environment to the select function }
procedure SelectObjTool.Draw; begin FigList.Select; end;

{ Used to interface the environment to the Duplicate routine }
procedure DuplicateObjTool.Draw; begin FigList.Duplicate; end;

{ Used to interface the environment to the Delete routine }
procedure DeleteObjTool.Draw; begin FigList.DeleteObj; end;

{ Used to interface the environment to the FlipToFront routine }
procedure FlipToFrontTool.Draw; begin FigList.FlipToFront; end;

{ Used to interface the environment to the FlipToBack routine }
procedure FlipToBackTool.Draw; begin FigList.FlipToBack; end;

{ Used to interface the environment to the Rotate routine }
procedure RotateObjTool.Draw; begin FigList.Rotate; end;

{ Used to interface the environment to the DeleteAll routine.
  Deletes all objects in the figure list. }
procedure DeleteAllObjTool.Draw; begin FigList.DeleteAll; end;

procedure CADChangeLineStyleTool.Draw;
{ Select a new line style from the line style pull-down menu.
  Note that this function overrides the same function used in the
  paint program (Chapter 11) to create a pull-down menu. Arrows
  have been added to the menu from the paint version. }
var
  WindowWidth, WindowHeight: integer;
  Offset, I, Mx, My: integer;
  T: boolean;
begin
  WindowWidth := LineWidth + Border * 6;
  WindowHeight := LineHeight * MaxLineStyles;
  Mouse.Hide;
  { Note: We're using the Win object declared in USERTOOL.PAS }
  T := Win.GPopup(LineWindowX,LineWindowY,LineWindowX+WindowWidth+Border,
                  LineWindowY+WindowHeight+LineHeight div 2,
                  SolidLn,GetMaxColor,SolidFill,Black);
  SetColor(GetMaxColor);
  Offset := Border;
  for I := 0 to MaxLineStyles-1 do begin
    if I >= 4 then begin            { Line styles 4, 5, and 6 have arrows }
      SetLineStyle(SolidLn,0,NormWidth);
      Line(Border*3,Offset+LineHeight div 2,Border*3+LineWidth,
           Offset+LineHeight div 2);
      case I of
        4: begin
           Line(Border*3,Offset+LineHeight div 2,
```

```
                 Border*3+2,Offset+LineHeight div 2-2);
             Line(Border*3,Offset+LineHeight div 2,
                 Border*3+2,Offset+LineHeight div 2+2);
             end;
          5: begin
             Line(Border*3+LineWidth,Offset+LineHeight div 2,
                 Border*3+LineWidth-2,Offset+LineHeight div 2-2);
             Line(Border*3+LineWidth,Offset+LineHeight div 2,
                 Border*3+LineWidth-2,Offset+LineHeight div 2+2);
             end;
          6: begin
             Line(Border*3,Offset+LineHeight div 2,
                 Border*3+2,Offset+LineHeight div 2-2);
             Line(Border*3,Offset+LineHeight div 2,
                 Border*3+2,Offset+LineHeight div 2+2);
             Line(Border*3+LineWidth,Offset+LineHeight div 2,
                 Border*3+LineWidth-2,Offset+LineHeight div 2-2);
             Line(Border*3+LineWidth,Offset+LineHeight div 2,
                 Border*3+LineWidth-2,Offset+LineHeight div 2+2);
             end;
          end;
      end
    else begin
      SetLineStyle(I,0,NormWidth);
      Line(Border*3,Offset+LineHeight div 2,Border*3+LineWidth,
          Offset+LineHeight div 2);
    end;
    Inc(Offset,LineHeight);
  end;
  Mouse.Show;
  { Don't put arrowheads on the line }
  LeftArrow := False;  RightArrow := False;
  while not Mouse.buttonpressed(LeftButton) do ;
  Mouse.GetCoords(Mx,My);
  Offset := Border;
  for I := 0 to MaxLineStyles-1 do begin
    if Mouse.InBox(LineWindowX+Border*3,Offset-LineHeight div 2,
                  LineWindowX+Border*3+LineWidth,
                  LineWindowY+Offset+LineHeight div 2,Mx,My) then begin
      Mouse.Hide;
      T := Win.GUnpop;
      Mouse.Show;
      if I >= 4 then begin
        case I of
          4: LeftArrow := True;
          5: RightArrow := True;
          6: begin LeftArrow := True; RightArrow := True; end;
        end;
        I := SolidLn;
      end;
      SetLineStyle(I,0,NormWidth);
      { Now set the global line style to the style just selected }
      GlobalLineStyle := I;
```

```
        while not Mouse.ButtonReleased(LeftButton) do ;
        Exit;
      end;
      Inc(Offset,LineHeight);
    end;
    Mouse.Hide;
    T := Win.GUnpop;
    Mouse.Show;
  end;

procedure ToggleGridTool.Draw;
{ Toggle the use of the grid and update the screen appropriately }
begin
  if GridOn then GridOn := False else GridOn := True;
  ClearDrawingArea;
  FigList.DisplayAll;
end;

begin
end.
```

• Listing 12.5. CADWINDW.PAS

```
unit CADWindw;
{ CADWINDW.PAS: Provides two support routines for the CAD program.
  They are included in this unit so that there aren't any circular
  references with other units. }
interface
uses
  Graph, Draw, Matrix;
var
 GridOn: boolean;                     { If True, grid is to be displayed }

procedure ClearDrawingArea;
procedure DrawGrid;

implementation

procedure DrawGrid;
{ Draw a background grid in the drawing window using six
  horizontal and vertical dotted lines. This function assumes
  that the mouse is NOT visible. }
var
  I, J, X, Y, SaveColor: integer;
  SaveLine: LineSettingsType;
  Vp: ViewPortType;
begin
  GetViewSettings(Vp);
  SetViewPort(0,0,MaxX,MaxY,True);
  SaveColor := GetColor;
  GetLineSettings(SaveLine);
```

```
      SetLineStyle(DottedLn,0,NormWidth);
      SetColor(GetMaxColor);
      for J := 1 to 5 do begin          { Place same number here as that }
        WorldToPC(0.0,0.0+J,X,Y);       { used in Set_Window in SetupScreen }
        Line(Wl,Y,Wr,Y);
      end;
      for I := 1 to 6 do begin          { Use same number here as that }
        WorldToPC(0.0+I,0.0,X,Y);       { in SetupScreen }
        Line(X,Wt,X,Wb);
      end;
      SetLineStyle(SaveLine.LineStyle,SaveLine.Pattern,SaveLine.Thickness);
      SetColor(SaveColor);
      SetViewPort(Vp.X1,Vp.Y1,Vp.X2,Vp.Y2,Vp.Clip);
    end;

    procedure ClearDrawingArea;
    { Clear the drawing window }
    var
      Vp: ViewPortType;
    begin
      GetViewSettings(Vp);
      SetViewPort(Wl,Wt,Wr,Wb,True);  { Set viewport to drawing window }
      Mouse.Hide;
      ClearViewPort;                   { Clear the drawing window }
      { Set viewport back to full screen }
      SetViewPort(Vp.X1,Vp.Y1,Vp.X2,Vp.Y2,True);
      { Draw a grid in the drawing window if the gridon flag is True }
      if GridOn then DrawGrid;
      Mouse.Show;
    end;

    end.
```

13

Three-Dimensional Graphics

In this chapter we will explore three-dimensional graphics. Our goal is to develop a graphics package that displays three-dimensional wire-frame objects from any vantage point. We'll begin by defining some of the terminology used in three-dimensional graphics. Next, we'll discuss various components of the three-dimensional viewing package and explain how it works. Finally, we'll give you a few sample three-dimensional object files for you to display and suggest some extensions you might try adding to the program.

Adding the Third Dimension

In the preceding chapters we have been limiting our discussion to programs with two-dimensional objects. For example, in the CAD program presented in Chapter 12, the objects that we created were all defined in world coordinates using only the x and y dimensions. This gave us objects with specific heights and widths. Now we will add depth to our objects by including a third dimension, z.

In the following sections, we'll develop a program called THREED.PAS that will allow us to view wire-frame objects as shown in Figure 13.1. In order to develop the three-dimensional program, however, we'll be developing a handful of new tools and explore various issues related to three-dimensional graphics.

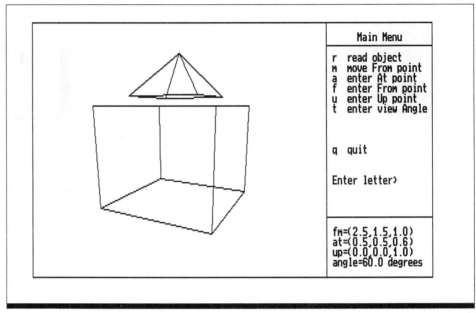

Figure 13.1. The environment of the THREED.PAS program

Using a Camera Model

Generating a scene of a three-dimensional object is similar to taking a picture of an object with a camera in that they both create a two-dimensional view of a three-dimensional object. In fact, we'll be using a camera model to help us specify how objects are to be displayed.

Basically, we will assume that we are using a pinhole camera where everything in view is in focus. In addition, we'll assume that the camera is located somewhere in world coordinates at a location called the *from* point, and that it is looking directly toward a location called the *at* point. The camera model also specifies a viewing angle that acts much like a lens in that it defines how much of the scene will actually be displayed. Finally, our camera model includes a parameter called an *up* vector that defines the orientation of the viewing plane with relation to the coordinate system. Figure 13.2 illustrates each of these viewing parameters as they appear in world coordinates.

Actually, since we are interested in how objects appear with respect to the screen, we will be using another coordinate system, called *eye coordinates*. It has its origin at the *from* point and the *at* point on the positive z axis as shown in Figure 13.3. The term eye coordinates comes from the fact that the coordinate system is oriented with respect to the viewer—in our case the camera.

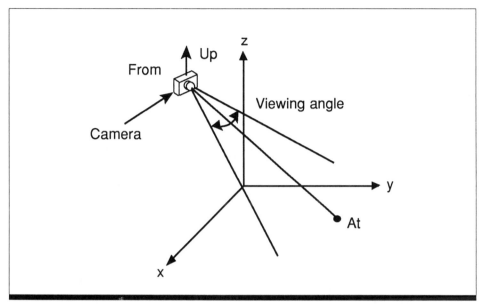

Figure 13.2. The from, at, up, and viewing angle parameters in world coordinates

Finally, our camera model uses a perspective projection of all objects. In other words, we will project all objects onto the viewing plane along rays that extend out from the from point as shown in Figure 13.4. Because we will be using perspective projection objects will appear distorted as illustrated in Figure 13.1. This gives a natural sensation of depth.

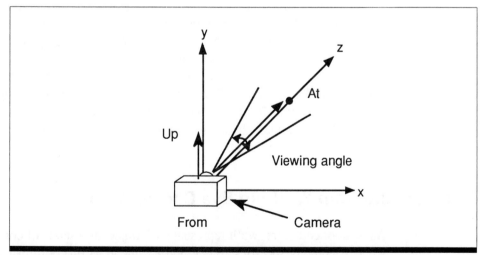

Figure 13.3. The viewing parameters as they appear in eye coordinates

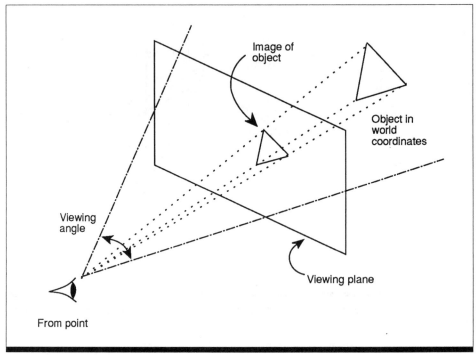

Figure 13.4. Projecting a three-dimensional object into two dimensions

Objects in Three Dimensions

To keep things simple, we'll be dealing exclusively with three-dimensional wire-frame objects like that shown in Figure 13.1. Each object is represented by a series of three-dimensional coordinate triplets that are connected by line segments to create the outlines of an object being displayed.

Each point, or *vertex*, as it is usually called, is specified as an (x,y,z) coordinate in world coordinates. The goal of a three-dimensional graphics package, therefore, is to transform these coordinates into two-dimensional screen coordinates and then connect them with line segments. This process requires numerous steps that we'll cover in the next several sections.

Transforming from World to Eye Coordinates

As mentioned before, we'll represent each object as a series of connected vertices where each point specifies an x, y, and z value in world coordinates. However, we are not so much interested in where these points are located in world coordinates as we are in where they are with respect to the viewer—the eye coordinates. In fact, one of our first steps will be to transform object points from the world coordinate system to an eye coordinate system. By doing this we will easily be able to determine what objects are in view and how they appear.

Unfortunately, transforming a three-dimensional point from world coordinates to eye coordinates is not a trivial matter. Basically, what we need to do is to apply a series of transforms that can align the world coordinate system with the eye coordinate system. This can be broken up into the following steps:

1. Translate the world coordinate system so that the location of the viewer (the from point) is at the origin of the eye coordinate system.
2. Rotate x axis so that the at point will lie on the positive z axis.
3. Rotate y axis similarly.
4. Rotate z axis.

At this point, objects can be projected onto the viewing plane situated along the z axis. The projection process is described in greater detail later.

Although the steps just described can be used to transform between world and eye coordinates, they require numerous mathematical operations. On a PC these calculations can make a system too slow to be practical.

Instead, we'll use a vector algebra technique that reduces the number of mathematical operations that must be made. The process begins, as before, by translating the viewer in the world coordinate system to the origin of the eye coordinates; however, to align the coordinate axes, we will not use a series of rotations. Instead, we'll replace these three steps with one as shown in Figure 13.5. We won't derive

Step 1: Translate points by $(-f_x, -f_y, -f_z)$

Step 2: Multiply result from Step 1 by V_{4X4} where

$$V = \begin{bmatrix} a_{1x} & a_{2x} & a_{3x} & 0 \\ a_{1y} & a_{2y} & a_{3y} & 0 \\ a_{1z} & a_{2z} & a_{3z} & 0 \\ 0 & 0 & 0 & 1 \end{bmatrix}$$

$$(A_1)\ (A_2)\ (A_3)$$

To compute A1, A2, and A3, let A' be a vector where $A' = A - F$

and $\quad A_1 = \dfrac{A' \times U}{\|A' \times U\|} \qquad A_2 = \dfrac{(A' \times U) \times A'}{\|(A' \times U) \times A'\|} \qquad A_3 = \dfrac{A'}{\|A'\|}$

Figure 13.5. Operations to convert world coordinates to eye coordinates

the matrix expression V that replaces the rotations described above, but let's look at what it is doing. Essentially, the matrix V specifies how the unit vectors A_1, A_2, and A_3 can be aligned to the eye coordinate system as Figure 13.6 illustrates. Therefore, by applying the matrix V shown in Figure 13.5 after translating the world coordinates, we can transform all world coordinates to eye coordinates.

In addition, we will apply the matrix:

$$\begin{bmatrix} D & 0 & 0 & 0 \\ 0 & D & 0 & 0 \\ 0 & 0 & 1 & 0 \\ 0 & 0 & 0 & 1 \end{bmatrix}$$

where D is

$$\frac{1}{\tan(\text{viewing\_angle}/2)}$$

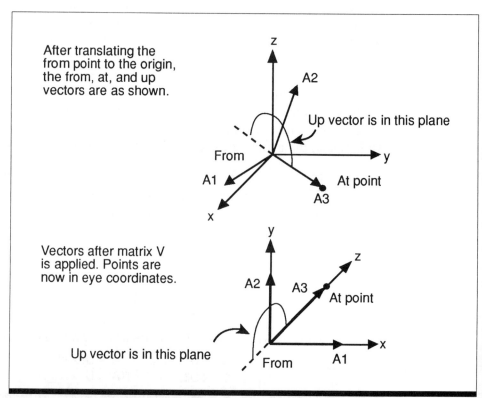

Figure 13.6. Vectors before and after the vector V is applied

after converting points to eye coordinates. The purpose of this matrix operation is to adjust the scene according to the viewing angle so that the object extends between the lines $y=z$, $y=-z$, $x=z$, and $x=-z$; this makes clipping a lot easier. We'll look at this presently.

Fortunately, we can combine the operations shown in Figure 13.5 and the matrix shown on p. 330 into a handful of equations. These resulting equations are used in the procedure **TransformSeg** to transform lines from world to eye coordinates in the three-dimensional program. Many of the values in **TransformSeg** are calculated in the routine **SetEye**, which must be called prior to transforming any line segments. You'll notice that **SetEye** performs most of the calculations outlined in Figure 13.5. Since many of these operations are vector operations, we have included a separate utility called VECTOR.PAS (see Listing 13.1) to perform these operations. A list of the routines in VECTOR.PAS is shown in Table 13.1.

Clipping in Three Dimensions

Thus far we have been fortunate in that the BGI has provided us with clipping algorithms to handle clipping of graphics figures as they are displayed. However, now we must develop our own code to clip objects in three dimensions. Essentially, what we want to do is to ignore all objects that do not project onto the projection plane or clip edges of objects that extend beyond the border of the viewport on the projection plane.

To accomplish this, THREED.PAS (see Listing 13.2) includes the routines **Clip3D** and **Code**, which clip three-dimensional line segments in *eye coordinates* to a *viewing pyramid* as shown in Figure 13.7. Note that all objects within the viewing pyramid will be projected onto the viewing plane and displayed on the screen. This is done at the end of **Clip3D**. We'll get back to this, but first, let's look at how the clipping algorithm works.

Table 13.1. Routines in VECTOR.PAS

Routine	Description
Subtract	Subtracts two vectors
Divide	Divides a vector by a scalar
Mag	Returns the magnitude of a vector
Cross	Calculates the cross product of two vectors

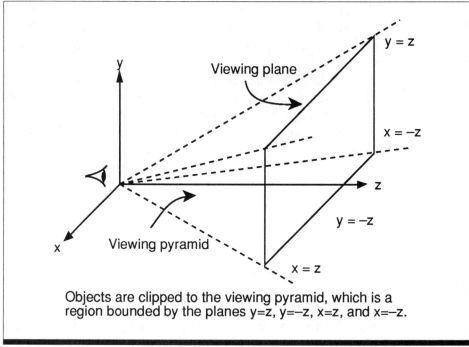

Objects are clipped to the viewing pyramid, which is a region bounded by the planes y=z, y=−z, x=z, and x=−z.

Figure 13.7. The viewing pyramid is used to clip objects in three dimensions

After we transform a line segment from world coordinates to eye coordinates, we'll pass it through the clipping process, which begins by calling **Clip3D**. Then **Clip3D** calls **Code** to determine on which side of the viewing pyramid the endpoints of the line segment fall. If one of the coordinates falls outside of the viewing pyramid, the appropriate bit in the variable **C** is set to indicate that the line might cross the edge of the viewing pyramid and must be clipped. The clipping is done in **Clip3D** by calculating where the line segment intersects the viewing pyramid. This intersection is then used as the new endpoint of the line and the resulting line is passed through the process again until the line is trimmed so that it is completely within the viewing pyramid. Then the line is displayed. As mentioned before, this is done at the end of **Clip3D**. Let's now examine how this is done.

Perspective Projection

All objects in the three-dimensional viewing program are displayed using perspective projection. The basic idea is to project all objects onto the viewing plane as shown earlier in Figure 13.4. Note that objects will be displayed only if a line connecting them and the viewer passes through the viewport on the viewing plane. Objects that do not intersect this region are clipped as described in the last section.

Assuming that we have a line segment that is within the viewport on the viewing plane, how do we know what size to draw it? Fortunately, we can use a simple geometric property of similar triangles as shown in Figure 13.8. Based on these values, a point (x,y,z) maps to $(x/z,y/z)$ on the viewing plane. This point is then converted to PC coordinates using the routine **WorldToPC** as is done in **Clip3D**. Note that we need to make sure z is not zero, so that we don't divide by zero! Once the points are converted to PC screen coordinates, the line segment is displayed using **Line**.

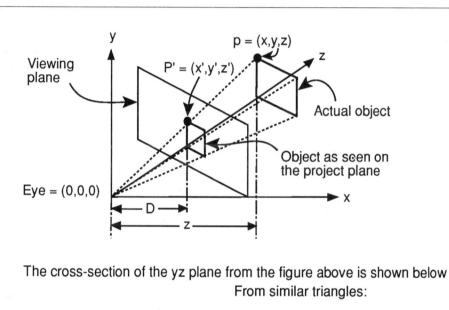

The cross-section of the yz plane from the figure above is shown below
From similar triangles:

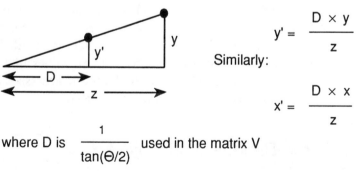

$$y' = \frac{D \times y}{z}$$

Similarly:

$$x' = \frac{D \times x}{z}$$

where D is $\dfrac{1}{\tan(\Theta/2)}$ used in the matrix V

Figure 13.8. Projecting objects onto the viewing plane

Object Files

The three-dimensional viewing program does not let you interactively create objects like the CAD program in Chapter 12. Instead, THREED.PAS is intended to merely display three-dimensional objects. Therefore, the program reads the objects that it displays from object files. This is done in the function **Read3DObject**.

In order to save space and simplify modifications, three-dimensional objects are saved in a special format. The file begins with a header that specifies the number of vertices in the object and the number of connections between the vertices, respectively. After the header is a list of the vertices that make up the object where each vertex is represented by three **real** values that correspond to the x, y, and z values of the point in world coordinates. The number of vertices in this list is specified by the first value in the header as mentioned earlier. Next is a series of indexes into this list of vertices that specifies which vertices should be connected to which. Essentially, they describe how the points read in above should be connected to draw the object. For example, if our object is a triangle with the vertices:

(0.0, 1.0, 0.1)	vertex 1
(1.0, 0.0, 0.1)	vertex 2
(1.0, 0.1, 1.0)	vertex 3

and we wanted them connected in this order, then the list of connections would appear as

    1 2 3 -1

This indicates that vertex 1 is connected to vertex 2, which is connected to vertex 3, which in turn is connected to vertex 1. Note that the last value is negative. This is a special marker in the connection list that indicates that the object has ended or at least that this face of the object is complete. The number of connections that must be read in is specified by the second number in the file header.

The procedure **Read3DObject** reads these values into the global variables listed in Table 13.2. Later, the values in **Points** are accessed according to the order specified in the array **Connect** to draw the object.

Displaying a Three-Dimensional Object

Now that we know how a three-dimensional object is read from a file, let's see how **Points** and **Connect** are used to display an object. This is accomplished by

Table 13.2. Global variables that store objects

Variable	Description
Vertices	Number of vertices in object
Length	Number of connections in vertices
Points	Array of vertices that are stored in world coordinates
Connect	Array of indexes into the Points array that specify how the vertices are to be connected

the nested **while** loops in the routine **View** as shown here.

```
I := 1;
while I < Length do begin
  Start := I;
  Inc(I);
  while Connect[I] > 0 do begin
    TransformSeg(Points[Connect[I-1]],Points[Connect[I]]);
    Inc(I);
  end;
  TransformSeg(Points[Connect[I-1]],Points[-Connect[I]]);
  TransformSeg(Points[-Connect[I]],Points[Connect[Start]]);
  Inc(I);
end;
```

The outer **while** loop sequences through the list of vertex connections contained in **Connect**. Remember that the negative values in **Connect** are used to denote the end of a series of connected points. The inner **while** loop sequences through the list of connected vertices until a negative marker is found. For each pair of connected points, **TransformSeg** is called to transform the two points and display a line connecting them if it is visible:

```
TransformSeg(Points[Connect[I-1]],Points[Connect[I]]);
```

When a negative value is reached in the **Connect** array, the current pair of points is displayed and then the last point is connected back to the first by the lines:

```
TransformSeg(Points[Connect[I-1]],Points[-Connect[I]]);
TransformSeg(Points[-Connect[I]],Points[Connect[Start]]);
```

This process continues until all values in the **Connect** are used.

Setting the Viewing Parameters

There are several parameters that must be set for the three-dimensional viewing package to work properly. For instance, before an object can be viewed the **From, At, Up,** and **Angle** variables must be all set. To simplify things, each of these are given default values or are designed to automatically calculate values that can be used. For example, the *at* location is set by **SetAt** each time a new object is read in. It calls the routine **MinMax** to determine the bounds of the object and then it sets the *at* point to the middle of the object. Similarly, **SetFrom** sets the *from* point so that it is far enough away from the object that the entire object will appear in the viewport.

In addition, there are several routines that allow you to interactively specify each of these values. They can be changed by selecting the appropriate options in the program menu.

Compiling the THREED.PAS Program

To compile the program THREED.PAS you will need the files listed in Table 13.3.

Using the Three-Dimensional Program

After you have your three-dimensional program compiled, you're ready to try displaying an object. In the following section, the file listings for two three-dimensional objects are shown. To display each of these objects, first type the data into two separate files and give them the names as indicated. The files can then be read by the three-dimensional program by selecting the read file command, which is done by typing the letter r. A pop-up window will appear in the center of the screen prompting you to enter the name of the file to be read. You should type this filename and press the Enter key. Once you press Enter, the object file is read and the object is displayed.

Table 13.3. Files used to compile the program THREED.PAS

Source file	Chapter
GTEXT.PAS	3
GPOPPAC.PAS	9
VECTOR.PAS	13
THREED.PAS	13

You can experiment with each of the viewing parameters by selecting the appropriate menu options from the screen. For instance, to change the *from* point, you can type the letter f, which will cause a pop-up window to prompt you for a new *from* point. For example, try changing the *from* point to the world coordinates (2,2,2) or even (0,0,0). The latter value should take you inside the object!

Another way to change the *from* point is to use the m menu option, which incrementally steps toward the object when you press the up arrow or away from the object when you press the down arrow.

Another area that you might want to try experimenting with is changing the viewing angle. This can be done by selecting the menu option which prompts you for a viewing angle—effectively allowing you to zoom in and out on an object.

Sample Objects

This section lists two data files for objects that you should try with your three-dimensional program. Here is the data file, called TEST1.DAT, for the object shown in Figure 13.9:

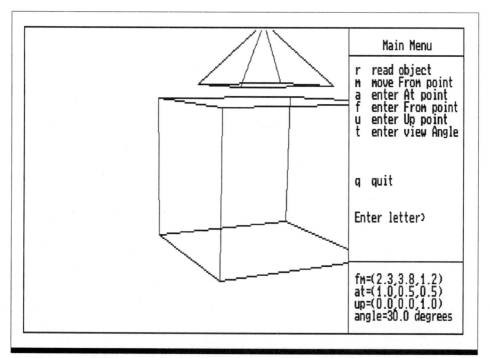

Figure 13.9. The object created by the file TEST1.DAT

```
13 40
1.0   1.0   1.0   1.0   1.0   0.0
1.0   0.0   0.0   1.0   0.0   1.0
0.0   1.0   1.0   0.0   1.0   0.0
0.0   0.0   0.0   0.0   0.0   1.0
0.8   0.2   1.1   0.8   0.8   1.1
0.2   0.8   1.1   0.2   0.2   1.1
0.5   0.5   1.5
1   5   8   -4   5   6   7   -8   6   2   3   -7   1   4   3   -2
8   7   3   -4   6   5   1   -2   9   10   -13   10   11   -13   11   12
-13   12   9   -13   12   11   10   -9
```

The next data file, called TEST2.DAT, generates the object shown in Figure 13.10:

```
38 54
1.0   1.0   1.0   1.0   1.0   0.0
1.0   0.0   0.0   1.0   0.0   1.0
0.0   1.0   1.0   0.0   1.0   0.0
0.0   0.0   0.0   0.0   0.0   1.0
0.25   0.0   0.25   0.25   0.0   0.75
0.75   0.0   0.75   0.75   0.0   0.7
0.3   0.0   0.7   0.3   0.0   0.5
0.6   0.0   0.5   0.6   0.0   0.45
```

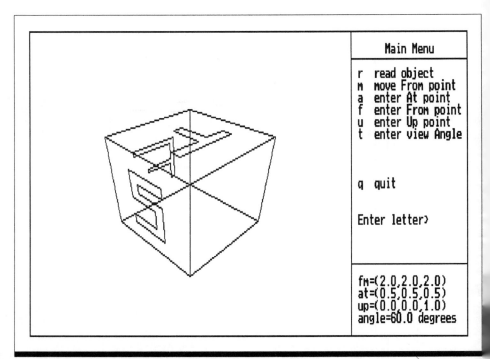

Figure 13.10. The display created by the file TEST2.DAT

```
0.3   0.0   0.45  0.3   0.0   0.25
1.0   0.3   0.2   1.0   0.3   0.3
1.0   0.6   0.3   1.0   0.6   0.5
1.0   0.3   0.5   1.0   0.3   0.8
1.0   0.7   0.8   1.0   0.7   0.7
1.0   0.4   0.7   1.0   0.4   0.6
1.0   0.7   0.6   1.0   0.7   0.2
0.4   0.3   1.0   0.4   0.6   1.0
0.2   0.6   1.0   0.2   0.7   1.0
0.8   0.7   1.0   0.8   0.6   1.0
0.5   0.6   1.0   0.5   0.3   1.0
1   5   8   -4   5   6   7   -8   6   2   3   -7   1   4   3   -2
8   7   3   -4   6   5   1   -2   9   10   11   12   13   14   15   16
17   -18   19   20   21   22   23   24   25   26   27   28   29   -30   31   32   33   34
35   36   37   -38
```

Extending the Program

There are several enhancements that you might try adding to the three-dimensional viewing package. The first thing you could do is put in routines to interactively draw three-dimensional objects. The difficulty here is in coming up with a clean way of drawing them. You will probably want to use several viewports that show the object at different perspectives in order to give yourself a good idea of what the object looks like.

Another possible extension of the program would be to add color or fill patterns to the objects that are drawn. Since our file format groups edges of the objects into faces by use of the **Connect** array, you can try using **FillPoly** to draw the faces of the object rather than drawing them a line at a time. This way you'll be able to make the faces of the objects solid. However, you'll find that the order in which the faces are painted is important in drawing the object correctly. Generally, this becomes a problem of hidden surface removal. For the ambitious, this is probably the direction you'll want to explore.

• Listing 13.1. VECTOR.PAS

```pascal
unit Vector;
{ A set of vector manipulation routines used in THREED.PAS }
interface
uses
  Graph;
type
  VectorType = record
    x, y, z: real;
  end;
```

```pascal
{ These functions are available to external routines }
function Mag(V: VectorType): real;
procedure Subtract(V1, V2: VectorType; var S: VectorType);
procedure Cross(V1, V2: VectorType; var C: VectorType);
procedure Divide(V: VectorType; Num: real; var D: VectorType);

implementation
function Mag(V: VectorType): real;
{ Calculate the magnitude of the vector }
begin
    Mag := Sqrt(V.X * V.X + V.Y * V.Y + V.Z * V.Z);
end;

procedure Subtract(V1, V2: VectorType; var S: VectorType);
{ Subtract two vectors }
begin
  S.X := V1.X - V2.X;
  S.Y := V1.Y - V2.Y;
  S.Z := V1.Z - V2.Z;
end;

procedure Cross(V1, V2: VectorType; var C: VectorType);
{ Cross-multiply the two vectors V1 and V2 }
begin
  C.X := V1.Y * V2.Z - V2.Y * V1.Z;
  C.Y := V1.Z * V2.X - V2.Z * V1.X;
  C.Z := V1.X * V2.Y - V2.X * V1.Y;
end;

procedure Divide(V: VectorType; Num: real; var D: VectorType);
{ Divide the scalar number into the vector V }
begin
  if Num <> 0 then begin
    D.X := V.X / Num;
    D.Y := V.Y / Num;
    D.Z := V.Z / Num;
  end
  else begin
    CloseGraph;
    WriteLn('Divide by 0 in Matrix Divide Operation');
    Halt(1);
  end
end;

end.
```

• Listing 13.2. THREED.PAS

```pascal
program ThreeD;
{ THREED.PAS: Displays three-dimensional wire-frame views of objects.
  Objects are read from files and displayed according to the settings
```

```
    of the from, at, up, and viewing angle. In some modes you may need to
    change the constants PCL, PCR, and PCT in order to get the program to
    display figures with the correct proportions.  }
uses
    Graph, GText, Matrix, GPopPac, Vector, Crt;
const
    NumConnections = 100;    { An object can have this many }
    NumVertices = 150;       { vertices and connections }
    PCL: integer = 1;        { Border of viewing region on }
    PCR: integer = 469;      { the screen }
    PCT: integer = 1;
    PCB: integer = 198;
    UpKey = #72;
    DownKey = #80;
    prompt: string[14] = 'Enter letter> ';

var
    A, B, C, D, DVal: real;
    From, At, Up: VectorType;        { Viewing parameters }
    Angle: real;                     { The viewing angle }
    A1, A2, A3: VectorType;          { Used in three-dimensional transform }
    Connect: array[0..NumConnections-1] of integer;    { Vertex connections }
    Points: array[0..NumVertices-1] of VectorType;     { Vertices }
    Length: integer;                 { Number of vertex connections }
    Vertices: integer;               { Number of vertices }
    ObjXMin, ObjXMax: real;          { Extent of three-dimensional object }
    ObjYMin, ObjYMax: real;
    ObjZMin, ObjZMax: real;
    TFrom: real;                     { Controls from-at point distance }
    OffsX, OffsY, OffsZ: real;       { Transform variables }
    Dist: VectorType;                { Distance to from-at point }
    { Pixel boundaries of viewing area }
    PCLeft, PCTop, PCRight, PCBottom: integer;
    MaxX, MaxY: integer;             { Size of the screen }
    Ch: char;
    Win: GWindows;                   { The object for the pop-up windows }

function MaxOf(Val1, Val2: real): real;
begin
    if Val1 > Val2 then MaxOf := Val1
        else MaxOf := Val2;
end;

procedure WorldToPC(XW, YW: real; var XPC, YPC: integer);
{ Converts clipped world coordinates to screen coordinates }
begin
    XPC := Round(A * XW + B);   YPC := Round(C * YW + D);
end;

procedure Init3DGraphics;
{ Must be called before program begins main execution. It sets up
  the dimensions of the screen and various default values. }
var
    GDriver, GMode: integer;
```

```
begin
  GDriver := Detect;
  InitGraph(GDriver,GMode,'\tp\bgi');
  MaxX := GetMaxX;  MaxY := GetMaxY;
  PCLeft := PCL;    PCRight := PCR;
  PCTop := PCT;     PCBottom := MaxY - 1;
  A := (PCRight - PCLeft) / (1 + 1);  { Set viewport/window }
  B := PCLeft - A * (-1);             { mapping variables }
  C := (PCTop - PCBottom) / (1 + 1);
  D := PCBottom - C * (-1);
  { Set default values for the from, at, and up vectors  }
  From.X := 1.0;  From.Y := 0.0;  From.Z := 0.0;
  At.X := 0.0;    At.Y := 0.0;    At.Z := 0.0;
  Up.X := 0.0;    Up.Y := 0.0;    Up.Z := 1.0;
  Angle := ToRadians(60);   { Use 60-degree viewing angle }
  TFrom := 1.0;
end;

procedure MinMax;
{ Returns the minimum and maximum values in the point array
  for the x, y, and z values }
var
  I: integer;
begin
  ObjXMin := 32000;  ObjYMin := 32000;  ObjZMin := 32000;
  ObjXMax := -32000; ObjYMax := -32000; ObjZMax := -32000;
  for I := 0 to Vertices-1 do begin
    if Points[I].X > ObjXMax then ObjXMax := Points[I].X
    else if Points[I].X < ObjXMin then
      ObjXMin := Points[I].X;
    if Points[I].Y > ObjYMax then ObjYMax := Points[I].Y
    else if Points[I].Y < ObjYMin then
      ObjYMin := Points[I].Y;
    if Points[I].Z > ObjZMax then ObjZMax := Points[I].Z
    else if Points[I].Z < ObjZMin then
      ObjZMin := Points[I].Z;
  end
end;

procedure SetAt;
{ Routine to provide a default value for the at point. It is set to
  the midpoint of the extents of the object. }
begin
  MinMax;
  At.X := (ObjXMin + ObjXMax) / 2.0;
  At.Y := (ObjYMin + ObjYMax) / 2.0;
  At.Z := (ObjZMin + ObjZMax) / 2.0;
end;

procedure SetFrom;
{ Routine that provides a default value for the from point. It
  is dependent on the at point and the view angle. }
```

```pascal
const
  Width: real = 1.73205; { Ratio used to determine from point }
                         { It is based on size of the object }
begin
  From.X := At.X + (ObjXMax-ObjXMin) / 2.0 + Width *
            MaxOf((ObjZMax-ObjZMin)/2.0, (ObjYMax-ObjYMin)/2.0);
  From.Y := At.Y;  From.Z := At.Z;
end;

procedure SetEye;
{ There must be a valid object in the Points array before calling this
  routine. It sets up the various variables used in transforming an
  object from world to eye coordinates. }
var
  AMarkMag, TempMag: real;
  Temp: VectorType;
begin
  DVal := Cos(Angle/2.0) / Sin(Angle/2.0);
  Subtract(At,From,Dist);
  AMarkMag := Mag(Dist);
  Divide(Dist,AMarkMag,A3);
  Cross(Dist,Up,Temp);
  TempMag := Mag(Temp);
  Divide(Temp,TempMag,A1);
  Cross(A1,A3,Temp);
  TempMag := Mag(Temp);
  Divide(Temp,TempMag,A2);
  OffsX := -A1.X * From.X - A1.Y * From.Y - A1.Z * From.Z;
  OffsY := -A2.X * From.X - A2.Y * From.Y - A2.Z * From.Z;
  OffsZ := -A3.X * From.X - A3.Y * From.Y - A3.Z * From.Z;
end;

procedure Clip3D(X1, Y1, Z1, X2, Y2, Z2: real);
{ Clips line segment in three-dimensional coordinates to the viewing
  pyramid }
const
  NoEdge: byte     = $00;
  LeftEdge: byte   = $01;
  RightEdge: byte  = $02;
  BottomEdge: byte = $04;
  TopEdge: byte    = $08;
var
  C, C1, C2: byte;
  X, Y, Z, T: real;
  XPC1, YPC1, XPC2, YPC2: integer;

function Code(X, Y, Z: real): byte;
{ Returns a code specifying which edge in the viewing pyramid
  was crossed. There may be more than one. }
var
  C: byte;
begin
  C := NoEdge;
```

```pascal
          if X < -Z then C := C or LeftEdge;
          if X > Z then C := C or RightEdge;
          if Y < -Z then C := C or BottomEdge;
          if Y > Z then  C := C or TopEdge;
          Code := C;
        end;

      begin
        C1 := Code(X1,Y1,Z1);
        C2 := Code(X2,Y2,Z2);
        while (C1 <> NoEdge) or (C2 <> NoEdge) do begin
          if (C1 and C2) <> NoEdge then Exit;
          C := C1;
          if C = NoEdge then C := C2;
          if (C and LeftEdge) = LeftEdge then begin
            { Crosses left edge }
            T := (Z1 + X1) / ((X1 - X2) - (Z2 - Z1));
            Z := T * (Z2 - Z1) + Z1;
            X := -Z;
            Y := T * (Y2 - Y1) + Y1;
          end
          else if (C and RightEdge) = RightEdge then begin
            { Crosses right edge }
            T := (Z1 - X1) / ((X2 - X1) - (Z2 - Z1));
            Z := t * (Z2 - Z1) + Z1;
            X := Z;
            Y := T * (Y2 - Y1) + Y1;
          end
          else if (C and BottomEdge) = BottomEdge then begin
            { Crosses bottom edge }
            T := (Z1 + Y1) / ((Y1 - Y2) - (Z2 - Z1));
            Z := T * (Z2 - Z1) + Z1;
            X := T * (X2 - X1) + X1;
            Y := -Z;
          end
          else if (C and TopEdge) = TopEdge then begin
            { Crosses top edge }
            T := (Z1 - Y1) / ((Y2 - Y1) - (Z2 - Z1));
            Z := T * (Z2 - Z1) + Z1;
            X := T * (X2 - X1) + X1;
            Y := Z;
          end;
          if C = C1 then begin
            X1 := X;  Y1 := Y;  Z1 := Z;
            C1 := Code(X,Y,Z);
          end
          else begin
            X2 := X;  Y2 := Y;  Z2 := Z;
            C2 := Code(X,Y,Z);
          end
        end;
        if Z1 <> 0 then begin
```

```
      WorldToPc(X1/Z1,Y1/Z1,XPC1,YPC1);
      WorldToPc(X2/Z2,Y2/Z2,XPC2,YPC2);
    end
  else begin
      WorldToPc(X1,Y1,XPC1,YPC1);
      WorldToPc(X2,Y2,XPC2,YPC2);
    end;
    { Draw the line after it has been clipped }
    Line(XPC1,YPC1,XPC2,YPC2);
end;

procedure TransformSeg(V1, V2: VectorType);
{ Transform the segment connecting the two vectors into the
  viewing plane. 3DClip clips and draws the line if visible. }
var
  X1, Y1, Z1, X2, Y2, Z2: real;
begin
  X1 := (V1.X * A1.X + A1.Y * V1.Y + A1.Z * V1.Z + OffsX) * DVal;
  Y1 := (V1.X * A2.X + A2.Y * V1.Y + A2.Z * V1.Z + OffsY) * DVal;
  Z1 :=  V1.X * A3.X + A3.Y * V1.Y + A3.Z * V1.Z + OffsZ;
  X2 := (V2.X * A1.X + A1.Y * V2.Y + A1.Z * V2.Z + OffsX) * DVal;
  Y2 := (V2.X * A2.X + A2.Y * V2.Y + A2.Z * V2.Z + OffsY) * DVal;
  Z2 :=  V2.X * A3.X + A3.Y * V2.Y + A3.Z * V2.Z + OffsZ;
  Clip3D(X1,Y1,Z1,X2,Y2,Z2);
end;

procedure View;
{ Index through the Points array containing the vertices of the object
  and display them as you go. This will draw out the object. }
var
  I, Start: integer;
begin
  I := 1;
  while I < Length do begin
    Start := I;
    Inc(I);
    while Connect[I] > 0 do begin
      TransformSeg(Points[Connect[I-1]],Points[Connect[I]]);
      Inc(I);
    end;
    TransformSeg(Points[Connect[I-1]],Points[-Connect[I]]);
    TransformSeg(Points[-Connect[I]],Points[Connect[Start]]);
    Inc(I);
  end;
end;

procedure Clear_Viewport;
{ Clear the viewport }
begin
  SetViewPort(PCLeft,PCTop,PCRight,PCBottom,True);
  ClearViewPort;
  SetViewPort(0,0,GetMaxX,GetMaxY,True);
end;
```

```pascal
function VectorToStr(V: VectorType): string;
{ Text output routine used to write vector values to graphics screen }
begin
  VectorToStr := RealToStr(V.X,3,1) + ' ' +
  RealToStr(V.Y,3,1) + ' ' + RealToStr(V.Z,3,1);
end;

procedure ShowValues;
{ Show the from, at, up, and viewing angle values in a window on
  the bottom right of the screen }
begin
  { Erase the area where the values are to be written }
  SetFillStyle(SolidFill,0);
  Bar3D(PCRight+1,19*8,GetMaxX,GetMaxY,0,False);
  GWriteXY(60*8,19*8+TextHeight('F'),'fm='+VectorToStr(From));
  GWriteXY(60*8,19*8+2*TextHeight('F'),'at='+VectorToStr(At));
  GWriteXY(60*8,19*8+3*TextHeight('F'),'up='+VectorToStr(Up));
  GWriteXY(60*8,19*8+4*TextHeight('F'),
    'angle='+RealToStr(Angle/0.017453293, 3, 1)+' degrees');
end;

procedure PopupError(Message: string);
{ Pop up an error message }
const
  Press: string[25] = ' Press ENTER to Continue ';
var
  Width: integer;
  Ch: char;
  T: boolean;
begin
  Width := TextWidth(Message);
  if Width < TextWidth(Press) then Width := TextWidth(Press);
  if Win.GPopup(MaxX div 2,MaxY div 2+20,MaxX div 2+Width+10,
      MaxY div 2+20+3*(TextHeight('H')+2),SolidLn,
      GetMaxColor,SolidFill,Black) then begin
    GWriteXY(5,5,Message);
    GWriteXY(5,5+TextHeight('H'),Press);
    Ch := ReadKey;
    T := Win.GUnpop;
  end
end;

function GetVector(Title, Message: string; var Nu: VectorType): boolean;
begin
  if Win.GPopup(MaxX div 2 - TextWidth(Title) div 2-5,
    MaxY div 2-4*TextHeight('H'),MaxX div 2+TextWidth(Title) div 2+5,
    MaxY div 2+4*TextHeight('H'),SolidLn,GetMaxColor,SolidFill,0) then
begin
    GWriteXY(5,5,Title);
    GWriteXY(5,5+2*TextHeight('H'),'Enter x y z coordinates');
    GWriteXY(5,5+3*TextHeight('H'),Message);
    GWriteXY(5,5+4*TextHeight('X'),'x> ');
    GWriteXY(5,5+5*TextHeight('X'),'y> ');
```

```
    GWriteXY(5,5+6*TextHeight('X'),'z> ');
    MoveTo(5+TextWidth('x> '),5+4*TextHeight('H'));
    if GReadReal(Nu.X) then begin
      MoveTo(5+TextWidth('y> '),5+5*TextHeight('H'));
      if GReadReal(Nu.Y) then begin
        MoveTo(5+TextWidth('z> '),5+6*TextHeight('H'));
        if GReadReal(Nu.Z) then begin
          GetVector := True;
          Exit;
        end;
      end
    end
  end;
  GetVector := False
end;

procedure GetFrom;
{ Interactively specify the from coordinates. It cannot be the
  same as the at point. }
var
  Nu: VectorType;
  T: boolean;
begin
  if GetVector('     Change the From Point     ',
               'of new From point.', Nu) then begin
    T := Win.GUnpop;
    if (Nu.X = At.X) and (Nu.Y = At.Y) and (Nu.Z = At.Z) then begin
      PopupError(' Invalid From Point ');
      Exit;
    end;
    From.X := Nu.X;  From.Y := Nu.Y;  From.Z := Nu.Z;
    Clear_Viewport;
    SetEye;
    View;
  end
  else
    T := Win.GUnpop;
end;

procedure GetAt;
{ Let the user change the at point. The at point should not be the same
  as the from point or the up vector. }
var
  Nu: VectorType;
  T: boolean;
begin
  if GetVector('     Change the At Point     ',
               'of new At point.', Nu) then begin
    T := Win.GUnpop;
    if ((Nu.X = From.X) and (Nu.Y = From.Y) and (Nu.Z = From.Z)) or
       ((Nu.X = Up.X) and (Nu.Y = Up.Y) and (Nu.Z = Up.Z)) then begin
      PopupError(' Invalid At Point ');
      Exit;
```

```
      end;
      At.X := Nu.X;  At.Y := Nu.Y;  At.Z := Nu.Z;
      Clear_Viewport;
      SetEye;
      View;
    end
    else
      T := Win.GUnpop;
end;

procedure GetUp;
{ Change the up vector coordinate to the user coordinates indicated.
  It should not be the same as the at point. }
var
  Nu: VectorType;
  T: boolean;
begin
  if GetVector('     Change the Up Vector      ',
               'of new Up vector.', Nu) then begin
    T := Win.GUnpop;
    if (Nu.X = At.X) and (Nu.Y = At.Y) and (Nu.Z = At.Z) then begin
      PopupError(' Invalid Up Vector ');
      Exit;
    end;
    Up.X := Nu.X;  Up.Y := Nu.Y;  Up.Z := Nu.Z;
    SetEye;
    Clear_Viewport;
    View;
  end
  else
    T := Win.GUnpop;
end;

procedure GetAngle;
{ Ask the user for a viewing angle. It must be between 0 and 180 degrees. }
const
  Title: string[34] = '     Change the Viewing Angle     ';
var
  nut: real;
  T: boolean;
begin
  if Win.GPopup(MaxX div 2-TextWidth(Title) div 2-5,
      MaxY div 2-3*TextHeight('H'),MaxX div 2+TextWidth(Title) div 2+5,
      MaxY div 2+4*TextHeight('H'),SolidLn,GetMaxColor,SolidFill,0) then
begin
    GWriteXY(5,5,Title);
    GWriteXY(5,5+2*TextHeight('H'),'Enter a new angle between');
    GWriteXY(5,5+3*TextHeight('H'),'0 and 180 degrees.');
    GWriteXY(5,5+4*TextHeight('X'),'> ');
    MoveTo(5+TextWidth('> '),5+4*TextHeight('H'));
    if not GReadReal(Nut) then begin
      T := Win.GUnpop;
      Exit;
```

```
      end;
    T := Win.GUnpop;
    if (Nut > 0) and (Nut < 180) then begin
      Angle := ToRadians(Nut);
      SetEye;
      Clear_Viewport;
      View;
    end
    else
      PopupError(' Angle must be between 0 and 180 ');
  end;
end;

procedure MoveFrom;
{ Interactively move the from point toward or away from the at point
  depending on user input }
const
  FromInc: real = 0.1;
var
  Nufx, Nufy, Nufz: real;
  StartV: VectorType;
  Ch: char;
begin
  StartV.X := From.X;  StartV.Y := From.Y;  StartV.Z := From.Z;
  TFrom := 1.0;
  GWriteXY(60*8,15*8,'Up arrow moves in ');
  GWriteXY(60*8,16*8,'Down to move away ');
  GWriteXY(60*8,17*8,'Any key to quit   ');
  Ch := ReadKey;
  while Ch = #0 do begin
    Ch := ReadKey;
    if (Ch = UpKey) or (Ch = DownKey) then begin  { Move in or out }
      if Ch = UpKey then begin
        if (TFrom > FromInc) then TFrom := TFrom - FromInc
      end
      else
        TFrom := TFrom + FromInc;
      Nufx := At.X + TFrom * (StartV.X - At.X);
      Nufy := At.Y + TFrom * (StartV.Y - At.Y);
      Nufz := At.Z + TFrom * (StartV.Z - At.Z);
      if (Nufx = At.X) and (Nufy = At.Y) and (Nufz = At.Z) then
        PopupError(' Cannot move to here ')
      else begin
        From.X := Nufx;  From.Y := Nufy;  From.Z := Nufz;
        SetEye;
        Clear_Viewport;
        View;
        ShowValues;
      end
    end;
    Ch := ReadKey;
  end;
  SetFillStyle(SolidFill,Black);
```

```
    Bar(60*8,15*8,MaxX-2,18*8-1);
end;

procedure Zoom;
{ By changing the viewing angle, zoom in and out toward the object }
const
  ZoomInc: real = 0.17453293;   { Increment this many radians }
var
  Ch: char;
begin
  GWriteXY(60*8,15*8,'Up arrow zooms in ');
  GWriteXY(60*8,16*8,'Down to zoom out  ');
  GWriteXY(60*8,17*8,'Any key to quit   ');
  Ch := ReadKey;
  while Ch = #0 do begin
    Ch := ReadKey;
    if Ch = UpKey then begin                        { Zoom in }
      if Angle > ZoomInc then begin
        Angle := Angle - ZoomInc;
        SetEye;
        Clear_Viewport;
        View;
        ShowValues;
      end
      else
        PopupError(' Cannot zoom in any closer. ');
    end
    else if Ch = DownKey then begin          { Zoom out }
      if Angle < ToRadians(179) - ZoomInc then begin
        Angle := Angle + ZoomInc;
        Clear_Viewport;
        SetEye;
        View;
        ShowValues;
      end
      else
        PopupError(' Cannot zoom out any more. ');
    end;
    Ch := ReadKey;
  end;
  SetFillStyle(SolidFill,Black);
  Bar(60*8,15*8,MaxX-2,18*8-1);
end;

function Read3DObject(FileName: string): boolean;
{ Reads in a file describing a polygon that adheres to standard
  described in the text. Returns True if file is read successfully;
  otherwise it returns False. }
var
  InFile: text;
  I: integer;
begin
  {$I-} Assign(InFile, FileName);
```

```
    Reset(InFile); {$I+}
    if IOResult <> 0 then begin
      PopupError('Could not open file.');
      Read3DObject := False;
      Exit;
    end;
    ReadLn(InFile,Vertices,Length);
    if (Vertices > NumVertices) or (Length > NumConnections) then begin
      PopupError('Object in file is too large.');
      Read3DObject := False;
      Exit;
    end;
    for I := 1 to Vertices do
      Read(InFile,Points[I].X,Points[I].Y,Points[I].Z);
    for I := 1 to Length do
      Read(InFile,Connect[I]);
    Close(InFile);
    Read3DObject := True;
end;

procedure Read3DObjectFile;
{ Prompts for the filename of the file to be read and then calls
  Read3DObject to read it. If the file is successfully read, it is
  displayed by calling view after setting the viewing parameters. }
const
  Title: string[28] = '  Reading a 3D Object File  ';
var
  FN: string;
  T: boolean;
begin
  T := Win.GPopup(MaxX div 2-TextWidth(Title) div 2-5,
       MaxY div 2-3*TextHeight('H'),MaxX div 2+TextWidth(Title) div 2+5,
       MaxY div 2+4*TextHeight('H'),SolidLn,GetMaxColor,SolidFill,0);
  GWriteXY(5,5,Title);
  GWriteXY(5,5+2*TextHeight('H'),'Enter filename:');
  MoveTo(5,5+3*TextHeight('X'));
  GWrite('> ');
  if GReadStr(FN) then begin
    if Read3DObject(FN) then begin
      T := Win.GUnpop;
      SetAt;
      SetFrom;
      SetEye;
      Clear_Viewport;
      View;
    end
  end;
  T := Win.GUnpop;
end;

procedure MainMenu;
{ Listing for the main menu }
begin
```

```
      Rectangle(PCRight+1,0,MaxX,19*8);
      GWriteXY(60*8,1*8,'      Main Menu');
      Rectangle(PCRight+1,0,MaxX,TextHeight('M')*2+2);
      GWriteXY(60*8,3*8,'r  read object');
      GWriteXY(60*8,4*8,'m  move From point');
      GWriteXY(60*8,5*8,'z  zoom in/out');
      GWriteXY(60*8,6*8,'a  enter At point');
      GWriteXY(60*8,7*8,'f  enter From point');
      GWriteXY(60*8,8*8,'u  enter Up point');
      GWriteXY(60*8,9*8,'t  enter view Angle');
      GWriteXY(60*8,12*8,'q  quit');
   end;

   begin
     Init3DGraphics;
     Win.Init;
     Rectangle(PCLeft-1,PCTop-1,PCRight+1,PCBottom+1);
     MainMenu;
     ShowValues;
     repeat
       GWriteXY(60*8,15*8,Prompt);
       MoveTo(60*8+TextWidth(Prompt),15*8);
       Ch := ReadKey;
       case(Ch) of
         'm' : MoveFrom;
         'z' : Zoom;
         'r' : Read3DObjectFile;
         'a' : GetAt;
         'f' : GetFrom;
         'u' : GetUp;
         't' : GetAngle;
       end;
       ShowValues;
     until Ch = 'q';
     CloseGraph;
   end.
```

Appendix:
BGI Function Reference

This appendix lists the procedures and functions provided in the BGI. Each routine includes a brief description along with its declaration and an explanation of its parameters and return value, if they exist. Remember, to use any of the procedures or functions in the BGI you must place the unit **Graph** in the **uses** section of your program files.

Arc

Draws a circular arc around a center point with a fixed radius. The arc is drawn counterclockwise from a start angle to a stop angle. Both angles are measured counterclockwise relative to the 3 o'clock position.

```
procedure Arc(X, Y: integer; StAngle, EndAngle, Radius: word);
```

X,Y	The center of the arc.
StAngle,EndAngle	The starting and ending angle specified in degrees.
Radius	The radius specified in pixels.

Bar

Draws a filled-in rectangular bar with the current drawing color and fill pattern. The **Bar** procedure does not draw an outline for the bar.

```
procedure Bar(X1, Y1, X2, Y2: integer);
```

X1,Y1	The pixel coordinates of one corner of the bar.
X2,Y2	The coordinates of the opposite corner of the bar.

Bar3D

Draws a filled-in three-dimensional rectangular bar with the current drawing color and fill pattern. To draw a bar with an outline, set the Depth to 0.

```
procedure Bar3D(X1, Y1, X2, Y2: integer; Depth: word;
                TopFlag: boolean);
```

X1,Y1   Coordinates of one corner of the bar.
X2,Y2   Coordinates of the opposite corner of the bar.
Depth   The three-dimensional depth of the bar specified in pixels.
TopFlag   If True, a top is placed on the bar. Set this to False if you want to stack another bar on top of the bar.

Circle

Draws a circle with a fixed radius around a specified center. The circle is drawn in the current drawing color. Circles can be drawn only with the default line style (solid line). The thickness of the line can, however, be set before drawing the circle using the **SetLineStyle** procedure.

```
procedure Circle(X, Y: integer; Radius: word);
```

X,Y   The center of the circle.
Radius   The radius of the circle.

ClearDevice

Erases the entire graphics screen with the background color and moves the current position (CP) to (0,0). The **ClearDevice** routine should be used whenever you need to clear the full screen, even if the viewport is set to a size smaller than the full screen. If you need to clear only the current viewport, you should use the **ClearViewPort** procedure.

```
procedure ClearDevice;
```

ClearViewPort

Clears the active viewport and moves the current position (CP) to (0,0) in the active viewport. Only the active viewport is cleared. The screen area outside the viewport is not altered.

```
procedure ClearViewPort;
```

CloseGraph

Shuts down the BGI graphics system and deallocates the memory set aside for the graphics drivers, fonts, and an internal buffer. The screen is restored to the mode it was in before the BGI was initialized.

```
procedure CloseGraph;
```

DetectGraph

Checks the hardware to determine which graphics driver and mode to use. This procedure always selects the mode that will give the highest resolution possible for the installed adapter. The codes for the graphics drivers and graphics modes are presented in the sidebar in Chapter 2: "Working with the Graphics Hardware." If for some reason **DetectGraph** does not detect a graphics adapter, the **GraphDriver** parameter is set to -2.

```
procedure DetectGraph(var GraphDriver, GraphMode: integer);
```

GraphDriver	Returns an integer code to indicate which graphics driver can be used.
GraphMode	Returns an integer code of the highest-resolution mode that can be used.

DrawPoly   Draws the outline of a polygon using the current drawing color and line style.

```
procedure DrawPoly(NumPoints: word; var PolyPoints);
```

NumPoints	The number of points (coordinate pairs) used to draw the polygon.
PolyPoints	An array of the points for the polygon. The unit **Graph** contains the **PointType**, which defines a record containing X and Y fields that can be used in the array. In order to draw a closed polygon, the first and last points in the array must be the same.

Ellipse   Draws an elliptical arc around a center point with a specified horizontal and vertical radii. The ellipse is drawn from the starting angle (**StAngle**) to the end angle (**EndAngle**). You can draw a complete ellipse by setting the starting angle to 0 and the ending angle to 360. The ellipse is drawn in a counter-clockwise direction, where 0 degrees is at 3 o'clock and 90 degrees is at 12 o'clock. You cannot change the line style of an ellipse, but you can set its thickness using **SetLineStyle**.

```
procedure Ellipse(X, Y: integer; StAndle, EndAngle: word; XRadius,
                  YRadius: word);
```

X,Y	The center of the elliptical arc.
StAngle,EndAngle	The starting and ending angles specified in degrees.
XRadius,YRadius	The horizontal and vertical radii in pixels.

FillEllipse   Draws and fills an ellipse using the current fill pattern and color. If you wish to draw a partial filled ellipse, use the **Sector** procedure.

```
procedure FillEllipse(X, Y: integer; XRadius, YRadius: word);
```

X,Y	The center of the ellipse.
XRadius,YRadius	The horizontal and vertical radii in pixels.

FillPoly   Draws and fills a polygon using the current line style and fill settings. If you want to draw a polygon without filling it, use **DrawPoly**.

```
procedure FillPoly(NumPoints: word; var PolyPoints);
```

NumPoints The number of coordinate pairs used to draw the polygon.

PolyPoints An array specifying the coordinates of the vertices of the polygon. The unit **Graph** contains the **PointType**, which defines a record containing X and Y fields that can be used in the array.

FloodFill   Fills a bounded region with the current color and fill pattern starting from the coordinate specified. If the point is inside a region bounded by the color passed to **FloodFill**, then the interior of the region is filled. If the starting point is outside a bounded region, everything but the bounded region is filled. This procedure does not work with the IBM 8514 driver.

```
procedure FloodFill(X, Y: integer; Border: word);
```

X,Y   The location of a region to fill.

Border The color of the border.

GetArcCoords   Retrieves the coordinates of the most recent arc drawing command. The coordinates returned are the arc's center point and its endpoints.

```
procedure GetArcCoords(var ArcCoords: ArcCoordsType);
```

ArcCoords A record of type **ArcCoordsType** used to return the coordinates of an arc. It is defined in **Graph** as:

```
ArcCoordsType = record
  X, Y: integer;
  XStart, YStart: integer;
  XEnd, YEnd: integer;
end;
```

GetAspectRatio   Returns two scaled values that effectively indicate the resolution of the screen. One can be divided into the other to calculate the screen's aspect ratio.

```
procedure GetAspectRatio(var Xasp, Yasp: word);
```

Xasp,Yasp Return the X and Y proportions of the screen.

GetBkColor   Returns the index in the palette that represents the background color. The background color can range from 0 to 15, depending on the graphics mode. If the 0th location in the palette is changed by **SetPalette** or **SetAllPalette**, **GetBkColor** returns 0.

```
function GetBkColor: word;
```

GetColor Returns the index in the palette that corresponds to the current drawing color. The drawing color can range from 0 to 15, depending on the graphics mode.

```
function GetColor: word;
```

GetDefaultPalette Returns the color codes contained in the default color palette. The default palette size for CGA is 4 colors in low-resolution mode and 2 colors in high-resolution mode. Both EGA and VGA have 16 colors in their default palettes.

```
procedure GetDefaultPalette(var Palette: PaletteType);
```

Palette A data structure that returns the palette information. The **PaletteType** is discussed with the **GetPalette** routine.

GetDriverName Returns the name of the currently installed graphics driver.

```
function GetDriverName: string;
```

GetFillPattern Obtains the bit setting for the user-defined fill pattern. The 64-pixel fill patten is represented as a sequence of 8 bytes, where each byte corresponds to 8 pixels in the fill pattern. If you need to determine the active fill color, use **GetFillSettings**.

```
procedure GetFillPattern(var FillPattern: FillPatternType);
```

FillPattern The user-defined fill pattern stored in an array of type **FillPatternType**, which is defined in **Graph** as:

```
FillPatternType = array[1..8] of byte;
```

GetFillSettings Retrieves the current fill pattern and color. The fill settings returned correspond to one of the codes listed in Table 2.7 in Chapter 2.

```
procedure GetFillSettings(var FillInfo: FillSettingsType);
```

FillInfo The data structure that contains the fill pattern and fill color. This data structure is defined as:

```
FillSettingsType = record
  Pattern, Color: word;
end;
```

GetGraphMode Returns an integer code indicating the current graphics mode for the installed graphics driver. The possible codes and constants for them are listed in the sidebar "Working with the Graphics Hardware" in Chapter 2.

```
function GetGraphMode: integer;
```

GetImage

Copies a rectangular screen image into memory. The image can be restored later by calling **PutImage**.

```
procedure GetImage(Left, Top, Right, Bottom: integer; var BitMap);
```

Left,Top	Top-right corner of the rectangular screen region.
Right,Bottom	Bottom-right coordinate of the screen region.
BitMap	References the location in memory where the screen image is stored.

GetLineSettings

Returns the current line style, pattern, and thickness. A list of the valid line styles is included in the section "Predefined Line Patterns" in Chapter 2. Note: the **Pattern** field of the **LineInfo** record is used only if the **LineStyle** field contains **UserBitLn**.

```
procedure GetLineSettings(var LineInfo: LineSettingsType);
```

LineInfo   Uses a predefined data type called **LineSettingsType** to return the line settings. The data type is defined as:

```
LineSettingsType = record
  LineStyle, Pattern, Thickness: word;
end;
```

GetMaxColor

Returns the largest index in the current palette. This is the maximum color that can be used with **SetColor**.

```
function GetMaxColor: word;
```

GetMaxMode

Returns the number corresponding to the highest resolution mode for the current driver.

```
function GetMaxMode: word;
```

GetMaxX

Returns the maximum horizontal coordinate for the active graphics mode.

```
function GetMaxX: integer;
```

GetMaxY

Returns the maximum vertical coordinate for the active graphics mode.

```
function GetMaxY: integer;
```

GetModeName

Returns a string containing the name of the specified graphics mode.

```
function GetModeName(ModeNumber: integer): string;
```

ModeNumber   An integer code that specifies the graphics mode.

GetModeRange   Returns the range of graphics modes for a given driver.

```
function GetModeRange(GraphDriver: integer; var LoMode,
                      HiMode: integer);
```

GraphDriver   A code specifying one of the BGI's drivers.
LoMode,HiMode   The lowest and highest modes possible.

GetPalette   Returns information about the active color palette including its size and colors. The default colors and sizes for the standard graphics adapters (CGA, EGA, and VGA) are presented in Chapter 2.

```
procedure GetPalette(var Palette: PaletteType);
```

Palette   Uses the predefined data type **PaletteType** to store the palette information. This data type is defined as:

```
const
  MaxColors = 15;
type
  PaletteType = record
    Size: byte;
    Colors: array[0..MaxColors] of shortint;
  end;
```

GetPaletteSize   Returns the size (number of index locations) in the currently active palette.

```
function GetPaletteSize: integer;
```

GetPixel   Returns the color (palette index) of a pixel at a specified location.

```
function GetPixel(X, Y: integer): word;
```

X,Y   The horizontal and vertical position of the pixel.

GetTextSettings   Obtains information about the current text settings.

```
procedure GetTextSettings(var TextInfo: TextSettingsType);
```

TextInfo   Uses the predefined data type **TextSettingsType** to return the current text settings. The data type is defined as:

```
TextSettingsType = record
  Font, Direction, CharSize, Horiz, Vert: word;
end;
```

GetViewSettings   Gets information about the current viewport. When the graphics system is initialized with **InitGraph,** the viewport is set to the dimensions of the full screen by default.

```
procedure GetViewSettings(var ViewPort: ViewPortType);
```

ViewPort   A predefined data type that returns the viewport settings. The data type is defined as:

```
ViewPortType = record
  X1, Y1, X2, Y2: integer;
end;
```

GetX   Returns the horizontal coordinate of the current position (CP).

```
function GetX: integer;
```

GetY   Returns the vertical coordinate of the current position.

```
function GetY: integer;
```

GraphDefaults   Resets the graphics attributes to their default settings. The default settings are listed in Table A.1.

```
procedure GraphDefaults;
```

Table A.1. Default graphics settings

Graphics attribute	Default setting
Current position (CP)	Upper-left corner (0,0)
Viewport	Full screen dimensions (0,0) to (width-1,height-1)
Palette	Default for the current adapter
Drawing color	The color in the maximum palette index
Background color	Color 0 in the palette
Line style	Solid line
Fill color	The maximum color
Fill style	Solid fill
Font size	1 for default font, 4 for stroke fonts
Font direction	Horizontal
Font justification	Left and top

GraphErrorMsg   Returns an error message string for the error code returned by **GraphResult**.

```
function GraphErrorMsg(ErrorCode: integer): string;
```

ErrorCode   The integer error code returned by **GraphResult**.

GraphFreeMem   Frees memory allocated by the BGI. This procedure is called internally by the BGI when the graphics system is closed. You can install your own routine to free graphics memory by setting the BGI variable **GraphFreeMemPtr** so that it points to your routine.

```
procedure GraphFreeMem(var Ptr: pointer; Size: word);
```

Ptr   Pointer to the memory area to free.
Size   The size of the memory area.

GraphGetMem   Allocates memory for the BGI. This procedure is called internally by the BGI when the graphics system is initialized to allocate memory for graphics device drivers, stroked fonts, and a buffer used by **FloodFill**. To provide your own memory allocation routine, set the variable **GraphFreeMemPtr** to your procedure.

```
procedure GraphGetMem(var Ptr: pointer; Size: word);
```

Ptr   Set to the memory allocated.
Size   The size of the memory block to allocate.

GraphResult   Returns the error code for the last graphics call.

```
function GraphResult: integer;
```

ImageSize   Returns the number of bytes needed to store a rectangular screen image. If the image size is greater than or equal to 64K, a 0 is returned.

```
function ImageSize(X1, Y1, X2, Y2: integer): word;
```

X1,Y1,X2,Y2   Coordinates of opposing corners of the rectangular region.

InitGraph   Initializes the graphics system by loading a specified graphics driver and setting the graphics mode. The **InitGraph** procedure must be called before using any of the BGI's drawing routines.

```
procedure InitGraph(var GraphDriver: integer; var GraphMode: integer;
                    PathToDriver: string);
```

GraphDriver	Contains a code specifying the graphics driver to be used. (See the sidebar "Working with the Graphics Hardware" in Chapter 2.)
GraphMode	Contains a code specifying the graphics mode to use.
PathToDriver	The directory pathname where the graphics driver and font files are stored.

InstallUserDriver Installs a new BGI device driver. This function is used to install third-party device drivers. It returns the driver number for the driver installed or a -11 if an error has occurred.

```
function InstallUserDriver(DriverName: string; AutoDetectPtr:
                          pointer): integer;
```

DriverName	The DOS name of a graphics driver (.BGI) file. The name can contain the full directory path.
AutoDetectPtr	A pointer to an optional autodetect function that is assigned to the new driver.

InstallUserFont Loads a user-supplied font file. It returns a code that can be used with **SetTextStyle** to select the font. If an error has occurred a 0 is returned, which effectively selects the default font.

```
function InstallUserFont(FontName: string): integer;
```

FontName	The DOS name of a stroked font file. The name can contain the full directory path.

Line Draws a line between two points. The line is drawn in the current color and line style. To change the line settings, call the **SetLineStyle** procedure before drawing the line.

```
procedure Line(X1, Y1, X2, Y2: integer);
```

X1,Y1,X2,Y2   The two endpoints of the line.

LineRel Draws a line from the current position (CP) to a position calculated by adding the offset (**Dx,Dy**) to the CP. After the line is drawn, the CP is updated.

```
procedure LineRel(Dx, Dy: integer);
```

Dx,Dy   The relative horizontal and vertical distance used to draw the line. These values can be positive or negative.

LineTo   Draws a line from the current position (CP) to the coordinate specified. The CP is updated to the location specified.

```
procedure LineTo(X, Y: integer);
```

X,Y   The endpoint for the line.

MoveRel   Adds the offset (**Dx,Dy**) to the current position (CP).

```
procedure MoveRel(Dx, Dy: integer);
```

Dx,Dy   The amount to move the CP.

MoveTo   Moves the current position (CP) to the coordinate specified.

```
procedure MoveTo(X, Y: integer);
```

X,Y   The new CP.

OutText   Displays a string at the current position. The text string is displayed with the current size, font, direction, and justification settings. The current position is updated only if a horizontal direction and left text justification are used.

```
procedure OutText(TextString: string);
```

TextString   The string to display.

OutTextXY   Displays a text string starting at the specified location. The current position is not updated.

```
procedure OutTextXY(X, Y: integer; TextString: string);
```

X,Y   The coordinate where the text is displayed.
TextString   The text string to display.

PieSlice   Draws and fills a pie slice with the current drawing color and fill style.

```
procedure PieSlice(X, Y: integer; StAngle, EndAngle, Radius: word);
```

X,Y   The center point of the pie slice.
StAngle,EndAngle   The starting and ending angles in degrees.
Radius   The radius in pixels along the horizontal axis.

PutImage   Copies a bit image onto the screen. This procedure along with **GetImage** is useful for performing animation.

```
procedure PutImage(Left, Top: integer; var BitMap; Op: word);
```

Left,Top Screen location to place top-left corner of the screen image.
BitMap Points to the image to place on the screen.
Op Code specifying how the image is to be combined with the screen's pixels.

PutPixel

Displays a pixel in the specified color.

```
procedure PutPixel(X, Y: integer; Color: word);
```

X,Y Position of the pixel.
Color The color to use.

Rectangle

Draws a rectangle in the current line style and color.

```
procedure Rectangle(Left, Top, Right, Bottom: integer);
```

Left,Top The upper-left corner of the rectangle.
Right,Bottom The lower-right corner of the rectangle.

RegisterBGIDriver

Registers a BGI graphics driver. A driver can be loaded from disk or can be linked to the program as an .OBJ file. It returns a code corresponding to the driver if the operation is successful; otherwise a value less than 0 is returned.

```
function RegisterBGIDriver(Driver: pointer): integer;
```

Driver A pointer to the memory containing the driver.

RegisterBGIFont

Registers a BGI font file. If **RegisterBGIFont** returns a value less than 0 an error has occurred; otherwise, it returns a code corresponding to the font loaded.

```
function RegisterBGIFont(Font: pointer): integer;
```

Font The font to register.

RestoreCrtMode

Restores the screen to the mode it was in before a graphics mode was selected.

```
procedure RestoreCrtMode;
```

Sector

Draws and fills an elliptical pie slice with the current drawing color and fill style.

```
procedure Sector(X, Y: integer; StAngle, EndAngle, XRadius,
                 YRadius: word);
```

X,Y   The center point of the pie slice.
StAngle,EndAngle   The starting and ending angles in degrees.
XRadius,YRadius   The horizontal and vertical radii in pixels.

SetActivePage   Specifies which page all graphics output is written to. To display what is on this page, you must call **SetVisualPage**.

```
procedure SetActivePage(PageNum: word);
```

PageNum   The page number to make active.

SetAllPalette   Changes all palette colors.

```
procedure SetAllPalette(var Palette);
```

Palette   Specifies the palette color information. The data structure used is described in the discussion of the **GetPalette** routine.

SetAspectRatio   Sets the X and Y aspect ratio for the active graphics hardware and mode. The aspect ratio is used by **Circle**, **Arc**, and **PieSlice** to draw symmetrical shapes.

```
procedure SetAspectRatio(Xasp, Yasp: word);
```

Xasp,Yasp   The new horizontal and vertical aspect proportions.

SetBkColor   Selects the background color by specifying which palette index to use.

```
procedure SetBkColor(ColorIndex: word);
```

ColorIndex   A code that specifies the new background color. A table of the background colors and codes is presented in Table 2.4 of Chapter 2. The value can range from 0 to 15, depending on the graphics mode being used.

SetColor   Sets the active drawing color. The maximum number of colors that are available for the given graphics adapter and mode can be obtained by calling **GetMaxColor**.

```
procedure SetColor(Color: word);
```

Color   Specifies which palette location is used as the current drawing color.

SetFillPattern   Selects a user-defined fill pattern and color. The user-defined fill pattern is created using bit settings. The technique of defining a pattern is described in Table 2.7 of Chapter 2.

```
procedure SetFillPattern(Pattern: FillPatternType; Color: word);
```

Pattern   Specifies the user-defined fill pattern.
Color   Specifies the fill color.

SetFillStyle   Selects the current fill pattern and color. The fill pattern selected is used by the routines: **Bar, Bar3D, FillPoly, FloodFill, PieSlice,** and **Sector**.

```
procedure SetFillStyle(Pattern: word; Color: word);
```

Pattern   Specifies one of the twelve BGI-supported fill patterns.
Color   Specifies the fill pattern's color.

SetGraphBufSize   Sets the size of the internal graphics buffer used by routines such as **FloodFill**. The default size is 4K. If this function is used, it must be called before calling **InitGraph**. It returns the number of bytes of the previously defined buffer.

```
procedure SetGraphBufSize(BufSize: word);
```

BufSize   The number of bytes to be used for the graphics buffer.

SetGraphMode   Sets the system to graphics mode and clears the screen. To use this routine, **InitGraph** must have been previously called.

```
procedure SetGraphMode(Mode: integer);
```

Mode   The graphics mode to use.

SetLineStyle   Sets the current line style and width.

```
procedure SetLineStyle(LineStyle: word; Pattern: word;
                       Thickness: word);
```

LineStyle   One of the line style codes specified in Table A.2.
Pattern   The user line style pattern specified as a 16-bit pattern.
Thickness   The line thickness. Two styles are supported: **NormWidth** (1 pixel wide) and **ThickWidth** (3 pixels wide).

SetPalette   Changes a color in the active color palette.

Table A.2. Line style codes

Value	Name
0	SolidLn
1	DottedLn
2	CenterLn
3	DashedLn
4	UserBitLn

```
procedure SetPalette(ColorIndex: word; Color: shortint);
```

ColorIndex   The palette index location to update.
Color   The new color.

SetRGBPalette   Changes a color in the active color palette on an IBM 8514 or VGA in 256 color mode.

```
procedure SetRGBPalette(ColorNum, RedVal, GreenVal, BlueVal: integer);
```

ColorNum   The palette entry to be updated.
RedVal,GreenVal,BlueVal   The components of the color.

SetTextJustify   Sets the text justification style. The justification codes are listed in Table A.3.

```
procedure SetTextJustify(Horiz, Vert: word);
```

Horiz   The horizontal justification code.
Vert   The vertical justification code.

Table A.3. Text justification codes

Constant	Value	Description
LeftText	0	Left-justify text
CenterText	1	Center text (for either horizontal or vertical text)
RightText	2	Right-justify text
BottomText	0	Justify text from bottom
TopText	2	Justify text from top

SetTextStyle   Defines the text settings to be used by the BGI.

```
procedure SetTextStyle(Font: word; Direction: word; CharSize: word);
```

Font   One of the font styles listed in Table A.4.

Direction   Font direction to use when displaying text. It can be either **HorizDir** (value = 0) for horizontal text or **VertDir** (value = 1) for vertical text.

CharSize   Amount to magnify characters displayed. Can be between 0 and 10. A value of 0 can be used only with stroke fonts and instructs the BGI to use the character size specified by **SetUserCharSize** or the default magnification (4).

SetUserCharSize   Specifies how much to scale the stoke font characters that are displayed.

```
procedure SetUserCharSize(MultX, DivX, MultY, DivY: word);
```

MultX,MultY   Specifies the height and width multiplication factors.

DivX,DivY   Specifies the height and width division factors.

SetViewPort   Defines the dimensions of the current viewport and whether graphics should be clipped to its boundaries.

```
procedure SetViewPort(Left, Top, Right, Bottom: integer;
                      ClipFlag: boolean);
```

Left,Top   The upper-left corner of the viewport.

Right,Bottom   The lower-right corner of the viewport.

ClipFlag   If True, it specifies that graphics are to be clipped to the viewport.

Table A.4. Font styles

Name	Value	Description
DefaultFont	0	8 by 8 bit-mapped font
TriplexFont	1	Triplex stroke font
SmallFont	2	Small stroke font
SansSerifFont	3	Sans-serif stroke font
GothicFont	4	Gothic stroke font

SetVisualPage Selects which graphics page is displayed. The number of pages available depends on the graphics mode being used.

```
procedure SetVisualPage(PageNum: word);
```

PageNum Specifies the visual page to use.

SetWriteMode Sets the writing mode to be used by the line-drawing graphics routines. The writing mode affects only these routines: **DrawPoly**, **Line**, **LineRel**, **LineTo**, and **Rectangle**.

```
procedure SetWriteMode(WriteMode: integer);
```

WriteMode Specifies the writing mode. The modes supported are: **CopyPut** (value = 0) and **XorPut** (value = 1). The **CopyPut** mode is used to overwrite whatever is currently on the screen with the new line that is drawn. The **XorPut** mode exclusive-ORs the color of the line being drawn with the pixels that the line overwrites.

TextHeight Returns the height of a text string in pixels. The current font size and scale factor are used to calculate the height of the string.

```
function TextHeight(TextString: string);
```

TextString The string to measure.

TextWidth Returns the width of a text string in pixels. The current font size and scale factor are used to calculate the width of the string.

```
function TextWidth(TextString: string);
```

TextString The text string to measure.

Index

Disk Order Form

The real fun in computer graphics is running programs—not typing them in. To help, we are making available a set of diskettes that contain all the source code presented in this book.

To order your disks, fill out the form below and mail it along with $15 in check or money order (orders outside the U.S. add $5 for shipping and handling) to:

> Robots Etc.
> Turbo Pascal 6 Graphics Disks
> P.O. Box 122
> Tempe, AZ 85280

To order your disks with Visa or Master Card, call (602) 483-0192.

- -

Please send me _____ copies of the Turbo Pascal 6 Graphics Disks at $15 each. (Orders outside the U.S. add $5 shipping and handling. Please make payment in U.S. funds drawn on a U.S. bank.) Make checks payable to Robots Etc.

_____

Name

_____

Address

_____

City   State   Zip Code

_____

Country   Telephone

                           Disk format: ❑ 5 1/4"   ❑ 3 1/2"